STO

**DO NOT REMOVE
CARDS FROM POCKET**

ELEMENTS OF TEXTILES

JULES LABARTHE

Late Professor Emeritus of Textile Technology, Carnegie-Mellon University

Contributors:

Donice H. Kelly *Abilene Christian College*

Barbara Densmore *The Pennsylvania State University*

ELEMENTS OF

Macmillan Publishing Co., Inc.
New York

Collier Macmillan Publishers
London

A portion of this material has been adapted from *Textiles: Origins to Usage,* by Jules Labarthe, copyright © 1964 by Macmillan Publishing Co., Inc.

MACMILLAN PUBLISHING CO., INC.
866 Third Avenue, New York, New York 10022

COLLIER-MACMILLAN CANADA, LTD.

Library of Congress Cataloging in Publication Data

Labarthe, Jules, (date)
  Elements of textiles.

  Bibliography: p.
  1. Textile industry and fabrics. I. Title.
TS1445.L19   677   73-20993
ISBN 0-02-367030-4
Printing: 1 2 3 4 5 6 7 8   Year: 5 6 7 8 9 0

Preface

It is estimated that there are 20 million young people between the ages of 14 and 24 in the United States at the present time. Because this age group will become an even greater factor in the purchasing of consumer goods during the next few years, to no other group does the textile industry cater more seriously in order to provide as great a diversity of texture, color, and textile properties in both apparel and household furnishings. These young consumers are more active in the market than their parents were; they show greater responsibility in selection and a more rapid life pattern of change as they express their preferences for textures, colors, and apparel designs. With an ever-widening variety from which to choose, this generation more than any other needs guidance in making careful selections and in utilizing the textiles available.

In this text, an effort has been made to provide in as simple, but complete, a form as possible, essential technological information aimed toward fulfilling these consumer needs. The technological information required for more serious professional work in textiles is left to more advanced courses of specialization. Although courses in professional career specializations for men and women in college are becoming more technology-oriented, intense specialization in any field, including those professionally oriented, conflicts with the desire of many colleges and universities to produce a well-rounded and useful citizen with broad interests.

This book has been designed to accommodate two diverse pressures placed on undergraduate students of textile science. First, it provides a basic knowledge of textile products not only in apparel, but also in household fabrics; second, it awakens a sense of consumership or the appreciation of the responsibility one has to oneself, to one's family, and to the economy to become a more informed selector of textiles and user of textile products. For this reason more than the usual amount of attention is given to textile finishing. In preparing an attractive product for the market, it is also essential to gain a knowledge of the physical and chemical properties of the fabric that are required for special uses. A great amount of attention has been given to two such finishes: fire-resistant and durable-press finishes. In the case of the fire-resistant finish, Federal legislation has set certain rigid requirements because it is a kind of merchandise failure that involves potentially fatal hazard to the consumer. The durable-press finish is emphasized because it is an outstanding labor-saving device for textile care in the home.

To accommodate these two diverse pressures in the training of home economists, some introductory courses may be combined at the elementary level to include both the technical data and the economic factors affecting both the selection and the use of textile products. This text is an attempt to fill that need.

Thus, it is hoped that *Elements of Textiles* will provide the student with a dependable base on which to build an advanced professional career in textiles or to become an informed consumer well ahead of the average shopper in the marketplace.

J. L.

Contents

ONE Basic Concepts 1

Consumership—Professional and Amateur *3*
Essential Properties of a Textile Fiber *7*
Textile Fiber Classifications *14*

TWO Natural Fibers: Cellulosic and Protein Fibers 18

Characteristics of Natural Cellulosic Fibers *18*
Cotton Fibers *19*
Flax Fibers *39*
Jute, Hemp, and Ramie Fibers *45*
Miscellaneous Bast Fibers *48*
Characteristics of Protein Fibers *49*
Wool *50*
Silk *75*

THREE Man-made Fibers 87

Rayon and Acetate Fibers and Filaments *89*
Organic Fibers *114*
Miscellaneous Inorganic Fibers *116*
Metallic Fibers *121*

FOUR Manufactured Fiber Families 124

Common Properties of Manufactured Fibers *124*
Nylons *126*

Acrylic Fibers   *140*

Modacrylic Fibers   *150*

Polyester Fibers   *154*

Olefin Fibers   *164*

Elastomeric Fibers   *171*

Miscellaneous Manufactured Fibers   *175*

Status of Manufactured Fibers   *180*

Man-made Fiber Exports   *184*

The Search for New Polymers   *188*

FIVE   Yarns: The Bones and Sinews of Textiles   191

Yarn Structure   *191*

Continuous Filament Yarns   *200*

Yarn Nomenclature and Measurement   *200*

Textured Yarns   *205*

Twinned Fibers   *209*

Stretchable Textured Cotton Yarns   *213*

Future Trends in Textured Yarns   *214*

Paper Yarns   *216*

SIX   Fabric Constructions   217

The Basic Weaves   *217*

The Count of Fabrics   *219*

Balance of the Fabric Structure   *221*

Ten Important Types of Woven Structure   *222*

The Identification of Fabrics   *234*

Novelty Weaves   *235*

Applied Patterns or Structural Design   *239*

Pile Weaves   *240*

Tufted Fabrics   *245*

Knitted Fabrics   *246*

Nonwoven Textiles   *266*

Layered Constructions   *278*

SEVEN   Finishing and Coloring Fabrics   284

Role of the Converter   284

General Finishes Affecting Consumer Selection   286

Special Processing for the Various Fibers   287

Growth of Textile Finishing   296

Fabric Preshrinkage   300

Water-repellent Finishes   301

Fire-retardant Finishes   304

New Federal Laws on Flammability   306

Antibacterial Finishes   313

Warmth Retention   314

Spot- and Stain-resistant Finishes   314

Mildew-resistant Finishes   314

Insect-repellent Finishes   315

Starchless Finishes   315

Static-resistant Finishes   316

Wash-and-wear Finishes   317

Soil-release Finishes   322

Color Applications   325

Deposited Design Finishing   339

EIGHT   Selecting Fabrics for Apparel and Household Uses   341

Textile Legislation   342

Flammability—Further Research   347

Aids to the Consumer in Selecting Textiles   348

Possible Limitations of the L-22 Standard   351

Producers' Aids to Fabric Selection Care   360

Technical Aspects of Selection   361

Psychological Selection Criteria   363

Apparel Consumership   375

Household Textiles   382

Development of Skills for Selecting and Using Textiles   407

Air Pollution and Textiles   422

Mechanical Attrition   423

The Future of Textiles   425

APPENDIX ONE   Bibliography   432

APPENDIX TWO   Tables   438

1. *Yarn Numbering and Count Systems*   *438*
2. *Conversion Factors of Importance to Textile Study*   *439*
3. *Conversion Factors: Count Values to Tex Numbers*   *440*

APPENDIX THREE   Approved Fiber Nomenclature with Definitions 441

INDEX   445

ELEMENTS OF TEXTILES

CHAPTER ONE

Basic Concepts

The basic concept guiding the preparation of the material for this book about textiles and the use of these materials in a textiles course at Carnegie-Mellon University has been that this information on fibers and fabrics should contribute to greater competence in consumership. It is felt that consumership is a basic ingredient not only in the professional competence of those who later train themselves for positions in the textile or clothing industries, but also for the homemaker.

For this reason, the following order of presentation, beginning with the simplest element, the fiber, and progressing through yarns, has been chosen: the formation of fabrics; the finishing and dyeing of these fabrics for their presentation to the market; and finally an elementary presentation of consumership, including the responsibilities of the consumer and some of the aids available to this textile product user. At every level the matter of quality of product and maintenance of uniformity of quality by means of mixing or blending is emphasized.

There is a general belief that there is no specific, rigid use condition for which some textile fiber cannot be designed, constructed, and finished. It remains, then, for the consumer to know in

1

advance the performance criteria needed for any specific end-use application. This knowledge will bring about a more intelligent selection of the most appropriate material. For example, in selecting a garment for protection from rain, it would be important to know the usual severity of the local rainfall and the degree of protection needed; that is, should the garment be rainproof and resistant to air permeability or could the repellency be more temporary, permitting greater comfort with an air-permeable material? These criteria involve physiology, thermal properties of fibers and fabrics, fabric structure, air permeability, effectiveness of special finishes, the chemistry of proper cleaning of the garment, and the importance of initial and afteruse appearance of the garment and fabric. Is protection the ultimate consideration, or should it be modified for a more fashionable appearance required by the purchaser? Is comfort the main factor, or might a heavier and more moisture-impervious fabric be tolerated? In the final analysis, it appears that consumership success depends on planning for use just as much as on planning the most successful and best-performing textile product at each step of production, from fiber to fabric to finished article.

It is possible to view planning on the part of the consumer as consisting of four basic steps.

1. *Selection.*   Information contributing to the intelligent selection of *which* of several competitive items would be the better buy and *why* this is true should provide the greatest degree of satisfaction with the purchase.

2. *Use.*   Users will be better satisfied and the product will last longer if the selection is well suited to the individual needs and requirements of the purchaser. This, again, is a part of the initial plan or purpose of the selection.

3. *Maintenance.*   When the most appropriate methods of care and cleaning have been adhered to, the consumer will be rewarded by increased service life and certainly by a much better appearance, whether of wearing apparel or some household textile material.

4. *Protection.*   This item, often overlooked, involves not only the physical protection of the textile product when not in use, such as the storage between the seasons, but also protection against the elements (such as fire danger and moisture seepage through a leaky wall or ceiling) and reasonable insurance for all household property against damage.

It will be noted that in the various steps leading to production of the final article, repeated attention is given to the matter of blending for uniformity of product. In maintenance and use, the consumer or user also benefits from the basic concept of blending. Here the blending is in the ordinary sensible in-use rotation of products. For example, towels, napkins, bedding and other household textiles should be rotated frequently, the freshly washed articles placed at the bottom of the pile, rather than at the top where they would be used and reused constantly. Another way in which the use pattern can be regarded as a blending operation is in the rotation of curtains about the house from sunny windows to shady ones. Thus, curtains are not always in the same exposure where sun fading or sun damage may occur. Similarly, when rugs are cleaned, their position should be reversed in order to equalize the wear. Stair carpeting also can be taken up for cleaning and then reversed.

CONSUMERSHIP—PROFESSIONAL AND AMATEUR

Changes and improvements in clothing and in the textiles of which they are made have contributed greatly to man's mobility and to his conquest not only of his own environment, but also of such extremes as outer space and inner space. Few of us are concerned, however, with these extremes. It is rewarding enough if in studying textiles and their applications to apparel and household comfort we become more selective and efficient buyers; learn how most effectively to wear, use, and care for what we buy; and know and fulfill our responsibilities as consumers.

Responsibilities

Consumer responsibility is not an idle phrase. It is real and applies to everything we buy or use; but as applied to clothing textiles, it affects not only our pocketbooks but also our public image. To purchase apparel for one's self or for one's family in a responsible manner requires taste in appropriate selection and factual knowledge of the textiles of which the apparel is made, the effects of the finishes applied, and the kind of care required for the best serviceability. We generally know *what* it is we want to buy when we visit a store, open a catalogue, or read an advertisement. What a challenging selection faces us! We must then decide *which* items we want to buy and are often guided by the esthetic qualities of color, texture, style, and other personal appeals. The best selection value can only be made when we know enough about materials to know *why* one is a better buy than the others. The informed and responsible consumer is familiar, too, with such guides as labels, booklets, and references to pertinent legislation and standards.

This responsibility does not end with the merchandise selection. Knowledgeable consumers are prepared for the kind of wear and care conditions required by the fabric structure, finish, and color. Armed with this knowledge, the consumer is qualified to judge whether a disappointing failure in serviceability is the result of a merchandise flaw or her own carelessness. Only under these conditions is she justified in filing a complaint with the store and seeking redress. Indeed, it is her responsibility to report any justifiable complaint. The store is then responsible for reporting such failure to its resource. Too often the first inkling of consumer disappointment coming to the attention of the garment manufacturer and then to the fabric resource is a sudden drying up of orders by retailers because their customers have found through sad experience that the esthetic qualities did not last through repeated washings or cleanings, or the special finish was nonpermanent, or the fabric failed to give the anticipated service. This applies to apparel and to rugs. These industries may never know why the orders stopped—was it the result of one of the failures mentioned here or was it a whim on the part of the public? At the risk of repeatedly belaboring a single point, it should be reiterated that only when merchandise of faulty nature is returned by the consumer and then channeled back through the market path can the nature and origin of flaws in the merchandise be determined. That element in the chain of textile production whose responsibility it is to make the necessary corrections can be notified in time to avoid widespread consumer disappointment during another market season.

Especially vulnerable are the producers of proprietary textile fibers whose products may be given a long-lasting bad name through no fault of their own but through some mishandling in finishing, dyeing, cutting, or inappropriate end-use application by the garment manufacturer. Publicly promoted textile-finishing processes are similarly vulnerable. The advantages to the consumer in purchasing a textile product identified by the proprietary label name of the primary source (the fiber or finish producer) are further emphasized in Chapter Eight.

Most of the research efforts of the textile industry have been devoted to the production of fibers of potential value to the consumer and to the finishing materials and processes involved in creating the qualities desired by the consumer in making a selection. With very few exceptions, less research has been done by the finishers of textiles and by the manufacturers of garments than by the chemical industry. Therefore, it is not surprising that with (1) the wide variety of materials from which to choose, (2) efforts to accelerate the time from the test tube to the store counter, and (3) the competitive dyestuffs and textile finishing agents available efforts to reduce the costs of the many processing steps frequently produce end-use items disappointing to the public. In other words, we are all of us participating in a gigantic experiment.

In this day of experimentation with the newest in fiber sources, styles, and textiles, and with constant pressure quickly to promote each new item or novel idea, the opportunities for error are magnified. Therefore, the consumer must participate more promptly and actively in helping the textile industry to fulfill *his* wants and needs better. To do so, much more must be known about textiles and their behavior and care. We cannot yet be in a position to collect all these facts, feed them into a computer, and come out with the ideal textile material for any special end-use. To supply this knowledge, the public really has only the home economist, trained in textiles and clothing, on whom to depend as a professionally qualified teacher with no axe to grind and no special interest to defend. Whether this home economist is employed by the textile industry; serves as a store buyer; is in the extension service; or teaches in a secondary school, college, or university, she *must* learn as much as possible about these new materials: how to care for them and how best to create a lively interest in the public in this very important matter of producing textiles better able to meet the need of the consumer.

Personal Needs

We might term the discussion thus far *social responsibility*, but the actual purchases are based on personal needs. We often disclose our ethnic origin and, indeed, our personal character as to neatness or sloppiness by the apparel we wear. Is our garb appropriate for the environment, physical or social, in which we find ourselves? The old adage, "Clothes make the man" pertains to this concept of the man being appropriately dressed for any occasion.

It is true that the textile industry can offer products more nearly ideal for the serviceability demanded for nearly every end-use product. There is still a somewhat obscure answer to the question of serviceability demanded: namely, by *whom*. Are these criteria advanced by the fabric producer who visualizes the greatest variety of possible end-uses for his fabric? Does the manufacturer of a dress define the fabric performance to be expected? Is the store buyer responsible for anticipating the style rightness, colors, and textures that will appeal to his clientele as well as the durability in use of garments and their constituent parts? Does the store buyer provide up-to-date guidance to the neophyte consumer as well as to those approaching senior citizenship who are thus a long way from their initial learning of facts? Do the store customers, the consumers of the goods, know enough about their own requirements to define the performance levels to be met in testing the goods to assure satisfactory use? Certainly none of these interested members in the development chain from fiber to home closet can be entirely responsible for shortcomings in satisfaction. It is, however, reasonable to conclude that the consumer is the one most keenly affected; his responsible judgment in selection and use will be greatly aided by an increased knowledge of textiles. It is the advanced amateur who achieves the greatest satisfaction in the purchases made and in their care. It is this same consumer who guides new market trends and products.

Basic Hypotheses

A few basic hypotheses are suggested here concerning the causes of our confusion in making choices and our inability to use to advantage some of the new tools available to us. Personal problems and needs cannot be answered by computer machines.

1. Good consumership is one definition of the fulfillment of the responsibilities of a consumer.
2. The measure of good consumership lies in understanding one's own or family's needs and buying textile products to that standard.
3. Confusion and uncertainty result from lack of knowledge and experience and thus create a feeling of frustration and suspicion during the decision making of many customers.
4. Few know and still fewer appreciate that the science and art of textile technology can be combined to produce *nearly* the perfect fabric for many of our end-use items and even for the stresses of extreme seasons.
5. Customers, and even some store buyers, do not appreciate the power for goodwill or for ill will possessed by textile finishers and dyers, the converters.
6. A fundamental knowledge of the characteristics and advantages of various textiles—including materials, constructions, and workmanship—is a prerequisite to the use of today's guides, such as laws, codes, or standards, as an aid in the decision making leading to good buying habits.

In considering the homemaker's responsibilities, it would be the easiest thing in the world to say, "Let her learn all the facts, then she will be a good, responsible consumer." The truth is that she does not have the background, the time, or the inclination to prepare herself. Looking at these six hypotheses, the second one seems to stand out. If that can be satisfied, the others all fall into line. Suppose we express this statement in another way.

The measure of a consumer's responsibility lies in her understanding *why* she selected one product over others to meet her needs and then, in her considered judgment, *how* it fulfilled those objectives. These two responsibilities would guide the consumer in future purchases.

We may boast that we are experienced buyers of clothing for ourselves and for our family and that these hypotheses do not apply to us, but experience is no longer a thoroughly dependable teacher in this age of rapid technological change and of increased attention to satisfying the needs of the public. Experience supplemented by knowledge will define the needs of our own household and thus specify the individual requirements these textile products must meet in order to be selected. They will also fortify our judgment as to the degree the merchandise has satisfied the performance characteristics required by use.

Textiles and Clothing: A Profession

The textbook is not the appropriate place in which to discuss the pros and cons of the expression *home economics* as the descriptive title of curricula offered by colleges of that name in many of our universities. It is a shelter, housing such varied professional courses of study as textiles and clothing, food and nutrition, family relations, child care, and teacher education. This writer has attempted to define the complexity of this course of study:

> Home Economics is synthesized by the elements of many disciplines derived from the physical sciences, the humanities, and the arts. It has a unique two-fold purpose in the college education of young women, which can only be achieved through the stimulating and intellectual challenges of these disciplines blended into an orderly course of study designed to provide the graduate with the foundation for a professional career and the more competent fulfillment of her traditional role of responsible citizen, wife, and mother.

Many of the professional positions open to graduates of what one might term a college of household engineering and management, majoring in textiles and clothing, are listed in the following table. Naturally, the closer the institution is to an area abounding in textile laboratories and mills, the more varied will be the local job opportunities.

ESSENTIAL PROPERTIES OF A TEXTILE FIBER

The definition of a fiber is not precise, and, in fact, textile terminology often makes no clear distinction between hair and fiber. In a general sense, a fiber can be regarded as the raw material used in the manufacture of textiles. Thus, it may be partly described as being a slender filament or fine strand of sufficient length, pliability, and strength to be spun into yarns and formed into cloth. Even within this definition, individual fibers vary greatly in appearance and length, from the almost endless filaments produced by the man-made fiber industry, including rayons and acetates and the new synthetics, to the short, hollow, twisted tubes identified as cotton fibers. They also vary between the relatively stiff monofilaments of saran, for example, and the soft, silky hair fiber of the angora rabbit. All these are textile raw materials.

Table 1-1 *Professional Opportunities for Textile and Clothing Majors*

	Fiber Producer	Fabric Producer	Dye and Finish Industry	Garment Manufacturing	Retailing	Retail Laboratories	Commercial Testing	Consulting Advisors (Magazines)	Laundry Industry	Dry Cleaning Industry	Government Laboratories	Agricultural Extension	School and College Teaching
Chemical researcher	X												
Consumer preference and/or satisfaction researcher	X	X	X	X	X	X	X	X	X	X	X	X	X
Use studies/performance researcher		X	X	X		X	X	X	X	X	X	X	X
Laboratory technician		X	X			X	X	X	X	X	X		
Technical writer			X		X	X	X			X	X		
Manufacturing representative		X	X	X					X	X			
Advisor to industry on consumer needs	X	X	X	X	X	X	X	X	X	X	X	X	X
Training director				X	X				X	X			
Buyer—retailer					X								
Stylist advisor			X	X	X						X	X	
Pattern designer		X	X	X							X	X	X
Clothing designer			X	X	X								
Writer of material of interest to public				X			X	X	X		X	X	X

Technologists sometimes differentiate three classifications of textile "fibers" on the basis of length. A **fibril** is a very small cell or a component of a fiber cell wall and is customarily measured in microns or millimicrons (one micron is 0.001-millimeter). A **fiber** is customarily measured in inches. A **filament** is an extruded fiber of extreme length, rarely measured but sometimes stated in yards or meters. Filaments may be cut to predetermined short lengths for spinning into yarns. These fibers are known as **staple fibers**. Only fibers and filaments are of interest to the textile industry and the consumer. Fibrils are of importance to researchers.

Fiber Properties: Essential Qualities

The spinnability of a fiber into a yarn depends very largely on its physical properties. These properties will be dealt with more fully in the sections devoted to the individual fibers and in discussion of the textile materials made from them. However, a brief reference to the physical and chemical properties is appropriate for laying a groundwork for the general definitions of these physical terms.

SPINNABILITY **Spinnability** includes several physical properties, each having an effect on the ability of the fibers to be spun into yarn. For example, staple fibers must be capable of taking a twist, they must have a certain degree of friction against one another to stay in place when pull is applied to the yarn, and they must be able to take and hold special finishes for lubrication during spinning or to provide additional surface resistance to soiling or abrasion. With fabric and yarn strength depending so much on the fiber-to-fiber contacts and friction effects, the strength of the individual fibers is incidental.

FIBER LENGTH A textile fiber must have sufficient **length** to be successfully spun into a yarn. Generally, a fiber must be at least 100 times as long as it is wide to be spinnable. Many fibers exceed this minimum by a large amount. Natural fibers vary in length from approximately ½-inch to 40 inches or more. Very fine, soft fibers such as kapok and milkweed fiber are too short for making a yarn, because the limit for economical spinning is approximately ½-inch. Generally, the longer the fiber, the stronger the yarn, and the more uniform its diameter. For best results in processing and in use, fibers should be relatively even in length in any spinning mixture.

FINENESS OR DIAMETER The **fineness** of a fiber is a relative measure of size, diameter, linear density, or weight per unit length. A variety of units are used. Rarely are fibers perfectly round in cross section; therefore, the geometrical cross section, wall thickness, and the diameter of the **lumen** or hollow center (if present) should be calculated if the fineness is to be determined with extreme accuracy for research or if precise grading problems are involved. The natural fibers vary greatly in fineness from place to place on an individual fiber. The man-made fibers are much more uniform in cross section and fineness as a result of their having been extruded through a metallic orifice called a spinneret and stretched.

CRIMP   **Crimp** is the waviness of a fiber. It is a natural quality in merino wools. Fine wools usually have many fine waves; coarse wool is more definitely curled rather than crimped. Crimp is often put into fibers for specific end uses; for example, carpet viscose rayon is given a permanent crimp in order to provide loftier or more vertical pile in carpeting. The synthetic fibers, being thermoplastic or heat-softened, can be given a more permanent crimp; this is a characteristic of some of the so-called textured yarns, which, unusually soft and bulky, are used for sweaters, socks, and suitings. Crimp is measured by the difference between the length of the crimped fiber as it lies at rest and of the same fiber stretched gently until it is perfectly straight. Crimp is expressed as the percentage of the unstretched fiber length.

TENSILE STRENGTH   **Tensile strength** is the ability to resist breakage as a result of stress or pull. Generally, it is expressed in terms of the force per unit of cross-sectional area—that is, kilograms per square millimeter or pounds per square inch (psi). The most common term for fiber and yarn strength is **tenacity**, which is the force per unit linear density; for example, where the yarn number is expressed as a weight per unit length, such as grams per denier. Tensile strength and tenacity are not the same, but there is a mathematical procedure for getting one from the other. (See Appendix II, Table 1.)

Wet strength is often an important characteristic, particularly in the vegetable fibers, which have a higher wet strength than their dry breaks, and in the protein fibers and rayon, which characteristically have lower tenacities when wet than when dry.

It should be noted that each of these physical properties contributes in some measure to property number one having to do with the spinnability of a fibrous material. It is not essential that all potential fibers possess all of these features; however, special techniques in spinning can compensate for some of the features that may be missing in any particular fiber. There are other physical characteristics that contribute to yarn formation and also to specific end-use applications of the fabric or apparel. These are what might be termed *wants*, by way of characteristics, as distinct from the *needs*, or the fundamentals, without which yarn formation would be more difficult. Elasticity is a case in point.

ELASTICITY   **Elasticity** is the property by which the fiber tends to recover its original length upon removal of a stress that caused deformation or stretch. Vulcanized rubber is an outstanding example of a highly extensible or elastic material that recovers almost immediately its original form and length when the load is released. Under certain conditions of heat and moisture, wool also shows considerable elasticity. On the other hand, certain of the cellulose fibers show so little extensibility as to be classed as brittle. Numerous research chemists probing into the structure of high **polymers** (or giant, chainlike molecules, such as rubber, nylon, and other man-made fibers) and cotton and wool are in substantial agreement that the key to differences in elasticity between fibers is associated with the chain structure of the simple chemical links of the various polymers. The **elastic limit** is the maximum load or stress to which a fiber or yarn can be subjected without the formation of a permanent set when the load is removed. This property affects the setting of crimp or curl in synthetic fibers.

COHESION   **Cohesion** is the property of clinging or sticking together in a mass. Usually, the more rigid the fiber, the lower its cohesion. Lack of cohesion on the part of one fiber will often make the uniform blending of this and a more cohesive fiber somewhat uncertain. It is generally assumed that a high degree of frictional resistance plays a part in cohesiveness. It is certain that external scales and neps (the surface irregularities on wool and flax, respectively) and the twists and irregularities in the diameter of cotton contribute to the ability of such fibers to hold together. Smoothly textured, uniformly surfaced fibers, such as most of the man-made types, do not possess this phenomenon of cohesion unless specially treated. It is not measurable by laboratory means.

DENSITY   **Density** is the mass or weight of material per unit volume generally expressed in grams per cubic centimeter. The **specific gravity** or **specific weight** of a material is the ratio of the mass weighed in air to the mass of an equal volume of water at 4°C. Because the exact volume is affected by the lumen in hollow fibers, the porosity (resulting from surface cracks), and the amount of crystallinity in certain sections of the individual fibers, the true density is very difficult to determine, and the specific gravity is generally the preferred method of expressing the weight of a textile fiber. In Table 1–2 the specific gravities of the principal textile fibers are given, beginning with the synthetics, which are the lightest, to asbestos and glass, the heaviest.

PLASTICITY   **Plasticity** is the property of a solid by which, under certain conditions of temperature or pressure, it can be made to take on the shape of any mold and to retain this shape after cooling. The synthetic fibers, being

Table 1-2   Specific Gravities of Fibers

Fiber	Specific Gravity	Fiber	Specific Gravity
Polyethylene	0.95	Wool	1.32
Polystyrene	1.05	Acetate	1.33
Nylon 66	1.14	Silk (raw)	1.33
Acrylics	1.14–1.22	Vinyon HH	1.34
Vicara	1.25	Polyesters	1.22 or 1.38
Silk (boiled off)	1.25	Cotton	1.50
Vinylons	1.30	Flax	1.50
Modacrylics	1.30–1.37	Cuprammonium rayon	1.52
		Rayon	1.52
		Saran	1.70
		Asbestos	2.10–2.80
		Teflon	2.30
		Fiberglas	2.56

SOURCE: J. J. Press, ed., *Man-made Textile Encyclopedia* (New York: John Wiley & Sons, Inc., 1959), Table II, p. 145.

thermoplastic materials, are all heat-softened. The heat setting of nylon hosiery to a predetermined size is an example of this phenomenon. The stretch yarns, many of which are of nylon—but which may be of other thermoplastic material—are other examples of plasticity applied to fibrous materials. Moisture may also contribute to some fiber plasticity. Under certain conditions, wool becomes somewhat plastic, so that a wool suit can be shaped or molded under the influence of steam and pressure to give a smoothly fitting shoulder or lapel.

RESILIENCE   **Resilience** is the springing back or recovery of a fiber when it is released from a deformation. Recovery from a compression is a desirable attribute in carpeting materials, for it enables the indentations from chair and table feet to disappear when the furniture has been moved. Resilience is also a desirable property in filling fibers for pillows and mattresses and in some types of wearing apparel. Other examples of resilience are recovery from bending (such as wrinkling) and restoration of shape after stretching.

ABSORBENCY   Because most textile fibers **absorb moisture** from the air, it is important that the market purchaser of fibers and yarns knows their moisture content so that he will not be paying fiber prices for water. The amount of moisture present is expressed as a percentage of the original weight of the material or of its oven-dry weight. In the first case, it is expressed as the percentage of moisture in the textile material as received; in the second case, it is referred to as the **moisture regain**, or moisture absorbed from a standard atmosphere (70°F and 65 per cent relative humidity) after exposure of the oven-dried sample. Storage conditions play a very significant part in the amount of moisture a fiber will absorb. For the consumer, absorbency is an important factor in the comfort of apparel. Briefly, the fibers that absorb moisture are more comfortable than those with low absorbency, especially in hot, humid weather when perspiration is removed rapidly by absorbent fibers. The warmth of wool in cold weather is unique.

CAPILLARITY OR POROSITY   These two terms express properties with a similar influence on the ability of a textile fiber or yarn to accept and hold a dye, a finish, a lubricant, or even a resin in order to increase the wrinkle resistance of a fabric or to give it a "wash-and-wear" finish. Liquids pass rapidly through small cracks or breaks in the outer surface of a fiber, bringing about absorption of a liquid through **porosity**. Porosity is the ratio of the volume of void or air contained within the boundaries of the material to the total volume (solid matter plus void), expressed as a percentage. In the case of the passage of these liquids through the hollow center, or lumen, in cotton or through small voids on the surface of a wool fiber, it is usually regarded as the effect of the mechanism termed **capillarity**. In either case, it is important that the desired material absorbed should then be retained in the fiber permanently. The rise of a liquid in a yarn or fabric is called wicking and is a property related to capillarity and absorbency.

COLOR   Most natural fibers have some **color**. For example, silk is yellow to tan; wool has a brownish tint; cotton is a creamy white or brown; most of the synthetic fibers, too, have a slight creamy or yellowish color. Fibers must, therefore, be bleached, boiled, or stripped of their color by some chemical process in order to produce as white a fiber and yarn as possible. This is necessary not only for white fabrics, but also for a more even dyeing of the fabrics for consumer use.

LUSTER   Generally, a certain amount of **luster**, or light reflectance, is desirable to give variable brightness intensity as the direction of light or of viewing are moved to show off brightness and any woven-in or printed pattern on the textile goods. It is an ornamental or an esthetic property rather than a necessity. Sometimes fibers have too much luster or brightness. Many of our man-made fibers, including rayon and acetate (but also a great many of the synthetics), are found on the market as bright, semidull, and dully textured fibers, filaments, yarns, and fabrics. A common dulling agent is titanium dioxide (TiO_2), known industrially as Titanox. It is also used today in many white paints.

FLAMMABILITY **Flammability** will be discussed in detail in Chapter Seven, but as a general fiber property, the mineral fibers, such as glass, asbestos, and mineral wool, do not burn. Dynel and Saran are also non-flammable, and undyed nylon is generally regarded as a nonflammable fiber. With these exceptions, all other textile fibers burn, some of them being highly combustible. Because fibers are so very fine and because a mass of fibers, unless very tightly packed, contains abundant air, they are readily ignited and may burn fiercely. The cellulosic fibers, cotton and rayon, are readily flammable in fabrics having a napped or raised surface and in extremely sheer nets. The first Flammable Fabrics Act (Public Law 88) was passed by the 83rd Congress and signed by President Eisenhower on June 30, 1953. The Flammable Fabrics Act as amended and revised now applies to all textile end-uses; it is discussed in detail on pp. 309–11.

STATIC ELECTRICAL RESISTANCE The phenomenon of **static electricity** creates a problem in the spinning and other processing of textile fibers, especially in rooms with very low relative humidity. The problem is much more severe in the case of synthetic fibers, which have extremely low **electrical conductivity** and generally absorb too little moisture to provide a path whereby the static charge can be carried away. Static electrical properties create problems in the packaging, in the sewing, and in the wearing of many of these textile products. The problem of static electricity will be discussed on p. 315.

As we now proceed to study the members of the natural fibers and of the man-made fiber families, we will note that all these different fibers are good and serviceable for a considerable number of types of apparel and for other textile products used in the home. Indeed, the successful use of some fibers for their end-use specialities may depend as much on the absence of a certain fiber property as the presence of another.

TEXTILE FIBER CLASSIFICATIONS

Recognizing the many physical and chemical differences between fibers of different origins, and being faced by an always increasing number of fiber names and claims for the expanding lists of man-made fibers, consumers were becoming confused and their selections were much more difficult to make in the retail market. In recognition of this, the Textile Fiber Products Identification Act was passed by the Senate and signed by President Eisenhower on September 2, 1958. It became effective 18 months later when the

Federal Trade Commission (FTC) was made responsible for the definitions, rules, and regulations affecting the administration of the Textile Fiber Products Identification Act (TFPIA).

The names of most of the fibers on the market are shown in Figure 1–1. In each family of man-made fibers, the fiber producers' trademark names are mentioned in the section in which that fiber family is discussed. It should be noted that the natural fibers are broken down into two groups, the cellulosic, or vegetable, and the protein, or animal, fibers. The man-made fibers are divided into two major categories: The first is the nonthermoplastic fibers which includes rayon, a regenerated cellulose fiber. Regenerated fibers are derived from natural materials and then, through chemical manipulation, are put into liquid form for extrusion. The second category, the thermoplastic fibers, includes the acetates, which are salts of cellulose, and the synthesized fibers. This group of man-made fibers has been described as **manufactured** fibers or **synthetic** fibers formed from materials of a non-fibrous nature that have been made to react together to form a giant molecule. Most of these are thermoplastic materials. There are three groups of inorganic man-made fibers that are regarded as non-thermoplastic in the ordinary conditions of use. These include the mineral, glass, and the metallic fibers of aluminium and other metal strips.

Economic Factors

If a fiber is to qualify for the textile industry, three basic economic requirements must be met:

1. It must be available in sufficient quantity.
2. It must be economical in cost or have excellent competitive value for use in certain textile products.
3. It must have satisfactory fineness to be readily spinnable into a yarn.

The man-made fibers face two other requirements for successful marketing in competition with the natural fibers:

4. Costly chemicals and solvents must be recoverable for reuse.
5. By-products must be marketable, and waste must be disposable at low cost.

To a lesser degree, these same additional qualifications must be faced by the natural fibers, for waste and byproducts are found in the waxes, oil, and gums in cotton, wool, and silk, for example. Then, too, contaminants, such as sand, burrs, leaves, and tangled fibers, called neps, are found in wool and other animal fibers. Contaminants of an organic nature are the waxes, gums, and woody materials in the stems from which are obtained such fibers as flax and ramie.

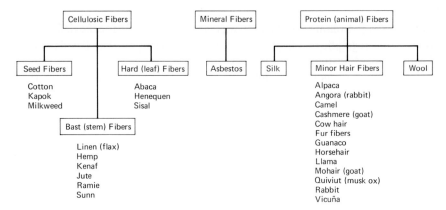

Figure 1-1 Classification of textile fibers of importance in the United States: Natural fibers.

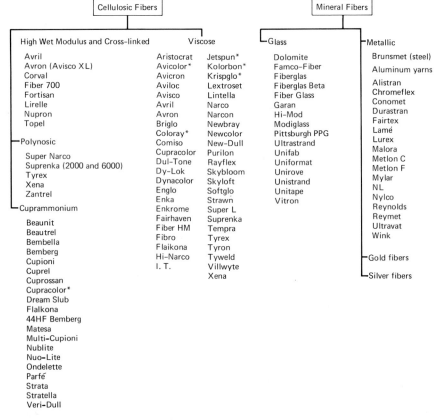

Note: Capitalized names are trademarks assigned to the manufacturer.

*Trademark names of solution–dyed fibers.

Figure 1-1 (*cont.*) Nonthermoplastic man-made fibers.

16

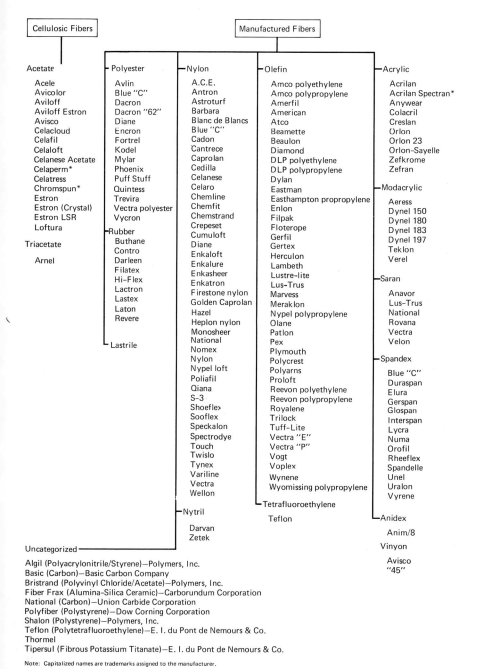

Cellulosic Fibers	Manufactured Fibers			

Acetate

Acele
Avicolor
Aviloff
Aviloff Estron
Avisco
Celacloud
Celafil
Celaloft
Celanese Acetate
Celaperm*
Celatress
Chromspun*
Estron
Estron (Crystal)
Estron LSR
Loftura

Triacetate

Arnel

Polyester

Avlin
Blue "C"
Dacron
Dacron "62"
Diane
Encron
Fortrel
Kodel
Mylar
Phoenix
Puff Stuff
Quintess
Trevira
Vectra polyester
Vycron

Rubber

Buthane
Contro
Darleen
Filatex
Hi-Flex
Lactron
Lastex
Laton
Revere

Lastrile

Nylon

A.C.E.
Antron
Astroturf
Barbara
Blanc de Blancs
Blue "C"
Cadon
Cantrece
Caprolan
Cedilla
Celanese
Celaro
Chemline
Chemfit
Chemstrand
Crepeset
Cumuloft
Diane
Enkaloft
Enkalure
Enkasheer
Enkatron
Firestone nylon
Golden Caprolan
Hazel
Heplon nylon
Monosheer
National
Nomex
Nylon
Nypel loft
Poliafil
Qiana
S-3
Shoeflex
Sooflex
Speckalon
Spectrodye
Touch
Twislo
Tynex
Variline
Vectra
Wellon

Nytril

Darvan
Zetek

Olefin

Amco polyethylene
Amco polypropylene
Amerfil
American
Atco
Beamette
Beaulon
Diamond
DLP polyethylene
DLP polypropylene
Dylan
Eastman
Easthampton propropylene
Enlon
Filpak
Floterope
Gerfil
Gertex
Herculon
Lambeth
Lustre-lite
Lus-Trus
Marvess
Meraklon
Nypel polypropylene
Olane
Patlon
Pex
Plymouth
Polycrest
Polyarns
Proloft
Reevon polyethylene
Reevon polypropylene
Royalene
Trilock
Tuff-Lite
Vectra "E"
Vectra "P"
Vogt
Voplex
Wynene
Wyomissing polypropylene

Tetrafluoroethylene

Teflon

Acrylic

Acrilan
Acrilan Spectran*
Anywear
Colacril
Creslan
Orlon
Orlon 23
Orlon-Sayelle
Zefkrome
Zefran

Modacrylic

Aeress
Dynel 150
Dynel 180
Dynel 183
Dynel 197
Teklon
Verel

Saran

Anavor
Lus-Trus
National
Rovana
Vectra
Velon

Spandex

Blue "C"
Duraspan
Elura
Gerspan
Glospan
Interspan
Lycra
Numa
Orofil
Rheeflex
Spandelle
Unel
Uralon
Vyrene

Anidex

Anim/8

Vinyon

Avisco
"45"

Uncategorized

Algil (Polyacrylonitrile/Styrene)—Polymers, Inc.
Basic (Carbon)—Basic Carbon Company
Bristrand (Polyvinyl Chloride/Acetate)—Polymers, Inc.
Fiber Frax (Alumina-Silica Ceramic)—Carborundum Corporation
National (Carbon)—Union Carbide Corporation
Polyfiber (Polystyrene)—Dow Corning Corporation
Shalon (Polystyrene)—Polymers, Inc.
Teflon (Polytetrafluoroethylene)—E. I. du Pont de Nemours & Co.
Thormel
Tipersul (Fibrous Potassium Titanate)—E. I. du Pont de Nemours & Co.

Note: Capitalized names are trademarks assigned to the manufacturer.

*Trademark names of solution-dyed fibers.

Figure 1-1 (*cont.*)   Thermoplastic man-made fibers.

CHAPTER TWO

Natural Fibers: Cellulosic and Protein Fibers

CHARACTERISTICS OF NATURAL CELLULOSIC FIBERS

Because the differences in the physical properties of fibers affect the formation of yarns and fabrics and even influence the cutting and sewing together of garments, it is well to scrutinize very carefully the physical properties peculiar to the natural fibers and to man-made fibers and filaments. There is no perfect fiber. In order to avoid as much confusion as possible between fiber properties and those of the fabrics and garments made of these fibers, principal emphasis here will be given to the *physical* rather than the chemical properties of the fibers themselves. The reader should be reminded that many of the physical properties of fibers become lost in the manufacture of the cloth and especially in its finishing. In discussing yarns and finished goods and the problems concerned with clothing selection and care in other areas of this book, the emphasis will be on the significance of the *chemical* properties of the fibers. The chemical properties of a fiber remain in the fabric except when special finishes are added to make a fiber more suitable for some new use.

COTTON FIBERS

It is difficult to appreciate the chemical and physical structure of the almost invisible cotton fiber pulled from a yarn or from a batting of absorbent cotton. In reality, cotton (of the botanical family **gossypium**) is a giant molecule, termed a **polymer**. This cellulose molecule is believed to contain 16,000 individual units or monomers (one omer) of glucose, a simple sugar, the chemical configuration of which is shown in Figure 2–1.

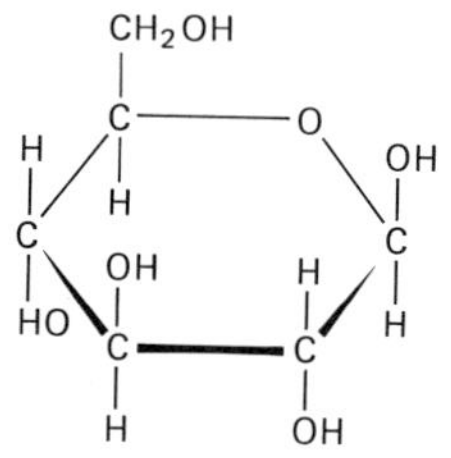

Figure 2-1 The glucose molecule. The cellulose chain in glucose units: The heavy lines in the rings represent linkages and portions of the glucose units projecting toward the observer. Light lines recede. This shows the spiral nature of the molecular structure. The six carbons in each glucose molecule are numbered to show how and where each substituent (that is, hydroxyl [OH]; alcohol [CH_2OH]; and glucosidic linkage) is located. In the ring structure the corner carbons are usually not shown. [E. Ott and H. Spurlin, eds., *Cellulose and Cellulose Derivatives* (New York: Interscience, 1954), p. 64.]

GLUCOSE   In the cellulose molecule, these glucose units form a chain. The method of attachment is by the splitting of a molecule of water between pairs of touching terminal carbon atoms. Cellulose is made up of 44.4 per cent carbon, 6.2 per cent hydrogen, and 49.4 per cent carbon.

Many of the chemical properties and chemical reactions of cotton, such as dyeing, processing, weather resistance, washability, and acid and alkali exposure resistance, are dependent on the alcohol or hydroxyl groups along the sides of the cellulose molecule.

Characteristics of the Fiber

The cotton fiber is a long cell made up of countless cellulose molecules. One of several concepts of the construction of the cellulose molecule is shown in Figure 2–2. The electron microscope, a tool much more powerful than the ordinary optical microscope, discloses structures that are invisible under the optical system. The cellulose wall from the cotton fiber is disclosed as a series of concentric growth rings somewhat similar in appearance to growth rings in a tree stump; within these are minute fibrous deposits, **fibrils,** that are laid down in a latticelike formation (see Figure 2–3). These fibrils have a minute coating of wax. They are not all of the same length. The center of the cotton fiber is a collapsed channel, the residue of the tube through which nutrients reach the fiber and enable it to grow to maturity. The outer surface skin of the fiber is termed the **Cuticle.** (See Figure 2–4.) To the

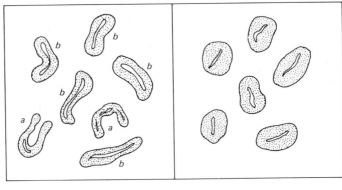

Nonmercerized

a, Immature—U–shaped thin wall;
lumen not prominent.
b, Mature—roughly bean-shaped
and flat; lumen visible, twisted.

Mercerized

Swollen to approximate
round cross section

Figure 2-2 Typical cross sections showing the microscopic appearance of cotton fibers. (Based on ASTM Committee D-13 Standards for Textiles, 1962, and data from fiber producers.)

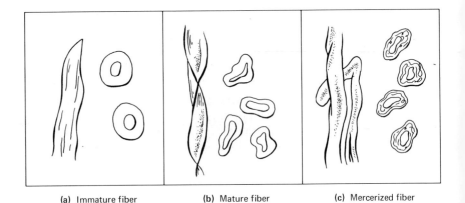

(a) Immature fiber   (b) Mature fiber   (c) Mercerized fiber

Figure 2-3 Sketches of the cotton fiber in three conditions.

naked eye, the cotton fiber exhibits a twisted structure. Under the microscope, it looks more like a flat, randomly twisted ribbon.

When cotton fibers are treated with sodium hydroxide in the **mercerization** process (see p. 286), the fibers swell and straighten somewhat; thus, they become more lustrous and are stronger. Various cotton fibers exhibit variations in flatness of cross section under magnification. Some have a comparatively regular shape resembling a lima bean; others are much more irregular and some are flat.

Tables 2–1 and 2–6 give the characteristics of the two principal cellulosic fibers, cotton and linen. Cotton varies considerably in fiber length and in

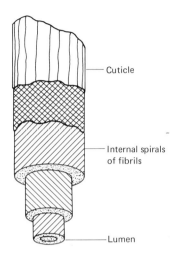

Cuticle

Internal spirals
of fibrils

Lumen   *Figure 2-4*   Concept of an idealized cotton fiber.

fineness or thinness of the fiber; it has very low luster. Fibers have a low breaking strength, but the twisted nature of the fibers and their cohesiveness enable a spinner to make a compact and tight yarn of excellent strength. Plant geneticists are constantly endeavoring to improve the type of cotton available in the United States and elsewhere in the world, and the organic chemist is greatly strengthening cotton by means of chemical reactions among the molecules in the individual fiber.

The spiral structure of the fibrils and their ability to slide under stress or pulling gives cotton a slight degree of elasticity. Linen has none. Cotton has a low conductivity of heat but is regarded as a cool, comfortable material largely because it absorbs moisture so rapidly. It is stronger when wet than when dry. Its resistance to dilute alkali makes it possible for cotton fabrics and garments to be washed in soap of almost any pH value. When exposed to strong alkali, cotton fabrics will shrink unless they are kept under tension, where, in the absence of air, cotton fibers become mercerized. Strong mineral acids destroy cotton rapidly, and it is weakened by dilute acid. Certain antiperspirant solutions containing metallic chlorides can release hydrochloric acid that will tender cotton by forming a structureless, easily powdered substance, **hydrocellulose**. Cotton is weakened by oxidation either from an excessively strong bleach or by intense sunlight. Fabrics can be pressed with a hot iron up to 400°F. It scorches at 475°F and is flammable in certain fabric constructions having a vast surplus of air in the fabric structure, such as in chenilles, cotton blankets and velvets, and the other napped or raised-surface fabrics of cotton. Cotton fibers, alone or blended with other materials, can be spun into firm, tightly twisted yarns or soft, lofty yarns capable of being napped. Cotton fabrics, therefore, will vary from crisp sheer organdies to heavy industrial ducks; or from fine broadcloth shirtings to canvas belts; or from sheer nets and curtain fabrics to heavy rugs and carpets. These uses are further enhanced by the ease of washing and caring for this fiber in fabrics. In cold weather clothing, cotton functions in two ways: it can provide a dense and compact fabric that is virtually impenetrable by wind to serve as an outer shell or it can be utilized in soft, bulky yarns knitted into the *brynje* vest worn by Scandinavian fishermen in cold weather, or as a fluffy inner shell in children's winter jackets. A windproof outer shell with bulky inner layers holding dead air constitutes the *layer principle* for clothing men in the Armed Forces in cold weather.

Chemical Constitution

The cotton fiber consists of about 89 per cent cellulose, with small quantities of gums and oils. Raw cotton fiber masses also retain small particles of the

Table 2-1 Characteristics of Cotton

Physical Characteristics	
Microscopic appearance	Flat tube, spiral twists
Length of fiber	¾-in. to 1½-in.
Diameter	0.0005-in. to 0.0009-in.
Color	Yellowish or cream; may be clean white
Luster	Not pronounced
Strength	Single fiber, 2–5 grams per denier
Elasticity	Lower than silk or wool; spiral structure makes it better than linen
Conductivity to heat	Fair
Regain or hygroscopic moisture	7–10 per cent
Capillarity and penetrability	Has capillarity
Composition	87–90 per cent cellulose; 4–6 per cent gums, proteins, etc.; 5–8 per cent water
Specific gravity	1.50–1.58
Preparation of fiber	Ginning to remove too short fibers
Chemical Characteristics	
Effect of light	Weakens
Mildew	Readily attacked
Heat	Withstands well; can be heated to 300°F with no damage; scorches at 475°F and burns
Water	Even boiling water has no action

Mineral acids
  sulfuric
  hydrochloric
  nitric
  hydrofluoric
	Concentrated acids destroy; cold dilute acids do not injure if washed out or neutralized; dilute solutions (3 per cent or less) of these acids, if allowed to dry, make tender and destroy

Table 2-1 (continued)

Volatile organic acids
  formic
  acetic
	No detrimental action

Nonvolatile organic acids
  oxalic
  tartaric
  citric
	Will tender slightly if not removed, especially if heat is applied

Strong alkalies
  caustic soda
  soda ash
	No injury, even if concentrated and even if heat is applied when air is excluded; concentrated solution will mercerize if cotton is under tension; otherwise, cotton will shrink

Weak alkalies
  ammonium carbonate
  borax
  sodium phosphate
  sodium silicate
  soap
	No injury

Oxidizing agents (potassium permanganate)	Destroys if not controlled
Metallic salts	Has practically no affinity for metallic salts
Affinity for dyestuffs	Less than that of silk and wool

Classes of dyestuffs met with in
  common use
	Direct
	Sulfur
	Basic with mordant
	Coloring matter developed on fiber
	  vat colors

Bleaching agents
  chlorine bleach or
  hypochlorites
	Cold dilute not detrimental to fiber (must be removed, as heat and concentrated solutions destroy)

Other oxidation bleaches
  hydrogen peroxide
  sodium perborate
  potassium permanganate plus
  bisulfite of soda
	No injury if properly controlled

Reduction bleaches
  sulfurous acid
  (sulfur dioxide plus water)
  hydrosulfite
	No injury if controlled

SOURCE: National Institute of Drycleaning (NID).

hard shells from the bolls and the cotton seed. The removal of such components is described in the topic on cotton finishing (p. 287). The characteristics of the cotton fiber from the standpoint of the various criteria set up for a successful fiber are shown in Table 2–1.

Cotton Linters

Mention should be made of the extremely short and fine cotton fibers called linters that cling to the seed but are too short to be spun into a yarn. Cotton linters are generally ¼- to ⅜-inch in length. For many years they have been one of the main materials for stuffing toys, dolls, and shoulder pads for women's dresses; for filling comforters; as a matted layer in mattresses and upholstered or overstuffed furniture; and for various surgical pads and compresses. Most cotton linters today go into the rayon and acetate industries and provide one of the sources of cellulose for these man-made fibers (Figure 2–5). The removal of these from the harvested cotton is by ginning.

Cotton Fabric Versatility

The versatility of cotton permits its use in many textile items that may require it to be subjected to one or more of many special functional finishes, such as water repellency, wrinkle resistance, durable-press, flame resistance, and protection from mildew and from bacteria, in addition to other resin and chemical treatments. It is not to be construed that every cotton fabric is given all these finishes. It is so readily dyed and can be given such a variety of textures that its application to consumer goods is practically limitless.

Sources of Cotton

Cotton was one of the treasures of the Orient that Columbus was seeking when he discovered the Americas. Even in his time, the beautiful and sheer cottons of India and China were quite well known in the trade of Europe. The long caravan routes were hazardous and costly to the textile traders of of Europe.

Although some cotton is grown in almost every country in the world, the United States is the most important cotton-producing nation, and despite the inroads of the man-made textile materials, cotton still accounts for 43 per cent (1969) of the fiber consumption in the United States. Cotton is a product commonly grown as far as 34° latitude on both sides of the equator. In the United States, it is concentrated in a band from the Atlantic to the Pacific, bounded on the north approximately by the Mason-Dixon line—

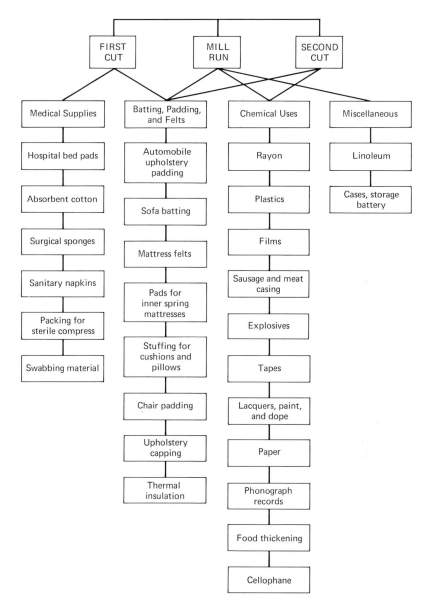

Figure 2-5　The use of cotton linters.

that is, along the tops of the states of Virginia, Tennessee, and Kentucky—
and extending south about 300 miles. As one travels from east to west, one
finds different types or varieties of cotton, each suited to the growing conditions of the region insofar as terrain, quality of soil, and amount of moisture
are concerned.

Until recent years, with the entry of very large acreages of cotton permitting the use of mechanized equipment, the growing of cotton, was essentially a hand-labor operation and was originally made possible in the United States through the importation of slaves to work the plantation fields in the South. (See Figure 2–6.) The question of slavery as a means of labor was

Figure 2-6   Hand picking cotton. (Courtesy of Burlington Industries, Inc.)

one of the principal incendiary issues leading to the Civil War. But from its earliest history, cotton marketing has been a source of international irritation both commercially and politically. It is interesting to note that this condition of conflict exists today. For example, Japan is one of our best customers for raw cotton. Our own textile industry is necessarily deeply concerned about the amount of finished cotton goods being imported back into the United States from Japan and other nations.

Cotton Production in the United States

For the past 15 years, the following states ranked from first to fourteenth in the production of cotton.

1. Texas	8. Tennessee
2. Mississippi	9. Georgia
3. California	10. South Carolina
4. Arkansas	11. Oklahoma
5. Arizona	12. New Mexico
6. Alabama	13. Missouri
7. Louisiana	14. North Carolina

Slight shifts in order have occurred occasionally. Small amounts of cotton are produced in other states within the cotton belt. The longest domestic staple cotton is produced in California, New Mexico, Texas, and Arizona.

The consumption and production picture of cotton in the world market is complex. Through the years the long-term leadership of cotton in consumption has gradually declined to an approximate 40 per cent in 1973, not only in the United States but elsewhere in the world. For many years, the United States government has had a variety of price-support products in areas of agriculture in which surpluses were so great they threatened the economy of other nations, as well as the bankruptcy of thousands of our own producers. This has been true especially of lower grade, and therefore less marketable, cottons. These government surpluses are drawn upon for the production of cotton products of lower durability here and abroad, as a supply of some of these standard grades for foreign manufacturers, and for nontextile use in this country. There ought to be a storage reserve against which producers of cotton goods can draw in times of low domestic production resulting from drought, flooding, disease, or some other catastrophe that has destroyed a large part of a crop.

Ten countries produce about 85 per cent of the total cotton supply. In 1967, the United States produced 20.3 per cent; the USSR, 19.1; Mainland China, 13.4; India, 9.4; Mexico, 4.6; Pakistan and the UAR, 4.3; Brazil, 4.2; Turkey 3.6; and the Sudan, 1.8 per cent. Production forecasts for 1968 and for 1970 indicate that the USSR is currently producing slightly more cotton than the United States.

The world mill consumption of cotton shows the United States and USSR first and second; with the United States, 21.8 per cent; USSR, 14.2; Mainland China, 13.4; India, 11.6; Japan, 6.2 Pakistan, 2.7; France, 2.4; Brazil and West Germany, 2.3 each; and Italy, 2.1 per cent.

Growing Cotton

The cotton boll is the seed pod that develops after the cotton blossom has fallen from the plant. As the vast number of individual cotton fibers develop in the boll, they are seen as slender, thin-walled, hollow-centered fibers, the development of which depends upon the life fluids flowing into the individual fibers through the plant stem and root system. As the boll matures and the cotton fibers reach their full growth of between ¾- and 1½-inches, depending on the species, the fibers dry, the inner canal or lumen collapses, and the fibers begin to curl and twist so that eventually they resemble flat and twisted ribbon sections. When the boll is fully matured, it cracks open. If the plant is allowed to stand in the field too long, the fibers will blow away, carrying the seeds from the plant with them.

In hand picking cotton, it has been the custom to go through the field two or even three times, with the worker picking only the mature bolls, because immature cotton does not dye as uniformly nor is it as strong as that which has been fully developed (Figure 2–7). In the relatively dry western states, cotton fields may be hundreds or even thousands of acres in extent, and where the terrain is relatively flat, the fields are irrigated and mechanized cultivation and picking are used. Under these conditions, to insure the uniformity of fiber, it is customary to spray the plants with a chemical to **defoliate** them, that is, to remove all the leaves. This exposes all bolls to direct sunlight so that they mature almost at the same time, and only one picking is then necessary.

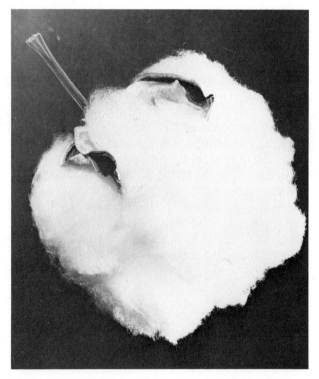

Figure 2-7   A ripe cotton boll. (Courtesy of Burlington Industries, Inc.)

Two of the most important of the United States cottons, the so-called Pima and Supima, have been genetically developed as hybrids from our **Sea Island** cotton and from fine Egyptian cotton stock. The **Pima** fibers grow as long as 1½ inches, almost as long as Sea Island; the Pima, the most treasured of our domestic cottons, has been pushed almost into the Atlantic Ocean by the boll weevil. The newly hatched beetle larvae develop and feed on the soft fibers before this longer and more slowly maturing Sea Island cotton matures. Shorter fiber length **Upland** cottons, which include the varieties grown in the south-central and eastern states, mature more rapidly and generally can be harvested before the weevil larvae become too active. It must be borne in mind that the longer the cotton fiber, the finer and more slender it is and the slower it is to mature. The Pima cottons are exclusively grown on irrigated land in Texas, California, and Arizona from carefully controlled seed stocks. Egyptian long-staple cotton is regarded as the finest in the world (Figure 2–8), and most of this now goes to Russia as part of an international agreement tied in with the Soviet government's completion of the giant Aswan Dam at the headwaters of the Nile.

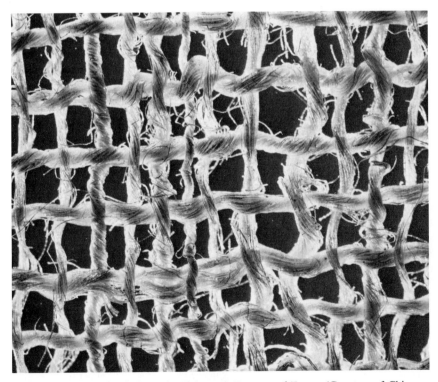

Figure 2-8   Cotton fabric from the Eighteenth Dynasty of Egypt. (Courtesy of Chicopee Manufacturing Company)

Cotton Grading and Marketing

After the ginning operation for the removal of the cotton seed (Figure 2–9), the cotton fibers are pressed into bales of about 500 pounds each and taken to the market. Here, the cotton is classified or graded as to fiber length, grade, and character. Sample bales are classified from each lot, and the price at which the shipment is auctioned off depends on this inspection.

    The staple length classification includes the following groups or classes (Figure 2–10): (1) Very short-staple cotton, less than ¼-inch, which is not suitable for spinning but is used in battings or fillings and as a nap for blankets. Most of this is an imported cotton. (2) Short-staple cotton, ¼-

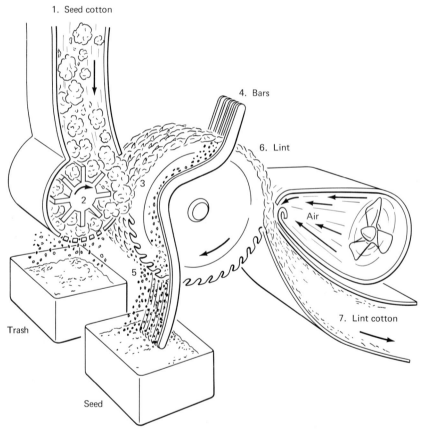

Figure 2-9 Operation of the cotton gin: (1) Seed cotton enters gin. (2) Roll throws seed cotton against fast-turning saws. (3) Saw teeth take cotton up and against bars. (4) Bars near to saws on both sides let lint pass through, but hold back seed. (5) Seed falls down into conveyor. (6) Lint on saw teeth is struck by blast of air and blown into (7) lint cotton conveyer pipe. (Courtesy of Bibb Manufacturing Company)

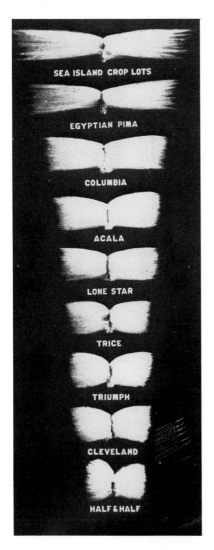

SEA ISLAND CROP LOTS

EGYPTIAN PIMA

COLUMBIA

ACALA

LONE STAR

TRICE

TRIUMPH

CLEVELAND

HALF & HALF

Figure 2-10 Combed fiber on the seed of varieties of cotton grown in the United States. (One-half natural size)

to $1\frac{5}{16}$-inch. This is used for coarser, inexpensive cotton goods where the many fiber ends are not objectionable. (3) Medium-staple cotton, $1\frac{5}{16}$- to $1\frac{1}{8}$ inches, which makes up the greater part of our Upland cotton from the foothills of the Blue Ridge Mountains to the Mississippi. Most sheetings and carded knitting yarns, print cloths, and twills are made of this grade. (4) Ordinary long-staple cotton, $1\frac{1}{8}$ to $1\frac{3}{8}$ inches, much of which comes from the Mississippi delta region for fine combed fabrics, such as lawns, piqués, and broadcloths. This is also known as the peeler variety. (5) Extra long-staple cotton, $1\frac{3}{8}$ and longer, are Sea Island and Pima cottons for fine woven goods and fine knitted fabrics (see Figure 2–10). The treasured Egyptian product is in this classification.

In the United States, there is also classification by grade, which describes the cotton as to its creamy whiteness with absence of dirt, leaf, or seed shells and freedom from matted masses of fiber. This system requires the skillful observation of cotton graders and seven grades are generally recognized: (1) Good-middling, (2) strict-middling, (3) middling, (4) strict-low-middling, (5) low-middling, (6) strict-good-ordinary, and (7) good-ordinary. The highest good-middling has a lustrous, silky appearance. It is absolutely clean and the grades decline in whiteness down to the good-ordinary, which contains considerable quantities of leaf particles, mold, dirt, sand, mats, and spots. Also affecting the grade are the color gradations from pure creamy white to spotted, slightly tinged, yellow-stained, and grey, the latter two color effects being contributed to by the presence of mildew.

The character classification refers to any other qualities, such as the maturity, the smoothness, and uniformity of the fibers, the fiber diameters, strength, and other factors that would contribute to the amount of finishing required to produce a good white fabric for commercial use. (See Figure 2–11.)

The various features, of course, deal with the conditions under which cotton is raised; they vary from season to season, even in the same field. It is

Figure 2-11 Bales of cotton about to be delivered by truck to the processing plant.

for this reason that the producers of cotton fabrics exercise great care in their selection and blend bales of cotton of the same grade representing the purchase of several years' products. In other words, the fabric producer wants to produce as uniform a product year in and year out as possible.

Cotton Price Support

Evelyn Stout gives an excellent account of the economic revolution that took place in the United States during and just after the great depression of the early 1930s, following the stock market crash of 1929. During that time the price of cotton dropped from the high of 35 cents per pound during World War I to 5 cents per pound in the 1930s. This economic debacle was disastrous to most farmers, many of whom were obliged to return to the cities, where they joined the city men who were out of work. Certain essential farm crops had to be price-supported by the Federal government in some manner in order to enable the growers to obtain seed, fertilizer, and equipment to reopen the market for their products. One of the most essential was cotton. According to Stout,

> Some of the measures taken by the Government were price supports based on price-cost relationships of the years 1909–1914 as a normal base referred to as a parity. Some direct payments were authorized to farmers who would sign up in acreage control programs in which a part of their crop was plowed under. All participants in the program were able to borrow on the cotton (another base crop) they produced from the Commodity Credit Corporation without waiting to sell them in the market of the country or the world. These loans, called non-recourse loans, worked this way. A farmer could borrow from the CCC up to a given percentage (this varied over different years from 65 to 105 per cent) of the anticipated value his crop would bring on the market. If he was then able to market his crop at a higher price than that of the loan, he could repay the loan, reclaim the cotton and sell it wherever desired, but if the price were lower than the loan, after June 30 of the crop year, the cotton was considered sold at the loan price to the CCC. This in effect put a floor under the prices farmers received and was an indirect method of income payment. This was a way in which high surpluses in various farm products began and continued building up because the loan price was often higher than the particular commodity would bring on the open market. Often no effort was made to sell in the market place. Within a few years, cotton exports had dropped to 40 per cent of the crop. With many products, the tendency was to produce varieties that would give them maximum yield per acre regardless of quality and much was too poor in quality to be used. During the year ending June 1971, the CCC paid the farmers $918 million or 16 cents per pound.[1]

[1] Evelyn Stout, *Introduction to Textiles*, 3rd ed. (New York: Wiley-Interscience), pp. 45–52.

Cotton Consumption Declines

The examination of numerous sources showing cotton consumption since 1925—the beginning of man-made fiber competition—shows several significant trends as a result of increasing competition.

1. Between 1925 and 1941, the consumption of cotton declined about 8 per cent (88.3 to 80.6) as the man-made rayon and acetate fibers advanced from 1.7 to 9.2 per cent; wool was 10 per cent in both years.

2. Between 1941 and 1950, cotton declined another 12 per cent (80.6 to 68.8); wool declined from 10 to 9.3 per cent, while rayon and acetate rose to 19.8 per cent, a twofold increase. The newer man-made fibers totaled 2.9 per cent.

3. In the 1960s, the growth was in man-made (noncellulosic) fibers, many of which entered the market during this time. These fibers increased to 9.3 per cent and the cellulose-based fibers were fairly constant, but cotton and wool declined to 64 and 7.3 per cent, respectively, in 1970, as shown in Table 2–3.

These patterns are continuing: Cotton has declined to 29.2 per cent—a loss of 37.1 per cent—because man-made fibers entered the market in quantity. The great growth is in the noncellulosics. These totaled only 2 per cent in 1950; 9.3 per cent in 1960; but 51.1 per cent in 1973 (excluding glass and waste). In 1973, the man-made fibers, including rayons and acetates, were 69.3 per cent; cotton 29.2 per cent; and wool accounted for only 1.5 per cent.

Table 2-2   Pounds per Capita of Fibers Consumed

Year	Population	Total Man-made	Cotton	Wool	Per Capita (lb)
1960	180.7	**10.1**	23.3	3.1	36.5
1961	183.7	**10.8**	22.1	3.0	35.9
1962	186.5	**12.6**	23.0	3.2	38.8
1963	189.2	**14.3**	21.8	3.1	39.2
1964	191.8	**16.2**	22.8	2.7	41.7
1965	194.2	**18.3**	23.9	2.9	45.1
1966	196.5	**20.2**	25.1	2.7	48.0
1967	198.6	**21.4**	23.5	2.2	47.1
1968	200.6	**26.7**	21.9	2.4	51.0
1969	202.6	**27.9**	20.9	2.2	51.0
1970	204.8	**27.8**	19.7	1.7	49.2
1971	207.0	**33.0**	20.1	1.3	54.4
1972	208.8	**37.7**	20.0	1.3	59.0
1973	210.4	**42.0**	18.4	1.0	61.4

*SOURCE: Figures based on *Textile Organon,* **45** (March 1974), p. 27.

Another view of this textile upheaval is shown by comparing the consumption of the several fibers on a pounds per capita basis. This is done by dividing the annual consumption in pounds by the population figure for each year. An estimate of the per capita consumption of major fibers is shown in Table 2–2. Between 1960 and 1969 the per capita consumption of man-made fibers rose from 10.1 to 27.9 pounds and cotton remained steady from 23.3 to 20.9. In 1973, the man-made fibers reached 42 pounds as the per capita consumption reached a new high of 61.4, approximately 70 per cent above 1960. (See Table 2–2.) It is interesting to note the mill consumption of major fibers in Table 2–4, shown in millions of pounds. These data should be restudied when the topics dealing with consumership are being discussed. Very briefly, the table shows that

1. Cotton consumption averaging 4713.8 million pounds and 33.9 pounds per capita in the 1940s had fallen only 522.9 million with a loss of 10.7 pounds per capita to 232 pounds in 1960 and had a further loss of 54.4 million pounds in 1968 but was down to 20.6 pounds per capita. Our population increase had softened the blow in terms of total marked decrease.

2. Man-made fibers (rayons, acetates, and manufactured) have increased from 845.9 million pounds and 6.1 pounds per capita in the 1940s to 5300 million pounds and 26.3 pounds per capita in 1968.

3. It was the noncellulosic, man-made fibers that accounted for most of this gain after about 1963.

In Table 2–5 the impact of blends on cotton fiber consumption in broadwoven goods is illustrated.

Based on millions of yards produced, the 100 per cent cotton fabric has dropped steadily from 73.5 per cent of the market in 1958 to 52.6 per cent in 1968. The 100 per cent man-made goods have remained rather steady at about 16 per cent of the market; cotton's share in blends has risen from 2.5 to 4.6 per cent in this same 10-year period.

It is in the polyester blends that profound increases are noted. The polyesters were of scant significance as late as 1964; they more than doubled between 1963 and 1965; and they doubled again from the 1965 total of 1310.5 million yards to 2775 million in 1968. Generally, the polyester cotton blends are 65:35 ratios.

Cotton Consumption Forecast

The decline in cotton consumption in the United States has been due primarily to man-made fibers. A contributing factor has been the increase in the use of fiber blends at the expense of cotton goods of 100 per cent cotton. This change, first noted in the apparel industry, is now expanding into household applications. Steadier fiber prices and the more stable quality from year to year, combined with such technological advances as durable-press and spot- and stain-resistant finishes, have resulted in greater reliance

Table 2-3   U.S. Mill Consumption, Major Fibers, in Millions of Pounds

Year	Rayon and Acetate	Noncellulosic	Textile Glass	Waste	Total Man-made	Cotton	Wool	Silk	Grand Total
1962	1,263.4	898.1	177.5	73.8	2,412.8	4,192.5	503.5	6.5	7,115.3
1963	1,440.2	1,075.5	182.0	77.3	2,775.0	4,028.9	486.5	6.4	7,296.8
1964	1,516.3	1,334.2	220.6	91.1	3,162.2	4,286.9	431.3	6.7	7,887.1
1965	1,550.4	1,693.3	268.2	102.2	3,614.1	4,452.6	457.0	5.8	8,529.5
1966	1,591.1	1,984.9	315.3	98.8	3,990.1	4,621.0	427.9	4.6	9,043.6
1967	1,500.2	2,317.4	303.7	124.0	4,245.3	4,414.2	366.6	2.8	9,028.9
1968	1,688.0	3,078.3	383.8	155.4	5,305.5	4,104.1	378.4	4.0	9,792.0
1969	1,614.9	3,337.6	460.5	139.2	5,552.2	3,972.6	354.9	3.3	9,883.0
1970	1,414.4	3,543.6	404.9	138.4	5,501.3	3,775.0	273.3	1.8	9,551.4
1971	1,489.4	4,392.9	466.7	186.4	6,535.4	3,885.7	218.8	1.7	10,641.6
1972	1,413.3	5,381.9	569.3	198.5	7,563.0	3,849.8	246.9	2.0	11,661.7
1973	1,389.9	6,375.9	676.0	210.1	8,651.9	3,641.7	182.4	3.3	12,479.3

Percentage of Total

Year	Rayon and Acetate	Noncellulosic	Textile Glass	Waste	Total Man-made	Cotton	Wool	Silk	Grand Total
1962	17.8	12.6	2.5	1.0	33.9	58.9	7.1	0.1	100.
1963	19.7	14.7	2.5	1.1	38.0	55.2	6.7	0.1	100.
1964	19.2	16.9	2.8	1.2	40.1	54.3	5.5	0.1	100.
1965	18.2	19.9	3.1	1.2	42.4	52.2	5.3	0.1	100.
1966	17.6	21.9	3.5	1.1	44.1	51.1	4.7	0.1	100.
1967	16.6	25.7	3.3	1.4	47.0	48.9	4.1		100.
1968	17.3	31.4	3.9	1.6	54.2	41.9	3.9		100.
1969	16.3	33.8	4.7	1.4	56.2	40.2	3.6		100.
1970	14.8	37.0	4.2	1.4	57.6	39.5	2.8		100.
1971	13.9	41.2	4.3	1.7	61.4	36.5	2.0		100.
1972	12.1	46.2	4.8	1.7	64.9	33.0	2.1		100.
1973	11.1	51.1	5.4	1.7	69.3	29.2	1.5		100.

Table 2-4 What Is Happening to Mill Consumption of Major Fibers?
(millions of pounds)

Year (Averages)	Cotton Total	Cotton Per Capita (lb)	Man-made Fibers Rayon and Acetate Total	Rayon and Acetate Per Capita (lb)	Noncellulosic† Total	Noncellulosic† Per Capita (lb)	Wool, Silk Flax Total	Wool, Silk Flax Per Capita (lb)	All Fibers Total	All Fibers Per Capita (lb)
1940–49	4,713.8	33.9	801.9	5.8	44.0	0.3	640.4	4.6	6,200.1	44.6
1950–59	4,361.2	26.6	1,264.7	7.7	412.3	2.5	462.0	2.8	6,500.2	39.7
1960	4,190.9	23.2	1,081.7	6.0	796.1	4.4	422.6	2.3	6,491.4	35.9
1961	4,081.5	22.2	1,155.6	6.3	905.1	4.9	424.8	2.3	6,567.0	35.7
1962	4,188.0	22.4	1,291.2	6.9	1,127.3	6.0	441.5	2.4	7,048.0	37.8
1963	4,040.2	21.3	1,471.0	7.8	1,316.8	7.0	424.8	2.2	7,252.8	38.8
1964	4,244.4	22.1	1,555.8	8.1	1,618.5	8.4	370.9	1.9	7,789.6	40.6
1965	4,477.5	23.0	1,593.3	8.2	2,030.8	10.4	400.3	2.1	8,501.9	43.7
1966	4,630.5	23.5	1,623.2	8.2	2,379.0	12.1	384.9	2.0	9,017.6	45.8
1967	4,423.0	22.2	1,520.4	7.6	2,723.3	13.7	322.9	1.6	8,989.6	45.2
1968	4,146.5	20.6	1,712.9	8.5	3,588.5	17.8	341.9	1.7	9,789.8	48.7

SOURCE: Bureau of the Census and the Textile Economics Bureau.
† Includes textile glass fiber.

Table 2-5 What Is Happening to Broadwoven Cotton Goods Production?
(millions of square yards)

Year	100 Per Cent Cotton		Cotton Blends		100 Per Cent Man-made		Polyester	Man-made Blends			Total
	Total	Share†	Total	Share†	Total	Share†		Other	Total	Share†	
1958	10,172.7	73.5	326.5	2.4	2,137.8	15.4	168.3	1,032.9	1,201.2	8.7	13,838.2
1960	10,676.9	73.6	468.1	3.2	2,032.8	13.9	385.6	959.5	1,345.1	9.3	14,512.9
1962	10,614.0	70.6	576.3	3.8	2,139.4	14.2	620.8	1,090.0	1,710.8	11.4	15,040.9
1963	10,112.5*	67.6	573.9*	3.8	2,194.8*	14.7	849.8	1,208.6*	2,058.4*	13.8	14,939.6
1964	10,521.0*	65.6	597.1*	3.7	2,821.5*	17.6	773.9	1,327.2*	2,101.1*	13.1	16,040.7
1965	10,898.8	64.0	577.8	3.4	2,731.1	16.0	1,310.5	1,518.3	2,828.8	16.6	17,036.5
1966	10,428.0	60.9	799.2	4.7	2,636.7*	15.4	1,686.2	1,583.8*	3,270.0*	19.1	17,133.9
1967	9,838.2	59.5	766.8	4.6	2,527.4*	15.3	1,869.4	1,538.2*	3,407.6*	20.6	16,540.0
1968	8,950.0*	52.6	775.0*	4.6	2,750.0*	16.2	2,775.0	1,750.0*	4,525.0*	26.6	17,000.0

SOURCE: Publications of the Bureau of the Census and the Textile Economics Bureau.
* Estimated.
† Shares may not add to 100 because of rounding.

38

on the part of manufacturers and consumers in both blended fiber compositions and in 100 per cent man-made fiber fabrics. When one considers
the greater amount of both cost and number of finishing operations preparatory to the dyeing of spun cotton yarns compared with the man-made
fibers, it is not surprising that approximately one-third of the cotton loss to
the man-made fibers in 1969 was sustained by fabrics of colored cotton
yarns. Significant losses were noted in bed sheeting and in men's shirting
fabrics, both broadcloth and oxford cloth. A major industrial loss was under-
gone by the cotton fiber industry when cotton sandbags were replaced by
acrylic and polypropylene plastic bags. During the fiscal years 1965–1968,
the Defense Department began using acrylic and polypropylene bags and
did not consume the approximately 500,000 bales of cotton it had in former
years.

FLAX FIBERS

Flax is a **bast** or stem fiber from the woody stalk of **Linum**. It is much longer
than seed fibers such as cotton. Flax fiber is botanically known as **Linum
usitatissimum** and may be from 6 to as many as 40 inches in length. Generally, however, these stem fibers are about 18 inches long. The outer appearance of this fiber is bamboolike with cross markings, or **nodes**, occurring
along its length, as shown in Figure 2–12. The lumen, or central canal, is

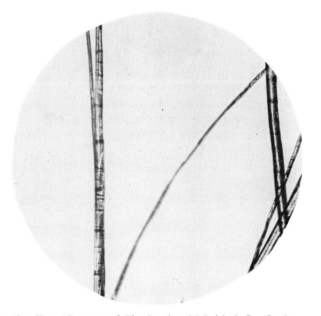

Figure 2-12   Flax fiber. (Courtesy of Glendenning, McLeish & Co., Inc.)

almost invisible in this fiber. Although the finest or most slender flax fibers are coarser than the finer cotton, the coarser fibers of the two are approximately equal. Flax ranges from 0.0047- to 0.0098-inch in diameter. It is more irregular in cross section and somewhat more difficult to spin. (See Figure 2–13.) The stem contains about 70 per cent cellulose, largely confined to these fibers, and has a considerable quantity of wax and a pectin substance that acts as a binder holding the fibers together in the stem. These noncellulosic materials and the woody tissue in the center (Figure 2–14) must be removed from the cellulose by a process known as **retting**. This is usually associated with water with a high bacterial content, or with exposure to dew for a long period of time, and, of course, it is now aided by chemical processing. In Table 2–6 some of the principal chemical and physical characteristics of the linen fiber are shown.

Properties of Linen

Further comments regarding some of these properties will highlight consumer interest in products from this fiber. It is not necessary to mercerize linen in order to develop a silky luster. The natural brightness is increased

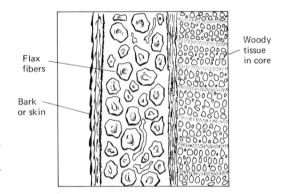

Figure 2-13 Sketch from a photomicrograph of a flax fiber. (Courtesy of Glendenning, Mc-Leish & Co., Inc.)

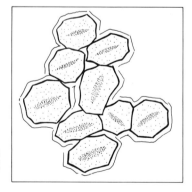

Figure 2-14 Cross section of clustered flax (linen) fibers. Note the polygonal outline of the fibers and the pronounced lumen.

if the fabric is pounded or passed through heavy calender rolls during processing. It is a common observation also that heirloom linens, such as fine damask tablecloths, become softer and more silky and beautiful as they are used and repeatedly washed and ironed.

Its lack of elasticity makes linen an easily wrinkled cloth unless it has been given a treatment to control wrinkling, such as in the commercial wash-and-wear processing. It also feels harder and smoother than cotton

Table 2-6   Characteristics of Linen

Physical Characteristics

Microscopic appearance	Number of small fibers cemented together; has cross markings at intervals; resembles bamboo pole
Length of fiber	Averages 18 to 30 in. long
Diameter	0.0047- to 0.0098-in.
Color	A yellowish buff to grey
Luster	Greater luster than cotton; characteristic silky luster
Strength	Stronger than cotton. Strength increases when wet
Elasticity	Not elastic
Conductivity to heat	Better conductor of heat than cotton
Regain or hygroscopic moisture	10 to 12 per cent
Capillarity and penetrability	Great wicking property, dyes readily
Composition	71.5 per cent cellulose; 10.7 per cent natural impurities; 9.4 per cent gums, proteins, etc.; 10 per cent fat, wax, and extractable materials
Specific gravity	1.50
Preparation of fiber	By retting flax (separating stalk from the fiber)

Chemical Characteristics

Effect of light	More resistant than cotton
Mildew	Attacked
Heat	About the same as cotton
Water	Being cellulose, this fiber generally shows the same chemical properties

Mineral acids
  sulfuric
  hydrochloric
  nitric
  hydrofluoric
	Concentrated acids destroy; cold dilute acids do not injure if washed out or neutralized; dilute solutions (3 per cent or less) of these acids, if allowed to dry, make tender and destroy.

Table 2-6 (continued)

Volatile organic acids formic acetic	No detrimental action
Nonvolatile organic acids oxalic tartaric citric	Will tender slightly if not removed especially if heat is applied
Strong alkalies caustic soda soda ash	No injury, even if concentrated and even if heat is applied when air is excluded; concentrated solution will mercerize if linen is under tension; otherwise linen will shrink
Weak alkalies ammonium carbonate borax sodium phosphate sodium silicate soap	No injury
Oxidizing agents (potassium permanganate)	Destroys if not controlled
Metallic salts	Has practically no affinity for metallic salts
Affinity for dyestuffs	Less than cotton
Classes of dyestuffs met with in common use	Direct Sulfur Basic with mordant Coloring matter developed on fiber Vat colors
Bleaching agents chlorine bleach hypochlorites	Cold dilute not detrimental to fiber (must be removed, as heat and concentrated solution destroy); more difficult to bleach because of presence of natural impurities
Other oxidation bleaches hydrogen peroxide sodium perborate potassium permanganate plus bisulfite of soda	No injury if properly controlled
Reduction bleaches sulfurous acid (sulfur dioxide plus water) hydrosulfite	No injury if controlled

SOURCE: National Institute of Drycleaning (NID).

and provides excellent summer suiting because of its good heat conductivity. The moisture regain is comparable to that of cotton but it has a much more rapid rate of moisture absorption; this makes it vastly superior for towelings and wiping cloths intended to pick up moisture from surfaces. Linen fabrics are usually smoother than cotton because of the much longer fiber length and, consequently, a greatly reduced number of loose fiber ends in the yarns. Smoothness makes it more resistant to the adhesion of bacteria and dirt. It is somewhat difficult to dye because of the lack of penetrability, and often the interior of a yarn when ravelled out will show that the fibers inside the yarn are less deeply colored than those on the outside.

The History of Linens

The oldest textile fragments still comparatively intact are of linen. These have been found in villages of the lake dwellers, a neolithic people, who dwelled in Switzerland. Fragments of clothing and pieces of nets have been found. Linen shroud cloths were used by the Egyptians for wrapping their Pharaohs and other nobility; these wrappings are found still in good condition in some of the burial tombs being opened after centuries. Its use is mentioned frequently in the Bible and in the histories of the Egyptians, the Greeks, and the Romans. Fiber flax is raised principally in Europe, the largest producer being the USSR with more than 70 per cent. Other important flax-producing countries are Poland, France, Germany, Holland, Belgium, Ireland, Italy, Latvia, Lithuania, and Egypt. In the United States, there is some flax fiber produced, but generally it is the oil from the seed that is sought. This linseed oil is an excellent drying oil used in paints and varnishes. The fibers from plants that have been allowed to mature for oil production are not of as high quality as that produced abroad principally for the fiber. After the linseed oil has been expressed, or pressed out from the seeds, the cake residue is an excellent cattle feed.

Flax Production

Moisture and a mild climate are required to produce flax. The flax seed is planted in the spring, much as grain crops are planted. In about three months, the plant is 2 to 4 feet high. It is generally harvested in late summer when the stalks begin to turn yellow and the seed begins to turn brown. It is common to pull the plants up by the roots in order to have as long an unbroken fiber as possible.

The combing operation, which consists of pulling the stalks through the teeth of an iron comb, either by hand or mechanically, is referred to as **rippling**—this removes the seeds. The stalks are then tied in bundles preparatory to retting, the chemical process previously referred to for the separation of the flax fibers from the woody constituents of the stalk and from the pectin binder. Retted flax generally consists of 65 to 70 per cent cellulose.

Two further processes for the separation and purification of the fibers are (1) **scutching**, or crushing the woody retted stalks under a series of fluted rollers, which tend to free the fibers from the woody or more brittle constituents; and (2) the **hackling** operation, corresponding roughly to the carding and combing of cotton, which is intended to lay the fibers parallel. The scutched fibers are pulled through a series of iron combs of increasing fineness to produce a fine **roving**. In the operation, of course, some short fibers and broken fragments stick to the comb or fall out onto the floor. These are referred to as **tow** and are used in cheaper linen fabrics and towels and in cloth intended to show a rough or irregular sized yarn. These tow linens differ greatly in appearance from the fine parallel fibers called line. The **line** fibers are used in fine table damasks, sheer linen fabrics, and handkerchiefs.

COUNT OF LINEN YARNS   In the United States and England, the weight of the yarn is expressed in numbers called counts. The standard or base of this **count** is called a lea and is a length of 300 yards. The count is the number of **leas** required to weigh 1 pound; thus, if 3000 yards of a linen yarn weigh 1 pound, the count would be 3000 divided by 300, or 10, and this would be expressed as a 10's yarn. Thus, the lower the count, the coarser the yarn. Fine yarns for laces may be as high as 400's; 25's linen are widely accepted weights for dress fabrics. However, there are coarser linens for suitings, down to 20's, producing fabrics weighing about 6 to 8 ounces per square yard. Men's linen suits and slacks from these generally are a somewhat lower count than women's year. Once popular for summer wear, they have been largely replaced because of their wrinkling tendencies by worsteds; by blends of linen and rayon; by blends of synthetic fibers with wool; and by wash-and-wear treated cottons. Dish towels use 16's yarns for greater moisture absorbency. Linen provides a fine, serviceable fabric, but overbleaching or overretting will weaken the fiber. One of the reasons for the greater cost of cellulose yarns from linen is the fact that the dry flax plant produces somewhat less than 10 per cent of its weight of finished linen fiber.

Flax Papers

Flax is used in fine papers. It imparts great flexibility and tear resistance to fine papers for currency and writing bond. Another extensive use, which annually consumes about $4 million worth of paper in the United States alone is in cigarette papers. Flax papers burn without odor.

JUTE, HEMP, AND RAMIE FIBERS

The second important bast fiber is **jute,** a fiber obtained from various species of **Corchorus,** native to India and the East Indian Islands. These plants, like flax, are annuals. Various species grow with straight, slender stems to a height of 5 to 15 feet. They thrive with an abundance of moisture and a warm climate. The plants are either cut or pulled when the setting of the seed pods begins. Jute also must be retted in order to remove the woody parts of the cane. The retting is complete when the fibrous layers can be separated freely from the cane itself.

The separated fiber is hung on poles to dry, and is then taken to a central collector where the fibers from various small farms or producers are gathered into small packages of about 80 pounds each. The packages are then taken to a larger collecting agency where they are resorted and baled for shipment to Calcutta where the bulk of the crop is manufactured. Quality fiber for export is identified as "first mark"; other symbols indicate the color, origin of growth, and other features of the baled fibers.

Jute Fiber

The yield of dried jute fiber is only about 4.5 per cent of the green weight of the stems. The bast cells of the jute fiber are from 0.05- to 0.19-inch in length. The cross section of the fiber (Figure 2–15) shows that these bast cells gather in small clusters and that each is of an irregular polygonal outline. Between clusters is a narrow median layer, and the fiber shows a pronounced lumen. In fact, the lumen is often larger in diameter than the thickness of the fiber wall. The fiber is smooth and lustrous.

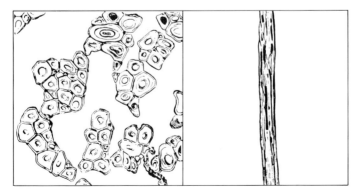

Figure 2-15 Cross section of jute. [J. Gordon Cook, *Handbook of Textile Fibres* (Textile Book Service, Metuchen, N.J., 1960), p. 58.]

The chemical composition is complex. The cellulose content is about 50 per cent; other forms of cellulose with glucose linkages from some of the side carbons amount to about 15 per cent.

USES   This harsh, brittle fiber is second only to cotton in the worldwide use of cellulosic fibers from natural sources. It is used mostly in coarse woven fabrics, such as gunny sacks and bags where cheapness is of primary importance. As a backing fabric, jute is used in the tapestry trade and also as a binding thread in the weaving of carpets and rugs. Novelty fabrics for dress goods have been made from jute, sometimes in combination with wool. Burlap skirts, a fad a few years ago among high school and college students, are an example of this fiber in wearing apparel with special softening finishes. Jute is the cheapest fiber used in textile manufacturing and is used widely in India where it is woven into mats and coarse fabrics. Some jute is used in paper.

Hemp Fibers

The **hemp** plant is related to the nettle family and produces soft, flaxlike fibers. It reaches a height of 6 to 12 feet and is grown extensively in Russia, Italy, France, India, and China. Because of the needs of the United States during World War II, about 350,000 bushels of seed were planted in the central states from Kentucky to Minnesota. Japanese hemp is of high quality and of very light straw color. It is believed by some to have been the first textile fiber to be utilized in Japan. Thus far, it has not produced sufficiently fine yarns for competition with flax. The cultivation of hemp closely approximates that of flax. When the lower leaves fall off and the tops of the stalks turn yellow, the crop is harvested, usually by hand pulling. The retting process for the removal of the fine fiber from the woody constituents is similar to that of flax. The scutching operation, consisting of kneading or crushing the dried, fully retted stems, removes the fibers but is a slow, arduous, and rather expensive operation, especially with the longer stems of up to 8 feet. Late in the nineteenth century, and until about 1914, a considerable quantity of hemp was grown in the United States. Subsequent to this, and until the emergency of World War II, production fell to almost zero. Much of this loss of market was a result of the cheapness of jute and because such fibers as sisal and manila hemp, or abaca, are superior for rope and cordage. Hemp contains about 78 per cent cellulose. It is generally gray or yellowish in color, although some varieties and sources produce a dark brown fiber. Its tensile strength is greater than linen but it is coarser. The luster is comparable to that of flax. The moisture regain in hemp, according to the

ASTM, is 11.75 per cent. It is principally used for cordage, twine, rope, and canvas.

Ramie, or China Grass

Ramie is a native to many parts of China and some Pacific Islands from Formosa as far south as Borneo and Vietnam. It requires a moist soil and comparatively warm weather. It is a perennial, with a yield from two to five crops of fiber per year, depending on the climate. The plants grow to a height of from 4 to 8 feet. The canes of this grasslike plant contain a series of bast fiber bundles that extend the full length of the cane and are held together by gums, waxes, and pectins. (See Figure 2–16.) The retting operation is difficult, and thus far, no chemical method has been evolved to free these fibers economically. In China, it is done by immersing the stems in water and then washing and partly drying them; the operations are repeated at frequent intervals until all traces of gum have been removed. Some operators use a bacteriological process for removing gums and pectins.

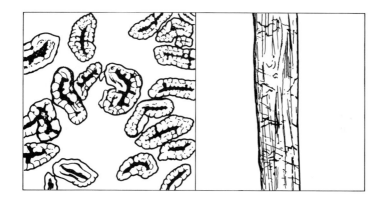

Figure 2-16 Cross section of ramie. [J. Gordon Cook, *Handbook of Textile Fibres* (Textile Book Service, Metuchen, N.J., 1960), p. 59.]

The bast cells in ramie are very large—from 0.78 to 9.84 inches in length. The fibers are very fine, the ratio of the length to its breadth being about 2400:1. After gum removal, the fiber is nearly pure cellulose (90 per cent) and the diameter is slightly greater than flax and cotton.

PROPERTIES The ramie fiber is the strongest and most durable of the vegetable fibers. It resists rot and damage from water, is almost white, and

Table 2-7   Fiber Diameters

Fibers	Fiber Diameter (mm)
Ramie	0.04–0.06
Linen	0.016
Cotton	0.014–0.024
Silk	0.009–0.024

is more lustrous than linen. However, the economics of its production, thus far, have hampered textile producers who want to produce ramie on a large scale in the western world. One of the more ancient fibers, ramie fabrics have been found in some of the wrappings in ancient Egyptian mummy cases.

MISCELLANEOUS BAST FIBERS

Sunn fiber is grown principally in India. It is comparable to jute but is whiter, somewhat higher in tensile strength, and more wear- and/or sun-resistant. It contains 80 per cent cellulose, about 15 per cent more than jute. Several other fiber-producing **legumes**, which may also be used as cover crops, are the **Colorado River** hemp of the United States and the **kudzu** hemp of China and India. Kudzu fibers are used for clothing in Asia.

Several varieties of hibiscus, principally **kenaf or ambari**, are commercially grown in India, in other Asiatic countries, and in Brazil. It appears to have been indigenous to Africa and produces a coarse fiber. The strongest fibers are harvested when the plant is in flower.

Certain varieties of mallow produce a bast fiber and are cultivated in Germany and France. One, cultivated in Sweden for the production of cordage and sailcloth, is called Swedish hemp.

Another very unusual fiber, found in the South Sea Islands, is utilized by the natives for preparing a fabric without spinning or weaving. This is the paper mulberry fiber, also known as the **tapa** fiber of the Fiji Islands. The cleaned fibers are laid out to form a regular surface, several layers being placed one on top of the other while wet. They are allowed to dry overnight and adhere so that the entire mass can be lifted as one piece. The dried web is beaten with a wooden instrument until it is spread out and matted together —it looks like a fine muslin. These layers can be made as thick or as thin as desired. Some varieties of tapa cloth are thick enough to look and wear like leather. The cloths are easily dyed and printed. The same fiber is grown in Japan, where the fiber is used for making paper.

Leaf Vegetable Fibers

The most important of the leaf fibers is **abaca**, a plant native to the Philippine Islands. These are the vein fibers in the leaf and outer stem of certain plants. This skin can be pulled away in narrow ribbons by making an incision just beneath the skin layer at the end of the leaf and giving a very sharp pull. The thin ribbon is then pulled across a knife edge to remove pulp and pithy material. Several varieties of **Agave** produce usable fiber in their leaves. **Sisal** was used by the Mexicans at the time of the Spanish Conquest, being utilized by Indians for cordage and for coarse cloth. The source is a plant known as the Agave **sisilana**. It has recently been introduced into the East Indies and into West Africa, from which sources the United States has obtained much of its imported sisal in recent years.

Another Agave plant produces a fiber known as **hennequen**. This is also native to Mexico and has been used by the Indians from the earliest recorded history of these people. This was the principal textile fiber used by Mexicans. The Mexican **maguey** is one of several useful fiber-producing Agaves. The pineapple plant produces a leaf fiber of extreme fineness. However, this plant has been principally cultivated for its fruit.

Miscellaneous Seed Hairs

A number of seed hairs have been used in the manufacture of buoyant materials and articles, such as lifesaving belts and boat cushions and for stuffing such varied articles as mattresses, pillows, and stuffed toys. Probably the best known of these is **kapok**, a ⅜- to ¼-inch floss from the seeds of a large tree, indigenous to India and known as **Bombay malabarica**. It was this fiber, unavailable during World War II, that was partly replaced for flotation accessories, such as life belts, by the floss from the common **milkweed**, so widely found in the United States. Kapok is very buoyant and becomes water-saturated at an extremely slow rate, losing about 10 per cent of its buoyancy after being held under water for 30 days. Even **cattail** floss is used for packing or shipping because of its water resistance and for soundproofing. These fibers have been almost wholly replaced for stuffings by extruded foams and the staple fibers of man-made origin.

CHARACTERISTICS OF PROTEIN FIBERS

Animal fibers are proteins, a much more complicated chemical structure than cellulose. Proteins, in turn, contain amino acids. The composition of

fibroin, the principal protein in silk, and of **keratin**, the principal protein in wool, are listed in Table 2–8.

Table 2-8   Composition of Protein Fibers

	Composition, in Per Cent	
	Keratin (wool)	Fibroin (silk)
Carbon	50	48.3
Nitrogen	16–17	19.2
Hydrogen	7	6.5
Sulfur	3–4	0
Oxygen (by difference)	22–24	26

It will be noted that they contain—in addition to carbon—hydrogen, oxygen, some nitrogen and, in the case of wool, a small amount of sulfur.

WOOL

Molecular Structure

Keratin, the protein constituent of wool, is a complicated polymer, or giant molecule, made up of various amino acids, so linked as to form a chain Figure 2–17. The unique feature of this molecule, contrasted with those in most textile fibers, is the cross linkage shown in Figure 2–18. One conception of the molecular structure, theorized by Steadman, shows these two linkages with the cystine linkage (S—S) in a narrower region in the space between the two adjacent chains, and a somewhat longer salt linkage forming longer

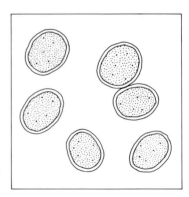

Figure 2-17   Cross section of wool fibers (approximately round).

"ladder rungs," where the wavy chains are more widely separated (Figure 2–18). This structural image offers a possible reason for the resiliency of the wool fiber; that is, these cross linkages permit the ends of the chain to move up and down, while the crimped position of the carbon-to-carbon bonds lengthwise in both chains can be straightened out when tension is applied to the fiber, and hence to the individual molecules. When stress is removed, these crimped positions and the natural waviness of the chains will return to their normal position and the cross linkages will regain their normal length, thus helping to strengthen the wool fiber. This conception

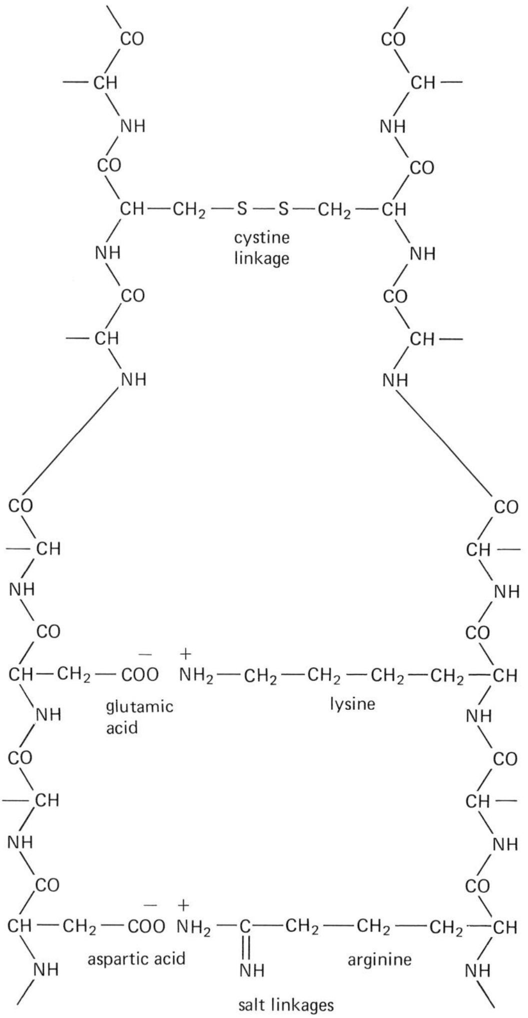

Figure 2-18 One of several structural formulas postulated for wool (Steadman's theory).

also suggests how such a naturally crimped fiber would show a high degree of resilience—recovery from pressure stress. No fiber approaches wool in this valuable property.

History of the Wool Fiber

The most important of the animal fibers is wool; and although sheep's wool is the principal type, the terminology also includes the hairy fibers from many other animals, such as goats, camels, llamas, and less common wool-bearing animals. Some of these specialty fibers will be dealt with after a general discussion of sheep's wool.

The pelts of sheep and other hair-bearing animals were undoubtedly among the first clothing worn by prehistoric man. The quality of the hair or wool of his sheep was considerably coarser and straighter than that found on sheep today. There are evidences of this in wool on sheep that have run wild or on very old animals. These long, straight hairs are, thus, a reversion to an original stock. Through several thousand years the selective breeding of sheep has brought about the domesticated sheep with its fleece coat.

> The care and raising of sheep appears to have been one of the earliest taken by man to provide him with food, shelter, and raiment. The oldest references to wool have come from Asia Minor, from the great mound of Tllasmar. Here archeologists exploring a succession of ruined cities found seals indicating a personal ownership of wool and flocks of sheep. The date set for this mound is 4200 B.C. and evidence is given that an active trade existed in this fiber as early as that time. According to the old testament Abraham prospered because of his flocks and herds. These are evidences that sheep and shepherding spread from Central Asia, and then traveled by trade or by conquest throughout the world.[2]

It is recorded that the sheep and the wool industry came to Europe as long ago as 3000 to 1000 B.C. In the Minoan period and in the succeeding civilizations in eastern Europe, the people maintained flocks of sheep through the wars and invasions of thousands of years. It was the Romans who spread sheep through western Europe and into the British Isles: as the armies advanced, they took the flocks of sheep with them to provide food and clothing. It is recorded that the first woolen factory in England was established in A.D. 50 by Roman conquerors. The quality of sheep's wool in the early years of recorded history was probably rather low. It is interesting to note that the best breeds of sheep now found virtually all over the world, insofar as wool quality is concerned, date back to A.D. 14 to 37 with

---

[2] Werner Von Bergen and Herbert R. Mauersberger, eds., *The American Wool Handbook*, 2nd ed. (Metuchen, N.J.: Textile Book Service, 1948), p. 63.

the introduction of the **merino** through the cross breeding of the fine Tarentine strain developed by the Romans with sheep from Asia Minor. When the Saracens conquered Spain in the eighth century, they introduced the merino strain to that country. Spain eventually became the richest sheep-raising country in the world, with the largest wool-weaving industry.

According to the booklet entitled, "The Wool Story," published by Pendleton Woolen Mills,

> Statistics at that time are in order here: 10 million sheep seeking pasture were herded seasonally over a 90-mile-wide trail under the guidance of 50,000 shepherds. Despite strict laws against the export of Merino strain animals from Spain, its prestige as the greatest wool-weaving country of the day gradually diminished. Even the death penalty for exporting these animals was not a complete deterrent, and in 1786 Spain permitted the importation into France of several hundred ewes which were crossed with the French sheep owned by King Louis XVI, and this developed the *Rambouillet* breed, the finest wool-producing sheep in France and one brought in considerable numbers to the United States. In the war between France and Spain at the beginning of the 19th century, Spain lost the greater part of her herds; and in desperation, fine Merinos were sold to England and to the United States. The jealous guarding of wool industries among the countries of Western Europe, France, England, and the various principalities making up these areas, now recognized as nations, was as bitter as the battles fought by them through approximately 300 years.

The first sheep introduced into United States came with the Spanish under Cortez in 1519. These were not fine merinos but sheep intended primarily for food. They were called *churra*. Later millions of sheep grazed in the Mexican-controlled southwest, some owned by the Spanish dons and others by Americans who had settled in the southwestern areas now known as Oklahoma, New Mexico, Arizona, Texas, and California. These were used primarily for mutton and gave wool of indifferent quality. The real quality wool industry began in the eastern part of the United States, and this was as strong a rebellion against the Stamp Act as the demonstrations of the Boston Tea Party. The production and use of illegal wool played a significant part in the textile industry of the Colonies. According to Pendleton Woolen Mills, "a Harvard graduating class of 1768 appeared 'to a man' in suits of black cloth made from Rhode Island wool."

Wool Growing

Sheep shearing is usually done in the spring by means of machine-powered shears, permitting a skilled operator to clip as many as 200 sheep a day. As in the case of the pickers or collectors of other agricultural crops, the sheep-shearing teams begin in the southern part of the United States early in the spring and gradually work northward. This makes it possible for many growers who do not own such equipment to have their animals machine-clipped by these more modern techniques. It is common in the United States for the fleece to be clipped off in one piece, which may weigh from 6 to 18 pounds, with an average fleece weight of 8 pounds of raw wool per animal. This, in turn, yields about 3 pounds of scoured, or cleaned, wool. (See Figure 2–19.)

Figure 2-19 Sorting shorn wool fleeces.

In Australia, and occasionally in the United States, recognition is made of the fact that the quality of wool varies in different parts of the animal. Thus, the superior wool from the sides and shoulders of the sheep would be treated as one fleece, and the wool from the head, belly, legs, and breech would be separated from the best and treated as a second quality product. These fibers are generally weaker and are more likely to be contaminated with burrs, twigs, and dirt. These would suffer much greater attrition in attempts to remove the contaminants to produce a scoured, clean product. This is particularly noticeable in the United States among the western and plateau region flocks, where the sheep are allowed to graze over wide areas, moving from the valleys in the early spring up into the higher meadows and grassy areas during the summer, and then being herded back to the warmer, protected valley areas for the winter. Merino wools from the eastern flocks are generally from pasture-grazed animals.The finest (80's) United States wool comes from pastured sheep from Texas. In Australia, sheep are grazed in large enclosures called paddocks, which keeps them as free from burrs and other contaminants as possible. Some wool, of course, is produced from animals that are killed for meat; this constitutes about 8 per cent of the apparel wool used in the United States. These are known as **pulled** wools and have the root intact. This closed end interferes with dye absorption, the fiber will also become somewhat weaker than fleece wool if chemicals are applied to help loosen the fibers.

A biochemical method is under experimentation. A pill that causes the wool to constrict and weaken at the skin level is fed to the animal a few weeks before shearing time. When the dose is discontinued, the wool fiber again grows naturally. When such animals are combed, the fibers break and a fleece is obtained. In merino wool, there is a certain amount of **kemp**, which is a straight, weak, somewhat coarse fiber—it is also more difficult to dye and, therefore, shows up as flecks in the finished cloth.

Wool Grading

The grade is based on a sampling of a percentage of the bales being marketed.

Wool fleeces are graded according to what the skilled inspectors, called wool classers, judge that the majority of the fibers in the bale may be. Figure 2–20 shows the distribution of the various kinds of wool on the sheep. The fiber classification is based on fiber diameter and is broken down into fine, medium, coarse, and carpet grades. There are 13 grades of wool as defined by the U.S. Department of Agriculture. Twelve were enacted into law on June 18, 1926, and the thirteenth (62's) was added in 1940, because it was a grade used by some mills. These figure grades and the American "blood" equivalents are shown in Table 2–9. The numbers are based on the English system and are recognized internationally.

A second classification is based on fiber length. This is judged by the **sorter** working for a mill. The longer fibers, **tops**, are of even fiber length and are classed as **combing** wools for use in worsted yards. The shorter-fibered wools, and the short fibers, or **noils**, removed during combing, are used in woolens. These woolen fibers are usually fewer than 2 inches long. Terms used are **strictly combing** for fibers over 2.5 inches long, **French combing** for fibers 1.5 to 2.5 inches, and **clothing** for less than 1.5-inch-long fibers. **Carpet wools** are long and coarse and come mainly from South Africa and mountainous areas, such as New Zealand, India, and Scotland.

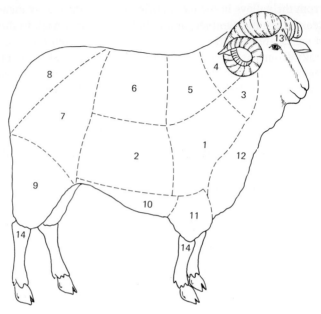

Figure 2-20 Sheep fleece showing distribution of wool fibers as classified by the sorter. (1) Shoulder wool is usually the best fiber and often referred to as *prime*. (2) Sides produce next grade, or *super*. (4-5-6) Back produces *choice* wool.

Table 2-9   Standard Wool Grades Used in the United States *

British System	United States System	Average Fiber Diameter (microns)
80's		17.70–19.14
70's	Fine	19.15–20.59
64's		20.60–22.04
62's		22.05–23.49
60's	Half-blood	23.50–24.94
58's		24.95–26.39
56's	Three-eighths-blood	26.40–27.84
54's		27.85–29.29
50's	Quarter-blood	29.30–30.99
48's		31.00–32.69
46's	Low-quarter-blood	32.70–34.39
44's	Common	34.40–36.19
40's		36.20–38.09
36's	Braid	38.10–40.20
Coarser		40.21 and over

* Full blood is 100 per cent merino.

The English classification system for **worsted** yarns is widely used. The wool is given the number showing the number of hanks of 560 yards that can be spun from it to weigh 1 pound. Thus, if one 560-yard hank can be spun, the wool is a No. 1; but if 40 such hanks, or 22,400 yards weigh 1 pound, the wool is a No. 40. Yarns below 40's are classed as coarse. According to the run-count system used in New England Mills, a No. 1 **woolen** yarn means that 100 yards of yarn weigh 1 ounce, or that 1600 yards weigh 1 pound. A No. 10 woolen yarn by this system is so fine that 1000 yards weigh 1 ounce.

Being a natural product, the quality may vary from year to year or from animal to animal, depending on the grazing conditions, the health of the flock—or the individual animal—and the damage to be anticipated in scouring. Therefore, for uniformly good products, fabric producers commonly retain a backlog of wool stock accumulated for two or three years to which wool of similar grade will be blended from the new crop. The object, of course, is to produce as great a similarity in fabric property from year to year as possible.

Wool Products Labeling Act

Because of the practice of some producers of introducing reworked wool into fabrics and selling them as new or virgin wool, the Federal Wool Products Labeling Act of 1939 was passed by the Congress and became effective July 14, 1941. It is administered by the Federal Trade Commission, which issued rules and regulations to guide business as to the correct manner in which to label and promote wool products. Some of the old terms describing wool were discontinued; since that date, fabrics and garments containing wool have had to be labeled as to fiber content. A few products were specifically exempted from the law; among these were rugs, mats, and upholstery fabrics.

Under this law, wool fabrics are classified as follows:

1. *Wool*: New wool fibers that have never been woven, knitted, or felted.
2. *Reprocessed wool*: Wool fibers that have been woven, knitted, or felted (but that have never been used by the consumer) reduced back to the fiber state and remade into a consumer product.
3. *Reused wool*: Wool fibers that have been used in consumer products, reduced back to the fiber state, and reformed into a consumer product.

The term **wool** can be used alone to describe only new wool in labeling advertising or by word of mouth at the time of sale. Although the term

virgin wool is not used in the Wool Products Labeling Act, it is still used in trade, because of a long-established custom, and it persists in the minds of consumers. The term *wool* must have the appropriate qualifying description in any kind of labeling or other commercial material. For example, a fabric made of a blend of 50 per cent wool, 30 per cent reprocessed wool, and 20 per cent reused wool must be so labeled. In the legal sense, this fabric is only 50 per cent wool or all-wool material. Similarly, the presence of any other fibers, whether wool-like or blended in for other purposes, must be labeled according to the order of presence of each. This would include mixtures of sheep wool with mohair, cashmere, camel, or other wool-like fiber, rayon, cotton, polyester, or other nonprotein fiber.

Because of the 1939 act, Congress did not include wool products in the Textile Fiber Products Identification Act of 1960. It is interesting to note that neither act covers the disclosure of the fiber compositions of upholstery fabrics, although slipcover materials not containing wool are included in the new law.

These names for the reworked wools are more exact in disclosure of the past history of the fiber and of the possible alteration or damage suffered through **garnetting**, the mechanical step required to reconvert it to the fiber state preparatory to again spinning, weaving, and finishing that fabric.

Properties

The general characteristics of wool are given in Table 2–10. (See also Table 2–12, in which the characteristics of wool and silk are compared.)

It must be kept in mind that wool is a hair originating in the skin. These grow thickly, and there are as many as forty to fifty thousand per square inch of surface. Under the microscope, the wool fiber appears to be a solid rod covered with horny scales that project slightly from the stem of the fiber and point outward slightly toward the tip. The coarser the wool fiber, the larger these scales and the more reflectant, or lustrous, the fabrics made from them. In these coarser wools, the scales do not project out as decidedly as in the finer fibers; thus, the reflective surface is more flat. An enlarged view of a wool fiber is shown in Figure 2–21. This figure shows that the fiber consists of three portions: the outer, horny portion, or **epidermis**, scaly material; the **cortex**, or cellular portion, just inside the scales, and the **medulla**, or central portion. The inner portions contribute the natural pigment coloring matter of the fiber. Wool color ranges from almost white to black. Most wools are sufficiently colored to require bleaching in their preparation. Research into the structure of the wool fiber has indicated that the cortex is made up of numerous, small, spindle-shaped cells varying from 0.0014- to 0.0025-inch in length.

Table 2-10   Characteristics of Wool

Physical Characteristics

Microscopic appearance	Solid rod with its surface covered with horny scales resembling fish scales
Length of fiber	Averages 1–3 in. worsted averages 3–8 in.
Diameter of fiber	0.005- to 0.0015-in.
Color of fiber	Yellowish to brown, sometimes black
Luster	High in coarse grades; low in good grades
Strength	Calculated to be 1–1.7 grams per denier
Elasticity	Elastic—average wool stretches 25–35 per cent of its length before breaking
Conductivity to heat	Poor
Regain or hydroscopic moisture	10–15 per cent
Capillarity and penetrability	Has both
Composition of fiber	Keratin: a mixture of nitrogen, sulfur, and amino-acid compounds
Method of preparation	Scouring, mainly to remove natural impurities, such as wool perspiration and wool grease

Chemical Characteristics

Effect of light	Changes chemical structure making its action toward dyestuff different (usually has greater affinity)
Mildew	Slightly attacked if left in *damp* condition for a period of time
Heat	At 275°F, dry heat, begins to decompose, if heated to 212°F in moist atmosphere, becomes plastic and can be shaped; retains new shape if cooled
Water	Temporary loss of 10–25 per cent when wet; may be steam pressed

Mineral acids
  sulfuric
  hydrochloric
  nitric
  hydrofluoric
	Acid dyes do not injure, even at a boil; concentrated acids destroy

Volatile organic acids
  formic
  acetic
	No detrimental action

Table 2-10   (continued)

Nonvolatile organic acids
  oxalic
  tartaric
  citric
	Not injurious if removed before pressing

Strong alkalies
  caustic soda
  soda ash
	Strong solutions injurious; cold solutions under 5 per cent not injurious if removed or neutralized; dilute solutions of soda ash produce weakening

Weak alkalies
  ammonium carbonate
  borax
  sodium silicate
  sodium phosphate
  soap
	Not injurious if action is controlled

Oxidizing agents (potassium permanganate)	Affect S=S bond
Metallic salts	Slight affinity for metallic salts, such as magnesium chloride or sulfate and zinc chloride
Affinity for dyestuffs	Good
Classes of dyestuffs in common use	Acid colors; chrome; some basic; direct

Bleaching agents
  chlorine bleach or
  hypochlorites
	Ordinarily harmful; under some conditions may produce chlorinated wool, which has high luster and is unshrinkable

Other oxidation bleaches	Hydrogen peroxide best bleach

Reduction bleaches
  sulfurous acid
    (sulfur dioxide plus water)
  hydrosulfite
	Damaged

Effect of insects	Damaged by larvae of clothes moth and carpet beetle unless treated

SOURCE: Fiber chart of the National Association of Dyers and Cleaners.

FIBER LENGTH   The wool fiber varies in length from 1.5 to 15 inches, depending on whether the sheep is shorn once or twice yearly, on the type of sheep, and on the location of the wool fiber on the animal. The longer apparel-wool fibers, of from 6 to 9 inches in length, are generally used in worsted goods; those for woolens are 1.5 to 5 inches in length. The longer fibers (9 to 15 inches) are coarser and are usually identified as carpet wools.

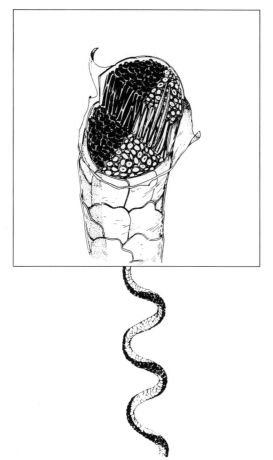

Figure 2-21 Schematic view of the wool fiber showing the spiral form and crimp of this scaly fiber. The greater magnification at the cross section reveals the cellular internal structure as theorized by many research chemists and physicists. The spindlelike cells in the cortex are smaller than those in the medulla.

ELASTICITY   The theory is that the strength and elasticity characteristics of the wool fiber depend on the structure of the cortex and on the movement of the cells when subjected to tension. Wool is the most elastic natural fiber and can be stretched from 25 to 30 per cent of its length before it breaks. This is a valuable characteristic, causing wool to shed wrinkles readily. The strength of wool for equal diameters is less than that of silk, cotton, or linen, but the stretching compensates for this. Wool is weaker when wet than when dry; conversely, the strengths of cotton and linen are greater when wet. On the basis of equal fiber diameter, the very fine Saxony merino fibers are stronger than the coarser wools. Another characteristic believed to depend on the cortical layer is the curl of the fiber. If the cells are uneven in growth or arrangement, the fiber will be wavy. Fine staple fibers are naturally more curly than the coarser ones. The springiness of wool fabrics is caused in part by this curl and also by the elasticity of the fiber. The intertwining of these curly fibers is believed to contribute to the felting property of wool.

HYGROSCOPIC MOISTURE   Wool normally carries 10 to 15 per cent moisture; the amount may be greater or less, depending on the temperature and humidity of the air. The hygroscopic property of wool makes it important that the testing of wool fabrics and the purchase of raw wool and of finished fabrics be done under known conditions. The standard condition for a testing room is 70°F and 65 per cent relative humidity. In purchasing wool, it is a generally accepted practice to add to the bone-dry weight an allowable **regain** or moisture weight of 11 per cent. It is easy to determine the moisture content of a wool fabric by laboratory test, but very difficult for a purchaser to judge by the feel or apparent weight of a fabric how much water it contains. In wet weather, wool contains as much as 30 per cent moisture without feeling damp. The fibers absorb moisture and dry out again slowly. A bather who is wearing a wool bathing suit is less chilled while the suit is drying out than the wearer of any other fabric.

CAPILLARITY AND POROSITY   These physical properties affect the readiness with which wool is dyed or bleached, for they influence the moisture penetrability of the fiber. Because *porosity* is the measure of the volume of voids or openings in a volume of fiber or other solid, the more irregular the outer surface of a fiber, such as wool, the greater the porosity and the greater the surface area. Both factors in wool serve to make it easier to dye and finish. If voids connect with one another, or if the void is a central canal, such as the medulla of wool, the passage of water and other solutions is promoted by **capillarity**. Shorn wool is more easily dyed than pulled wool because the medulla in the fiber is open at one end and available for capillary transmission of water. In wool, however, the scaly structure makes porosity the more significant factor in moisture penetration.

Chemical Behavior

EFFECT OF LIGHT   Sunlight affects the strength of all textile fibers. Some investigators ascribe the effect to the ultraviolet rays. Others believe that ozone is developed, which, with the presence of moisture, affects the fibers. Experience has shown that, whatever the actual mechanism, wet, woolen fabrics exposed to ultraviolet light are more severely faded and weakened than are dry fabrics.

MILDEW   Raw wool may have mildew spores that are inactive until it is wet. Wool is attacked by mildew only after being damp for some time. It is much more resistant than cellulose fibers.

EFFECT OF HEAT[3] When heated to 212–220°F, moist wool becomes bone dry and harsh to the touch. The original softness is not fully restored even after the hygroscopic water is regained by exposure to the air. If heated to 212°F in a moist atmosphere, such as in steam pressing, wool becomes plastic, can be shaped and creased, and will retain the new shape after it has cooled. It is superior to all other fibers for tailoring. Wool begins to decompose at 275°F dry heat.

ACTION OF WATER[4] Wool is slightly weaker when wet than when dry. Prolonged boiling, however, has been found to dissolve and decompose small amounts of the fiber. Boiling water also reduces luster and promotes the felting of wool fabrics. It is decomposed by high pressure and dry steam.

ACTION OF ACIDS[5] Very dilute mineral acids, even if boiled, do not injure wool. Wool fibers are treated with acids to remove burrs from the fleece or to similarly carbonize cotton and reworked wool. It is weakened with 5 per cent acid. Concentrated mineral acids destroy wool if the fabric is soaked in them for more than a few minutes, or if the acid dries on the fabric. Formic acid and acetic acids are not detrimental to wool. Oxalic, citric, and tartaric acids are not injurious if the acid is washed or sponged off the fabric. Fruit, citrus juices, and soft drinks are acid enough to weaken wool if they are not washed out before the garment is pressed.

ACTION OF ALKALIES Wool is very susceptible to damage by alkalies. Weak alkalies, such as soap, sodium phosphate, ammonia, borax, and sodium silicate, will not damage wool if the temperature is kept below 68°F. Wool must be washed with soaps containing no free alkali. Wool is dissolved in a few minutes when boiled in a 5 per cent solution of sodium hydroxide. Concentrated alkalies below 68°F impart an increased luster and strength to wool, probably by fusing the scales together. This is called mercerized wool.

EFFECT OF BLEACHES Chlorine and hypochlorite solutions (Javelle water) are harmful to wool. Products sold as liquid chlorine (hypochlorite) will yellow wool and can dissolve it at room temperature. Chlorine in various forms is used to make **chlored** or **unshrinkable wool**. When viewed under the microscope, it is shown that the scales have been more or less destroyed. This wool is weaker and less elastic than untreated wool and has no felting properties. Its dye affinity is also greater. In Italy, chlored wool may be mixed with **lanital**, a man-made protein fiber from casein for more even dyeing than is possible with untreated wool-lanital mixtures. Reducing

---

[3] G. H. Johnson, *Textile Fabrics* (New York: Harper & Row, Publishers, 1927), p. 47.
[4] Ibid., p. 48.
[5] Fiber chart of the National Association of Dyers and Cleaners.

agents do not harm wool, but their bleaching action on the coloring matter in wool is not permanent. Under normal conditions, oxidizing agents will not tender wool. Widely used bleaches are potassium permanganate, sodium peroxide, and hydrogen peroxide.

Care of Wool Garments and Articles

Wool clothing exhibits all of the chemical features of wool and, to a greater degree than in most fibers, also reflects the physical characteristics of the wool fiber; that is to say, its natural resiliency permits wear wrinkles to hang out in garments and dresses, increasing comfort during wearing, and allows expert and permanent tailoring. The care of wool garments is discussed in Chapter 8, as far as protection against insect larvae is concerned. It should be said here that permanent protection against moth and carpet beetle larvae removes one of the objections some people have to this unique fiber, which, in so many ways, is superior to any other on the market for articles of wearing apparel.

With the chemical behavior of the wool fiber and wool fabrics freshly before us, it might be well to give a brief outline of the proper way to wash wool fabrics.

These chemical facts suggest a few salient points in the home washing of wool.

1. Use lukewarm water to avoid softening the scales on the wool fibers and meshing the yarns.

2. Subject the wool fiber to the mildest soap or detergent available. By no means should a built or general utility soap powder or detergent powder be used, because of the action of alkalies on these proteins.

3. Wash wool products by hand or with a minimum of mechanical agitation. It is the wringing and twisting of wet wool that aid in the tangling of the fibers with one another to produce felting. Repeated washings at moderate temperatures might produce as much felting and shrinkage as would a single washing at too high a temperature.

4. A very light wash load should be used at the cool setting if an automatic washing machine is used.

5. Squeeze dry; do not wring or spin dry. Use no bleach if possible. If bleach is necessary, add peroxide or a perborate type. Read the labels on the commercial bleaches. Any containing hypochlorite should not be used.

6. A heavy article, such as a blanket or a washable suit, may be put in the dryer at a low heat, preferably with but a single article to avoid rubbing and felting; the article should be removed from the dryer before it is completely dry.

7. Final drying should be on a line, preferably over a double or triple line, to avoid too great tension on one single fold. Garments should be dried on hangers. Knits, such as sweaters, should be dried flat.

Processing Worsteds

Even the normal cleaning of newly shorn wool preparatory to its being spun results in a considerable amount of weight loss or **shrinkage**. In the United States, this loss is estimated to average nearly 60 per cent in territory wools from the free-ranging sheep of the western states. If all the burrs and other vegetable matter are not removed in the scouring operation, it may be necessary to carbonize the fleece by burning the cellulose materials with a flash flame. Another method sometimes used is to freeze the fleece at a very low temperature to harden the grease and to make the burrs brittle enough to be brushed or shaken out, as shown in Figure 2–22.

The fibers are first scoured to remove the wool grease, dirt, and dried perspiration, or **suint**. Wool grease is purified to yield **lanolin**, a product widely used in ointments and cosmetic creams. The alkaline solution is used to remove the grease, and the soap and water to remove the dirt and perspiration.

Figure 2-22   Wool fiber scouring.

The wool fibers are then carded in much the same way as cotton. (Figure 2–23). The card consists of several cylinders equipped with fine wire teeth that lay the fibers in a soft sheet or web, much as a rake lays grass stems roughly parallel. The web is gathered into a soft strand called a sliver.

For worsted cloths, the fibers are then combed out as nearly parallel as possible. The pattern of the woven cloth is clearly shown, and it is necessary that the short fibers be combed out; these combings are the **noils**. The slivers are drawn out narrower than they were in the carding machine and are slightly twisted. The individual fibers are all of about the same length after combing. The dyeing operation commonly follows the combing. Yarn-dyed

Figure 2-23 Wool carding. A web of carded wool emerges from the first card, having been pressed at high pressure under the rollers. These heavy, metal rollers crush all seeds and other foreign vegetable matter remaining in the wool fibers. (Courtesy of The Wool Bureau, Inc.)

cloths have a more uniform color as a result of the pressure-dyeing process; dye circulation is more complete, and the fastness of the color to service conditions is better than if the cloth were dyed after weaving. In the latter case, the color is not always uniform throughout the yarn, and different shades of color may show up during wear.

Spinning puts the desired twist in the yarn. The speed and tension of winding the slivers are regulated to give the yarn the desired twist as it progresses from one spool to another. Worsted yarns are usually given a greater twist and are firmer than woolens. The count or size of worsted yarns has already been defined in terms of the number of hanks required to weigh 1 pound. Weavers purchase the yarn on the spool or in hanks. Worsted yarns may be single-ply, two-ply, three-ply or four-ply. Multi-ply yarns are graded according to the number of plys and the size of the individual ply strands making up the twisted yarn.

Manufacture of Woolen Yarns

The shorter wool fibers are used for woolen yarns. The merino wool fibers are specially suited for this use. Woolen cloths are characterized by softness in handling and texture, indistinctness of pattern, and often a slight napping of the surface. The properties of blankets, typical woolen cloths, are discussed in Chapter 8.

Woolens may be made up entirely of virgin wool fibers or in combination with reprocessed or reused wools or other textile fibers such as cotton, rayon, or synthetics. In low-grade woolens, the fiber content may be nearly all reclaimed fibers, or other textile fibers may constitute a high percentage. The napping of woolens, the indistinct pattern, and the slight felting in the finish make possible the use of fibers of varying lengths and render it difficult to distinguish the identity of the fiber types that have been spun into the yarn.

Wool fibers, whether new or reworked, are customarily scoured and garnetted before they are used (Figure 2–24). The carding operation of yarns for woolens is not intended to straighten all the fibers but to separate them. Woolen yarns are, therefore, not combed. The final yarn is fuzzy, is less tightly twisted than the worsted yarn, and can be easily napped after weaving. The fuzzy structure retains or traps air, and thus woolens are warmer than worsteds. These yarns can be carded several times. They are usually dyed before weaving and are described as **stock-dyed** if at the sliver stage, **yarn-dyed** if at that step, or **piece-dyed** if colored after the cloth has been woven.

A reprocessed yarn made from unfelted knit goods may be superior in durability to a virgin wool yarn made up of fibers from the belly or legs of the sheep. It is difficult to distinguish a fabric made of reworked wool from

Figure 2-24 Pilot plant for wool processing, Albany, Calif., showing some of the equipment for the operations from carding through weaving. Various chemically treated wools are studied here for processibility and the products prepared are subjected to performance testing. (Courtesy of the U.S. Department of Agriculture)

one composed of virgin wool. Microscopic examination might show more broken or flattened scales on the fibers, but even an expert cannot always find conclusive differences between virgin wool and a good shoddy yarn, such as that from Botany wool. If there is a great difference in the length of individual fibers, and if there are fibers of many colors in the cloth, it can be assumed that some reworked wool has been used in the fabric. Garnetting fabrics may damage the fiber scales and may also break some fibers.

Performance Characteristics of Wool

Among the words of highest praise that producers of synthetic fibers can give their products is the brief descriptive claim, "This fiber produces a wool-like fabric." Wool fibers can be spun into compact, tough, strong yarns or into loose, fluffy, soft yarns. Thus the fabric is suitable for heavy-duty work clothes or dress garments, for soft-textured knitted sweaters or blankets, and for such durable materials as upholstery fabrics and carpeting. The fiber possesses a natural crimp, lending itself to easy spinning into yarns and providing fabrics with a built-in ability to absorb shock, such as sudden stresses. When the crimped fibers straighten out, the interlocking surface scales release their grip between adjacent fibers and, finally, the natural resiliency of the fibers takes over. Wool fabrics are not brittle, and they will not break under moderate stress.

Low wet strength is a disadvantage, but it can be compensated for in this stretchability of the yarns.

It has been said that wool stands head and shoulders above all other textile fibers when one moves from a heated and dry indoor atmosphere on a winter day to a cold, damp exterior. The process of rapid moisture absorption by wool actually produces heat through the heat of moisture absorption. When a solid substance absorbs moisture, heat is produced. Under these same conditions, the wearer of any other natural fiber or any synthetics of comparable weight would be chilled to the bone within a matter of a few minutes.

Wool can hold about a third of its own weight of water without feeling wet to the touch. Under these same conditions, other textile materials would be clammy and cold and cling to the body. This same property of wool—moisture absorbency—combined with the ability of the fiber to be manipulated when subjected to steam, enables the tailor to produce a more perfect garment structure as far as fit is concerned in the shoulder area and lapel roll.

The shrinking characteristics of wool are generally recognized and usually do not constitute a problem to the consumer who knows how to wash wool blankets, sweaters, and similar articles; however, one would not dare experiment with a woven suiting unless labeled "washable." Washable wools and even permanently mothproofed wools are available as the result of special finishes developed by science to widen the application of this fiber and to avoid what were the two principal complaints voiced by homemakers. Rarely have complaints been voiced about the loss of color in wool garments during service.

Even this fiber has benefited from technological advances. In addition to the finishing improvements mentioned here, modern concepts for protective wearing apparel for wet-cold exposures utilize wool. A lightweight windbreaker shell of closely woven cotton replaces a thicker, heavier wool fabric and permits the use of the much lighter-weight wool shirt or other undergarment combination to help keep in body heat during extremely cold weather. It is the modern technologist's approach to the Eskimo dress, which in winter has the vapor-barrier skin surface worn outside the heavy winter garment and the hair side or insulator toward the wearer's body. Less wool is used than previously with the adoption of this layer principle for protection.

Just as the properties of the wool fiber indicate the reason for some of the unique advantages possessed by wool in garments, certain disadvantages appear as well. For example, the scaly surface that will become softened by excessively warm water and by alkaline soaps requires the special conditions described on p. 64. At best, the vast majority of wool clothing items are woven; unless given special treatment, they cannot be washed even by approved methods. They require a more costly dry cleaning in order to keep them looking well pressed.

The susceptibility of wool to insect damage also places it at a disadvantage with all other textile fibers, for the wool fiber is the only one that sustains the life of the larvae feeding on it. Thus, wool requires special finishing, either by the use of a toxic substance or by destruction of the sulfur-sulfur bond in the protein that these larvae require. The chemical nature of the protein causes an allergenic reaction when in contact with the skin of some persons of unusual sensitivity. All textile fibers are known to affect some persons, but wool is by far the worst offender as a result of its unique composition, combined possibly with the rubbing effect of the rough-surfaced wool fiber against the skin of these sensitive individuals. For these persons, wool cannot be used.

Another disadvantage to which the moisture absorbency and the chemical receptivity of the fiber may contribute is the tendency of wool to pick up odors from vapors in the air and from odorous materials spilled on the fabric. This factor combined with the fact that wool cannot be made sterile by boiling prevents the use of wool in any kitchen clothing. It also cannot be used by individuals working in laboratories in which the air has a strong odor. Other proteins exhibit this same phenomenon; for example, protein foods as well as fats pick up the odor of other foodstuffs in a refrigerator or in a storeroom.

Specialty Hair Fibers

There are many special fibers that are commercially valuable because of their wool-like characteristics or because in combination with wool they produce fabrics with interesting properties. Figure 2–25 shows the various animals yielding these special fibers.

MOHAIR   The United States is the principal producer of **mohair** fiber, the wool-like hair of the mohair or Angora goat. Texas is the largest producer, followed by Arizona, California, New Mexico, Oregon, and Utah. The second national producer is Turkey. Much of the United States production, 56 to 66 per cent in the 1960s, was shipped to England. Another name for this animal is the Angora goat, from which the yield of wool has been greatly increased through scientific breeding. Pure bred animals may pro-

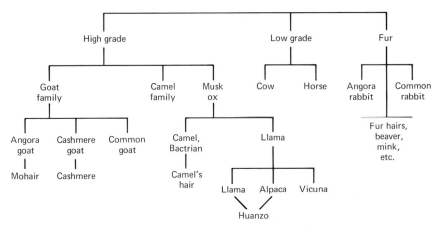

Figure 2-25 Specialty hair fibers. [W. von Bergen, *Wool Handbook*, 3rd ed. (New York: Interscience, 1963), Vol. 1.]

duce anywhere from 7 to 9 pounds per year, and, generally, these animals are clipped twice, as in the case of range-bred sheep. The wool, especially in the under parts of the animals, is likely to be badly matted and soiled. There are three types of fleeces, **tight lock** (ringletted the whole length), **flat lock**, and **fluffy fleece**.

The principal properties of mohair, as well as the other specialty fibers, are compared with wool in Table 2–11. It is interesting to note that although the mohair fiber is similar to wool, there are certain structural differences aiding in its identification; for example, the epidermal scales are only faintly visible and fit so closely to the fiber that a shiny, smooth surface is produced. Mohair, therefore, is a much more lustrous fiber than is apparel wool. It is widely used in men's clothing, often in combination with wool and with silk, or with other fibers. In women's apparel, mohair blends are found in bouclés, velours, and worsteds. It is also more wiry and slippery than wool and has excellent resistance to abrasion and wear. Thus, it has for many years been used in upholstery material where a great deal of wear is to be encountered. In fact, the standard upholstery fabric on the railroad pullman cars and automobiles for many years was mohair fabric. Mohair also makes a fine, durable lining fabric.

CASHMERE This type of wool is produced from the **cashmere** goat (or Kashmir), which is native to Tibet, India, Iran, Iraq, and southwestern China, and is finer in texture than wool. The true cashmere fiber is a soft, fine undercoat that underlies the heavy, coarse, hairy growth of this animal. These goats are not shorn, the hair is pulled out by hand in the late spring when the animal begins to molt or shed its surplus hair that had afforded winter protection. Shreds of the soft wool, as well as certain amounts of the outer hair, are collected from bushes and shrubs against which the animals rub in the pasture when grazing. A separate classification, **pashm wool**, is given these fibers bought from the natives as a mass of fine hair; they contain dust and bark collected from the grazing area of the animals. Of the yield of approximately 8 ounces of hair per animal, only 3 to 5 ounces are the valuable cashmere fiber. The United States consumes approximately 100,000 to 200,000 pounds of cashmere each year. The fiber is naturally wavy and glossy. It is extremely difficult to identify cashmere wool from fine quality sheep's wool. Indeed, only a microscopic examination showing a higher content of fine fiber in a given sample can identify cashmere from a sample of wool. Chemically, it behaves like wool. Extremely fine sweaters, infants' wear, and luxury fabrics for men's and women's coats and for dress goods may be of cashmere. The U.S. Census estimates (1970) that if all cashmere fibers on the market were genuine cashmere, 16 to 20 million goats would be required at 8 ounces of wool per animal.

CAMEL HAIR   With the greater amount of camel hair fiber coming from eastern Asia (from Mongolia, Pakistan, and the northwestern provinces of China), it is understandable that to the Western world the fiber is only available in limited quantities. This fiber comes from the two-hump, or Bactrian, camel, rather than from the one-hump Dromedary type, found in Arabia and Egypt. These camels, serving as beasts of burden in Central Asia, are hybrids of the two types and have a shaggy coat capable of withstanding both heat and cold. Camel hair is "harvested" in the form of the loose clumps of hair that fall from the animals as the caravans move slowly across the desert or when the animals are resting. Most of the hair is collected in the spring, the time when animals shed surplus hair, although some is collected the year round. Generally the last few camels in the line of march in a caravan carry great sacks in which the camel hair that is dropped from the animals ahead is placed when it is picked up by boys and men. Again, it is the soft wool undercoat that constitutes the prized, genuine camel hair. The coarse outer hair is known as **beard hair**. It is separated in the combing machine as **noils**. The fine camel hair tops or undercoating goes into fine coating fabrics or knitting yarns.

The finest grades of camel hair wool are finer than cashmere and, as in the case of that fiber, the epidermal scales are more visible than in wool and mohair. The fibers have a distinct medulla, and small colored granules are found in this canal portion, as well as in the cortex. The properties of camel hair are shown in Table 2–11.

Wools from the Llama Family

Llamas of several species are native to the mountains of western South America and produce fine wool-like fleeces. They are approximately a

Table 2-11   Minor Hair Fibers*

Fiber	Animal Source	Habitat	Average Fiber Length (in.)	Average diameter (μ)	Strength	Principal Uses
Alpaca	Alpaca goat	Peru	4–8 (fine) 7–11 (coarse)	27	Strong	Men's summer suits and linings
Camel hair	Camel	Africa, Asia. China, Russia	2.5–3 (fine) 4–10 (coarse)	18	Like wool	Oriental rugs, gloves, sweaters, coatings, blankets, piece goods
Cashmere	Cashmere goat	Himalaya Mts, Kashmir, Tibet	1¼–3½	17	Like wool	Infants' wear, shawls, sweaters
Horsehair	Horse—mane, tail	North and South America	Variable	110 140	Strong	Braid, fur, upholsteries
Kasha	Tibet goat	Tibet		14		Kasha cloth
Llama	Anchenia goat	South America, Andean plateau	10–12	23		Coatings, rare in United States
Mohair	Angora goat	Asia Minor (Turkey), Cape Colony, United States	9–12 (year's growth)	57	Like wool	Upholsteries, draperies, summer suitings, braids, lining, riding clothes, gloves, plush, brushed wool sweaters, socks, mittens
Quiviut	Musk ox	Arctic regions	3–5	15	Like wool	Knitted garments
Rabbit hair	Angora rabbit	Turkey	0.4–0.8	13		Felt, knitted garments blended.
Vicuña	Vicuña goat	South America		13		Very rare — museum pieces

*Fine wool 20μ; medium 28μ; coarse 37μ.

73

quarter the size of a camel but are somewhat camel-like in their general appearance. Although they lack humps, they are known as the **Camelidae**, and there may have been a common ancestor between these llamas and the true camels, for fossil remains of camels have been found in several parts of both North and South America. The llama and alpaca have been domesticated and are the principal beasts of burden in the mountains of South America, both in the Andes and in the foothill regions. The guanaco and the vicuña are wild animals, although the Indians have domesticated the guanaco to some extent. There are several cross strains that have been developed for special fleece characteristics. The Spaniards, in their conquest of South America, found the llama and alpaca serving as beasts of burden and as a source of clothing fabric. Even today, much of the wool from these various animals comes from the high Andean regions of southern Ecuador, Peru, Bolivia, and northwestern Argentina. This region, generally known as llama land, is a large, almost uninhabited plateau, known as the Puña, lying between the two great ranges forming the Andes.

The llama has a thick, coarse coat consisting of a soft fleece and a coarse, straight outer hair. The fibers are generally brown, although there are some that are white. The outer hair is often white. Being the beast-of-burden for the Indians, it is estimated that there are about two million of these animals in Bolivia and about one million in Peru, with scattered thousands in the other countries. The alpaca is a superior fleece. This animal is smaller than the llama, being about 3.5 feet high instead of 4 to 5 feet. It has a heavier body and its hair hangs in long, tangled strands from 8 to 16 inches in length. Again, brown shades predominate. The fleece fiber is very silky, fine, and strong, and there is no coarse outer hair. The range is restricted to elevations of 13,000 to 16,000 feet on this Andean plateau because its chief food substance, the Ychu grass, is only found here. The government has prohibited exportation of alpacas to other countries even though it has never been found to thrive elsewhere. Cross-bred animals from the llama and the alpaca do not have wool as good as either parent strain. These animals are shorn after the winter rainy season.

The finest fiber producer is the **vicuña**, the smallest of the group; it exists in a wild state in the high mountains of Peru. It weighs only about 100 pounds and has remarkably soft, chestnut, or fawn-colored, fleece. It is very wily and has resisted all attempts at domestication. Thus, the animal must be killed to obtain the fleece. The vicuña is protected by the Peruvian government and only about 15,000 pounds of fleece are obtained per year. A man's topcoat of this fiber would require the fleece of 40 animals, and the cost would be in excess of $1,000. Only 10,000 fleeces are permitted each year, and in the late 1960s the fabric was as high as $150 per yard.

MINOR WOOL HAIRS Some very low-grade carpet yarns have small amounts of cow hair mixed with wool, and some felts contain cow hair, horse hair, or pig hair mixed with wool. The musk ox is a valued fiber source for the people of Lapland and Finland and has been introduced into northern Canada and Alaska. The fine underhair is wool-like and known as **Quiviat**. Experiments are being made at the University of Alaska in using this rather weak fiber in blends with other wools for commercial distribution. Various fibers from fur-bearing animals produce special effects in women's soft-textured dress fabrics and knitting yarns. The most important of these is the fur of the Angora rabbit. This is one of the softest of all fibers and has been useful mainly as a trimming material or blended with wool in fine soft-textured sweaters. Genuine fur fibers, such as mink, beaver, skunk, muskrat, pony, and rabbit, among others, have been blended with wool to produce soft and novel types of yarns.

Fur Fibers and Fur

Fur fibers are the fine individual fibers shorn from the pelts of fur-bearing animals for the purpose of blending with wool or other fibers to produce fabrics of special textures. Generally, the fibers are straight and blend well with the wavy wool fibers. The term **fur** refers to the pelt of the animal with the fur intact. Thus, in furs, we have the fiber surface on one side and the leather on the other.

In labeling, the identification of the fiber in these two types of garments would be under different acts of Congress. In the case of fur fibers blended with wool, the type and amount of fur fiber present would be expressed under the Wool Products Labeling Act of 1939. The fur coat, or other textile product with the pelt intact, would fall under the Fur Products Labeling Act, as amended March 15, 1961. It requires that the furs be correctly identified as to animal type, as whether it has been dyed or color-altered in any way, and as to the country of origin of the fur pelt. Fur fiber products blended with fibers other than wool must be labeled in accordance with the Textile Fiber Products Identification Act of 1958, amended under the FTC Rules of 1960.

SILK

Silk is a **filament**, an extremely long fiber of several thousand feet in length. It is formed in two glands to produce two parallel strands that emerge from a tiny opening in the mouth of the silkworm, called a spinneret. These strands are bound together at the opening by a natural gum of protein nature, termed **sericin**, formed by two other glands. The protein in silk is fibroin. The silk of commerce is produced by the worms of the mulberry silkworm, the **Bombyx mori**. This type has been developed over thousands of years as an egg-laying machine.

Although silk today is commercially an unimportant fiber, it is still regarded as the ultimate luxury fiber by the world of fashion. Then, too, the objective toward which the first researches in man-made fibers were striving was to produce a silklike filament.

The origin of silk is obscure, but history places it back some 4000 years into China and India. Even then, it was identified as the source of fabrics principally for the nobility. Legend has it that eggs were secreted in the clothing of itinerate merchants from China into India. A Chinese princess was said to have carried the two seeds necessary for the silk industry in her headdress, the silkworm eggs and the seeds of the mulberry tree upon whose leaves the caterpillars live.

In *The Story of Textiles*,[6] Walton says that it was Alexander the Great who brought the first knowledge of silk to Europe after his conquest of India in 356 to 323 B.C. However, this report must have disappeared because four hundred years later, the Romans appeared to have obtained silk from Greek tradesmen, and the scholars of the day had fantastic ideas as to the source of this wonderful fiber. Some thought it grew on trees; others thought it was grown from flowers; and Pliny described the Bombyx but identified it as being a native of Assyria. The Roman nobility used silk in the days of Julius Caesar—its price was its weight in gold. In A.D. 436, two Persian monks, acting under the command of the Emperor Justinian, brought back from China complete knowledge of the combination of the silkworm and the processing of the silk, together with seeds of the mulberry tree and silkworm eggs concealed in hollow staves. This established the silk industry in Europe.

Sporadic attempts have been made to develop a silk-fiber-producing industry in the United States, but high labor costs, as a result of the hand removal of the silk strands from the cocoons, have always brought about its failure. Attempts to develop the industry were made from Colonial days up until the early part of the twentieth century. At that point, silk imported from Japan arrived at West Coast ports on ships and was put on high-speed express trains to the Eastern Seaboard where most of the silk mills are located (in Connecticut; Philadelphia, Pennsylvania; and Paterson, New Jersey). This valuable cargo is now largely air-borne.

The development of the synthetic fiber industry, especially that of nylon just prior to World War II, virtually ended the women's hosiery market in the United States as far as silk was concerned. Many months before Pearl Harbor worsening relations between United States and Japan brought about a freeze of all silk into the United States for military use, for the silk fiber was used almost exclusively for parachutes for humans, and for powder bags for heavy naval guns.

[6] Perry Walton, *The Story of Textiles* (Boston: J. S. Lawrence, 1912).

Sericulture

Sericulture refers to the technique of cultivating and raising the silkworms and collecting the silk from the cocoon. It is essentially a cottage industry in Japan and China; in fact, some of the procedures, particularly the stripping of the silk from the cocoon, cannot be done as effectively by mechanical means as by hand. The life cycle of the silkworm is shown in Figure 2–26.

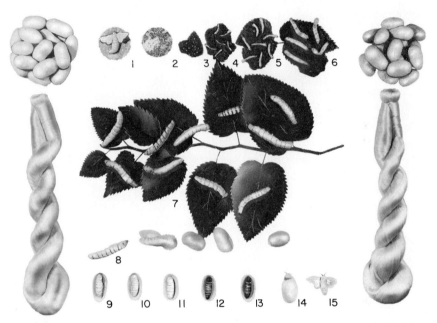

Figure 2-26   An exhibit of the life cycle of the silkworm. (1) Laying of eggs. (2) Hatching. (3) First age. (4) Second age. (5) Third age. (6) Fourth age. (7) Fifth age. Silkworms feeding on mulberry leaves. (8) Spinning cocoons. (9, 10, 11, 12) Stages of pupa. (13, 14, 15) Stages of moth. (Courtesy of International Silk Guild, Inc.)

In the modern silk industry, the tiny eggs, called seeds, are deposited by the carefully bred female moth on cards or strips of cloth. These are stored in a cool, dry place until a new incubated crop of silk worms is desired (Figure 2–27). The cards are then distributed to peasants and the eggs are incubated in the cottages or homes by mild warmth. Sometimes they are worn under the clothing until the tiny silkworms are hatched. At this point, they must be fed day and night with shredded, fresh mulberry leaves, as shown in Figure 2–28. The worms cling to and feed on these mulberry leaves on feeding trays. The weak worms are discarded. The stronger

Figure 2-27   Silk moths laying eggs. (Courtesy of International Silk Guild, Inc.)

specimens are fed five to six times a day, and during their life period of approximately one month, they will shed their skin four or five times at about five-day intervals. During this time, the worm grows from a 3-millimeter length to 8 or 9 centimeters; its weight is a thousand times greater than that of the newly hatched worm or ant. After about a month, it seeks something on which to spin its cocoon (Figure 2–29), at which time it is transferred to a special frame containing trays or troughs. The cocoon begins as a net forming a shell around the insect's body. The two strands are excreted from the **spinnerets** in the lower jaw and this fluid solidifies in contact with the air (Figure 2–30). If the cocoon is permitted to stand for

Figure 2-28 Workers feeding silkworms with mulberry leaves. (Courtesy of International Silk Guild, Inc.)

two weeks, the moth will develop and will then escape through the bottom of the cocoon, breaking the silk by the action of an alkaline solution secreted in the moth. Only enough of these developed moths are permitted to hatch in this manner to maintain a breeding stock (Figure 2–31). The vast majority of the cocoons, therefore, are treated with heat in order to kill the **chrysalis**, or undeveloped moth. The female moths are in the heavier cocoons and these are the ones principally saved. Each female moth, after hatching, will lay about 700 eggs, thus beginning a new cycle. The male mates live slightly longer than the females, which generally die about a week after they mate and lay their eggs.

Wild silk is that produced from other types of moths that have not been domesticated. These cocoons are found in trees and bushes; most of them have already been pierced when found; thus, wild silk filaments are shorter and of irregular lengths.

Properties

The silk filament has unique properties. Raw silk still containing the sericin appears under the microscope to have a rough, dense structure similar to

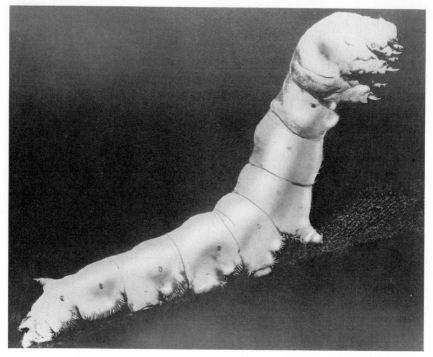

Figure 2-29 Microphotograph of full-grown silkworm ready to spin. (Courtesy of International Silk Guild, Inc.)

that of a piece of wood (see Figure 2–32). When the sericin is removed by boiling it off with soapy water, the fibers appear to be structureless, somewhat resembling hollow glass rods. The principal properties of the fiber are shown in Table 2–12, along with the characteristics of wool.

When sericin is removed, the warm, rich luster of the fiber is fully disclosed. This is capitalized on in many silk fabrics by weaving long floats to give reflectance in the woven cloth, such as in satin. It is difficult to describe the luster of silk, but it is safe to say that it is warmer, softer, and more subtle than that of the more highly reflective brilliance of the man-made fibers. Another factor contributing to the appearance of silk fabric is, of course, the fact that a filament fiber has few loose ends (such as are common in short-fiber fabrics), and it sheds dust and dirt readily. Silk can also be cut into shorter lengths for so-called spun-silk fabrics.

Throwing the Yarn

In the making of silk yarn, the filaments of four or more cocoons are drawn together to form a single strand of raw silk of uniform diameter. As the silk

Figure 2-30 Photomicrograph of silkworm cocoons, showing how the filament is spun in the form of a figure 8. (Courtesy of International Silk Guild, Inc.)

is withdrawn, the cocoons bob up and down in a basin of warm water as the figure-8 cast filaments are pulled into this continuous strand. Each cocoon contains between 300 and 1000 yards of fiber. These raw silk strands are transformed into a yarn by **throwing**—that is, by twisting two or more strands together. It is common to soak these skeins in a soap solution before throwing, or yarn forming, in order to remove the sericin gum still adhering to the raw silk (in an amount of approximately 25 per cent by weight).

The count, or size, of reeled thrown silk is based on the denier system. A denier is a legal coin weighing 0.05-gram. The size is expressed as the weight in deniers (International Denier of 450 meters of the silk). A mul-

Figure 2-31 Sorting out the cocoon crop. The collection of the cocoons takes place on the third or fourth day after the silkworms begin to spin their cocoons. (Courtesy of International Silk Guild, Inc.)

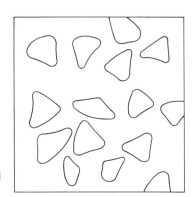

Figure 2-32 Cross section of a silk fiber (rounded corner, triangular).

tiple of 20 is used in expressing the denier of man-made fibers. Thus denier is the weight in grams of 9000 meters of yarn or filament ($20 \times 450 = 9000$).

The American silk industry grades silk on a clean or gum-free basis.

Silk from fifty bobbins is wound around a black frame, on which individual skeins are graded as to uniform size, evenness, and freedom from defects.

Spun-silk Yarn

The waste silk is made into spun-silk yarn by the same process as yarns from other short fibers are fashioned. The pierced cocoons, wild cocoons, and the **frisons**, or silk-waste, compose the raw materials for spun silk. The silk is degummed by boiling off in soap suds. It is then dried and cut into 9-inch lengths. The cut fibers are combed in order to straighten them. The yarns are twisted on a spinning frame, which gives them a tighter twist than is needed for the long-filament thrown-silk yarn. The spun-silk yarn is less lustrous than thrown silk because of the tighter twist; it is less elastic, less strong, and has a harsher feel or handle. It is less expensive and is suitable for filling yarns in woven cloth. Spun-silk sizes are computed by two methods, the English and the French. The English method sets 840 yards equal to 1 pound (as for cotton). A yarn size of 20-2 would have 840 yards of two-ply yarn times 20, or 16,800 yards. The French system base is the number of 1000-meter skeins weighing 1 kilogram.

Silk Weighting

Silk is purchased in the raw state on a weight basis, and the 20 to 30 per cent of gum it contains is charged for as if the yarn were all silk. It is customary to replace some of this gum, which will be boiled off, with metallic salts before dyeing the yarn. Silk has a great affinity for the salts of tin and iron and for tannin. An insoluble tin phosphosilicate is the usual weighting material. A **pure silk** or **pure dye silk** is one that is defined by the FTC (Trade Practice Conference, April 21, 1932) as containing no more than 10 per cent of weighting, except in black silk, which can have 15 per cent. This amount is not injurious to the serviceability of the silk. It is possible to **load**, or dynamite, silks to the extent of approximately three times the weight of the raw silk (before degumming). Weighted silks purchased by the consumer commonly contain between 40 and 60 per cent weighting calculated on the basis of the finished cloth.

Heavily weighted silks containing in excess of 40 per cent are not serviceable, but they appear to be dense and firm. The fiber strength is low; the fibers are inelastic; sunlight and perspiration rapidly deteriorate the fabric; the fabric spots readily; and it is difficult to wash and dry-clean. Salt water deteriorates weighted silk.

When a label reads, "pure dye silk," it refers to the amount of weighting,

Table 2-12 Characteristics of Wool and Silk Fibers

Physical Characteristics	Wool	Silk
Microscopic appearance	Rodlike with scales on surface	Double fiber
Length of fiber	1–3 in. in woolen fabrics 3–8 in. in worsted fabrics	Averages up to 4000 ft
Diameter of fiber	0.005- to 0.0015-in.	0.00054- to 0.00118-in.
Color of fiber	Yellowish, but may be brown to black	Yellowish
Luster	Coarse fibers, high; fine fibers, lower	Bright with gum out
Strength	15-30 grams per fiber	5-28 grams per denier
Elongation	Will stretch 25–35 per cent before break	1/7–1/5 of length
Conductivity to heat	Poor	Low
Regain or hygroscopic moisture	10-15 per cent	11 per cent
Capillarity and penetrability	Has both	None
Composition of fiber	Keratin, contains carbon, hydrogen, nitrogen, and sulfur amino-acid compounds	Fibroin with sericin gum
Method of preparation	Scouring to remove natural contaminants, such as wool grease and perspiration	Boil off with soap to degum
Chemical Characteristics		
Effect of light	Changes chemical structure, increases affinity of dyestuffs	Weakened
Mildew	Attacked if left damp for too long	Slight
Heat	At 275°F dry heat begins to decompose At 212°F wet heat becomes plastic	At 231°F dry heat, begins to yellow Above 330°F disintegrates
Water	Boiling reduces luster and strength, promotes shrinkage	Temporary loss of 10–25 per cent when wet. May be steam pressed
Mineral acids sulfuric hydrochloric nitric	Dilute acids do not damage even at boil; concentrated acids destroy wool	Acid dyes do not injure, even at a boil; concentrated acids destroy silk; dilute cold mineral acids (except HCl) do not injure silk

Volatile organic acids formic acetic	No damage	No damage unless heated
Nonvolatile organic acids oxalic tartaric citric	Not injurious if washed out	Must be washed out quickly to prevent weakening; perspiration weakens fiber
Strong alkalies caustic soda	Weakened by strong solutions Dilute cold solutions not injurious if neutralized	Damaged
soda ash	Dilute solution of soda ash may be used in lukewarm water if removed quickly	
Weak alkalies ammonium carbonate, borax, sodium silicate, sodium phosphate, soap	Not injurious under careful use	Alkalies weaken silk; built soaps must be avoided in washing
Oxidizing agents (hydrogen peroxide and potassium permanganate)	Like cotton	No damage if aftertreated with reducing agent and rinsed
Metallic salts	Has affinity	Great affinity
Affinity for dyestuffs	Good	Good
Classes of dyestuffs in common use	Chromic, acid, some basic dyes and direct	
Bleaching agents chlorine bleach hypochlorites	Harmful, if used with care, can produce a brittle, nonshrinkable wool	Yellow and tender fibers
Reduction bleaches sulfurous acid (sulfur dioxide plus water) hydrosulfite	Same as cotton	After treatments to be rinsed out
Effect of insects	Consumed by larvae of carpet beetle and clothes moth	Safe

which is a trade expression handed down through the trade industry and does not, in any way, refer to the dyestuff used. The presence of excess weighting is disclosed by the silk identification burning test. Instead of the melting of the fiber ends and the formation of the hard black bead characterized by burning pure dye silk, the fragile ash from a strip or strand of weighted silk retains the fabric or fiber structure. After burning away the organic protein material, the metallic weighting remains as a solid residue.

CHAPTER

Man-made Fibers

Man-made fibers include rayon and acetate fibers and filaments, organic fibers, metallic fibers, and miscellaneous inorganic fibers. They have several general characteristics in common, whether they are derived from cellulose fibers as the rayons and acetates, or from the polymerization or combination of one or more simple chemicals to form a synthetic fiber such as nylon, polyester, or acrylic. Glass fiber has some of these physical properties.

1. Man-made fibers are generally quite slippery because the walls of the spinneret have a tendency to polish the filament as the liquid is extruded.
2. They are generally quite lustrous or bright; therefore, it is not uncommon for a delustrant to be incorporated within the spinning solution to make the fibers more opaque and dull.
3. There is a general tendency for the fibers to have a thin skin or outer layer. The thickness and toughness of this outer layer depends on the rate of the solidification of the extruded mass forming the fiber.
4. After a filament has been spun, it may be cold-drawn (tension spun) to give it greater strength and to increase its ability to stretch.

Fiber Spinning

The term **spinning** has several different meanings in the textile industry, one of which refers to the gathering together and ultimate twisting of individual fibers into a yarn suitable for subsequent fabric formation, either by weaving or knitting. (See Figures 3–1 and 3–2.)

Figure 3-1 A rayon spinneret. (Courtesy of American Viscose Corporation)

The formation of man-made fibers by forcing a syruplike substance through tiny holes and then hardening the minute strand is also called spinning. The role of the finely perforated metal cup, called a spinneret, is thus like that of the spinning glands of silkworms.

Not all man-made fibers are emitted in the same fluid state or chemical combination, nor are they all hardened in a like manner. (See Figure 3–3.) We recognize three major forms or conditions in fiber spinning. When the thick, syruplike material is forced through a **spinneret** into a chemical bath to harden or be converted into an insoluble substance or regenerated fiber, the spinning method is described as **wet spinning**.

When the polymer, or chemical derivative, is dissolved in a solvent that can be evaporated, the filament is left to harden simply by dry air flow; this process is termed **dry spinning**.

When the polymer or other fiber-forming substance, including glass fiber, for example, is melted and extruded through the spinneret to be hardened by cool air, the process is termed **melt spinning**.

The term **spun**, or **spinning**, is used in the man-made textile industry in several other connotations; for instance, if the hardened filament is stretched

Figure 3-2 Spinneret for the extrusion of man-made filaments. (Courtesy of American Viscose Corporation)

during the process of hardening, it is said to be undergoing **stretch spinning**. Also, the hardened fiber may be given additional stretching. This cold stretching is sometimes termed stretch spinning and is intended to give fibers additional strength, stretchability, and fineness.

Man-made fibers can be produced in short lengths similar to the natural fibers and thus can be gathered and twisted or spun into yarns just as are the natural fibers.

Because of difficulty in dyeing, some of the man-made fibers require that the dyestuff be added to the liquid material in the feed tank before the fiber is actually spun into a fiber. This is sometimes called solution dyeing, spun dyeing, or dope dyeing, and means that the color is added prior to spinning.

RAYON AND ACETATE FIBERS AND FILAMENTS

In the 1920s when the man-made cellulosic filaments were first produced in quantity and their marketing became a large-scale operation, the Rayon Rules, set in 1923, did not distinguish between those fibers that were re-generated pure cellulose and those that were salts of cellulose (See

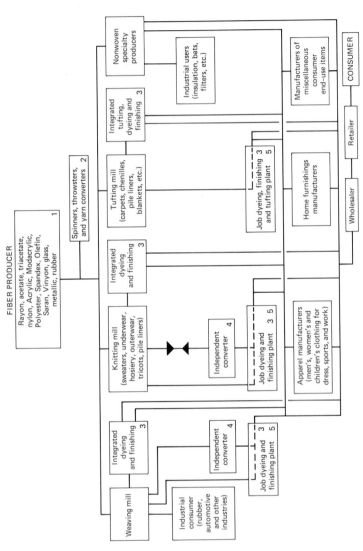

Figure 3-3 The flow of man-made fibers from producer to consumer. (1) Man-made fibers are used in the textile process either alone or in blends with each other or with natural fibers. (2) Spinners produce yarn from short fibers. Throwsters add to yarn additional twist, bulk, and so on. Yarn converters dye or otherwise prepare yarns for fabrication. Many weaving, knitting, and tufting mills perform these processes. (3) Dyeing and finishing plants dye or print fabrics and apply finishes for wash-and-wear, crush resistance, water and soil repellence, flame proofing, and so on. (4) Independent converters own stock in a process, but the processing is done by others. (5) Job dyeing, finishing, and tufting plants contract work from weaving, knitting, and tufting mills and from independent converters.

Figure 3–4.) The FTC clarified this confusion in the 1951 interpretation (effective in February 1952) of the official definitions of rayon and acetate. The two classes of fibers in these categories are expressed by the American Society for Testing Materials, as follows:

> *Rayon*: A generic term for man-made fibers, monofilaments and continuous filament yarns, composed of regenerated cellulose with or without lesser amounts of nonfiber-forming materials (*Note*: Regenerated cellulose fibers made by the complete saponification of cellulose esters are rayons.)
>
> *Acetate*: A specific term used for man-made fibers, monofilaments, and continuous filament yarns composed of acetylated cellulose with or without less amounts of nonfiber-forming material.[1]

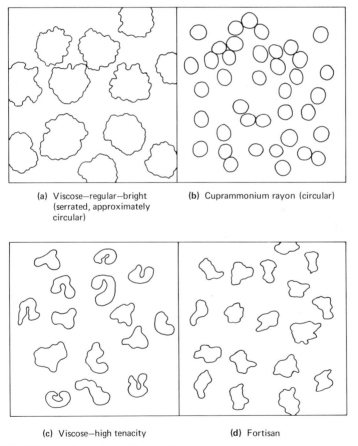

(a) Viscose—regular—bright   (b) Cuprammonium rayon (circular)
(serrated, approximately
circular)

(c) Viscose—high tenacity   (d) Fortisan

Figure 3-4   Cross sections of typical rayon fiber cross sections.

[1] American Society for Testing Materials, Committee D-13 on Textile Materials.

The key words in these two definitions are **regenerated**, in the case of rayons, and **acetylated**, connoting the idea of an ester or organic salt. It is an oversimplification in referring to the regenerated cellulose fibers as rayon to assume that all brands available are alike. Including the several types of regular rayon for apparel and household fabrics—the high-tenacity rayons, those with the irregular cross sections, and the many degrees of fiber fineness available in each—there are roughly 300 distinct rayon filaments marketed. (The characteristics of 50 rayons are listed in Table 3–1.) Many of those are

Table 3-1   Rayons

Tradename/General Classification	Producer	Type and Special Characteristics*	End-use Area*
Avicolor	American Viscose Division	F or S (solution-dyed)	AH
Avicron	American Viscose Division	F	H
Aviloc	American Viscose Division	F	I
Avisco	American Viscose Division	F or S	AHI
Avril (Fiber 40)	American Viscose Division	F or S (modified)	AH
Beau-Grip	Beaunit	F (high tenacity)	I
Beaunit Rayon	Beaunit	F (spun-dyed)	AH
Beaunit Rayon	Beaunit	F (flat filament)	A
Beaunit Rayon	Beaunit	F	AHI
Bemberg	Bemberg Industries	F	AH
Briglo	American Enka	F (bright luster)	AHI
Coloray	Courtaulds	S (solution-dyed)	AHI
Comisco	Beaunit	ST (super high strength)	A
Cupracolor	Bemberg	F	AH
Cuprel	Bemberg	F	AH
Dynacor	American Enka	F (improved adhesion)	TC
Dynacor	American Viscose Division	F (improved adhesion)	TC
Dynacor	Beaunit	F (improved adhesion)	TC
Dynacor	IRC Fibers	F	TC
Englo	American Enka	F (dull)	AH
Enka Rayon	American Enka	FS	AHITC
Enkrome	American Enka	FS (acid-dyeable)	AH
Fiber 700	American Enka	S (high wet modulus)	AHI
Fibro	Courtaulds	S	AHI
Flarkone	Beaunit	F (flake subcupro)	AH
Jetspun	American Enka	F (solution-dyed)	AHI
Kolorbon	American Enka	S (solution-dyed)	AH
Lintelle	Beaunit	F (thick and thin)	AH
Multi-Cupioni	Bemberg	F	AH

Table 3-1 Rayons (continued)

Tradename/ General Classification	Producer	Type and Special Characteristics*	End-use Area*
Narco	Beaunit	F (normal)	A
Narcon	Beaunit	ST (super high strength)	A
Purilon	American Viscose Division	S	I
Rayflex	American Viscose Division	F	I
Skybloom	American Enka	S (super crimp)	AH
Skyloft	American Enka	F (bulked natural or solution-dyed)	AHI
Softglo	American Enka	F (semidull)	AH
Super Rayflex	American Viscose Division	F	I
Super White	American Enka	S (optically bright)	A
Suprenka	American Enka	F (high tenacity)	I
Suprenka Hi-Mod	American Enka	F (low shrinkage super high tenacity)	I
Suprenka M	American Enka	F (super high tenacity, high elongation)	I
Suprenka MS	American Enka	F (super high tenacity, low elongation)	I
Suprenka 2000	American Enka	F (high tenacity)	ITC
Suprenka 6000	American Enka	F (super high tenacity)	ITC
Tyrex	American Enka	F	TC
Tyrex	American Viscose Division	F	ITC
Tyrex	Beaunit	F (super high tenacity)	ITC
Tyrex	IRC Fibers	F	TC
Tyron	IRC Fibers	F	HITC
Zantrel 700	American Enka	S (improved high wet modulus)	AHI

SOURCE: Based on data from *Modern Textiles Magazine* (March 1971).
A—Apparel
H—Home furnishings and carpets
I—Industrial fabrics
C—Tire cord
Type F—Multifilament
S—Staple fiber
T—Tow

available also in staple or short-fiber form. Similarly, the term **acetate** includes not only the conventional cellulose acetate but the newer triacetate named **Arnel**. These are available in numerous deniers, or degrees of fineness.

The general properties of rayons are given in Table 3–2. **Viscose** rayon is by far the most important commercially; it is also actually lower in price than cotton. The cuprammonium type rayon, or **Bemberg**, is similar in many of its properties. Rayon has a lower strength than cotton because the cellulose molecules in the regenerated fiber are shorter in length. In recent years, however, the wet and dry strength values for rayon have been constantly climbing because of the development of a longer molecule of cellulose. The cold stretching or spinning increases the filament or fiber tenacity of rayon and other man-made fibers.

Cold-stretched Rayon

The general concept of a fiber is that it consists of a large number of long molecules that although invisible, are vastly longer than they are wide. This concept is justified by a number of physical measurements, such as the behavior of light rays, X rays, and other sources of energy. If such a fiber were to be formed through a spinneret without any tension or lengthwise stress, even that of gravity, and without any friction from the spinneret lining, conceivably a perfectly amorphous or helter-skelter arrangement of these molecules or micelles would result. Figure 3–4 (a) represents such a completely random arrangement of molecules in the amorphous fiber.

When such an amorphous filament is stretched, as in cold stretch or stretch spinning, there is a tendency for those randomized molecules to become more parallel and to lie lengthwise along the length of the fiber. In the parallel or oriented fiber, the micelles tend to resemble crystals in their X ray photographs.

Most fibers, after being stretched from five to seven times their original length, tend to have molecules that appear in an amorphous or scattered arrangement in the crystalline areas. It must be kept in mind that when these fibers are stretched, let us say to five times their original length, the diameter becomes finer or more slender by the same amount, whereas the volume of the fiber is constant. Compacting alone would tend to force the individual molecules more and more closely together. This compacting could lead to a certain amount of both physical and chemical joining of adjacent molecules, which would cause the fibers to swell somewhat less under high moisture content and to show a slightly increased tensile strength or tenacity. One has only to look at the amorphous fiber and at the amorphous areas in the fiber to realize that those molecules lying crosswise to the length or axis of the fiber would contribute little or nothing to the strength of the fiber under tensile stress application; on the other hand, the more perfectly crystalline or oriented the individual molecules are, the greater will be the tenacity, because all the molecules will then contribute whatever their individual tensile strengths might be. Similarly, the stretchiness of the oriented fiber is increased, because when pulled within limits of the breaking strength of the rayon, nylon, or other man-made fiber, the stretchiness of each micelle and its ability to go back to the original length comes into play. Similarly, when stretched, individual bonds of attachment between the adjacent molecules

Table 3-2 *Important Use Properties for Rayon Types*

Type		Viscose Regenerated Cellulose Filament and Staple			Cuprammonium Regenerated Filament	High Wet Modulus Rayons			Crosslinked Rayon	High-tenacity Rayon Filament
		Regular	Medium	High		Avril	Lirelle	Zantrel	Corval	Fortisan
Tenacity [grams per denier (gpd)]	Standard	1.5–2.6	2.4–3.2	3.0–5.1	1.7–2.3	5.0	5.0–5.5	3.4	2.1–2.4	6–7
	Wet	0.7–1.8	1.2–1.9	1.9–3.9	0.95–1.35	3.5	4.0	2.7	1.2–1.3	5.1–6.0
Elongation at break (per cent)	Standard	15–30	15–20	9–26	10–17	18	6.5	10	12–15	6
	Wet	20–40	17–30	14–34	17–33	21	7.0	12	21–17	6
Specific gravity		1.50–1.53			1.52–1.54	1.5	1.53	1.51	1.53	1.5
Water absorbency standard (per cent)		13 (11 is commercial standard)			12.5	13	12.5	11.5	13	9.6–10.7

Rayons

Effect of heat	Lose strength at about 300°F and scorch at about 450°F Fortisan scorches at 68° above other rayons
Effect of acid and alkalies	More sensitive to acids than is cotton Swell and weaken in alkali
Resistance to mildew, sun, and aging	Clean rayons are rarely attacked by mildew unless left damp Viscose more resistant to light than silk but less than Corval, Avril, and Fortisan; resistant to aging weakening
Effect of bleach	Weakened rapidly by acid bleaching

will endeavor to restore themselves to their shortest length, and fibers will tend to cling together rather than be pulled apart by the rupture of these minute bonding forces. It is the amorphous section into which water penetrates most easily in rayon fibers; and when rayon is wet, it is approximately 40 per cent weaker than when it is dry. The entry of moisture also causes the rayon fibers or filaments to swell laterally—that is, in width; they also tend to lengthen slightly. For this reason, a fabric with a viscose warp is not a good drapery material—it will be longer on a wet or humid day and shorter on a dry day. In Table 3–2 rayon is shown to have about 11 per cent regain under constant temperature and humidity conditions. However, rayon can imbibe, or absorb, its own weight in water and rather rapidly, thus making it a good fabric for towels and for wearing apparel in which rapid moisture and perspiration absorbency are desired. Because wet rayon tends to cling to the skin, some people say that when it is wet, it is clammy to the touch.

In most chemical behaviors, rayon resembles cotton and, if the fabric is not too delicate, it can be washed and handled like cotton.

Production

Man-made fibers derived from cellulose totaled slightly over 7776 million pounds in the world production of 1968, with about 40 different countries producing this fiber.

The name **rayon** was chosen for the man-made cellulosic fibers in 1923. At the time, the term included both cellulose and cellulose acetate. The new rayon rules on labeling and advertising of this fiber were promulgated on September 11, 1951, by the FTC. The same identifications appear in the Textile Fiber Products Identification Act of 1960. Both types of fiber were first produced from cotton linters, but industry has outgrown this supply, and today, most rayon and acetate fibers are produced from wood pulp.

Purification of Cellulose Raw Material

The key to a fine rayon fiber lies in the purification of the cellulose raw material and in the uniformity of this product. Although German scientists, as early as 1918, were using spruce wood as a source of cellulose for their rayon industry, the producers in the United States were slower to turn to wood as the primary source of cellulose. The strategic priority assigned to cotton linters during World War I made them unavailable for the textile industry and, thus, accelerated the change. The greater abundance of cellulose at lower prices and improved technical knowledge as to processing have combined to keep spruce wood at the head of the materials selected for this textile industry. Other woods are now being used, but generally they require different chemical cooking methods for the removal of other constituents.

Logs are transported to the pulp mills by truck or are floated in great rafts along river or lake waterways. The water method is much cheaper, and for that reason many pulp mills are located on the banks of rivers or the shores of inland lakes adjacent to large forest areas. The logs are cut into lengths of about 20 feet, and the bark is stripped off by means of hydraulic pressure jets. The skinned trunks are then taken to a chipper, a large machine with revolving blades against which the conveyor holds the logs. This cuts the wood into small chips about 1-inch square and approximately a ¼-inch thick. These chips are transformed into a pulp by treatment with strong alkali and sodium sulfide and a pretreatment with a sulfate. This method produces a very pure white cellulose that is free of pigment and contains about 90 per cent **alpha cellulose**. (See Figure 3–5.) This pulp commonly is bleached to make it perfectly white. This is a purer grade of cellulose than that produced by the sulfite process for newsprint. The alpha cellulose predominant in the cellulose pulp for the textile industry is generally referred to as chemical cellulose. (See Figure 2–2, for the structure of cellulose.)

This watery pulp is then laid down on screens in the form of a large sheet, which then closely resembles white blotting paper; it is wound on rolls and

Figure 3-5 Books of chemical cellulose for viscose production. (Courtesy of American Viscose Corporation)

shipped to the fiber-producing plant. In order to maintain quality control when these large rolls are used, two or more are shredded at the time and fed into the vat in which the cellulose is to begin its transformation from blotting paper to luxury fiber. (See Figure 3–6.) Some alpha-cellulose pulp is shipped in tank cars to the manufacturers of rayon or of tissue-grade papers.

Figure 3-6 Chemical cellulose blotters about to be shredded for viscose production. (Courtesy of American Viscose Corporation)

The Viscose Process

The English chemists Cross and Bevan prepared the alkali-cellulose Xanthate and patented the process in 1895. This first viscose yarn was exhibited in 1900, but the yarn was weak. In modern technology, the viscose process involves nine steps and produces a strong fiber.

In Figure 3–7 a simplified flow chart for the production of viscose-type rayon from chemical cellulose is shown. The various steps follow:

1. Cellulose from a mixture of sheets of spruce wood with or without cotton linters is the preferred source of the *chemical cellulose* used in this process. Other woods are used also. The chips are cooked in a sodium bisulfite solution, washed with clear water, and then bleached with hypochlorite.

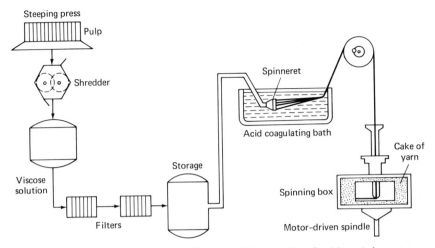

Figure 3-7 Viscose rayon flow chart. (Courtesy of *Modern Textiles Magazine*)

2. The sheets are steeped in caustic soda to produce *alkali cellulose*, which is shredded into crumbs, as shown in Figure 3–8.
3. The crumbs are aged.
4. The alkali-cellulose crumbs are changed into *cellulose Xanthate* by treatment with carbon disulfide.
5. The Xanthate is dissolved in dilute caustic alkali to produce *viscose*.
6. The viscose is filtered and aged until it is the right consistency for spinning—almost like molasses.
7. The viscose from several vats is forced through the spinneret into a dilute sulfuric acid solution. A typical spinneret may have 60 holes in it to produce strands. The holes are usually round, but may have other shapes to produce a special filament with new features, such as dyeability, luster, cover power, and so on. This wet-spinning process *coagulates* the filaments, which are simultaneously regenerated into pure cellulose, and the hardened mass of filaments is in the form of cakes.
8. The filaments are wound onto a skein, and the sulfur is removed by means of an alkaline sulfide bath.
9. The washed filaments are bleached and graded.

The chemical composition of viscose is shown in Figure 3–9.

The Cuprammonium Process

In 1857 Schweitzer dissolved cellulose in an alkaline copper solution, and Despeisses developed a method in 1890 to make a filament. The two methods

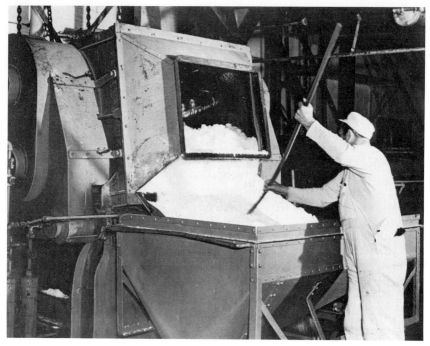

Figure 3-8 Shredding the alkali cellulose. The cellulose sheets are crumbled by the revolving blades of the shredding machine. (Courtesy of American Viscose Corporation)

have been modified until now the finest diameter of any of the rayons can be produced by the cuprammonium process.

1. Cotton linters afford the greatest purity and are the preferred source of cellulose. These fibers are cleansed by cooking in a mild caustic alkali and bleached with chlorine.
2. The purified **chemical-cellulose** is washed, dried, and treated with basic copper sulfate and ammonia.
3. The viscous solution is forced through spinnerets into water, which removes much of the copper and ammonia.
4. The filaments are passed through a mild sulfuric acid bath to coagulate and harden them and to remove the copper.
5. The skeins are washed and rinsed.
6. The yarns are sorted according to denier.

This yarn is capable of withstanding a hot iron and has the greatest wet strength per denier and permanent whiteness of any of the rayons, except special-tenacity fibers.

$$(C_6H_{10}O_5)_n + nNaOH \longrightarrow (C_6H_9O_4ONa)_n + nH_2O$$
cellulose   caustic soda   soda cellulose

$$(C_6H_9O_4ONa)_n + nCS_2 \longrightarrow [SC \overset{\diagup SNa}{\diagdown OC_6H_9O_4}]_n$$
soda cellulose   carbon   sodium cellulose
                    disulfide   Xanthate

The reaction has taken place on No. 2 carbon. Thus, the conversion of Xanthate to viscose on a structural basis might be considered to be

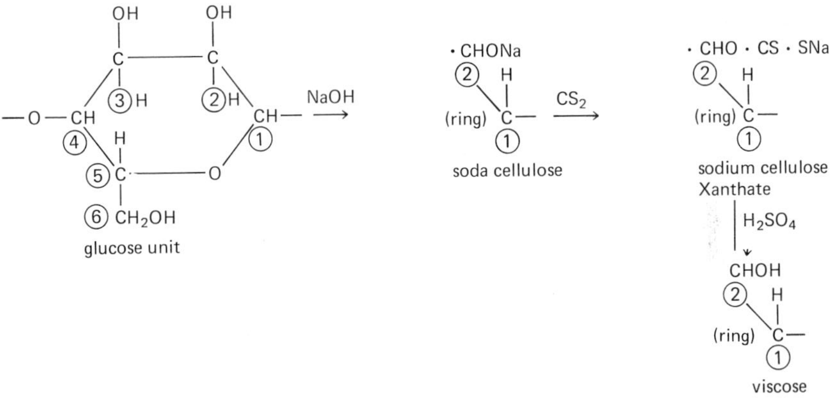

Figure 3-9 Chemical reaction in viscose rayon. Viscose is chemically identical to the purified cellulose, but each molecule of cellulose contains fewer glucose molecules. Thus, *n* is about 9000 in cotton, somewhat less in wood pulp, and 350–500 in viscose.

Physical Properties of Commercial Rayons

Rayons are the second most important textile family, being exceeded only by cotton in their worldwide volume in consumer goods. Rayon fibers are marketed in clusters of **tow** fiber, in continuous **filaments** of infinite length, or in cut or **staple** lengths. Practically all blends of rayon with other fibers are of staple yarn, with the fibers cut to approximately the same length as the natural fiber or other man-made fiber or fibers with which the rayon is blended. Wide ranges of fiber size and strength are available; therefore, there is no simple rayon performance classification so that to assign a set of test values to this fiber would be misleading. Rayon can, in fact, be tailored to almost any kind of end-use. The difference between what technologists consider to be typical viscose or typical cuprammonium rayon of moderate strength and the so-called high-tenacity or high-strength rayons is shown in Table 3–2. In this category, another important rayon, **Fortisan,** must be recognized as one of the most promising of the rayon fibers for household decorative use.

Sizes of Rayon Yarns

There are several sizes, or counts, of rayon yarns (Figure 3–10) identified as to fineness by denier. In the United States, the denier of a yarn is computed from the weight of 450 meters (492.2 yards) of yarn. The legal, or International, denier is a skein of yarn 450 meters long weighing 5 centigrams, or 0.05-gram. This corresponds to the ASTM definition: "The denierage of a yarn is the weight in grams of a length of 9000 meters of a yarn." Thus, a 2-denier yarn or filament is calculated in the following terms: If 450 meters of yarn weigh 0.1 gram, then 9000 meters of yarn weigh 2 grams. The average size of rayon apparel yarns is between 100 and 200 denier. The finest is 15 denier, made by the cupra-rayon process.

Manufacture of Staple

Production methods for viscose rayon staple and tow are the same as those for continuous filament yarns, up to the coagulating bath step. But here,

Figure 3-10   Rayon tow. (Courtesy of American Viscose Corporation)

instead of being wound on bobbins or formed into cakes, the mass of filament emerging from the coagulating bath is cut into any desired length to provide staple-length fibers. Ingenious modern machines providing tow-to-top, or direct, spinning permit the spinning of yarn in the form of a rope made up of the gathered filaments from 2000 to 3000 holes in the large spinneret used for staple or for tow filament spinning. The purchaser then breaks this rope into whatever lengths he desires of his own purpose. (See Figure 3–11.)

Figure 3-11 Viscose rayon cake. Filament rayon ready for the market. (Courtesy of American Viscose Corporation)

Properties of Rayons

All rayons are regenerated cellulose, and regular (or normal) rayons lose approximately the same percentage of strength or tenacity when wet. It is for this reason that the industry has sought to improve the tenacity of certain types of rayons in order to permit them to be used for fabrics requiring a greater amount of stress while wet, in addition to greater utility where normal wear is rigorous. Thus, cold-stretched or high-strength viscose has been produced and, by a special chemical treatment, the high wet modulus group shown in Table 3–2, the cross-linked Corval rayon, and the saponified rayon named Fortisan. Weather also causes the viscose rayon to creep or elongate when wet; this has already been mentioned as the reason rayon is not used in the warp of glass curtains that may be subjected to rain water. Usually, the original dimension will be restored after some days of hanging, especially if the ambient humidity is very low and the curtains are given a chance to become completely dry. The rayons, especially the viscose and cuprammonium types, have low resiliency and elasticity and wrinkle badly unless given a special treatment. They may also wrinkle in washing and drying. It is to overcome this and the abnormal swelling of rayon when it absorbs water that the special types, such as the high wet modulus, the cross-linked, and the high-tenacity rayons were developed. Modern rayons can be pressed at temperatures approaching that used for cotton; however, they lose strength under dry heat at about 300°F.

Properties of Cross-linked Rayons

For approximately 15 years organic chemists specializing in the field of cellulose chemistry have been actively seeking methods of stabilizing the dimensional variations of rayons when wet—that is, to reduce the swelling and the wet elongation, and also to reduce the characteristic loss of strength when water has been absorbed into the molecular structure. These researches led first to the cross-linked rayons, **Corval** and **Topel,** by Courtaulds North American, Inc. They have since been replaced by another class of rayons that are not only cross-linked but have an unusually high wet modulus. Representative of these are the FMC Corporation, American Viscose Division fiber **Avril,** and **Zantrel** made by the American Enka Corporation. **Lirelle,** a high wet modulus rayon made by Courtaulds, has replaced Corval on the market.

An attempt has been made to have a separate classification of these fibers on the basis of their unique physical properties as compared with conventional rayons. However, the Federal Trade Commission has maintained that the chemical nature of these fibers—that they are regenerated cellulose— makes it inadvisable to have a separate classification. Distinguishing between these two types of rayon, it is sufficient only to visualize inserting an organic radical between the CH_2OH side chains of the original cellulose-forming units. A rather crude analogy would be to stabilize two long pieces of lumber with cross steps as in a ladder, the wooden slats being the cross links holding the two side pieces together.

In 1969, the high wet modulus rayons accounted for approximately 20 per cent of the production of cellulosic fibers in the United States, roughly 1 billion pounds. These high wet modulus rayons are made by the viscose process with some modification. A cross section is round, being somewhat different from that of regular rayon, and the fibers are multifibrillar, very closely resembling the polynosic rayons in properties. Depending on the aftertreatment, they may have a very high tensile strength or elongation both dry and wet, or they may be intermediate in tensile strength.

These rayons will be increasingly important as blending fibers with cotton or with polyester and will give increased competition to the traditional cotton and polyester blends in shirtings, broadcloths, and sportswear. The growth of these high wet modulus rayon blends has increased nearly 600 per cent since 1962. The two-blend levels of high wet modulus rayons and polyesters have been found to give a clean, smooth fabric that has a soft hand and a good dyeability. The polyester high wet modulus rayons in 65:35 and 50:50 blends have been well received by manufacturers and consumers in sportswear and rain wear, as well as in sheeting and dress fabrics, which include broadcloths and crimped gauze. These blends have also been given durable-press treatments, but the 100 per cent high wet modulus rayon does not react to this treatment satisfactorily. Tests conducted by textile manufacturers have indicated that the 50:50 blend has the greater wear life after repeated launderings. Both the type 128 and type 140 muslins of 50:50 blend show greater fabric weight per square yard than do the traditional all-cotton muslins of the same types; 4.75 ounces per square yard for the type 128 and 5.2 ounces for the type 140 muslin in the blend as against approximately 4.2 and 4.6 for the all-cotton. According to American standards, the breaking strengths of these blended materials by the grab test exceed the minimum standards by approximately 10 per cent.[2]

If this cross linkage is carried out when the fibers are crimped or bent, this conformation is retained, and the resultant fiber has a degree of permanent loftiness. This brings about a certain amount of springiness under a compression load, and these cross-linked rayons are finding a number of applications in floor coverings, alone or blended with other carpet fibers.

The initial research on the high wet modulus fibers was done in Japan by Schozo Tachikawa, and his fiber was reported under the tradename of **Toramomen.** The principal fibers of this type made in the United States are Polynosic and Zantrel of the American Enka Corporation, and Moynel of Courtauld's (Alabama) Inc. The term **polynosic** is said to mean multifibrillar, thus suggesting a rayon fiber the cross section of which would exhibit a cluster of extremely fine molecules resembling the fibrillar structure of natural cellulose or cotton. The polynosic fiber producers have endeavored to have the FTC approve the following definition: "a manufactured cellulose fiber with a fine and stable microfibrillar structure, which is resistant to the action of 8 per cent sodium hydroxide solution down to 32°F, which structure results in a minimum wet strength of 2.2 gpd and a wet elongation of less than 3.5 per cent and a stress of 0.5 gpd." The arrangement of these fibrils is stated to be regular, and they lie more perfectly parallel to the lengthwise axis of the fiber than in the ordinary rayons (in which the fibrillar structure is less completely developed, and in which the molecules lie more or less in random

[2] Bibliography for high wet modulus rayon (noted in the articles as H. W. M. Rayon): "High-Wet Modulus Rayon and Its Blends," American Association of Textile Chemists and Colorists Seminar, p. 19; David Z. Goldenberg," Characteristics and Properties of H. W. M. Rayon," pp. 20, 394; Ervin Welch, "Fabrics Made of H. W. M. Rayon and Its Blends," pp. 24, 398; William Wygand, Jr., "Dyeing of H. W. M. Rayon and Its Blends," pp. 27, 401; A. Graham Fisher, "Finishing of H. W. M. Rayon and Its Blends," pp. 35, 407; *Textile Chemist and Colorist,* **1**, No. 19 (Sept. 10, 1969).

directions even after cold stretching). Details of the manufacture are secret. Zantrel polynosic rayon and other similar rayons are produced in a manner somewhat resembling the production of viscose rayon, but with some of the steps eliminated or drastically modified by the use of additional chemicals and catalysts. They have a subdued luster and are competitive with cotton in price and in many uses. They can also be mercerized. Shirtings, dress fabrics, curtains, and cellulose-containing draperies all offer excellent prospects for the utilization of these fibers, alone or in blends with others. Like many of the man-made fibers, these were first introduced, and others are still being introduced, under code identifications of letters and numbers. However, when they reach consumer acceptance and meet the standards of the L–22, which is basically the one passed by Avril and Zantrel, they will then be given the proprietary names representing the manufacturers. The name **polynosic** was granted to American Enka Corporation.

High-tenacity Rayons

The oldest and still the best-known of these rayons is Fortisan, which is produced by the acetate process. It is properly characterized as rayon, however, because all the acetic acid is removed, leaving the pure cellulose. This chemical process is known as **saponification.** Fortisan rayon has greater resistance to ultraviolet light and to weather degradation than other rayons. Therefore, it has become a popular material for curtains, generally, with Fortisan in the warp direction and some other fiber in the filling, in order to reduce the cost. It is still in somewhat short supply, which is another reason for its being mixed with other fibers in fabrics. The filaments are stretched to ten times their original length. The strength and its elongation properties are shown in Table 3–2, in comparison with other rayon fibers.

The future of Fortisan is clouded because of its relatively high price and because it has poor wrinkle resistance and limited recovery. Thus, it will probably continue to be a fiber sensitive to mussing not only in curtains, but also in wearing apparel. Consumers should treat the material as if it were made 100 per cent of the more sensitive and delicate fiber. Thus, in curtains, fabrics containing combinations of other fibers with Fortisan should generally be treated as if they were 100 per cent of the more sensitive fiber. Fortisan can only lend limited extra durability and light-fastness.

Acetate

Acetate is defined in the TFPIA as "a manufactured fiber in which the fiber-forming substance is cellulose acetate. Where not less than 92 per cent of the hydroxyl groups are acetylated, the term triacetate may be used as a generic description of the fiber."

The cellulosic acetate salt, or ester, was the first of the **thermoplastic fibers**. Thermoplastic refers to a fiber that is softened rather than decomposed or ignited when exposed to sufficient heat; in this respect acetate resembles the majority of our synthetic fibers. During World War I, cellulose acetate was produced in a solution in acetone and used as a protective finish or dope for the fabric wings of the war planes. The purpose was to make the cotton wing fabric more resistant to fire and to subzero weather. This necessitated the building of many plants for the manufacture of the primary chemical, acetic anhydride.

At the end of the war these plant facilities were utilized in the preparation of man-made fibers. The properties of cellulose acetate and of Arnel, the triacetate, are given in Table 3–3. These properties suggest special care in the use and particularly in the ironing of acetate garments. It is really for the safe ironing of acetate that many electric irons still have the so-called rayon setting. This is a misnomer, however, because rayons, being pure cellulose, can be ironed at virtually the same temperature as cotton. Even below their melting points, acetate and Arnel triacetate tend to become soft and show a marked tendency to glaze. This is actually the softening of the surface of the individual fibers to give a more planar and, therefore, a more reflective surface. Acetate garments should be pressed on the wrong side to avoid glazing. When burned, acetate forms a glassy bead and melts ahead of the flame. Sometimes the odor of acetic acid can be detected. This burning characteristic differs from that of viscose, which burns like cotton or paper and with the customary acrid odor. Acetate burns at a slower rate than cotton and rayon. It has reasonably good resistance to sunlight and does not degrade as rapidly as some of the synthetics, especially nylon.

Production

Like rayon, acetate was first made from cotton linters, the purest of the natural cellulose sources for the production of fibers. Today, however, much spruce wood is used as an alternate source. Although the reaction can be written simply as the esterification of one glucose unit and three molecules of acetic acid, or the complete esterification to the triacetate form, the reactant chemical used to supply the acetate is acetic anhydride:

The formula for acetic anhydride suggests the combination of two molecules of acetic acid bound together to form the anhydride with the splitting out of one molecule of water.

The chemical formula for cellulose acetate is considered to be as shown in Figure 3–12. The formula for Arnel triacetate is illustrated in Figure 3–13. Cross sections of acetate and triacetate fibers are shown in Figure 3–14.

The absence of many reactive hydroxyl (OH) groups is one reason for the difficulty in dyeing acetates. Another difficulty is in the low moisture absorbency shown in Table 3–3. Special classes of dyes have been developed,

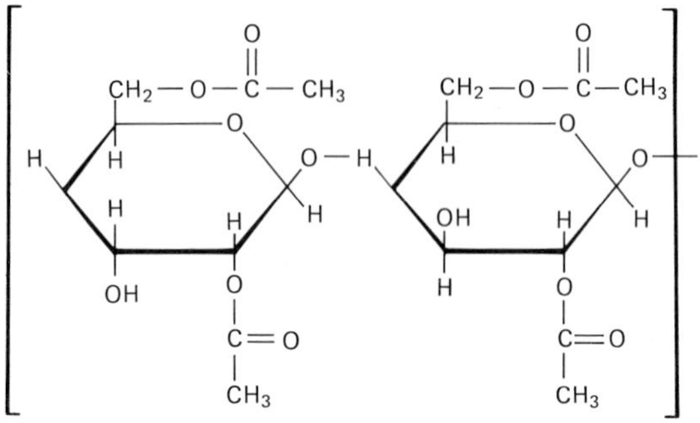

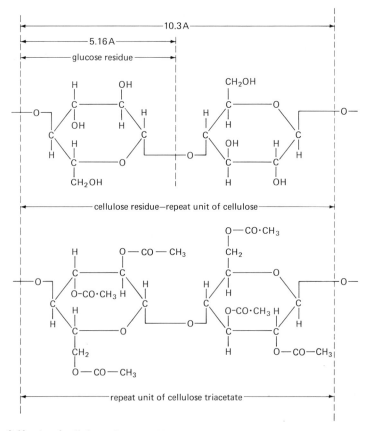

Figure 3-12 A possible formula for cellulose acetate.

Figure 3-13   Arnel cellulose triacetate. (Courtesy of Celanese Corporation of America)

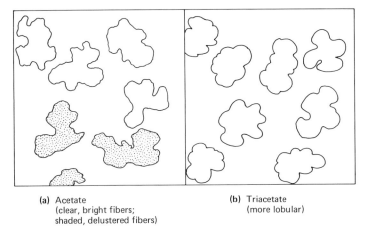

(a) Acetate
(clear, bright fibers;
shaded, delustered fibers)

(b) Triacetate
(more lobular)

Figure 3-14   Cross sections of acetate fibers.

including the dispersed-base dyestuffs, which are formed into a paste with water and a wetting agent. Acetates are generally fast to washing and have a reasonable fastness to sunlight.

This group of dyes does present two difficulties, however: Some shades have a pronounced tendency to fade when exposed to certain atmospheric oxides of nitrogen as well as a tendency to **sublime**—that is, to evaporate from the fabric and to redeposit on uncolored garments where a white and a colored area are in contact. The gas or **atmospheric fading** phenomenon and the sensitivity of certain colors, mostly light blues, to acids such as perspiration frequently cause the discoloration of acetate garments whenever the light blue component dye has been used to produce such shades as greens, lavenders, grays, and browns. Some stabilizing finishing agents can hold these colors for as long a time as the finishing agents stay in the fabric, but the more modern method of controlling such atmospheric fading is by dope or **solution** dyeing. In this process, the dyestuff is incorporated into the acetate solution prior to spinning the filament. It is, thus, an integral part of the final strand. A complication at that point is that the color cannot be removed for redyeing if it is not acceptable to the public.

Chromspun (Tennessee Eastman), **Celaperm** (Celanese Corporation), and **Colorspun** (American Viscose Corporation) are examples of the solution-dyed acetates. This same procedure is sometimes used for other man-made fibers.

A simplified flow chart, for the production of cellulose acetate is shown in Figure 3–15.

The various stages of the process for acetates follow:

1. *Cellulose purification.* Cotton linters, purchased in bales, or chemical cellulose in the form of large sheets already described here under rayon production, are treated with an alkali for several hours, after which

Table 3-3 *Important Fiber Properties of Acetates*

		Acetate	Triacetate Arnel
Microscopic cross-section		Shape very irregular	Shape rather bulbous
Tenacity (gpd)	Dry	1.4	1.2
	Wet	0.9	0.8
Elongation at break (per cent)	Dry	25	20–28
	Wet	35	35–40
Specific gravity		1.30–1.35	1.38
Water absorbency (per cent) regain		6.3–6.5	3.5
Effect of heat		Melts at about 450°F with decomposition; loses strength about 300°F; tacky at about 350°F; slightly flammable	Melts about 580°F but sticks slightly about 100° lower; can be heat-set in pleats, etc.
Effect of acids		Decomposed by strong acids; dissolved by acetic acid	Damaged by strong acids; slightly affected by dilution
Effect of alkalies		Saponified to cellulose; weak alkali; little effect on short exposure	Good resistance to dilute alkali
Resistance to mildew, sun, and aging		Not affected by mildew; weakened by sunlight; slight strength loss on age	Like acetate
Effect of bleach		Unaffected in cold solution	Stable to most common bleaches
Static electrical effects		Noticeable under winter conditions	Like acetate

SOURCE: *R. W. Moncrieff, Man-made Fibers,* 5th ed. (New York: John Wiley & Sons, Inc., 1971).

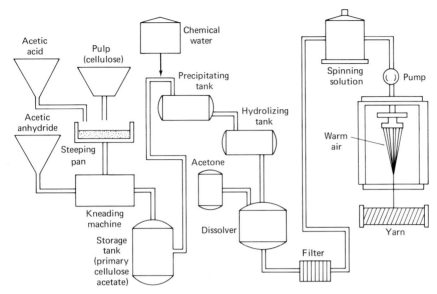

Figure 3-15 A simplified flow chart for cellulose acetate. [Redrawn from Leonard Mauer and Harry Wechsler, *Man-made Fibers* (New York: Rayon Publishing Corp., 1953), p. 17.]

they are rinsed, washed, and, if necessary, bleached with sodium hypo-chlorite, followed by another washing and drying.

2. *Acetylation.*   The cellulose is often allowed to soak in glacial acetic acid to make it more reactive and thus shorten the time required for the ace-tylation or esterification process. The cellulose is then placed in a closed vessel that is equipped with a powerful stirrer. Acetic anhydride and an ex-cess of glacial acetic acid are introduced into the vessel and are mixed thoroughly. A trace amount of sulfuric acid dissolved in an excess of glacial acetic is then added. This is the real acetylating agent. Although the sulfuric acid is actually used up in the process—as distinct from the usual catalyst, which remains unchanged—its role is primarily that of a catalyst. It is neces-sary to cool the reactant vessel because of the great amount of heat produced by this exothermic reaction. Too high a temperature would result in too great a chemical reaction on the cellulose, causing a shortening of the cellu-losic chains and thus producing a weak fiber. The reacting material becomes viscous, and in about eight hours the cellulose becomes completely acety-lated to the primary cellulose acetate and is completely in solution.

3. *Hydrolysis.*   The primary acetate is run into water and allowed to stand for approximately a day. During this time, acid hydrolysis takes place and the mixture is poured into an excess of water. The acid is now so dilute that it can no longer hold the cellulose acetate in solution, and the product precipitates out in white flakes. This is **secondary acetate** (the commercial

compound) and is soluble in acetone. The acetic acid is then extracted from the water by an organic solvent to be reconcentrated for use in another batch.

4. *Solution.* The secondary acetate flakes from several different batches are blended in order to produce as uniform a product as possible, and these batches are mixed with about three times their weight of acetone in a closed vessel with very powerful stirring. In about 24 hours of processing, the solution will be complete.

Spinning

The dope is a viscous, molasses-textured solution containing somewhere between 25 and 35 per cent cellulose acetate. The fibers or filaments spun from this solution would normally be shiny and lustrous. If a dull acetate is to be prepared, the delustrant material, usually titanium dioxide (Titanox), is added to the mass prior to spinning. This gives a permanently white yarn and fabric. It is at this stage also that many dyestuffs are added to acetate in order to produce the dope-dyed acetates (see Chromspun and Celaperm, p. 109). The flow of dope from the feed tank is carefully controlled, and the heavy liquid flows through the spinneret—which is shaped like a metal plate into which numerous small orifices have been drilled. The filaments emerge into a heated cabinet that immediately evaporates the acetone solvent, leaving a solid strand. This may be given a light stretching at this point by having the take-up rolls operate at a slightly higher speed than the flow of the solution through the jets or openings in the spinneret. The acetone is recovered and reused. Note that no receiving solution is involved in the spinning of acetate. This is characteristically a **dry spinning** operation, simpler and less costly to carry out. To a considerable measure this more costly fiber is also aided competitively by the near-complete recovery of the acetic acid and of the acetone as well as by the properties of the cellulose acetate.

Cellulose Triacetate Fiber (Arnel)

The properties of Arnel, as shown in Table 3–4, are generally similar to those of regular acetate; however, it can be regarded as a superacetate, having somewhat similar tenacity both wet and dry; better extensibility; a 100°F higher melting point; a lower moisture regain; and a superior colorfastness, both with and without dope dyeing. In use, Arnel has been found to give a crisp feel, excellent draping qualities, and beautiful colors. Alone and in combination with other fibers, it has been featured in most of the high fashion magazines. Arnel can be given a much more permanent pleat than can acetate, and it exhibits better resistance to sunlight than any of the other cellulose derivatives. The tradenames of several acetate fibers are shown in Table 3–4.

Table 3-4   Acetate Fibers

Trademark/General Classification	Producer	Type and Special Characteristics*	End-use Area
Acele	du Pont	F	AH
Arnel (triacetate)	Celanese	FST	AHI
Avicolor	American Viscose Division	F (solution-dyed)	AH
Avisco	American Viscose Division	F	AH
Celacloud (Type F)	Celanese	S	AH
Celafil (Type K)	Celanese	S	H
Celanese A	Celanese	FST	AHI
Celaperm	Celanese	F (solution-dyed)	AHI
Chromspun	Eastman	F (solution-dyed)	AH
Estron	Eastman	F (uncolored)	AH
Estron "SLR"	Eastman	F (dull, resistant to weather and sun)	H
Fiber 25	American Viscose Division	F	AH

SOURCE: Based on data from *Modern Textiles Magazine* (March 1973).
*A — Apparel
  H — Home furnishings and carpets
  I — Industrial fabrics
Type F — Multifilament
         S — Staple fiber
         T — Tow

Arnel Manufacture

A pure form of cellulose is used as the raw material in the manufacturing of Arnel. The initial steps in its manufacture are essentially the same as in the preparation of the regular cellulose acetate—that is, the purified cellulose is treated with acetic anhydride, acetic acid, and a sulfuric acid catalyst. When the esterification is complete, all the cellulose will have gone into solution. At this stage in the preparation of acetates, some of the acetic groups are hydrolyzed off the glucose units; however, in the case of triacetate, all these acetic groups are left in place. A mild hydrolysis of the mixture also is made in order to remove any sulfuric ester groups that might have adhered to some of the cellulose molecules. If any sulfuric acid is left in the cellulose, the fiber will be greatly weakened. After hydrolysis, the triacetate, also classified as **primary acetate,** is passed into water, where it precipitates as flakes and is washed and dried. The dried flake is dissolved in methylene chloride, in a concentration of about 20 per cent; then the solution either is forced through the spinnerets to produce continuous filament Arnel, or the emerging filaments are crimped and cut and deposited as tow or staple fibers. The solvent evaporates rapidly because its boiling point (107.6°F) is lower than that of acetone (134.6°F). Cool condensers at the top of the column cause the vapor to recondense as a liquid, which is collected, purified, and reused. Often an antistatic finish is added to these fibers and filaments because of Arnel's low moisture absorption and its susceptibility to building up static electricity. (See Figure 3–16.)

Figure 3-16 Celanese yarn inspection. (Courtesy of Celanese Corporation of America)

ORGANIC FIBERS

The Azlons

The FTC has defined azlon as "a manufactured fiber in which the fiber-forming substance is composed of any regenerated naturally occurring protein." [3] The sources for the naturally occurring proteins have been casein from skim milk, zein from corn, and the proteins from soybeans and peanuts.

---

[3] Federal Trade Commission Rules and Regulations under the Textile Fiber Products Identification Act, effective March 4, 1960.

Dissolving the naturally occurring proteins in strong alkali and then extruding the solution into an acid bath for hardening produces a protein that is not identical with the original. In this sense, then, regenerated is not as exact a term as in the case of rayon, which is true cellulose chemically the same as the source.

Organic fibers are not produced or used to any extent in the United States today. Their production during and shortly after World War II was primarily dictated by the need for a fiber to be blended with wool, during which time men's felt hats and certain other wool apparel were required to contain a minimum of 15 per cent of other wool-like fiber. Aralac, utilizing casein from skim milk, and Vicara, made with zein, were the most important azlon fibers.

The fairly close chemical similarity between Aralac and wool is shown in Table 3–5.

Table 3-5   Chemical Composition of Aralac and Wool

Element	Aralac (per cent)	Wool (per cent)
Carbon	53.0	49.2
Hydrogen	7.5	7.6
Oxygen	23.0	23.7
Nitrogen	15.0	15.9
Sulfur	0.7	3.6
Phosphorus	0.8	nil

The important azlons in the world market, most of which have now been discontinued, include Aralac (casein), United States; Ardil (peanut fiber), Britain; Lanital (casein, the first azlon), Italy; Merinova, Italy; Caslen (heavy industrial casein fiber), United States; Sarelon (peanut fiber), United States; Silkol (soybean), Japan; Vicara (zein), United States; and Wiplon (casein), Poland.

Properties

Azlons generally burn like wool with a similar odor and leave a brittle ash residue. They have a lower tenacity when dry and lose considerably more strength than wool when wet. This has been one of the factors entering into their application in blends rather than their use alone. They are water-absorbent and resist static build-up; being smooth-walled, extruded fibers, they do not felt. Vicara was of use for a longer period of time in the United States than other organic fibers because of its extreme softness and the feeling of richness that it gave when blended with wool in the finer, softer fabrics. Only the extra advantage of strength, especially when wet, enabled Creslan acrylic to replace Vicara in some of the finer woolen suitings. Most have a slight creamy color.

All azlons use food source materials. Because of the need to provide food for an increasing world population, there seems no justification for utilizing potential food proteins in textile fiber production.

MISCELLANEOUS INORGANIC FIBERS

Experimentation in the production of fibers and yarns from glass has been carried out over many years. The first successful method of spinning glass into fiber form was developed in 1931 by the Owens-Illinois Glass Company and the Corning Glass Works. These companies have since joined to form the Owens Corning Fiberglas Corporation. The growth of textile glass fiber has been phenomenal, and the quality of the product has improved vastly through new techniques and careful quality control. What was originally an individual batch process is now continuous. The ingredients, silica sand, limestone, and other inorganic materials, are also introduced at one end, and the completed glass filaments are extruded at the far end of the plant. Depending on the serviceability requirements, chemicals such as oxides of various metals and borax for special glasses may also enter the melt.

The properties of glass fiber are unique, for this is the only man-made inorganic fiber of commercial importance. Some of its properties are shown in Table 3–6. The glass formulations suitable for fiber making produce a cross-linked and linearly linked inorganic polymer network that is mobile— that is, it can flow at 2000°F. When cooled, the viscosity increases until a rigid structure is produced. Fiber production depends on the ability of this material to be formed.

Glass Fabric Uses

In consumer use, many of these fiber properties become significant. For example, glass fabric is completely nonflammable and has high strength. One would, of course, not expect it to be attacked by insects, mildew, or bacteria; and it has good chemical resistance. Decorative glass is colored by adding metal salts to the mix before melting. However, because it absorbs no moisture, glass is difficult to dye. In dyeing, the coloring matter is introduced into the melt bath in the form of an inorganic pigment; the extruded filaments are thus colored throughout. This involves a stockpiling problem to many producers. Generally, glass fiber fabric is printed with a paste pigment mixture that develops excellent fastness after a heating treatment, but it is subject to

Table 3-6   Typical Properties of Continuous Filament Glass Fibers*†

Tenacity, gpd	6.3–9.6
Wet	5.4–6.0
Loop	2.0–4.0
Knot	2.0–4.0
Elongation, per cent	3–4
Wet	2.5–3.5
Elastic recovery, per cent	100
Tensile stress, psi	204,000–220,000
Initial stiffness, gpd	307
Specific gravity	2.54
Water absorbency	Up to 0.3 per cent (surface)
Effect of heat	Will not burn; strength begins to decrease at 600°F and continues to decline to limiting temperature of about 1000–1500°F; softens at 1350°F
Effect of sunlight	None
Effect of acids	Attacked by hydrofluoric and hot phosphoric only
Effect of alkalies	Attacked by hot solutions of weak alkalies and cold solutions of strong alkalies
Effect of organic solvents	Insoluble
Dyes used	Resin-bonded pigments; also suitable dyes for special coatings

SOURCE: J. J. Press, ed., *Man-made Textile Encyclopedia* (New York: John Wiley & Sons, Inc., 1959), Table 1, p. 135.
* At standard conditions unless otherwise mentioned.
† From *Textile World*, **105**, No. 9 (Sept. 1955), pp. 82–102.

wearing away through rubbing. One problem is that the broken fiber ends, despite their extreme fineness, do have sharp points, and the skin of sensitive people may develop a dermatitis after prolonged rubbing. This has been noted in such items as ironing board covers. A new, ultrafine fiber has the finest diameter known heretofore. It is called Beta Fiberglas and is said to be so fine and supple that skin irritation is negligible. With this one exception, users associate glass fiber with industrial uses or as a decorative household material.

The greatest demand for glass fiber in the home is in curtains and draperies (see Table 3–1). Nearly 25 per cent of all custom-made draperies are of glass fiber. Strength, sun resistance, and fire resistance are its principal advantages. Vast quantities are used in industry in braids, tapes, battings, fire blankets, mailbags, and in heavier fabrics impregnated with plastic for boat hulls, bath tubs, fishing rods, vaulting poles, tennis racket frames, and

Table 3-7   Glass Fibers

Trade Name/ General Classification	Producer	Type and Special Characteristics*	End-use Area*
Trianti	PPG Industries	F	H
Beta	Owens Corning Fiberglas	F	AHI
Fiberglas	Owens Corning Fiberglas	FS (all types)	HIPTC
Fiber glass	Kaiser Glass	Roving	P
Fiber glass	Johns-Manville	SF (all types)	IP
Fiber glass	PPG Industries	F (all types)	HITC
Glass	Gustin-Bacon	F (chopped)	P
HI	Ferro	F (chopped strand)	P
NUF	Ferro	FM (strand, mat)	IP
Ply-Mat	Johns-Manville	F (chopped, woven)	P
Activa	Owens Corning	F	H
Aero Rove	Kaiser Glass	F	P
Ultra Strand	Gustin-Bacon	F	P
Uniroving	Ferro	FT (roving yarn)	IP
Unistrand	Ferro	FT (roving yarn)	P
Vitro-Flex	Johns-Manville	F (chopped strand)	HIP
Vitron	Johns-Manville	F (roving)	HITCP
Vitro-Strand	Johns-Manville	F (milled fiber)	IP

SOURCE: Based on data from *Modern Textiles Magazine*, **54**, No. 3 (March 1973), pp. 21–22.

*A —Apparel	Type M — Monofilament
H — Home furnishings and carpets	F — Multifilament
I — Industrial fabrics	S — Staple fiber
TC — Tire cord	T — Tow
	P — Plastics

golf club shafts, among many others. In 1965, 30 million pounds of glass fiber, about 30 per cent of production, were used for boat hulls alone.

Manufacture

The making of glass filaments does not differ greatly from the formation of glass for any other purpose, because silica sand and limestone with one or more other constituents must be melted at about 3000°F in a furnace. The molten glass can then be formed into a flat surface for window glass; it can be molded or blown into bottles or other containers; or in the case of filaments, it can be made to flow via gravity through fine holes—more than 200 of them—in the bottom of a flat-bottomed container called a bosking box. The strands that flow out of the holes harden in the air and are given a pro-

Figure 3-17 One of the steps in preparation for weaving at Burlington Industries' Altavista weaving plant is the "drawing in" process, typified by the hand working with strands of fiber glass. (Courtesy of Burlington Industries, Inc.)

tective sizing to prevent abrasion damage. They are wound onto a rapidly revolving tube and are thus drawn out into very fine filaments (Figure 3–17). Intermittent air blasts against the fibers extruded through the orifice holes pull the glass into short fibers for glass staple roving to be spun into staple yarns. Glass is regarded by the scientist as a solid solution or a supercooled liquid, one so thick that it will not flow perceptibly at room temperature. There are no definite chemical compounds and no evidences of crystallization in glass filaments.

Although sand, limestone, soda ash, and similar inorganic materials are generally regarded as the raw materials from which glass fiber is formed, the preparation of continuous filaments first began as a batch process with an intermediate product. The glass formed in the furnace was allowed to fall in the molten state from a high tower. As it fell, it formed perfect spheres, and, when cooled, this **cullet** of uniform glass marbles of about ⅝-inch in diameter was the raw material for the fibers. These marbles were carefully inspected for air bubbles, discoloration, or the presence of any undissolved particles or ingredients. The inspected marbles were remelted to 2500°F in an electric furnace, and the molten mass was allowed to flow down into a spinneret having about 100 orifices. These filaments were drawn together, given a slight oil lubrication, and wound into a strand. One marble, weighing about ⅓-ounce, might produce 100 miles of filament in the finest denier spun.

Continuous Production

Newer glass-fiber-producing plants bypass the marble step. They thus avoid one heating of the mass. Fibers for staple sliver yarns or for batting are prepared in a similar manner. The composition can be altered, depending upon the chemical nature of the material against which a particular batch is to be resistant. Again, the molten glass comes through fine openings in the bottom of the furnace, but in this case, a very strong jet of air or steam blows against the filaments, tearing them into varying short lengths. Bats, or loose masses, of other inorganic fibers, such as rock wool, slag wool, and so on, are formed in a similar manner and used for heat insulation in homes, freezers, ovens, and air-conditioning units. Four or five plants are under construction for the direct production of glass bat fibers from the original melt. This type of product is *not* included in data referring to textile glass fiber. By definition, *textile glass fiber* is produced in two forms: namely, continuous strand (filament) and staple sliver.

In the early days of glass fiber curtains and draperies, the material was found to be stiff and to have an ungraceful fold. The **Coronizing process** widened the application of glass fiber as a truly decorative material. This heat treatment at 1200°F, for 5 to 20 seconds, reduces its weight, improves its hand and dimensional stability, and enables it to hold a crimp. It is reported that the process involves coating glass fibers or filaments with colloidal silica, such as **Syton,** after which it is heat-set. The fabric is passed through a hot oven and the fiber is given a slight crimp. The fabric may be passed into a bath containing pigments for coloration.

If a glass fabric is to be printed, this is usually done after Coronizing; the pigment resin is then set by a similar heat treatment.

The difficulty with glass fiber fabrics is their relatively poor resistance to intense rubbing. Thus, if a Venetian blind rubs frequently against a glass curtain, or the curtain rubs against the back of a sofa or chair, not only may the print pattern be removed but the glass fiber filament may break. The same weakness exists in the washing operation. Thus, curtains or draperies are very satisfactorily washed if done one at a time, preferably by hand or in a tumbler-type washer. It is the wet rubbing or mechanical action that causes the most severe attrition to glass fiber articles. Furthermore, curtains or draperies should never be pressed, because despite the relatively good pliability of these fibers, they cannot stand a sharp, compressed bending without fracturing.

Glass fiber fabrics totaled about 286.2 million linear yards in 1970 but 332.5 million linear yards in 1973.[4]

METALLIC FIBERS

The FTC defines metallic as "a manufactured fiber composed of metal, plastic coated metal, metal coated plastic, or a core completely covered by metal." [5]

The fact that these metallics are compounded of two or more solid component parts would indicate that, technically speaking, they should be classified as yarns; however, they are used today predominantly for decorative and esthetic effects as threads. Until methods were perfected for coloring aluminum and other lightweight metals as thin ribbons or very fine wires, the precious metals, gold and silver, were used for finer quality fabrics. Nonprecious metals were too subject to staining by oxidation, by perspiration, or by prolonged weathering.

History reports the use of these precious metal fibers in clothing royalty and in fabrics for vestments and other church fabrics. Gold was the best of these metals because of its nontarnishing characteristics, but both gold and silver are heavy. The development of transparent films of cellulose acetate, of polyester **(Mylar),** and other water- and air-impermeable materials, made it possible to coat fine metal strips such as aluminum to give durable stain-resistant fibers. Generally, these yarns are multilayered. Very fine aluminum foil or a transparent film on which aluminum has been vaporized serves as a core layer; and adhesive is applied on each side; and then the sandwich is made complete with a transparent film on the outer layers. The laminate is made in varying widths of from 20 to 54 inches and is then cut in the desired strip width. These can be used as monofilaments or cut into staple lengths. If aluminum foil is used, the aluminum is rolled to a thickness of about 0.00045 inch and polished on both sides. In some of the newer metallics, polyester (usually Mylar) is coated with vaporized aluminum in a high vacuum. This is so lustrous that it does not require polishing. The advantage of the polyesters as outer coatings is their heat resistance, and apparel using these metallics can be pressed up to 350°F.

Because these metallics are used almost exclusively for decoration, it is

---

[4] *Textile Organon*, **45**, No. 5 (May 1974), p. 60.
[5] Federal Trade Commission Rules and Regulations under the Textile Fiber Products Identification Act, effective March 4, 1960, p. 5.

Table 3-8   Metallic Fibers

Trade Name/ General Classification	Producer	Type and Special Characteristics*	End-use Area*
Alistran (metallic)	Multi-Tex	F (flat laminated)	AH
Brunslon (metal)	Brunswick	FM	H
Brunsmet (stainless steel)	Brunswick	FST	AHIT
Chromeflex	Metal Film	M (flat)	AHI
Dura-Stran	Multi-Tex	F (flat laminate)	AH
Fairtex	Rexham	M (flat)	AHI
Hudstat	Hudson Wire	M	H
Lurex	Dow Badische	M	AH
Malora	Malina	M (flat)	AH
Metlon F	Metlon	MS (flat)	AH
Metlon FR	Metlon	M (flat)	AH
Metlon LMP	Metlon	M (flat)	AH
Metlon LR	Metlon	M (flat)	AH
Metlon P150	Metlon	M (flat)	AH
Metlon Ultrathin	Metlon	M (flat)	AH
Raybrite C. F. (metalcellophane)	Raybrite	M (cellophane foil)	AH
Raybrite MF Metallic	Raybrite	M (mular foil)	AH
Raybrite MM Metallic	Raybrite	M (metallized mylar)	AH
Zefstat F-100	Dow Badische	M (antistatic)	H

SOURCE: Based on data from *Modern Textiles Magazine,* **54**, No. 3 (March 1973), p. 26.
*A —Apparel   Type M — Monofilament
  H — Home furnishings and carpets   F — Multifilament
   I — Industrial fabrics   S — Staple fiber
                             T — Tow

understandable that their volume will fluctuate with the taste of the consuming public. Metallized surfaces on garments, however, are utilized in protective garb for fire-fighting crews. *America's Textile Reporter* lists nearly 30 types of metallics, but in many cases, from 4 to 6 of these will have the same proprietary name identified for end-use application by code number or letter. Important metallic "family" origins are listed in Table 3–8.

Some of these fibers are stiff and strong enough to be used unsupported; others, described as being ultrathin, are wound around a core or strengthening yarn. In apparel these yarns have been used in dresses, blouses, shoes, handbags, coats, suits, millinery, and in a yard goods, in which they have been used in combination with natural fibers as well as synthetic ones. Decorative fabric uses have included carpets and rugs, upholstery materials, wall coverings, and table covers.

Steel Staple Fibers

Very fine extruded steel wire has been used as a gimmick in hosiery, but it is being applied experimentally in carpeting in an attempt to reduce static electrical accumulation. In this application, the steel staple fibers account for less than 1 per cent of the fiber in the pile. Results have been good, but some of the constructions have not been sufficiently durable because of the cutting action of the steel. These fine steel fibers can be woven or knitted; their use has been suggested in a number of industrial applications, including automobile tires.

The Carborundum Company and Union Carbide Corporation have made fibers of graphite. They have unusual strength and stiffness for their weight and have been applied in aerospace and other aircraft applications. One of the trade names for this type of fiber is **Thornel.**

Voltex, a fabric made of carbon yarn and Beta glass fiber, is being used by some utility crews of electric power companies. The cloth is made of carbon yarns prepared by the Union Carbide Corporation.

CHAPTER

FOUR

Manufactured Fiber Families

The term **manufactured** refers to textile fibers formed by synthesis to create a giant molecule. Several thousand units of chemical compounds of low molecular weight add on to one another to form a long continuous chain made up of links of one or more individual simple chemicals. Such giant molecules are **polymers**. The process of their formation through heat and pressure is **polymerization**. The simple chemical constituents are referred to as **monomers**. Though the term synthetic carries no stigma of inferiority, the Federal Trade Commission has called for the word *manufactured* for these fibers, which are quite different from any of our naturally occurring polymeric fibers, such as cotton and wool. The FTC uses the phrase "manufactured fiber" in its definitions. The individual polymeric fibers differ in performance, especially in consumer use, between family or generic groups. But within each family, there is some similarity. This, of course, is of great benefit in guidance for consumer use.

124

Fortunately, too, all synthetics have some properties in common and are sufficiently similar so that the purchaser of a nylon dress, polyester blouse, acrylic sweater or other synthetic fiber product, alone or blended with other fibers, can expect certain similar performances in use and care.

1. The first property common to all of these fibers is that of **thermoplasticity**. In the case of cellulose acetate and Arnel triacetate, the property of thermoplasticity, or heat softening, has been discussed. Although this property is somewhat to the disadvantage of the consumer in that ironing requires a cool iron as a general precaution with any of these fibers to avoid melting or glazing, there is also the hazard of holes being melted in these materials from lighted matches, cigarette ash, and other sources of heat. On the other hand, this property has certain distinct advantages in merchandising and end-use applications: many articles composed of synthetic fabrics can be heat-set to a predetermined size or shape and will not deviate from size in subsequent washings. Noteworthy in this regard is nylon in women's hosiery. Furthermore, without this thermoplasticity feature, one would not be able to have permanently pleated skirts; crease-retentive suits, dresses and blouses; or the wrinkle-resistant characteristics of wash-and-wear garments and durable press made of these fibers. An exception to thermoplasticity is **Nomex aramid**.

2. These fibers are **hydrophobic**. In simple terms, this means that they do not absorb much moisture, either in the form of normal regain under standard conditions or even when allowed to stand for a long time in hot water. (One might say that these fibers had a phobia against water.) This property is a disadvantage in the dyeing of these materials, and some rather unique methods have had to be adopted in order to get dyestuffs into them. The lack of moisture absorbency also contributes to the phenomenon of static electricity, which is objectionable in the handling of these fibers, both in spinning and in weaving. It is also troublesome in consumer use, and everyone is familiar with the static spark created when these fibers are rubbed against protein substances and certain other materials on a cold, dry day or in a home interior that is too dry. Were there sufficient moisture in the fibers in the form of regain, this water would form a conductor by which the electric charge could be carried away rather than stored up for discharge upon contact. Even more significant to consumer use, however, is the advantage of this hydrophobic nature of the fiber when it comes to resisting water-carried spots and stains—water flows off the fabric. Thus, inks, soft drinks, muddy rain water, and other soiling materials will not be absorbed in these fibers. Generally, they are more quickly washed and at a lower temperature and are more rapidly dried than those fibers that absorb water (the hydrophilic fibers).

3. Manufactured fibers are generally regarded as being resistant to natural deterioration through bacteria, mildew, and the textile destroying insects, such as carpet beetles and clothes moths. This reduces some of the problems of the consumer in storing garments between seasons of use.

4. Most manufactured fibers are lighter in weight—that is, they have a lower specific gravity—than natural fibers. This feature combined with the fluffiness or bulkiness of the yarns made from some of the synthetics provides lighter-weight fabrics of comparably equal yarn diameter and of the same yarn count per inch.

5. From the standpoint of comfort, these fibers do not perform as well as the natural fibers. This is largely a result of moisture absorbency and the resultant entrapment of moisture vapor on the surface of the skin underneath the wearing apparel on a hot day. To some extent, the springiness of certain fabric constructions—notably the knits—and the bulkiness and lightness of the yarns will compensate for this moisture and heat entrapment.

6. For the most part, these fibers, especially monofilaments, are slippery. This causes some difficulty in sewing, in order to keep the seams from pulling out when sudden stress is applied. In furniture coverings, this slippery property requires special sewing reinforcements at all seams.

Many of these polymers have the unfortunate ability to absorb oil and grease, of both vegetable and animal origin. The problem is serious because, unless such stains are removed promptly, they may become permanent and eventually show up as gray discolorations on such fabric surfaces as rugs and carpets; upholstery material; or on the fronts of wearing apparel on which gravy or salad oil have been spilled and not promptly removed. This tendency is not so serious in some of the synthetics as in others, but general precautions should prevail with any synthetic.

These fibers will be discussed in approximately the chronological order of their initial generic introduction to the public and according to their commercial significance.

NYLONS

Nylon is now defined as "a manufactured fiber in which the fiber-forming substance is a long-chain synthetic polyamide in which less than 85 per cent of the amide linkages are attached directly to two aromatic rings." [1] This fiber, of such varied use, was the first synthetic, or manufactured, fiber defined by the Federal Trade Commission. Its development was unique, for it demonstrates what can be accomplished by intensive team research in pure science without any immediate thought of commercialization. In 1928, Wallace H. Carothers was placed in charge of a team of research scientists to explore a field of pure, or fundamental, research devoted to the preparation of large molecules. Carothers chose to work in the field of polymerization, in which small molecules are made into very large ones with

[1] *Man-Made Fiber Fact Book*, Man-Made Fiber Producers Association, Inc., 1974, p. 18.

molecular weights of 10,000 to 20,000 or more. The results of this research placed the E. I. du Pont de Nemours & Co. of Wilmington, Delaware, actively in the field of textiles of synthetic origin. Among the several kinds of polymers being studied by this research team were those made from dibasic acids and dihydric alcohols. These are organic acids and alcohols with a reactive group at each end of the molecule, the reaction being similar to simple esterification, or organic salt formation.

Simple Esterification

$$C_2H_5OH + CH_3COOH \longrightarrow CH_3COOC_2H_5 + H_2O$$

ethyl alcohol + acetic acid   ethyl acetate

Polymerization by Esterification

$$HO(CH_2)_6OH + HOOC(CH_2)_4COOH \longrightarrow HO(CH_2)_6OCO(CH_2)_4COOH + H_2O$$

active group

When enough of these two simple chemicals were added one to another to produce a long end-to-end straight-chain polymer (much as dominoes are matched end to end), a polyester, or multisalt, was formed. This research was later modified to use dibasic acids and diamines as the monomers, with the result that a better fiber was produced. Various treatments, new catalysts, and modifications in polymerization changed their physical properties, and finally, after about five years of research, certain combinations and molecular weights were produced that could be drawn out into fine filaments while hot. Further drawing or pulling after the filaments cooled made them more transparent, stronger, more flexible, and more elastic. Here were products suitable for the textile industry, but, even then, years of patient research and development were required before the first nylon stockings were made available in stores all over the United States in the summer of 1940. So completely has this fiber taken over the women's hosiery market that many consumers do not order stockings; they simply order "nylons" when they go into a store.

Today's nylon has a wide variety of uses and properties, depending upon the raw materials and the method of processing. The raw materials commonly used are dibasic acids and diamines. There are many of each of these kinds of simple chemicals, and the variety of types of nylon are, therefore, almost infinite. Some types are suitable for molding plastics, transparent sheeting, bristles, or even adhesives; however, relatively few of them are suitable for the production of the fine filaments required for our textile industry. (See Table 4–1.)

The name, nylon, is no longer a proprietary one belonging to E. I. du

Table 4-1   Nylon Fiber Names

Trademark/ Name of Classification	Producer	Types and Special Characteristics*	End-use Areas*
Actionwear	Monsanto	F (producer-textured)	A
ANSO	Allied	F	H
ANSO-X	Allied	FS	H
Antron	du Pont	FST	AH
AstroTurf	Monsanto	Ribbon	I
Ayrlyn	Rohm and Haas	FM	AH
Barbara	Sauquoit	F (nontorque stretch)	A
Beaunit Nylon	Beaunit	F (multilobal)	H
"Blue C" also "C"	Monsanto	F	AHITC
Cadon, C-Cadon	Monsanto	F (multilobal)	AH
Camalon	Camac	FM	AH
Cantrece	du Pont	FM (bicomponent)	A
Caprolan	Allied	FMS	AHITC
Captiva	Allied	F	A
Cedilla	Fiber Industries (Celanese)	F (bulked)	AH
Celanese Nylon	Fiber Industries (Celanese)	F	AHITC
Chadolon	Chadbourn Industries	FM	A
Chemstrand Nylon	Monsanto	F	AHITC
Cordura	du Pont	F	LI
Courtaulds Nylon	Courtaulds	F	A
Crepeset	American Enka	M (crepe boiltin)	A
C-Cumuloft	Monsanto	F (textured)	AHI
Cumuloft	Monsanto	F (textured)	H
Diane	Sauquoit	F (stretch)	A
du Pont Nylon	du Pont	FSTM	AHITC
Enkaloft	American Enka	F (textured, multilobal)	H
Enkalure	American Enka	F (multilobal, soil delay)	AH
Enkalure II	American Enka	F (improved)	H
Enka Nylon	American Enka	MFS (type 6)	AHITC
Enkasheer	American Enka	M (modified torque)	A
Formelle	Rohm and Haas	F (color spun)	AH
Hanover Nylon	Hanover	MF	AI
Hazel	Sauquoit	M (stretch)	A
Industrial Wire and Plastic Nylon	Indiana Wire and Plastic	M (flat and round)	AHI
Multisheer	American Enka	F (stretch)	A
MX 108	Shakespeare	M (round, opaque)	I

128

Table 4-1 *(continued)*

Trademark/ Name of Classification	Producer	Types and Special Characteristics*	End-use Areas*
NM 1000	Monofilaments	M (clear, melt-dyed)	AHI
NM 1200	Monofilaments	M (clear, melt-dyed)	AHI
NM 1400	Monofilaments	M (clear, melt-dyed)	AHI
Nomex	du Pont	FST	AHI
Nypel Nylon	Nypel	M	I
Nytelle	Firestone	MF	AITC
Phillips 66 Nylon	Phillips Fibers	FMS	AHI
Qiana	du Pont	M	A
Recall	Fiber Industries (Celanese)	MF	
Ruvea	du Pont	M (ribbon)	AHI
S-3	Shakespeare	MF	A
Shareen	Courtaulds	M (clear, melt-dyed)	I
Shoeflex	Shakespeare	M (clear, melt-dyed)	I
Shoeflex	Shakespeare	M (clear, melt-dyed)	I
Soo Valley Nylon	Shakespeare	M (round)	I
Source (N-Polyester)	Allied	FA	H
Spectradye	American Enka	F (warp-dyed)	H
Spectradye II	American Enka	F (new sharper)	H
Star Nylon	Star Fibers	S	AHI
Stryton	Phillips Fibers	F (undulating variable)	AH
Super Bulk	American Enka	F (high bulk)	H
Sunlon	Nylon Engineering	FS (solution-dyed, textured and nontextured)	HI
Superflex	Shakespeare	M (clear, melt-dyed)	I
Synflex-N	Wall Industries	M	H
Ultron	Monsanto	F	A
Uniroyal Nylon	Uniroyal Fiber and Textile	M	I
Variline	American Enka	F (random color combinations)	AH
Vylor	du Pont	M	I
Wellon	Wellman	S	AHI
Wellstrand (Nylon and Polyester)	Wellman	S (monofilament)	HI
X-static	Rohm and Haas	F (antistatic)	AH
Zefran Nylon	Dow Badische	FS	AH

SOURCE: Based on data from *Modern Textile Magazine*, **54**, No. 3 (March 1973), p. 31.

*A — Apparel	Type M — Monofilament
H — Home furnishings and carpets	F — Multifilament
I — Industrial fabrics	S — Staple fiber
TC — Tire cord	T — Tow

Pont de Nemours & Co., the original manufacturer. Therefore, nylon is properly spelled with a small "n." Du Pont has licensed numerous other manufacturers to use their nylon patents.

Nylon Manufacture

The principal type of nylon in the United States is designated as Nylon 66 and is so described because both the dibasic acid (adipic acid) and the diamine (hexamethylene diamine) contains six carbon atoms. Other nylons are similarly known to industry by the number of carbon atoms in the monomers.

$$HOOC(CH_2)_4COOH + H_2N(CH_2)_6NH_2 \longrightarrow HOOC(CH_2)_4COHN(CH_2)_6NH_2 + H_2O$$

adipic acid   hexamethylene
diamine

In Figure 4–1 the flow chart of the production of nylon is illustrated, beginning with the two monomers and ending with the cold drawing of the filament. Measured amounts of the two reactants are entered into this stirrer-equipped reactor vessel and are thoroughly mixed to form the nylon salt. This salt, with a small amount of water, is fed into the evaporator, in which the solution is concentrated by evaporation of the desired amount of water to give the proper concentration of salt. This is then passed into the jacket autoclave, in which the reaction of polymerization is carried out. This is simply the condensation, or adding on, of molecules, one to another, until the desired molecular chain length and weight have been attained. This reaction is carried out by increasing the pressure and temperature in the reactant vessels, accompanied by constant stirring. This is termed a **condensation polymerization** because, as the two monomers combine, a molecule of water is condensed and evaporated. In any condensation reaction, a by-product chemical, such as water or ammonia or some other simple

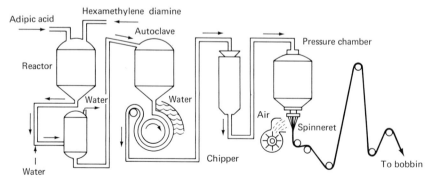

Figure 4-1   Nylon flow chart. (Courtesy of E. I. du Pont de Nemours & Co.)

compound, is produced. During this reaction, nitrogen is passed through the autoclave in order to prevent contact with air, the action of which would oxidize the polymer. As the molecules reach the desired size, a chemical is added to stop the reaction before the molecule becomes too long and losses its fiber usefulness. The mass becomes solid and is melted in the autoclave and extruded as a thick, whitish ribbon that is solidified by contact with a spray of cool water. This polymer can be delustered or dyed in the autoclave during the process of polymerization. These ribbons of solid nylon are taken from the casting wheel and transported to the chipper, in which the ribbons are broken into small flakes, or chips; it is these chips from which the nylon fiber is made.

Production of Nylon Filament

In the actual spinning operation, the flakes from several different batches are customarily mixed for the sake of greater uniformity of the product. Although the flakes can be dissolved in various solvents and extruded through spinnerets to form filaments, a common process for this synthetic fiber is high-temperature extrusion, or melt spinning, during which the molten nylon is forced through the fine openings of a spinneret. A nitrogen atmosphere is maintained, because oxygen would discolor the nylon (yellow) at the high temperature. This filament is generally rather weak because the constituent molecules are in a helter-skelter arrangement in the individual filaments. When this extruded filament is cold, it can be given a cold stretch, during which time it is stretched from two to seven times its original length. The fiber particles become oriented—that is, they tend to lie in a straight line—and the resultant filament is clear, lustrous, strong, and elastic. The long chains in the molecule are lined up side by side, the fiber is more crystalline, and, in effect, molecules reinforce one another so that the tensile strength is more than doubled. Nylon filaments can be spun over a wide range of diameters (see Figure 4–2). The textile nylon deniers vary from 10 within the fine filament classification up to 200 for the coarse; heavier monofilaments suitable for the toothbrush industry may reach 2000 denier. Wide varieties of types of yarn are used in textile products; even nylon hose, for example, may be monofilaments as fine as 10 to 15 denier or as heavy as 60-denier, 20-filament yarns. If staple nylon is desired, the filaments are cut after the cold drawing. The fibers may be given a permanent heat-set crimp and then are baled for shipment.

Nylon Properties

For many end-uses a dull, or less lustrous, surface is desired than that produced by the cold-stretch method. This can be done by putting a small

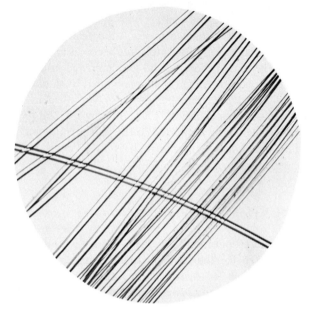

Figure 4-2 Nylon (longitudinal view). The smooth, rodlike translucency of continuous filament yarn manufactured from man-made textile fibers is demonstrated by these filaments. The filaments are magnified 160 times. (Courtesy of E. I. du Pont de Nemours & Co.)

quantity of delustrant, such as an inorganic oxide or sulfate, in the molten polymer. Another method is to roughen the surface. Unfortunately, the dull nylon has proved to be sensitive to ultraviolet light and has a tendency to sun rot, but at a rate less than that of silk. The bright nylon is more sun-resistant. Nylon is stable chemically and resists all the solvents commonly used in dry-cleaning operations. It is not affected seriously by dilute (less than 3 per cent) mineral acids, such as hydrochloric and sulfuric; however, it is weakened at an increasing rate, as the acid is more concentrated. If it is boiled for several hours with concentrated hydrochloric acid, the reaction is reversed and the adipic acid and hexamethylene diamine salt are recovered. Strongly acid chemical vapors and fly ash from heating plants using high sulfur coal can, under certain conditions of humidity, cause damage to nylon fabrics on which they fall. This accounts for the mysterious popping of nylon hose that has constituted a newspaper story on several occasions. The acid-weakened nylon yarns can no longer bear the strain as the wearer walks. Its resistance to alkali is very great. The more common solvents in which nylon is soluble are formic acid, cresol, and phenol.

The specific gravity of nylon (1.14) is lower than that of cotton and rayon. Thus, fabrics tend to be somewhat lighter in weight. On the other hand, the fact that the filaments are round in cross section causes them to pack densely in the yarn; thus, nylon fabrics have a transparent appearance.

Nylon does not absorb moisture (about 4.2 per cent at 70°F and 65 per cent relative humidity). This means that the fabric resists water-carried spots and stains and, when laundered, it dries rapidly. An important property of nylon is that certain articles, such as women's hosiery, can be molded into a permanent size and shape. Similarly, it is possible to heat-set pleats with fair success, although other synthetics surpass nylon in this regard. The Chemstrand Corporation advises that if pleats or preset creases are to be altered, the conditions of temperature and moisture under which the patterns were first set must be exceeded.[2] Although the melting point of nylon is 482°F, it is generally preferred that an iron setting not exceeding 300°F be used—sticking begins to develop at about 356°F. When heated in air at a temperature of about 300°, nylon tends to become yellow, not as rapidly as silk and wool, but more rapidly than the cellulosic fibers. Nylon does not burn if undyed; however, certain dyestuffs may render nylon slightly flammable. In general, however, it melts rather than burns, leaving a glassy globule at the end of the yarn. In common with all synthetics having a low moisture regain, nylon produces a considerable charge of static electricity when rubbed, particularly under ambient or room conditions of low relative humidity.

Regular nylons have a tenacity of 3 to 6.5 gpd for Nylon 66 and 6 to 6.8 gpd for Nylon 6. The high-tenacity type of each is about 8.59 gpd. These fibers are at least 85 per cent as strong when wet. The high tenacity of nylon combined with its flexibility contribute to its durability in full-fashioned or circular knit hose for women (Figures 4–3 and 4–4). Military lines, tow lines for aircraft, and sewing threads also depend on the combination of these two features. Sometimes this flexibility and stretchiness, 26 to 32 per cent for regular nylons and about 20 per cent for high tenacity, have a slightly detrimental effect on the end-use application. This can be true in sewing thread if the tension is too high. In this case, the nylon thread stretches during the sewing operation, and when it relaxes, the seam puckers. Somewhat the same objection is held against nylon for mooring ropes for boats and vessels. If such lines are used, the moored vessel may ease out of its normal position by the stretching of the nylon line in bad weather or high seas, but this same stretchiness is desirable when a sharp pull is to be exerted on the rope, reducing the shock of the sudden jerk. This is also true in the case of climbing ropes for mountaineers and explorers and in tow ropes for picking up gliders.

Stretchiness in nylon is further enhanced in the stretch yarns (Chapter Five), many of which are made of nylon staple. Cross sections of typical nylon fibers are shown in Figure 4–5.

An outstanding attribute of nylon is its resistance to wear. Indeed, this fiber can wear away most other textile fibers that rub against it. Thus, the occasional wearing away on the inside of the hem of a skirt or the gradual

[2] The Chemstrand Corporation, *Nylon Service Manual*, p. 19.

Figure 4-3 Nylon filament yarns awaiting shipment to knitting mills. Nylon's debut in 1938 climaxed years of work by hundreds of du Pont chemists and engineers in the company's fundamental research program. It shortly surpassed the competition of silk, long dominant in the hosiery field, and soon was on its way to uses varying from machine bearings to ropes for tugboats. Here, nylon, used in 124 million dozen pairs of women's stockings in 1970, is checked at du Pont's Seaford, Delaware, plant, where the fiber was made. (Courtesy of E. I. du Pont de Nemours & Co.)

disappearance of hem binding is caused more by the rubbing action of the nylon stocking than by any flaw in the other textile fabric. In a later discussion (Chapter Five) dealing with blends, the effectiveness of nylon as a strengthening fiber will be more fully demonstrated.

Perlon, the British equivalent of nylon, Nylon 6, and Allied's **Caprolan**, are the **polycaprolactam** type. Nylon 610, made from hexamethylene diamine and sebasic acid, has a greater resiliency than Nylon 66 and is being used in carpets. Despite its low moisture regain, it feels much like wool.

Dyeing

The hydrophobic nature of nylon—that is, its resistance to moisture absorption—has made the dyeing of this fiber difficult; the more crystalline the fiber is, as a result of cold stretching, the more resistant it is to the access of water. This is a distinct advantage of the fiber and nylon when it comes to

Figure 4-4 Each of these 1100 bobbins represents a different type of nylon that du Pont produces. Each differs in denier size, twist, brightness, or number of filaments. (Courtesy of E. I. du Pont de Nemours & Co.)

resistance to water staining—that is, discoloring from water solutions of soil, ink, beverages, or other water-carried material; it is also a barrier to the easy entry of dyes. Special procedures have had to be adapted to this fiber, both through special dyestuffs and also through the use of higher pressures.

Considering the technical problems of the level or uniform dyeing of nylons, it may seem inconsistent that white nylon appears to be so easily discolored in washing. White nylon articles washed with colored garments tend to absorb any loose dye in the wash water. Of course, this accidental

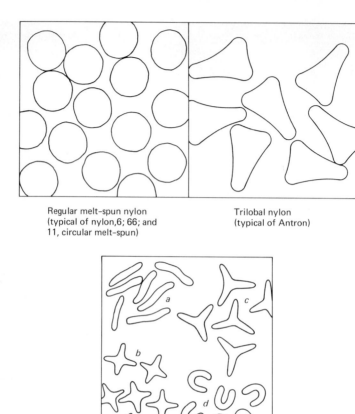

Regular melt–spun nylon
(typical of nylon,6; 66; and
11, circular melt–spun)

Trilobal nylon
(typical of Antron)

Miscellaneous special
nylon shapes for
unique fabrics:
a, flat;
b, cruciform;
c, triangular; and
d, closed *C'*

Figure 4-5 Cross sections of typical nylon fibers.

dyeing is objectionable no matter how even or uneven the discoloration of the formerly white garment may be. Thus, white nylon should never be washed with colored fabrics of any type, and nylon trimming on colored garments is a somewhat dubious form of decoration from the consumer's standpoint.

Early Disappointments with Nylon

The properties of nylon filament, staple and stretch yarn, differ according to the degree of cold-stretching orientation to which the yarn has been subjected and the amount of presetting of yarn or fabric. This synthetic fiber is widely used despite several physical disadvantages that limit its application in end-uses. Sensitivity to sun rotting and low moisture absorbency are its main limitations. Thus, the properties of the nylon fibers and of the yarns and fabrics made from them influence the suitability of any fabric construction for specific end-uses.

In the early days of nylon fiber use, acute discomfort was often experienced. Beautiful fabrics were closely woven in order to minimize the transparency of the fabric, especially in light shades, when the garments became wet with perspiration. The fabrics did not absorb body moisture. The result was that the human body, endeavoring to cool itself, produced more and more perspiration and the water-vapor level, or humidity between the skin and the fabric became higher and higher. Many nylon garments were discarded after very few wearings; they were simply intolerable in warm weather.

When one asks why it is that nylon tricot has become such an important textile for women's undergarments, one must recognize that the answer lies in the fabric construction. This tricot knit structure (see Knitted Fabrics, Chapter Six) is more open than the woven fabrics. Thus, there is more opportunity for moisture vapor and air to pass through the fabric, and this air and moisture transmission increases with the movement of the body. The elasticity, or stretchy nature, of knit fabrics serves as a pump, forcing air through the fabric with every movement of the body. The same weight of nylon in woven form continues to be uncomfortable in articles of wearing apparel in contact with the skin in warm or humid weather. These observations as to comfort are not new; they existed even in the days of the first nylon stockings, when these were made of heavier yarns, 30 to 35 denier. Some women complained that their feet were cold in winter and hot and moist in the summertime. This was a physiological effect, and the condition was probably noticed more by individuals who perspire profusely and whose skin surface is generally moist than by the average person. The comfort factor cannot be overlooked in any new fiber.

Cantrece Nylon, A Bicomponent Fiber

A unique filament extensively used for sheer stretch hosiery for ladies, for panty hose, and other knitted articles is a unique form of nylon yarn called Cantrece. This bicomponent yarn is made of two different types of nylon extruded simultaneously through the spinneret to produce a strand composed of both constituents, as shown in the cross section, Figure 4–6. These two nylons differ considerably in physical properties and react differently when exposed to heat or steam. One type shrinks and its filament takes on a curled or spiral structure. (Bicomponent fibers will be discussed in Chapter

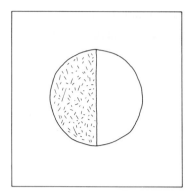

Figure 4-6 Cross section of Cantrece.

Five.) However, at this point it may be said that these bicomponent filaments, such as Cantrece, fill two needs in apparel. When they are knitted tautly, as in the production of hosiery, the final product clings flatteringly to the legs of the wearer. If, however, the apparel is knit in a relaxed manner, as in sweaters and other outer apparel, a bulky effect is achieved.

Nomex Aramid

In the early 1960s, du Pont announced a new type of nylon using an aromatic hydrocarbon product as one of the monomers. This fiber was originally given the code name HT-1; then, in 1967, when it went into production, it was named Nomex (see p. 126). The HT probably stood for high temperature, for this fiber and fabrics made from it are unaffected in strength, flexibility, stretch, and wear resistance through a temperature of 500°F. It is resistant to most chemicals and has less flammability hazard than the earlier commercial nylons. The greater part of this production will undoubtedly go into protective clothing of various types, in which chemical resistance and flame or burning characteristics are important. Not only is this fiber difficult to ignite, but the flame also disappears when the source of ignition is removed. Another advantage in its burning characteristic is that it does not melt but chars at a temperature of about 700°F. However, there is the danger of severe flesh damage from melt burns from thermoplastic fibers.

Nomex has extremely poor resistance to damage from ultraviolet light and is rapidly degraded. It has been used by the military for flight suits and for suits for fire-protection crews on aircraft carriers, usually with a reflective metal surface. It is claimed that this fiber can now be dyed in colors other than white and military green—the only two shades in which it appeared as late as mid-1969. It was solution-dyed for these colors.

Qiana Nylon

Because **Qiana** is formed by the amide linkage polymerization, it is called a nylon. Its other chemical constituents, or monomers, are new and their identity has not been disclosed. It is because of these substances that Qiana has such unique chemical and physical properties; it seems to stand alone among the nylons insofar as many consumer use applications are concerned. It is more readily dyed than the conventional nylons and will accept four classes of dyestuffs: disperse, acid, basic, and fiber reactive colors. It is more silklike in luster and texture than other manufactured fibers. Du Pont claims that it is comfortable to wear because it has high covering power combined with porosity, so that heat and perspiration are dissipated. The fiber wicks moisture much as silk does. Other claims for unusual performance characteristics are that it is dimensionally stable (neither shrinking nor stretching), can be washed or dry-cleaned, does not water spot or glaze, and can be pleated so permanently that it can be boiled without damaging the pleats. Whites are claimed not to yellow from oxidizing agents or from sunlight. Its density of 1.03 is lighter than any other manufactured fiber except the olefins. It is said not to wrinkle.

No new fiber has all plus factors or advantages working for it without disadvantages as well. Qiana, for example, requires very special handling in weaving, dyeing, and finishing in order to avoid soiling prior to heat setting. This is, of course, especially important in whites and pastels. It is more vulnerable to oil and grease setting or staining than many manufactured fibers even after finishing; unless these stains are removed promptly, they will become permanent. In putting in the seams, the apparel manufacturer must be particularly careful to have the fabric in a relaxed state rather than held taut; in sewing, the tension must be low to avoid puckering in the seams. This area is vulnerable also when it comes to the final pressing of the apparel. Generally, a woolen setting is adequate for Qiana garments.

Some properties of Qiana, or Type 472, nylon follow:

Properties	Number
Specific gravity	1.03
Tenacity, gpd	3.3
Elongation, per cent	30
Modulus	30
Moisture regain, per cent	2.5
Iron temperature, °F	365
Shrinkage (before heat setting) per cent	10

Du Pont's top market innovators felt confident that the production of the fiber was justified, but before spending many millions of dollars for its further development—and not wishing to risk large production from pilot plants for commercial development—took advantage of the cottage industry type of manufacture popular in Europe; that is, the use of weavers who devote themselves on a small scale to the perfection of the fabric they are making. These producers in France, Italy, and Switzerland used the yarn in very small quantities. These first fabrics were sold only in high-priced couturier apparel.

ACRYLIC FIBERS

The generic term **acrylic** refers to "a manufactured fiber in which the fiber-forming substance is any long-chain synthetic polymer composed of at least 85 per cent by weight of acrylonitrile units.[3]

$$(-CH_2 - CH-) ''$$
$$|$$
$$CN$$

Trade names of acrylics are listed in Table 4–2.

Table 4-2   Acrylics

Trade Name/General Classification	Producer	Types and Special Characteristics*	End-use Area*
A-Acrilan	Monsanto	FST	AHI
Acrilan	Monsanto	F (solution-dyed)	AH
Acrilan Plus	Monsanto	S	AH
Acrilan 2000 +	Monsanto	F (solution-dyed)	H
Acrylic 500	Dow Badische	S	I
Bi-Loft	Monsanto	S (bicomponent)	A
Colacril	Monsanto	FS	AH
Creslan	American Cyanamid	ST	AHI
Nomelle	du Pont	ST	AH
Orlon	du Pont	ST	AH
Orlon Sayelle	du Pont	S (bicomponent)	A
Zefkrome	Dow Badische	S (solution-dyed)	AH
Zefran	Dow Badische	ST (dyeable)	AH

SOURCE: Based on data from *Modern Textiles Magazine*, **54**, No. 3 (March 1973), p. 28.
*A — Apparel   Type F — Multifilament
  H — Home furnishings and carpets   S — Staple fiber
  I — Industrial fabrics   T — Tow

[3] Federal Trade Commission Rules and Regulations under the Textile Fiber Products Identification Act, effective March 4, 1960, p. 4.

The investigation of this polymeric structure was begun by du Pont as early as 1940. Experimental fibers carrying the code designation Fiber A appeared shortly thereafter both for military and for consumer use. In the latter case, an initial introduction was in the form of curtains. This polymer was named **Orlon** in 1948, and commercial production began in 1950. Some difficulties with fiber properties were found shortly after the introduction of this Fiber A. It was difficult to dye and posed a pronounced fire hazard in continuous filament form. The polymer was modified with changes in the other 15 per cent constituent and in the method of manufacture. Orlon acrylic fiber, type 42, produced today, is markedly superior to the original. However, it is marketed only in the staple yarn form. In Figure 4–7 typical cross sections of acrylic fibers are shown.

The fiber properties for Orlon acrylics are reflected in consumer use in the following manner. The Orlon filaments are less highly oriented than nylon, and the tenacity is considerably lower, being only about 2.3 gpd on an average. Acrylics have a low specific gravity, 1.17 and give good covering power with light weight. Moisture regain in percentages under standard exposure conditions varies from 1.2 for the Acrilan acrylic to 2.5 for Zefran. Acrylics retain 95 per cent of their strength when wet. The safe ironing temperature for acrylics is approximately 300°F for all except Zefran, which can be pressed at a temperature of 350°F. This, too, is higher in its softening point, or sticking temperature, than the other acrylics (490°F as compared to 408–455°F). All acrylic fibers are flammable. Orlon has a tendency to yellow under too high a temperature. The breaking elongation is between 20 and 28 per cent, except for Acrilan acrylic at 34 to 50 per cent. Although the water absorbency or regain is lower than that of nylon, being only 1.5 per cent, moisture does not cling to the surface of the fibers, it travels between the individual fibers and yarns by capillary action. Thus, Orlon shirts are more comfortable than nylon because the moisture vapor can escape from the skin surface and be evaporated more readily. However, rain water striking an Orlon garment will go through almost instantly.

Today's Orlon is generally given a fire-retardant finish in order to reduce the flammability characteristic of its fibers. Orlon's greatest advantage over other fibers is its resistance to sun degradation. Although the new Orlon is not quite as good as the original fiber, it can last for years in sun exposure without excessive deterioration. The characteristic cross section of Orlon is the well-known dog-bone shape (Figure 4–7 (*a*) and (*b*)), a unique configuration that naturally renders Orlon yarns very fluffy or bulky, even with a fairly high twist. This characteristic is defined as a **low-bulk density**, so that a yarn of Orlon and one of wool of approximately the same diameter will have a lightness of weight in favor of Orlon by as much as one third— meaning that the Orlon yarn of equivalent size will weigh only two thirds as much as wool. Hence, in sweaters, Orlon provides good warmth and covering power with less weight. The heat setting of Orlon is not as efficient as with nylon. Pleats or creases are most permanent when put in at right

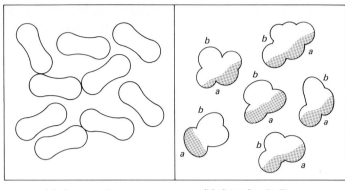

(a) Orlon acrylic
fibers (dog bone
shape)

(b) Orlon Sayelle fibers.
(a, Stained to show
the 2-component structure
b, Unstained)

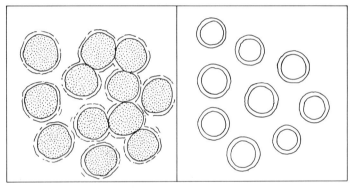

(c) Acrilan cross section
(generally round)

(d) Creslan
(round, shows thick skin)

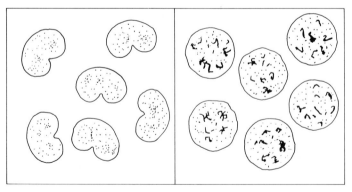

(e) Acrilan Spectran
(solution-spun-dry)

(f) Acrilan 42
(solution-spun-wet)

Figure 4-7 Cross sections of various acrylic fibers.

Table 4-3 *Comparison of Acrylic Staple Fibers*

	Orlon 42	Acrilan	Acrilan Spectran	Creslan	Courtelle (British)	Zefran
Tenacity (dry), gpd	2.2–2.6	2.0–2.7	2–2.6	2.0–3.0	3.0	3.3–4.2
Tenacity (wet), gpd	1.8–2.1	1.8–2.2		1.6–2.7	2.5	2.9–3.6
Extensibility (per cent), dry	20–28	34–50		40–55	30	30–36
Specific gravity	1.16	1.17	1.17	1.18	1.17	1.18
Average toughness	0.40	0.46		0.50–0.70	0.60	0.58–0.67
Cross-section shape	Dog bone	Round	Bean	Round	Round	Round
Moisture regain (per cent), standard	1.5	1.2	1.5	1.5	2.0	2.5
Sticking temperature (°F)	455	455	455	408	446	490
Safe ironing temperature (°F)	300	300	300	300	300	350
Chemical resistance to strong acids	Fair	Fair	Fair	Fair	Fair	Fair
Chemical resistance to weak acids	Very good	Good	Good	Good	Good	Good
Chemical resistance to strong alkali	Poor (yellow)	Poor	Poor	Poor	Fair	Fair
Chemical resistance to weak alkali	Good	Good	Good	Fair	Fair	Good
Chemical resistance to sunlight	Excellent	Good	Good	Excellent	Good	Good
Ease of dyeing	Excellent	Excellent	Excellent	Excellent	Good	Good
Flammability	Burns	Burns	Burns	Burns	Burns	Burns

angles to the Orlon yarns in mixed fabrics with Orlon used in the filling.

Unless Orlon is cold-stretched, it will shrink in hot water. An interesting extra high-bulk, or very fluffy, Orlon yarn has been produced by spinning or twisting two different Orlons in the yarn. This is not the same as a true bicomponent filament, such as Cantrece. However, Orlon Sayelle synthesized by du Pont was announced as a true bicomponent fiber, one component of which shrinks when heated to form a curly, wool-like texture. This is self-blend in which one Orlon has been cold-stretched and mixed with one that has not been treated. When such a yarn is treated with hot water or boiled, the unstretched component will shrink about 15 per cent. This leaves a self-blended yarn of very twisted and lofty structure, well suited for sweaters and for men's and boys' hose.

Manufacture of Orlon Acrylic

The usual equation representing the polymerization of acrylonitrile to form Orlon acrylic polymer is as follows:

$$CH_2 = CHCN + CH_2 = CHCN + CH_2 = CHCN$$

$$acrylonitrile \longrightarrow -CH_2 - \underset{\underset{CN}{|}}{CN} - CH_2 - \underset{\underset{CN}{|}}{CH} - CH_2 - \underset{\underset{CN}{|}}{CH} -$$

or

$$-\left(\underset{\underset{CN}{|}}{CH_2 CH} \right)_n - \quad \text{Orlon acrylic polymer}$$

As previously stated, this monomer, acrylonitrile (or vinyl cyanide), is represented as adding to itself with no splitting out of water or other by-products characteristic of condensation polymerization. Therefore, this particular process is referred to as an example of **addition polymerization**. At intervals in this chain units of the second monomer will appear, up to 15 per cent as the maximum. The identity and the order of these interspersed units are trade secrets. The polymer is usually regarded as a giant molecule consisting of approximately 2000 units.

1. The acrylonitrile and other monomers are heated in the reactant chamber shown in Figure 4–8, with an appropriate catalyst and with stirring.
2. The polymer, when formed, precipitates from the water solution in which the ingredients were first blended in the reactant chamber.
3. The precipitate is filtered out, dried, and then dissolved in a secret patented solvent from which it can be spun into the heated evaporation chamber.

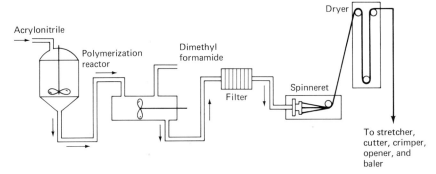

Figure 4-8 Orlon flow chart. (Courtesy of E. I. du Pont de Nemours & Co.)

4. As the filaments extend downward, there is an upward current of warm air, or nitrogen, or other atmosphere, that carries away the solvent for condensation and reuse.
5. The hardened filaments are stretched to several times their original length, usually under moderate heat.
6. The filaments are then cut to the appropriate staple length desired.

Uses of Orlon

Like the other acrylics, Orlon is constantly expanding into new textile fields while suffering minor losses in some of those in which it was used previously. For wearing apparel, Orlon can be either knitted or woven. It is widely used for knitted outerwear, such as sweaters and scarfs. It has been used in blends with wool, rayon, and other fibers for overcoatings and for relatively heavy suitings. Knitted jerseys of Orlon have had wide acceptance, as a result of their freedom from care and the ability of the fabric to hold its shape. A contributing factor, of course, is the saving of weight due to the lofty yarn. It has been blended with wool for men's socks and suitings and with cotton for dress fabrics and shirtings. In this latter use, it is interesting to note that even though Orlon has a lower moisture absorbency than nylon, Orlon is more comfortable to wear in hot weather. Orlon, alone or blended with cotton, is not as comfortable a shirting or dress fabric as all-cotton, but it is vastly more comfortable than nylon.

Household applications of Orlon acrylic fiber include blankets and rugs, and one can find upholstery fabrics in blends. For draperies, awnings, tents, tarpaulins, tops for convertible automobile models, and similar sun-exposure applications, this fiber is superior to almost anything else on the market. Helpful, too, in outdoor application is its resistance to chemicals, especially to acids in industrial areas. Thus, furniture covers and webbings of Orlon will vastly outwear any other material. Even though an awning or tarpaulin is not made of Orlon, its life will be enhanced if it is sewn with Orlon thread.

Other Acrylic Fibers

The principal acrylic fibers, Orlon, Acrilan, Zefran, and Creslan, are very similar in their performance. Therefore, they would be expected to be competitive in the consumer market for many of the same uses. The fact that their properties and uses are not discussed as fully as for Orlon does not, in any way, disparage or minimize these other fibers. The purpose is simply to avoid too much repetition. Therefore, only the unique properties of these other acrylics will be discussed in any detail.

ACRILAN ACRYLIC **Acrilan** acrylic fiber was patented by the Chemstrand Corporation and is now owned and marketed by the Monsanto Chemical Company in Decatur, Alabama. The method of production is shown in Figure 4–9. The first Acrilan fiber came on the market in 1952, but the initial fiber was rather brittle and tended to splinter (fibrillate) when pressed, especially at the cuffs and creases in men's suits and coats. An improved Acrilan, rounder in cross section, was introduced and found ready acceptance in 1954. Being round, this fiber does not have the high-

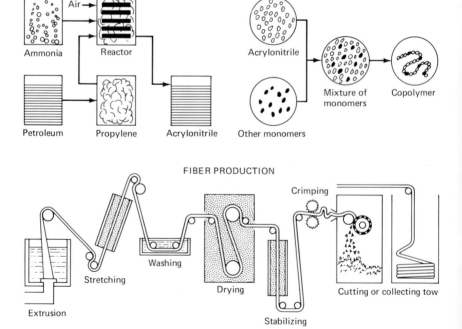

Figure 4-9 Production of acrylic fiber.

bulk qualities characteristic of Orlon. The second monomer used in Acrilan with acrylonitrile is distinctly different from that used in Orlon (vinyl acetate is used mostly). Acrilan is much more readily dyed, thus proving distinct chemical differences in this minor component. It is wet spun from solution, resulting in this round cross section, and it has scarcely any surface indentations along the fiber axis. Being a more compact yarn, Acrilan has fewer and smaller spaces in it through which water can enter. Therefore, one would not expect Acrilan garments to have quite the degree of water passage of Orlon apparel. This could be an advantage or a disadvantage, depending upon the end-use application. Acrilan is slightly flammable but safe for wearing apparel; even in carpets where Acrilan does burn at a slow rate, the rate is less than that of cotton or rayon carpets and rugs that have been used with satisfaction for many years without any great fire risk ever being considered. Acrilan does not have quite the same degree of sun resistance as Orlon, but it is comparable. Because Acrilan is not produced in filament form, one is not concerned with it in window curtains. The Acrilan-Spectran promoted by the Chemstrand Corporation is a solution-dyed high-bulk yarn with an unusually even dye distribution within the fibers (see Figure 4–10). This acrylic fiber is widely used in men's and boys' socks and sweaters and in a variety of knitted outer wear garments, including women's sweaters. Acrilan is blended with wool, cotton, rayon, or other fibers for many items of clothing. It has been unusually popular as a blanket material because of the beautiful permanent shades of color, an unusual dimensional stability, and the ability of this fiber to retain its gloss and softness of nap. Acrilan carpetings have been among the most popular of all those produced

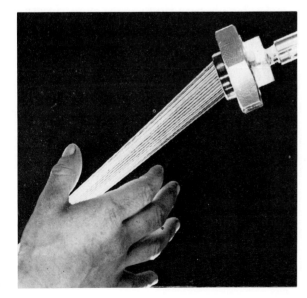

Figure 4-10 Strands of newly spun Acrilan acrylic fiber are processed at the Chemstrand Corporation's plant at Decatur, Alabama.

from synthetic fibers. There is some indication that Acrilan is less prone to static electricity than Orlon.

Zefran Acrylic

Zefran and **Zefkrome** are two acrylic fibers produced by the Dow Chemical Company generally marketed under the name Zefran. The essential difference is that the Zefkrome is dope- or solution-dyed for extra color fastness. These fibers have been commercially important since 1962, but were previously introduced under carefully controlled market supervision by the fiber manufacturer in order to see to it that the fibers went into appropriate end-uses and that quality control was assured. The polymerization of Zefran is highly secret and appears to be unique among the acrylics, in that the acrylonitrile units copolymerize and the other monomer or monomers hook on as side chains for side links. It is believed that the superior absorbency and dyeability of this fiber are the result of this adsorbent tail feature. The polymerization reaction forming Zefran is said to be unique, and some have described this polymer as being an alloy—that is, the intimate blending of two or more constituents into a solid mass.

Thus far, Zefran has been available as a crimped staple or as tow. It is not available in filament form. The breaking tenacities are between 3.3 and 4.1 gpd; when wet, it retains 95 per cent of its strength. The moisture regain is 2.5, higher than any other acrylic fiber. The cross section of the fiber is round, and it is white in color. Alone or in blends, the fiber is soft and has excellent draping qualities. It is more resistant to pilling than its more slippery sister fibers. Its use, thus far, has been mostly in the more expensive and high-fashion merchandise, generally in blends with wool in suitings or with rayon and cotton in dress fabrics.

Zefran is dyed with a wide range of colors by means of naphthol, sulfur, direct, and other types of dyestuffs. This polymer has the highest tenacity of any of the staple fibers but is somewhat lower in elastic recovery. It has a higher melting point than any of the other acrylics—as a matter of fact, it does not stick until a temperature of 490°F is reached. Zefran has greater resistance to acid than any of the other acrylics, and fair to good resistance to alkalis, solvents, and bleaches. Its resistance to sunlight and abrasion are good—not quite equivalent to Orlon, but better than the other acrylics.

Creslan Acrylic

Creslan acrylic fiber is the development of the American Cyanamid Corporation through experimental fibers X-51 and X-54, marketed on a test basis in the early 1950s. Creslan became important to the market in 1959 because of its unusual fiber softness. Indeed, fine Creslan staple blended with wool produces fabrics of a cashmerelike texture and feel and increases the wet strength of the fabric over one that is all wool. Luxury shirting fabrics have been produced of blends of Creslan and cotton giving the texture an appearance of spun silk. There are two types of Creslan: the first is designated as type 58 by the manufacturer; the other is type 61. These two types are produced in order to permit various kinds of dyes to be used. It is claimed that type 61 produces a clearer white and, thus, pastel shades will be brighter and fresher. It is interesting that blends of these two acrylics in a yarn or fabric produce cross-dyed effects.

The breaking strength of Creslan is between 2 and 4.2 grams per denier. It is similar to Orlon and Acrilan acrylics in most properties. The cross section is round, and it has a thicker skin than that of other acrylics. The spinning of this copolymer of acrylonitrile and some other chemical compound is done by wet spinning into a cold bath for coagulation. Details are unrevealed, and the filaments are crimped after some degree of cold stretching and are cut into staple lengths for blending.

A new type of Creslan, No. 63, is being produced in a staple. It is said that there are two types, one for industrial use and the other for apparel. It is readily dyed with basic or with dispersed dyes.

MARKETS AND USES   Acrylonitrile, the principal monomer used in acrylics—which by definition must contain a minimum of 85 per cent by weight of this chemical—and in modacrylics—which must contain between 35 and 85 per cent—is in abundant supply. This availability plus improve-

Table 4-4   Growth of Acrylic and Modacrylic Fibers*

(millions of pounds)

Year	Knits	Home Furnishings	Carpets and Rugs	Wigs	Pile Fabrics
1965	—	—	138.1	—	—
1968	—	—	—	4.3	60
1969	195	—	—	—	—
1970	—	6	184.3	6.5	70
1974	270	—	—	—	—
1975	—	20	290.0	8.0	90
1980	325	48	425.0	—	—

* *American Fabrics Magazine*, No. 88 (Fall 1970), p. 5, forecasts a business of a billion pounds for the acrylic/modacrylic fibers by 1980.

ments in dyeing techniques have greatly expanded the market potential[4] for the acrylic fibers.

The number of manufacturers is constantly expanding, not only in the United States but in the world market. In 1968, production of acrylic and modacrylic fibers together was 521 million pounds in the United States and 1611 million pounds as a world total. By 1973, production had reached 742 and 3453 million pounds for the United States and the world, respectively.[5]

MODACRYLIC FIBERS

The modacrylic is defined by the FTC as "a manufactured fiber in which the fiber-forming substance is any long-chain synthetic polymer composed of less than 85 per cent but at least 35 per cent by weight of acrylonitrile units." [6] These, then, are copolymers in which acrylonitrile can be a minor instead of a major monomer component; that is, the acrylonitrile can be less than 50 per cent by weight.

The characteristics of modacrylics are given in Table 4–5.

Table 4-5 Modacrylics

Trade Name/General Classification	Producer	Type and Special Characteristics*	End-use Area*
Dynel 150	Union Carbide	T (uncrimped)	AI
Dynel 180	Union Carbide	S (crimp T)	AHI
Dynel 183	Union Carbide	S (high-bulk crimp)	A
Dynel 297	Union Carbide	S (modified cross section)	H
Elura	Monsanto	T	H, wigs
Orlon	du Pont	ST	AH
SEF	Monsanto	FMS	AH
Verel	Eastman	S (assorted types)	AHI

SOURCE: Based on data from *Modern Textiles Magazine*, **54**, No. 3 (March 1973), p. 26.
*A — Apparel
  H — Home furnishings and carpets
  I — Industrial fabrics

Type M — Monofilament
  F — Multifilament
  S — Staple fiber
  T — Tow

[4] John E. Nettles and Frank Stevens, "Acrylic Fibers: Yesterday, Today, and Tomorrow," *Textile Chemist and Colorist*, **22** (Oct. 22, 1969), pp. 84–87.

[5] *Textile Organon*, **45**, No. 6 (June 1974), p. 71.

[6] Federal Trade Commission Rules and Regulations under the Textile Fiber Products Identification Act, effective March 4, 1960, p. 4.

Dynel Modacrylic

The modacrylic polymer bearing the name **Dynel** is a copolymer containing approximately 60 per cent vinyl chloride and 40 per cent acrylonitrile; the polymer is dissolved in acetone for spinning into a water bath in which it is coagulated. The stretching operation for giving extra strength and stretch characteristics is not done in the cold—as it is for most manufactured fibers—but when the fibers are hot and the stretch is as much as 1300 per cent. The fibers are usually cut into staple lengths and are crimped; much of its use as staple is in blends. The tenacity ranges from 2.5 to 3.5 gpd, and the elongation is from 32 to 40 per cent. It has an unusually low moisture regain, 0.4 per cent. This modacrylic is slightly heavier than the acrylics, being 1.31. It has outstanding resistance to acid, alkalies, and most chemicals. The softening temperature is 220°F. Thus, it is impossible to press an all-Dynel fabric, even with an ordinary household iron set at the cool setting. Blends can be pressed perfectly with a pressing cloth if the blending fiber is one with a fair amount of moisture content, such as a wool, cotton, or rayon. They cannot be steam-pressed safely.

Dynel Production

Dynel was announced in 1949 by Union Carbide Corporation and came on the market in 1951 in staple yarn form. It is a copolymer of vinyl chloride

$$(CH_2 = CH)$$
$$|$$
$$Cl$$

and acrylonitrile

$$(CH_2 = CH)$$
$$|$$
$$CN$$

Polymerization takes place in a heated autoclave to produce the high molecular weight polymer. The cross section in Figure 4–11 of an individual fiber is somewhat ribbonlike in that it is much greater in one dimension than in the other. It is nearly white in color and can be bleached. Dynel can be dyed by several classes of dyes including dispersed cationic and some direct colors. Originally, the acetate dyes were used, but these have the same color-fastness problem with regard to acid exposure and atmospheric fading as they do on acetate.

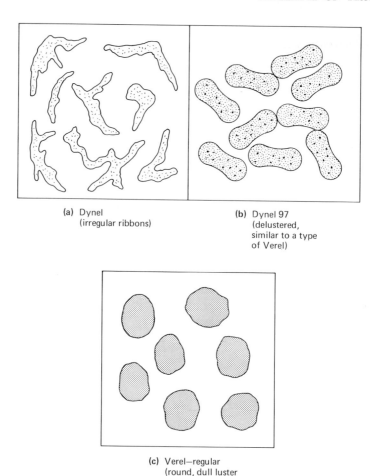

(a) Dynel
   (irregular ribbons)

(b) Dynel 97
   (delustered,
   similar to a type
   of Verel)

(c) Verel—regular
   (round, dull luster
   fibers)

Figure 4-11   Cross sections of several modacrylic fibers.

Consumer Use

The outstanding property of Dynel is its extremely high resistance to burning. This is doubtless a result of the content of chlorine in the vinyl chloride monomer. A blowtorch can be used on Dynel without causing it to burn. However, it does melt under flame as do other thermoplastics. One use for this fiber is in blends with some of the soft-textured synthetics, such as Creslan acrylic, Orlon acrylic, and Dacron polyester fibers; another use is in artificial wool-like or furlike coats. Here Dynel helps to reduce the fire hazard of the fluffy surface of more flammable materials. When formed into a round shape, either by knitting or weaving, a Dynel fabric can be molded over a heated hat form. Some of the simulated straw hats or textured fiber hats now so popular with men for summer wear are Dynel. The almost total lack of moisture absorbency contributes to the tendency of this fiber to store up static electricity. This was one of the handicaps encountered in making infants' blankets of Dynel. Considerable quantities of Dynel go into industrial usage, where its excellent resistance to acids, alkalies, and most chemicals makes it highly desirable for protective clothing for laboratories and industry.

The resistance of modacrylics, and especially Dynel modacrylic, to fire and its ability to take a permanent shape or crimp made it popular for wigs for dolls in the 1950s. However, Dynel is a more costly fiber than saran, and even though it is superior in softness and hairlike texture than the stiffer saran, the latter fiber has replaced it in most toy applications. The wig market as early as 1960 was $30 million and this had increased to $50 million by 1964. By 1970 it rose almost vertically to an estimated $700 million at retail prices. The advantages are, of course, flame resistance, permanency of styling of the hair, durability, lightness in weight, nonallergenic properties, and a subtle blending of fiber colors resulting in human hair tones. The original wigs worn by women of fashion prior to the entry of Dynel into the market were made of human hair, and they required about as much attention and as frequent care by the hairdresser as did a woman's own hair. The durability of Dynel in its styling is a tremendous advantage. All the advantages of Dynel make it especially useful for women in the public eye—for professional women golfers, for example, whose hair must always be attractive and must withstand the ravages of sun and rain. One prominent golfer known for her short temper has been known to rip off her wig when she makes a bad shot and beat it with a golf club; after venting her wrath, she would pick up the wig and don it once more. This, of course, is an extreme test of durability, but no other material with the advantages of Dynel could possibly equal the requirement.

Wigs, many of which are made in the Orient, are a sewing machine product. Fibers of the desired colors and length are blended together and then stitched into a weft. This is then stitched firmly after doubling the weft over, and the fibers are thoroughly locked in place. The wefting is then curled on heated tubes and, after cooling, is permanently curled. The desired length of this curled weft is then sewn onto a stretched fabric base, often a knit, to give the wig style and curl pattern desired. It is then thoroughly brushed and shipped to the consumer market.

Aeress Modacrylic

Aeress is the name of a new modacrylic fiber made by the Union Carbide Corporation and is essentially the same as Vinyon N. It is produced in medium to high denier and, thus far, has found most of its applications in industrial fabrics. The extensibility is lower than Dynel, only 12 to 16 per cent, compared with 30 to 42 per cent. It sticks at 150°F and melts at 240°F.

Verel Modacrylic

Introduced experimentally in 1956 by the Eastman Chemical Products Company, this fiber is currently widely used in staple and tow forms in a number of different fabric types that vary in crimp intensity and permanence. In cross section, the fiber resembles a peanut. It is not quite as uniform in cross-section shape as the dog bone of Orlon. Like Dynel, it will not support combustion, but the sticking temperature is 390–400°F. The tenacity of Verel is somewhat lower than that of Dynel, being only 2.5 to 2.8. It has approximately 3 per cent moisture regain, compared to 0.4 for Dynel. It has excellent resistance to acids, even in high concentrations; although not weakened by alkali, it can be damaged by becoming somewhat yellow. Most dry-cleaning solvents and chemicals will not affect it, but it is soluble in warm acetone. Verel has excellent resistance to sunlight and aging and has a high degree of softness and a luxurious texture. It has therefore been blended with wool and used in many high-fashion fabrics. When blended with cotton, Verel produces very soft-textured shirtings and dress fabrics and comfortable textiles for underwear, pajamas, and nightgowns. Some types shrink in boiling water. Thus, Verel, type 1, is sometimes used as a backing yarn for artificial fur coats so that the base fabric can be made more compact after boiling and thus hold projecting "fur" fibers more securely. A high-bulk fiber, type 1 has a high shrinkage, 19 to 23 per cent in boiling water, and as much as 25 to 28 per cent dry heat at 300°F. This fiber gives a high-bulk yarn that has been well accepted in socks, sweaters and other heavy knit articles. The irregular round- to peanut-shaped cross section helps to provide a high-bulk yarn.

POLYESTER FIBERS

E. I. du Pont de Nemours & Co. produced the first commercial polyester fiber (Dacron) in the United States in 1953. This fiber corresponds to the British Terylene, the first such fiber to be patented.

The official Federal Trade Commission definition for a polyester is "a manufactured fiber in which the fiber-forming substance is any long-chain synthetic polymer composed of at least 85 per cent by weight of an ester of a dihydric alcohol and terephthalic acid (p—HOOC—C_6H_4—COOH)." [7] Here p — refers to the para or end linkage in the benzene ring.

[7] Federal Trade Commission Rules and Regulations under the Textile Fiber Products Identification Act, effective March 4, 1960, p. 4.

Table 4-6 Polyester Fibers

Trade Name/ General Classification	Producer	Type and Special Characteristics*	End-use Areas*
Avlin (fiber 200)	American Viscose Division	FS	AH
Beaunit Polyester	Beaunit	F	TCA
Blue "C"	Monsanto	F	AHITC
Dacron	du Pont	FST	AHITC
Diane	Souquoit	F (textured)	A
Ektafill	Eastman	S (fiber-fill)	H
Encron	American Enka	FS	AHITC
Encron MCS	American Enka	S (modified cross section)	AH
Enkalure II (polyester-nylon)	American Enka	FS (multilobal, delayed)	H
Enka Polyester	American Enka	FS	AHITC
Esterweld	IRC Fibers	F (treated)	I
Fortrel	Fiber Industries (Celanese)	FST	AHITC
Fortrel 7	Fiber Industries (Celanese)	T	AH
Goodyear Polyester	Goodyear Tire	F	TC
Hystron	Hoechst	SFT (high-tenacity, low pilling for natural fiber systems)	AHI
Kodel	Eastman	FS (several types)	AHI
Monsanto Polyester	Monsanto	ST	AHTC
MX 6020	Shakespeare	M (round)	I
MX 6020 H	Shakespeare	M (round, hydrolysis ves. reg., mod. and low shrink)	I
Newton Polyester	Newton	F	I
NM 3100	Monofilaments	M (melt-dyed)	AHI
Polar Guard	Fiber Industries (Celanese)	FT	AI
Polybest	Beaunit	F	TC
Polyester	IRC Fibers	F	TC
Quintess	Phillips Fibers	F	AHI
Soo Valley Polyester	Soo Valley	M	I
Source (nylon-polyester)	Allied	FS	H
Spectran	Monsanto	S	A
Strialine	American Enka	F (thick and thin)	AH

Table 4-6 (continued)

Trade Name/ General Classification	Producer	Type and Special Characteristics*	End-use Areas*
Trevira	Hoechst	FST (high-tenacity)	AHI
Vycron	Beaunit	FS	AHITC
Wellene	Wellman		HI
Wellstrand (nylon and polyester) (heavy density)	Wellman	S (monofilament)	HI
Xtra-Tuf	Beaunit	S (high-tenacity)	A
Zefran	Dow Badische	F	A

SOURCE: Based on data from *Modern Textiles Magazine*, **54**, No. 3 (March 1973), pp. 28–32.
*A — Apparel
H — Home furnishings and carpets
I — Industrial fabrics
TC — Tire cord

Type M — Monofilament
F — Multifilament
S — Staple fiber
T — Tow

In Table 4–6 the most important polyester fibers made in the United States are listed.

Dacron Polyester

POLYMERIZATION OF DACRON POLYESTER The following equation shows the two monomers. The acid shown has the benzene ring with COOH at either end, at each of which can be added one hydroxyl or OH group from the dihydric alcohol shown here as ethylene glycol.

$$HOOC - \langle \text{benzene ring} \rangle - COOH + HO(CH_2)_2OH \longrightarrow$$

terephthalic acid   ethylene glycol

$$HOOC - \langle \text{benzene ring} \rangle - COO(CH_2)_2OH + H_2O$$

$$\text{Dacron is } HO - \left[OC - \langle \text{benzene ring} \rangle - COO(CH_2)_2O \right]_n H + (2n-1)H_2O$$

This is a condensation polymerization because each time there is a linkage between the two monomers, one molecule of water splits out, combining any number of molecules of each of the monomers, such as n. The flow chart for this reaction is shown in Figure 4–12. The polymerization takes place

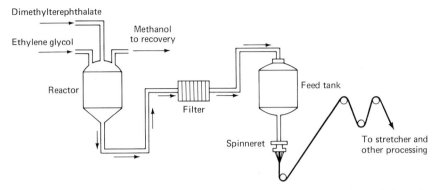

Figure 4-12 Simplified flow chart for Dacron polyester fiber. (Courtesy of E. I. du Pont de Nemours & Co.)

here at a high temperature and under a vacuum. After the monomers are introduced into the reaction vessel or autoclave, the following steps take place.

1. The molten polymer flows out of the reaction vessel onto a smooth casting wheel and solidifies in the form of a thin ribbon.
2. When thoroughly solidified, this ribbon is broken into small chips or blocks, approximately 4 millimeters square. These chips from several batches of polymer are mixed for a more uniform product.
3. The assembled chips are dried to remove any trace of moisture that may have condensed on them during storage.
4. They are then heated to the molten state.
5. The fluid material passes through very fine spinnerets typical of a melt-spinning operation.
6. The filaments harden rapidly, and as they emerge are gathered in the form of loose sliver and wound on cylinders.

PROPERTIES In Table 4–7 the physical and chemical properties of Dacron are shown in comparison with other polyester fibers. It will be noted that the tenacity can be doubled in the high-tenacity type as compared to the regular. This, however, results in a considerable loss of elongation, from a maximum of 25 in the case of regular Dacron to as low as 14 in the case of high tenacity. The polyesters are slightly higher in specific gravity than the acrylic fibers, 1.22 to 1.38, as against 1.17. The moisture regain is virtually nil. Although the melting point is 482°F, the safe ironing temperature is approximately 325°F. Dacron has good resistance to most chemicals including strong acids and alkalies and has excellent resistance to bleaching damage.

The customer has generally specified the amount of plying and twisting

Table 4-7　Properties of Common Polyester Fibers

| | Dacron | | | Kodel | Fortrel | | | Vycron | |
| | Filament | | Staple and Tow | Staple and Tow | Filament | | Staple and Tow | Type 2 | Type 5 |
	Regular	High-tenacity			Regular	High-tenacity		Low-density Monofilament	High-density Monofilament
Tenacity, gpd (both wet and dry)	4.4–5.0	6.3–7.8	3.2–4.3	2.5–3.0	4.5	7.5–8.0	4.85	5.3–8.0	5.0–5.5
Elongation to break, dry (per cent)	19–25	10–4	25–36	24–30	25–30	8–10	45–55	30–40	35–45
Specific gravity	1.38			1.22	1.38			1.38	
Water regain (per cent)	0.4–0.8			0.2	0.4			0.6	
Softening point (°F)	480			564	485–510			410	455
Ironing—safe limit (°F)	385			425	350			330	
Resistance to acid, strong	Good			Good	Good			Fair	
Resistance to acid, weak	Good			Good	Good			Good	
Resistance to strong alkali	Good			Good	Poor			Poor	
Resistance to weak alkali	Good			Good	Good			Good	
Resistance to bleach	Excellent			Excellent	Excellent			Excellent	
Class of dyes used	Acetate disperse and cationic with carrier			Same as Dacron	Same			Same	
Cross section	Round			Round	Round			Round	

he wants for spinning his own yarn. Usually, Dacron is stretched to five times its original length, making the cross section one fifth of the original diameter. The twist given the yarn will vary depending on the end-use application. After twisting, the yarn is usually passed through an oven in order to heat-set or stabilize the structure. In the case of high-tenacity Dacron, more stretch is given than the fivefold amount characteristic of yarns for wearing apparel. This process is primarily that for filament Dacron. The procedures for staple fiber are the same up to the spinning operation. Usually, for staple Dacron a much finer spinneret is used—that is, one with many more and smaller orifices. The tow laid down is much thicker; and because the individual filaments are finer to begin with, they need be stretched to only about three times their length. The amount of crimp depends on the fiber with which the Dacron is to be blended. Thus, both crimp and fiber length are designed to be as close as possible to these characteristics of the other fiber—that is, wool, cotton, or another synthetic. The uses for Dacron are many, both alone and in blends. Some blends used in great quantity have already reached a state of relatively exact standards. Typical examples are blends of Dacron and wool in 50:50 composition or 60 Dacron:40 wool; a great variety of cotton cloth items, such as dresses, blouses, sport shirts, and children's wear are now 65 Dacron:35 cotton.

In Figure 4–13 the processing routes are shown for cotton fibers and Dacron polyester staple to be spun into a blended yarn. Fewer processing steps are required for the manufactured fibers as compared to cotton prior to blending. The Dacron staple is cut to 1½ inches in length for blending with cotton fibers of 1- to 1½-inch staple to make the yarn more uniform.

New du Pont Dacron Polyesters

A new type of Dacron, type 655, has been found well suited for double-knit machinery and fine gauges for men's wear, such as sport coats, slacks, and suits. Du Pont has found that textured filament and spun yarns can be run on the same knitting machine at the same time. In another application, this Dacron polymer can be blended with Orlon of a high-bulk resilient bicomponent type (type 27) for sweaters and hosiery.

Properties Affecting Use

Despite the low moisture regain, the polyesters, like Orlon acrylic, permit moisture to pass through the fabric readily along the outside of the fibers by wicking action. It is, therefore, a comfortable fabric for summer wear, lying part way between cotton (the most comfortable) and nylon (of the same fabric yarn count or weight but the least comfortable).

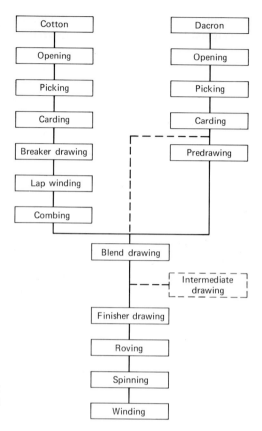

Figure 4-13 Processing routes for Dacron polyester and combed cotton blended yarn.

Dacron polyester also returns to its original shape after a considerable amount of wrinkling. This is a result of the heat setting of the crimp in the fibers, and it is one of the reasons for the successful wash-and-wear garments made out of Dacron and cotton blends. Like most melt-spun fibers, Dacron is round in cross section; therefore, it can pack rather densely in the yarn, unless it has been given sufficient crimp to resist the compacting. The fact that Dacron can be heat-set permits its use in many garments, such as sweaters and socks, which will retain their shape and size after washing. Crimped Dacron tow has been used in pillows and as an interlining material in winter wear under the name of **Fiber-Fill**, its use depending on its resiliency in the crimped form, its resistance to crushing, and its nonallergenic property. These qualities and the fact that it can be washed with ease and dried quickly make it a highly successful substitute for down or feathers. Its industrial uses are many because of its great chemical resistance and its strength. It is used in filter cloths and conveyer belts. Another industrial use is in the laundry trade, where it can be used for the sheeting to cover calender rolls; for padding; for blankets used in presses; and for laundry bags. In the field of sports and recreation, Dacron fabrics are now virtually the standard cloth for almost all sailboats from the smallest bon-boy scooter or sailfish to the big international race yachts. Its durability, lightness in weight, great flexibility, and satisfactory resistance to sunlight make it a valuable fabric for all kinds of outdoor exposure.

In Chapter 3, in which the modern metallic yarns are discussed, reference was made to a clear plastic sheet called Mylar. This is the same polymer as Dacron, but instead of being in fiber form, Mylar is in a wide, clear, transparent sheet of great strength and resistance to sun and moisture. This same film can be twisted into yarns or cords to serve as webbing for outdoor furniture. It is also used in photographic film.

The nonallergenic and nonreactive nature of Dacron enables it to be used in forming flexible tubing in surgery to replace arteries and other tubular elements in the body, and a mass of Dacron fiber or twisted Mylar strips has been used as latticework to reinforce damaged body tissues. With these inert polymers, the natural tissues grow through the interstices of this lattice, or mass structure.

Other Important Polyester Fibers

The uses and properties of **Fortrel**, **Kodel**, and **Vycron** and of the other polyester fibers are comparable with those of Dacron. However, each has certain features resulting from differences in the monomers, their concentration, the catalyst used, the reaction conditions, the method of solidifying, the spinning procedure, the extent of crimping, and the amount of stretching. Therefore, only the essential differences between these and the first one produced will be mentioned here.

FORTREL POLYESTER   The original Dacron license granted to the du Pont Company has expired. The Celanese Fibers Company, a subsidiary of the Celanese Corporation of America and Imperial Chemical Industries, Ltd. (ICI), produces a polyester fiber called Fortrel, which is virtually the same as Terylene polyester made by ICI in England. The first deviation from the usual Dacron polyester is that instead of using terephthalic acid, Fortrel utilizes the dimethyl terephthalate. This has a CH_3 group in the place of the hydrogen at the end of the COOH or carboxyl group. Condensation proceeds, as in the case of Dacron, with the splitting out of one molecule of water for each pair of monomers combined. Fortrel has a slightly higher melting point than Dacron, 485–500°F, compared with 482°F. The tenacity of both the regular and high-tenacity filaments are on the high side or on a rather wider range. In tenacity Fortrel has a higher breaking elongation than Dacron; but the high-tenacity type is somewhat more brittle and has a lower breaking elongation. A special Fortrel tow of a moderate tenacity of

1.3 to 1.5 is being used in nonwoven fabrics (see Chapter Six). This is referred to as a binder fiber and can be used alone or with other fibers (either natural or synthetic) to produce specialty synthetic papers, filtration pads, electrical insulation sheeting, and heat-forming cores for molded rugs. Its use as a blending fiber with cotton or wool is being expanded rapidly. In this use, Fortrel resembles other polyesters.

KODEL POLYESTER   Eastman Chemical Products, Inc., announced its new fiber polyester, named **Kodel**, in 1958. It is produced mostly in staple and tow, although there has been a small amount in filament form. Kodel is the whitest of the polyesters.

In comparison with other polyesters, Kodel has a somewhat lower tenacity of 2.5 to 3.0 gpd for the regular and 4.5 to 5.5 for the high-modulus types; however, it has a higher elongation than Dacron or Fortrel polyesters and is comparable with Vycron. These superior elongations make it an excellent fiber for blending not only with cotton, but also with wool. Kodel has the highest melting point of any of the polyesters, 554°F for the regular and 482°F for the high modulus. The principal advantage of this would be in the pressing of fabrics made of blends of polyester and cotton, in which polyester is the predominant fiber and might be in danger of being softened by heat. The factors of elongation and melting point make this fiber one of the more easily cared for of the blends.

VYCRON POLYESTER   **Vycron** is a product of Beaunit and is similar to the other polyesters shown in Table 4–7. It is produced in two types, designated as II and V. Type II has the lower softening point, 410°F, compared with 455°F for type V. The melting point in each case is approximately 40° higher than the softening point. Vycron is produced in filament and staple form for industrial fabrics and for cotton or wool blends for apparel. The fiber has good shape-retention and ease-of-care properties. Garments made from it can be shaped to size and given permanent creases and pleats when desired. Like the other polyesters, it is an excellent blending fiber for specialty fabrics and for minimum-care and durable-press apparel. The claim is made that it pills less than other polyesters, possibly because the difference in its chemical constitution and its irregular, round cross section makes the fiber more cohesive.

POLYESTER WD-2   The Monsanto Company has announced the introduction of a new polyester fabric made of fibers called WD-2. Because of some unusual fiber properties, they expect this new product to qualify for many end-uses. One claim for it is that it has unusually good resistance to oil stains. It gives excellent drapeability. It was first scheduled for introduction in women's and children's wear, with men's wear to follow, for the fall of 1970. It is said to retain the characteristic polyester qualities of wrinkle resistance, resiliency, washability, dimensional stability, quick drying, and a melting point of approximately 480°F. The stain-resistance factor would be an advantage in table linen and in uniform fabrics.

TREVIRA POLYESTER FIBER Reference was made in the section on nylon to the development of varied cross sections in fibers as the result of grinding and shaping the orifices in the spinneret to geometrical shapes other than round. **Trevira** polyester star fiber, made by Hoechst, is an example of this technique in the production of a polyester having a cross section that is pentalobal when extruded from a star-shaped molding orifice. These fibers combine the properties of bulkiness and luster, or light reflectance, in a wide variety of fabric weights and thicknesses. The bulkiness results from the inability of irregular, geometrical sections to pack as closely in the yarns as do perfectly round cross-section fibers. The enhanced luster in these pentalobal star structures results from an impinging beam of light being reflected from the side of one star point of the fiber to an adjacent one—two light beams are thus reflected back. In other more or less random multilobal fibers, the narrow light beam will be reflected in a random manner on the surface—most of these are duller than perfectly round fibers.

POLYESTER CHARACTERISTICS Most of the producers of polyester fibers produce both filament and tow fibers for staple yarns. Wide variations in denier are produced and these fibers may vary from bright to semidull to dull luster depending on the end-use contemplated. Dacron in the proper fiber lengths for blending with other fibers produces fabrics with a wide variety of properties—notably excellent wash-and-wear and durable-press fabrics that wash easily, dry quickly, and wear well. As previously noted, polyesters have good resistance to strong acids, except sulfuric acid, and in the case of a few of them to weak acids and to alkalies. Generally, they are not affected or yellowed by chlorine bleach.

Being melt spun, the cross sections are generally round, although filaments can be modified in such irregular cross sections as the trilobal, T, and the star or pentalobal shown in Figure 4–14. This can be done by changing the orifice shape in the spinnerette. These fibers can be vat- or solution-dyed, generally with acetate colors or with disperse and cationic dyes with carriers. They can be given unusually fast whiteness by the use of an optical whitener in the solution prior to spinning. As in the case of other manufactured fibers, producers are always open to suggestions of modifications that will make their products more useful to potential customers. There are very few articles of apparel in which polyesters are not used, either alone or in combination with other fiber. They are useful in sewing thread, high-pressure fire hose, tapes, belts, ropes, tire cord, silk cloth, and industrial fabrics.

The polyester fibers have a greater weakness in resistance to pilling than

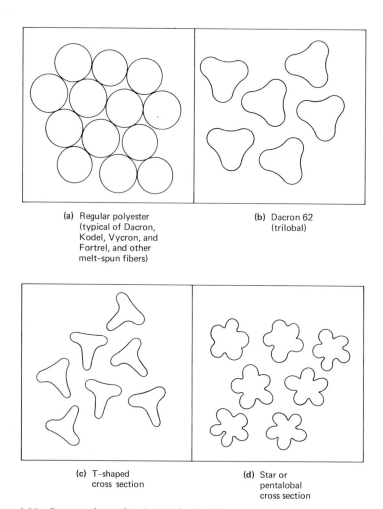

(a) Regular polyester
    (typical of Dacron,
    Kodel, Vycron, and
    Fortrel, and other
    melt-spun fibers)

(b) Dacron 62
    (trilobal)

(c) T-shaped
    cross section

(d) Star or
    pentalobal
    cross section

Figure 4-14   Cross sections of various polyester fibers.

do many other manufactured fibers. This property results in limiting the amount of polyester fiber in blends for fabrics intended to withstand hard wear. One example is in the collars of men's shirts. Like other synthetic fibers, the polyesters have an affinity for oily stains; some claim that polyesters are more subject to this problem than nylon and acrylics.

Table 4–8 gives the distribution of polyester used in 1970 and 1973.

OLEFIN FIBERS

An **olefin** fiber is, by definition, "a manufactured fiber in which the fiber-forming substance is any long-chain synthetic polymer composed of at least

Table 4-8   Polyester Fiber in Use by Categories

(millions of pounds)

Use Categories	1970	1973
Broadwoven (except carpets)	714.1	1,072.0
Carpets	196.4	207.6
Circular knit	252.7	976.9
Flat knit	18.4	81.8
Fiberfill	74.8	134.6
Tires	147.9	260.3
Other uses	31.6	117.6
Total	1,435.9	2,850.8

SOURCE: *Textile Organon*, **45**, No. 1–2 (Jan.–Feb. 1974) pp. 6–7.

85 per cent by weight of ethylene, propylene, or other olefin units." [8] The two polymers, the polyethylenes and the polypropylenes, have been on the market for several years in the form of cast articles or, even more commonly, as transparent film materials. The latter form is probably more familiar to the homemaker as the plastic film bags in which dry-cleaned or laundered articles are returned to the home. Some of the unique properties of these polymers—their low cost and ready availability from the natural gas industry—make them of great potential interest to many manufacturers, as is shown in the list of manufacturers and better-known trade names in Table 4–9.

Properties of Olefin Fibers

The olefin fibers are lower in specific gravity than any other fiber (0.91) and will float on water. A cross section of a fiber is shown in Figure 4–15. A fabric composed of Orlon yarn would require 1.3 pounds to cover the same area as 1 pound of polypropylene monofilament yarn. Cotton would require as much as 1.71 pounds for coverage equal to 1 pound of olefin. The tenacity of the polyethylene is relatively low in the monofilament; but in the higher density yarn, 3.5 to 6 gpd, it is comparable to the other synthetics. The moisture regain is virtually zero, so the properties would not be affected in any way in the presence of moisture. Polyethylene has a somewhat lower melting point, 300°F. The fibers may shrink at 165–212°F. In the high-

[8] Federal Trade Commission Rules and Regulations under the Textile Fiber Products Identification Act, effective March 4, 1960, p. 5.

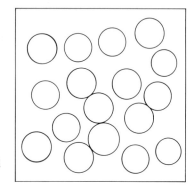

Figure 4-15 Cross section of olefin fiber (typical of polypropylene).

density polyethylene, the softening point is 240°F and the melting point is 255°F. Polypropylene is somewhat higher, softening at 285–330°F and melting at about 325–350°F. The chemical reactions are extremely important.

Both polyethylene and polypropylene fibers have excellent resistance to acids and alkalies but are affected by oxidizing agents. The fibers have good resistance to bleaches and solvents below 150°F. However, they swell and are damaged by chlorinated hydrocarbons. The olefin fibers are flammable. For carpet protection flame-resistant materials are being applied to the backing fibers and fabrics. The sunlight resistance is lower than that of some of the other synthetic fibers but is considered to be somewhat better than that of nylon. There is a tendency for these fibers to creep or gradually to extend under a weight or load applied for a considerable period of time and to permanently compress under a prolonged pressure. This can result in a permanent distortion of the garment or other article. Both fibers and fabrics have a waxy feel, especially the polyethylenes.

MANUFACTURE   The monomer for polyethylene is, of course, ethylene, an unsaturated compound with a double bond, $CH_2=CH_2$. Polypropylene is the next higher number in the homologous family with $CH_3-CH=CH_2$. The polymer formation is one of addition with the saturation of the double bond. The molecular weight sought is usually 20,000 to 25,000, with the pressure and time for the reaction generally determining the extent of this polymerization. The equation for olefins is

$$CH_2=CH_2 + CH_2=CH_2 + CH_2=CH_2 \longrightarrow -CH_2-CH_2-CH_2-CH_2-CH_2-CH_2-$$

ethylene   polyethylene

Both polyethylene and polypropylene polymers are melt-spun, and although they have been used in tubular form and in sheets for many years, the spun fiber is a relatively new product. A special class of dyes have been

Table 4-9   Olefin Fibers

Trade Name/ General Classification	Producer	Type and Special Characteristics*	End-use Areas*
Amco Polyethylene (PE)	American Manufacturing	M (includes split filament)	I
Amco Polypropylene (PP)	American Manufacturing	M (includes split filament)	I
American PE	American Manufacturing	M (includes split filament)	I
American PP	American Manufacturing	M (includes split filament)	I
Autotwine	Indian Head Yarn	Slit (processed)	R
Chadolene	Tennessee Fibers	F (fibrillated)	HI
Diamond	Metlon	M (flat)	AH
DLP 17 PE	Thiokol	M (round, shrunken)	I
DLP 21 PE	Thiokol	M (round)	I
DLP 31 PE	Thiokol	M (ribbon)	AHI
DLP 40 PP	Thiokol	M (round and flat)	HI
DLP 47 PP	Thiokol	M (round and flat)	HI
DLP 50 PP	Thiokol	M (round and flat)	HI
DLP 57 PP	Thiokol	M (round and flat)	HI
DLP 61 PP	Thiokol	M (round, high tension)	I
DLP 67 PP	Thiokol	M (round, high tension)	I
DLP 70 PP	Thiokol	M (ribbon)	I
DLP 77 PP	Thiokol	M (ribbon)	HI
DLP 90 PP	Thiokol	FSTM	AHITC
Durel PP	Celanese	F (slit processed)	H
Fibergrass	Pathogue-Plymouth	F	H
Fabrilawn	Fibron	F (fibrillated)	HI
Fribrilon	Fibron	F (fibrillated)	HI
Goldcres	Shuford Mills	M (flat)	AHI
Herculon	Hercules	F (bulked) FST	AHI
Lo-Pic	Fibron	M (flat)	HI
Lustreloft	Fibron	F (fibrillated)	HI
Marvess	Phillips Fibers	FSTM	AHI
Marvess III	Phillips Fibers	F (BCF modified cross-section high luster, solution-dyed)	H
Marvess CG	Phillips Fibers	S (heavy duty, solution-dyed)	H

Table 4-9   (continued)

Trade Name/ General Classification	Producer	Type and Special Characteristics*	End-use Areas*
Microwarp	Fibron	M (flat)	H
Montrel	Wellington Synthetic Fibers	(low shrinkage)	HI
Olefin	Indian Head Yarn	(slit film, high modulus)	IP
Olefin	Waltrich	M	AHI
Oletex	Poncar Plastic	M	IR
Parapro	Wall Industries	F	H
Polycrest	Uniroyal Fiber and Textile	F (textured dyeable)	H
Polyloom I	Chevron	F (fibrillated)	HI
Polyloom II	Chevron	F (fibrillated)	HI
Polypropylene	Moultrie		I
Polywrap	Indian Head Yarn	Slit processed HM	R
Poncar	Poncar Plastic	M	I
Pro-Tuft	Bemis	P (ribbon)	H
Shurti	Shuford Mills	F (fibrillated)	R
Tufflite	Tuff-Lite	M (round or flat)	HI
TyEZ	Indian Head Yarn	Slit processed H-19	R
Tytite	Indian Head Yarn	Slit processed H-19	R
Unifil	Wall Industries	M	H
Vectra	Enjay Fibers	MFTS	AHI
Voplex	Voplex	M (round or flat) PP and PE	I
Wall PP	Wall Industries	M	I
Waltrich PP	Waltrich	M and ribbon	I
WSF PE	Wellington Synthetic Fibers	M (round HT)	I
WSF PP	Wellington Synthetic Fibers	M (round HT)	I

SOURCE: *Modern Textiles Magazine*, **54**, No. 3 (March 1973), pp. 28–31.
*A — Apparel
 H — Home furnishing and carpets
 I — Industrial fabrics
TC — Tire cord
 R — Twine

Type M — Monofilament
       F — Multifilament
       S — Staple fiber
       T — Tow
       P — Plastics

developed that is dissolved in the melt prior to spinning so that the resultant fiber resembles solution or dope-dyed acetates and other man-made fibers. The color range is limited in order to achieve satisfactory light-fastness. The highest percentage of textile yarn fabrics from the olefins is formed from olefin sheets.

Sheets of polymers are generally referred to as films and can be used to form yarns by cutting them into narrow tapes that may be twisted into yarns and used in carpet backings, bags of various types for foodstuffs, and similar heavy-duty purposes. Some can be twisted into very tight, dense cords for wrapping purposes. A more modern method—and one capable of greater variation in the final yarn and the fabric is fibrillation. This process was pioneered by a German chemist, Heinrich Jacqué, who discovered that polyvinyl chloride films when stretched in one direction tend to become very weak in the other. If the films are then subjected to such mechanical actions as twisting, rubbing, brushing, or other friction-producing treatment, the film edge tends to break into fibers. In the polymer, polypropylene and polyethylene fibers are not bound together by chemical union or forces of energy; thus, they lend themselves to this splitting.

Another force splitting polymer films into fibrillar form is ultrasonic electric energy. These are extremely short waves or energies above the sound level. Fibrillated film yarns are being used extensively as cordage. The first appeared for use as agricultural baling materials in 1964. The shiny, very strong cords used by some merchandising establishments for package wrapping look like glass fiber, but they are often of these fibrillated fibers. Another extensive use of the yarns is in indoor-outdoor carpeting, in which the face yarns are made from the high-polymer film and needled into soft-surface floor coverings for patio or locker room floors, for pool edges, and as artificial turf.

The polymer **Herculon**, made by the Hercules Powder Company, has a high melting point. The polymer containing coloring material and other ingredients is melted and extruded as a film in this molten state. The film is then cooled in cold water, or by casting it onto a cool surface, or, if the film is in tubular shape, it is dried with a blast of air. All these methods are used for producing a solid film. These fibrillated sheets form discontinuous holes, and the mass—which appears to be honeycombed—gives an excellent tough base. Considerable variations in toughness, brittleness, density, uniformity, and other physical factors can be given to this material depending on the afterprocessing and the method of twisting.

In woven and knitted textiles, the olefins are losing some impetus in apparel markets, such as in underwear and hosiery. However, they are in increasing use in automobile upholstery fabrics; outdoor furniture, window screening; webbings for shoes; paddings; and insulators, including electrical insulation. They are being blended with other fibers in suitings and dress goods, and show a great potential for use in carpets and rugs, although some difficulties in cleaning have been encountered. The yarns do not seem to have sufficient resiliency in avoiding traffic lanes; thus, a long-continued compression or a long-continued tension may cause distortion of the fabric. Laboratory technicians use these fabrics extensively in their protective clothing. A unique fabric of olefins is made by the United States Rubber Company under the name **Trilok**, a tight fabric of polyethylene warp with either rayon or cotton in the filling. After this fabric is woven, it can be boiled in finishing, causing a 50 per cent shrinkage in the warp direction of the poly-yarns, thus making the fabric very compact.

Properties of Olefin Fabrics in Use

In 1970, two large producers of olefin fibers in Japan withdrew their polyethylene and polypropylene yarns of apparel denier monofilaments from the market. This tended to put a break on the rapid expansion forecast for the olefins when they were introduced into the market in the early 1960s. Several significant problems appeared regarding their acceptance as suitable apparel fibers: (1) difficulty in dyeing, (2) objectionable static electrical properties, (3) tendency to sag, and other manifestations of poor shape retention, (4) low regain, (5) objectionable oleophylic tendencies (oil staining), (6) flammability, (7) yellowing under ultraviolet light, and (8) a low melting point.

The laundering problem has been a difficult one to solve, and a number of the preceding physical properties all contribute to staining and soiling (for example, the strong electrostatic charge impinging against the fabric and the difficulty in removing it by washing). Then, too, this same static charge causes garments to creep and cling. This charge and a feeling of clamminess in cool, damp weather are a result of the zero moisture regain. The melting point for polyethylene is under 280°F and for polypropylene it is under 380°. These temperatures are low enough to cause some troubles in glazing with the use of an iron that is too hot—the heat effect becomes noticeable at a temperature of approximately 100 and 80°F, respectively, below the true melting point.

The low cost and high strength of olefin fibers led to an original over-optimism, and the temperature effect and creep have both made it impossible to use these fibers for automobile tire cord, for example. One of the early widespread uses of this material was in sand bags, both for military protection purposes and for the use on levees in flood control. These polymers are degraded rapidly by ultraviolet light in sunlight. It is true that there is an ultraviolet light-stabilized polymer in the propropylene group, but this is a higher-priced material.

The olefins can also be formed into stretched tapes and spun-bonded. In these forms, the olefins accounted for about 320 million pounds in 1968 and reached three times that amount in 1973. This application of manufactured fibers has not been included in any of the world figures given in this book because, to a very large extent, the stretch tapes, split yarns, and spun bondeds have all run into the appplications formerly held almost exclusively by manila hemp and other cordage fibers that (inconsistently) have not been included in most statistics on "textile" fibers.

The widening use of these fibers is shown in Table 4–10.

Table 4-10   Consumption of Polypropylene Fibers in
the United States

(millions of pounds per year)

	1968	1971
Continuous multifilament	43	75
Staple	60	55
Synthetic grass		10
Nonwovens	15	35
Monofilament	50	50
Tape	110	100
Total	280	325

SOURCE: *Textile Chemist and Colorist*, **4**, No. 6 (June 1972), p. 30.

ELASTOMERIC FIBERS

The term **elastomer** is applied to fibers that have a true elasticity to some degree; that is, after the fiber or filament is stretched to several times its original length it will return rapidly to its original dimension. One piece of terminology is that these are rubberlike; however, none of them has as rapid a recovery after stress as does natural rubber. **Lastex** yarn is rubber around which a filament thread of silk, nylon, rayon or cotton has been twisted. For many years it was the standard material for garments intended to control body conformation, such as corsets, girdles, elastic hose, and other articles. The ultimate objective toward which all elastomeric fibers are aimed is the elastic nature of natural rubber. Filaments of natural rubber include many of the physical properties of thermoplastic manufactured fibers insofar as exposure to heat and fire are concerned. They also are affected by light and by oxidizing agents. The principal advantage of rubber is its almost instantaneous recovery when tensile stress is removed.

During World War II, there was an immediate need for rubberlike materials because the supply of raw rubber, or latex, was cut off from us in the South Pacific. A crash program on rubber research led to three types that are now defined by the Textile Products Identification Act as "a manufactured fiber in which the fiber-forming substance is comprised of natural or synthetic rubber including the following categories: (1) a manufactured fiber in which the fiber-forming substance is a hydrocarbon, such as natural rubber, polyisoprene, polybutadiene, copolymers of dienes and hydrocarbons, or amorphous (noncrystalline) polyolefins; (2) a manufactured fiber in which the fiber-forming substance is a copolymer of acrylonitrile and a diene (such as butadiene) composed of not more than 50 per cent but at least 10 per cent, by weight of acrylonitrile units[9]

$$(-CH_2-CH-)."$$
$$\qquad\quad |$$
$$\qquad\quad CN$$

The term *lastrile* "can be used as a generic description for fibers falling within category (2); (3) a manufactured fiber in which the fiber-forming substance is a polychloroprene or a copolymer of chloroprene in which at least 35 per cent by weight of the fiber-forming substance is composed of chloroprene units" [10]

$$(-CH_2-C=CH-CH_2)."$$
$$\qquad\quad |$$
$$\qquad\quad Cl$$

These various rubber fibers are customarily wrapped in cotton, silk, rayon, or other fibers for softness, and for an attractive exterior color and hand. The core filaments are heat-sensitive and are damaged both by direct heat and strong detergents and bleach. The manufactured rubbers are more sluggish in their recovery and they lack the degree of extensibility or elasticity of natural rubber. Over a period of time, garments made of these elastomers tend to sag and lose their body-support qualities.

To a considerable extent, lastex has been replaced by a group of fibers known as **spandex** fibers. This generic name refers to "a manufactured fiber in which the fiber-forming substance is a synthetic polymer comprised of at least 85 per cent by weight of a segmented polyurethane." [11] The first of these fibers was du Pont's **Lycra**, originally called Fiber K. In the late 1950s, it found rapid acceptance in foundation garments and in elasticized materials connected with wearing apparel.

Lycra Formula

The equation for the polyurethane fiber, Lycra, is

$$(HO-R-OH)_n \ - \ (O=C=N-R-N=C=O)_n$$

glycol   di-isocyanate

$$(-C-N-R-N-C-O-R-O-)_n$$
$$\quad ||\ \ |\qquad\ |\ \ ||$$
$$\quad O\ \ H\qquad H\ \ O$$

---

[9] Federal Trade Commission Rules and Regulations under the Textile Fiber Products Identification Act, effective March 4, 1960, p. 5.

[10] Ibid.

[11] Ibid.

The molecular chain of this polyurethane has been created with alternating hard and soft sections. Within the soft sections, the molecular chains lie in a completely tangled state, but when stress is applied they orient themselves to lie parallel and close to each other. The hard section, at the same time, provides a permanence of structural form and seems to tie the chains together. When the stress is relaxed, the individual molecular chains go back to their tangled states.

The cross section of Lycra spandex fiber is a dog bone in shape. Individual fibers can be detected in Figure 4–16, which shows that the indi-

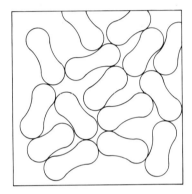

Figure 4-16 Cross section of Lycra fiber showing large adhering filaments.

vidual filaments tend to coalesce into an irregular mass with each separate fiber appearing to be closely connected to its neighbors. It is interesting to note that the polyurethane foams discussed earlier are essentially the same chemically as the spandex fibers. However, in this case, instead of being extruded as a fiber, quantities of air are sprayed into the mass in the kettle and it is run out into a form of a bun or loaf. At that time it cures, or sets, quickly into the foam structure. Thinner sheets of this same polyurethane are used in multilayer fabrics and as a foamlike lining in wearing apparel.

PROPERTIES OF SPANDEX FIBERS The tenacity of spandex fibers is usually 0.6 to 0.8 gpd. However, the elongation at the break is from 500 to as much as 700 per cent for these filaments. The moisture regain is low, 0.3 per cent for most of them, but Lycra is 1.3 per cent. The spandex fibers are light in weight, with a specific gravity of about 1.25. This lightness in weight and the fact that the spandex fibers do not have to be covered (although they may be) provides a lightweight, comfortable garment. The cross-sectional shapes are irregular; **Lycra** and **Spandelle** have a dog-bone shape whereas **Glospun** is very irregular and lobal. **Vyrene** is larger in diameter than any of the other spandex fibers and is produced only in monofilament; it is almost round in cross section.

The properties suggest that spandex can be used in surgical stockings, girdles, elastic belts, elasticized waistbands, hosiery tops, and as a stretching component in athletic and sports wear. These fibers can be ironed, but it is well to use a low heat. Vyrene is the most heat-sensitive of these fibers.

By definition, spandex yarns are elastic—that is, they are elastomers and retract or recover after stretching, giving a positive support to the body of the wearer when used in girdles, elastic belts, elasticized hose, and other apparel. In many of their uses, they will overlap the so-called stretch yarns, which give with the body but do not exert any positive support. Examples of this, of course, are Ban-lon nylon, Helanca nylon, and other stretchy yarns. A new application of spandex yarn is in the corner inserts of contour sheets; the yarns permit a tight, snug fit. Similar uses, of course, are in table covers, in slip covers for furniture, and in dust-protective textile devices. In wearing apparel the yarns appear in swim wear, antigravity suits for astronauts, outer wear, dresswear, and hosiery. Much attention will be given these rather miraculous fibers. It is forecast that they will be used extensively in football pants, in golf-ball windings, and as protective fabrics for swimming pools and outdoor furniture.

These spandex yarns may be covered, as is customary in the case of lastex, or used without winding. Sheerer and more lightweight batistes, satins, and laces are possible with Vyrene as a result of the process developed by the United States Rubber Company for a single cover on their spandex yarn—as compared with the double cover customary on Lycra, and other elastomers. Few articles are made of 100 per cent spandex yarn, and any percentage figure refers to the percentage of spandex in the portion of the garment in which it occurs.

One of the newest of the spandex fibers is **Numa**, made by the American Cyanamid Company. It is claimed that this spandex fiber has superior whiteness, both initially and after exposure to bleach or sunlight. The elongation is rated at about 550 per cent. The specific gravity is 1.2. The tenacity is

Table 4-11   Spandex Fibers

Trade Name/ General Classification	Producer	Type and Special Characteristics*	End-use Areas*
Glospan/Cleerspun Spandex	Globe	F ( )	AHI
Lycra Spandex	du Pont	F	A
Numa Spandex	Aneclistex	F (fused)	AHI
Unul Spandex	Union Carbide	F	A

SOURCE: *Modern Textiles Magazine*, **54**, No. 3 (March 1973), pp. 28–32.
*A — Apparel   Type   F — Multifilament
  H — Home furnishings and carpets
  I — Industrial fabrics

relatively high—that is, 0.8 gpd. Like other spandex fibers, it is somewhat difficult to dye, but it makes an excellent core for covered yarns. In cross section, it appears to be a complex of fused multifilament fibers resembling a bead necklace lying on a table in a tangled state with each bead being made up of a mass of monofilament ends. Like the other spandexes, it is finding wide use in women's intimate apparel, dresses, skirts, sports blouses, fabric shoes, suiting materials for men and women, slacks and sport coats, sport shirts, ties, and pajamas. Numa is also being used for outer wear, infants' wear, and swim wear.

Anidex Fibers

Anidex fibers are defined as "a manufactured fiber in which the fiber-forming substance is any long-chain, synthetic polymer composed of at least 50 per cent by weight of one or more esters of a monohydric alcohol and acrylic acid, $CH_2{=}CH{-}COOH$." [12]

Anim/8, made by the Rohm and Haas Company, is the first of the fibers in this new category. A major feature is its color-fastness to chlorine bleach and to repeated washings and dry cleanings; the excellent elasticity of this new elastomer is not affected by these treatments.

The fiber shows excellent elastomeric properties and can be used either bare or in covered yarns. Initial experiments indicate that it makes a good core filament and can be applied with other fibers. Among the covering yarns used thus far are cotton, acetate, nylon and polyester. Anim/8 has resistance to acids and, although it is slightly stiffened and discolored by 2 per cent NaOH (alkali), stronger solutions do not appear to have any ill effect. It will probably be used most widely as a blending filament in stretch-type apparel and in home furnishings.

MISCELLANEOUS MANUFACTURED FIBERS

Saran

The fiber whose generic and proprietary name is saran is defined as "any long-chain synthetic polymer composed of at least 80 per cent of vinylidene chloride units $({-}CH_2{-}CCl_2{-})$." [13] This polymer was extruded as a heavy

[12] Federal Trade Commission Rules and Regulations under the Textile Fiber Products Identification Act, effective March 4, 1960; added to the list of generic fibers after the original regulations were published.
[13] Federal Trade Commission Rules and Regulations under the Textile Fiber Products Identification Act, effective March 4, 1960, p. 5.

monofilament nearly 25 years ago and was early appreciated for its extreme durability and its resistance to weather. Ultraviolet light from the sun darkens saran. It was a product of the Dow Chemical Company in about 1940. Other sarans, as they have been classified since the passage of the Fiber Identification law, are **Velon**, a product of Firestone Rubber Company; **Lus-Trus**, made by Southern Lus-Trus Corporation; **Saran** of Enjay Fibers and Laminates, Inc.; the British fiber **Tygan**; and lesser-known saran-type materials made in France and Japan. The polymer has been important to the homemaker in the form of a clear, strong, durable, and self-sealing film known as **Saran Wrap**. Chemical modifications and changes in the production method through the years have enabled the Dow Chemical Company to produce a filament of increasing fineness suitable for staple yarns in rugs and carpets. However, the fibers are still somewhat stiff and wiry, even in finer deniers, and sarans have not made much of an impact in the apparel field. The monofilaments made by Dow Badische Company have been given the tradename **Rovana**. They have a unique cross section called microtape, which is formed by folding the thin slit film into a continuous strand.

FIBER PROPERTIES   Saran monofilaments, being melt-spun, are round in cross section. They have a heavier denier than other synthetic fibers. The tenacity is 1.2 to 2.3 gpd, lower than that of most other manufactured fibers; but being coarser, the strength is adequate for most consumer use. It is also stiffer and more wiry and has a lower elongation to the break, the value being somewhere between 15 and 30 per cent. The specific gravity is greater than that of other synthetics, ranging from a little over 1 to as much as 1.75. It is virtually nonmoisture-adsorbent. Sarans have a high abrasion resistance and withstand weather and sunlight well. Another objection to saran is in wearing apparel—or, in fact, in any textile use requiring ironing. The safe limit is 150°F. It softens around 320°F, and the sticking temperature is close to the boiling point of water, 210–220°F. The melting point is 340–350°F. Saran is generally pigmented during the manufacture, and therefore is a dope-dyed product. A most important property is its unusual fire resistance, as one might assume from the chemical nature of the product—that is, from its chlorine content. It also has good resistance to acids, alkalis, and to most solvents.

USES   Saran monofilament fabrics are used for upholstery in automobiles, both in the original seat covering and in replaceable seat covers. Heavy-denier monofilaments are used for porch and garden furniture webbing; artificial rattan; plastic window screens; and for heavy-duty covers for furniture in public transportation vehicles, stores, restaurants, and hotels. Saran has appeared in shoes and hats; has been twisted into ribbons and braids for belts and webbings; and has been used for woven wall coverings.

MANUFACTURE   The following equation shows the chemical structure of saran assuming copolymerization with vinyl chloride units.

$$CH_2=CCl_2 + CH_2=CHCl + CH_2=CCl_2 \longrightarrow -CH_2-CCl_2-CH_2-CHCl-CH_2-CCl_2-$$

The polymerization can be accelerated by a wide variety of catalysts, and it will be noted that the addition of one monomer to another results in saturating the compound—that is, removing the double bond—creates a single bond between the adjacent carbons in the monomer. It is evident that any other vinyl product can be used in varying concentrations up to the allowable 20 per cent maximum. Thus, vinyl chloride, $CH_2=CHCl$, or acrylonitrile, $CH_2=CHCN$, can be introduced into the chain. Polymerization is carried out in an autoclave under heat and pressure, and the molten polymer is extruded at a temperature of about 350°F, solidifying immediately upon extrusion. The usual cross section is round, but with the rather heavy deniers spinnerets of other shapes, elliptical or almost ribbonlike, can be used. It is common to cold stretch these filaments in order to give added strength and a higher degree of orientation.

Vinyon

Vinyon fibers are made by three manufacturers in the United States at the present time: **Avisco** vinyon is made by the American Viscose Division of FMC Corporation; **Voplex** vinyon is made by the Vogt Manufacturing Corporation; and **45** is made by the Polyarns Corporation. Vinyon is a copolymer of two or more derivatives of vinyl alcohol. For example, one type is made of vinyl chloride and vinyl acetate. Moisture regain under standard conditions is virtually zero. In boiling water, the filaments or fibers shrink about 60 per cent.

Vinyon is defined by the FTC as "a manufactured fiber in which the fiber-forming substance is any long-chain synthetic polymer composed of at least 85 per cent by weight of vinyl chloride units ($-CH_2-CHCl-$)." [14] The filaments are of rounded cross sections and show little evidence of crystallinity in their molecular structure. The fiber has good resistance to sunlight and to most acids and alkalies. However, exposure to elevated temperatures shows disadvantages in consumer use. It cannot be ironed at temperatures over 130°F, because it softens at as low a temperature as 170°F, becomes slightly sticky at 150°F, and melts at 260°F.

Vinyon also has a pronounced static electrical capacity. The material

[14] Federal Trade Commission Rules and Regulations under the Textile Fiber Products Identification Act, effective March 4, 1960, p. 5.

can be used as a binder to seal together layers of other fibers or fabrics and to apply felts to the base of articles. It finds some application as a binding fiber in papers and nonwoven textiles. Small amounts of vinyon staple fiber in rugs and carpets produce a three-dimensional or molded surface effect as the result of the action of hot water or dry heat on the carpet fabric. These conditions produce a shrinking in the vinyon.

Vinal Fibers

Vinal is defined by the Federal Trade Commission as "a manufactured fiber in which the fiber-forming substance is any long-chain synthetic polymer composed of at least 50 per cent by weight of vinyl alcohol units ($-CH_2-$ CHOH$-$), and in which the total of the vinyl alcohol units and any one or more of the various acetal units is at least 85 per cent by weight of the fiber." [15]

The Air Reduction Chemical Company is the only one producing this fiber on a commercial basis. There are two brand names: **Vinylon** and **Airco Vinal**. It is a strong fiber with excellent resistance to abrasion. This material is being used in rain wear and in bathing suits. It is wool-like in feel and texture when spun on the woolen system. Its moisture absorbency is somewhat higher than the other hydrophobic fibers, approximately 5 per cent. The fabric has a tendency to wrinkle badly in use, and this has limited its application in wearing apparel. Another shortcoming is that ironing at a temperature as low as 250°F will cause damage to the surface. Kuralon is a vinal fiber imported from Japan.

Tetrafluoroethylene Fiber

TEFLON FLUOROCARBON   Teflon fluorocarbon fiber is a fiber formed of long-chain carbon molecules with all available bonds saturated with fluorine. Thus, it is vastly different from the other synthetic fibers. A product of the E. I. du Pont de Nemours & Co., it is used only in industrial fabrics and therefore does not come under the Textile Fiber Products Identification Act. The basic raw materials are fluorspar (CaF_2) and chloroform. The fiber is very heavy; its specific gravity is 2.3. The tenacities are about 1.7, both wet and dry. Teflon has no moisture regain whatever, even at the boiling point. It has a phenomenal resistance to chemicals and to other natural agents causing destruction. It is widely used for felts and woven fabrics for use in gaskets, filtration media, pump packing, and electrical tapes and can be used at temperatures up to 570°F.

[15] Federal Trade Commission Rules and Regulations under the Textile Fiber Products Identification Act, effective March 4, 1960, p. 5.

NYTRIL FIBERS **Darvan** was a trade mark of the Goodrich Rubber Company but eventually was licensed to two companies in Germany under the joint ownership of the Celanese Corporation of America and a German textile producer. It is wool-like in many of its properties—such as handle, resiliency, softness, and other esthetic features—therefore, it was felt that its commercial development might be more rapid in Europe than in the United States.

According to the Textile Fiber Products Identification Act, a nytril is "a manufactured fiber containing at least 85 per cent of a long-chain polymer of vinylidene dinitrile ($—CH_2—C(CN)_2—$), where the vinylidene dinitrile content is no less than every other unit in the polymer chain." [16] It is approximately a 50:50 polymer of vinylidene dinitrile and vinyl acetate and is spun into a coagulating water bath, after which the filaments are heat stretched and drawn. The principal use of nytril thus far has been in staple, usually with a crimp for superior blending properties with other fibers or wool-like textured fabrics. Its specific gravity is 1.18 and it has 30 per cent elongation. It has good resiliency and wrinkle resistance. It burns readily, and the regain is 2 to 3 per cent. There seems to be some question as to whether or not it will reach the apparel market because of other competition.

SOURCE **Source** is a unique type of combined fiber, because two dissimilar generic fibers are spun together. It is a **biconstituent** fiber. In Source, a trademark fiber of Allied Chemical Corporation, the constituents are 70 per cent polyamide and 30 per cent polyester, although the portions may be varied greatly. Reference has been made on p. 137 to the bicomponent nylon fiber, Cantrece, in which two different nylons are spun simultaneously. The importance of this discovery is that a wide variety of combined fibers are possible with great differences in their physical and chemical properties. An ultramicroscopic examination of the cross section of this fiber shows the center or matrix to be polyamide, or nylon, surrounded by fibrils of the polyester. No hard-and-fast values can be assigned to any of the physical properties because of wide variations that depend on the constituents. Source is dyed like nylon, but it is said to have a more satiny and less metallic shine, probably due to the effect of the exterior fibrils of the polyester constituent. Its useful features are the resilience and high rating for abrasion resistance that are found in most other nylon matrix fibers. Its use, therefore, in carpets and upholstery fabrics should be almost limitless, provided that the price is satisfactory.

Another term used to describe these fibers is **conjugated**. Generally, the term **bicomponent** is applied where both fiber components are of the same generic family, as in Cantrece. Orlon Sayelle (p. 140) and Fiber E rayon

[16] Federal Trade Commission Rules and Regulations under the Textile Fiber Products Identification Act, effective March 4, 1960, p. 5.

(p. 179) are other examples of bicomponents. Biconstituents, on the other hand, are of different generic origins, as is Source.

STATUS OF MANUFACTURED FIBERS

Inferences are that the 1973 output of man-made fibers was about 24.8 billion pounds, a gain of more than 13 per cent as compared with 1972. Of this total, approximately 3.01 billion pounds were rayon and acetate yarn and 5.07 billion pounds were staple, giving a total of 8 billion pounds for the cellulosic fibers (Figure 4–17). Noncellulosics are estimated to have totaled

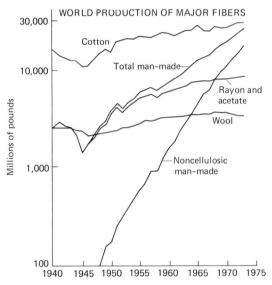

Figure 4-17   World production of major fibers as of 1973. (*Textile Organon,* June 1965 and 1974).

8.4 billion pounds of yarns and 8.3 billion pounds of staple for an output of 16.7 billion pounds. Thus, the synthetic fibers have outgrown the cellulosics. Not included in the cellulosics total, however, was the acetate cigarette-filter tow production that is expected to have totaled about 460 million pounds.

With the man-made fibers accounting for a little more than 50 per cent of the fiber consumption in the United States in 1969 (Figure 4–18), and assuming that there will be no great increase in the production of the natural fibers—cotton and wool—various textile marketing experts have projected continued fiber consumption to 1980 and some even to the year 2000. Even some of the more conservative estimates are that in 1980, 75 per cent of the textile-fiber consumption in the United States will be man-made. For 1975, the Textile Economics Bureau's estimates of the world's production capac-

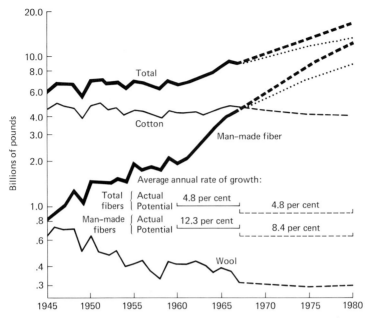

Figure 4-18 United States mill consumption of fibers, 1945–1968 and projections to 1980. (Courtesy of J. C. Pearson, Celanese Corporation of America)

ity of fibers will be 34 billion pounds annually for man-made fibers. The production capacity in man-made fibers is well above the present consumption. In Tables 4–12 and 4–13 world production of the major fiber-producing countries is shown.

In addition to the generic groups discussed, there are a few fibers still uncategorized by the Federal Trade Commission. For the most part these represent research explorations by a single company as indicated in Table 4–14.

The uses of these polymers appear to be highly specialized and limited in scope. Generally, their cost and special properties would make them appropriate for industrial applications.

The great growth in the world production of synthetic fibers has been demonstrated in Figure 4–17: In 1950 there was a total production of 1.39 million pounds, of which nylon accounted for 80 per cent; acrylics, 5 per cent; and others, 15 per cent. With the introduction of many additional fibers in these groupings, and the expansion of the polyesters, the 1973 figure shows the total of 18.2 billion pounds, with nylon accounting for 33 per cent; polyester, 38 per cent; acrylics, 19 per cent; and others 10 per cent. It is interesting to note that even today the category of "other fibers" is comparatively insignificant in the over-all market of synthetic fibers. This other category includes such fiber generic groups as olefin, vinal, azlon, spandex and elastomeric, alginate, saran, vinyon, and fluorocarbon. To some

Table 4-12   Major Fiber-producing Countries and Their 1973 Production
(in millions of pounds)

Country	Rayon/Acetate	Noncellulosic (except olefin)	Total	Per Cent of World Total
United States	1357	5823	7180	29.0
Japan	1128	2748	3876	15.6
West Germany	333	1779	2112	8.5
USSR	1197	633	1830	7.4
United Kingdom	582	1001	1583	6.4
Italy and Malta	356	724	1080	4.4
France	298	592	890	3.6
East Germany	371	159	530	2.1
Belgium, Netherlands, and Luxembourg	164	360	524	2.1
Spain	149	288	437	1.8
Taiwan	111	282	393	1.6
Poland	210	178	388	1.6
Brazil	130	227	357	1.4
India	265	57	322	1.3
Canada	95	218	313	1.3
Mexico	79	216	295	1.2
Austria	221	35	256	1.0
Romania	141	115	256	1.0
Korea, Republic of	17	233	250	1.0
Czechoslovakia	145	90	235	0.9
Yugoslavia	149	39	188	0.8
Switzerland	14	163	177	0.7
China, Mainland	121	43	164	0.7
Argentina	39	102	141	0.6

SOURCE: *Textile Organon*, **45**, No. 6 (June 1974), pp. 72–73, 76–77.

Table 4-13 The Changing Fiber Picture—World Production

(millions of pounds and per cents)

| | Man-made Fibers | | | | | | | | Natural Fibers | | | | | | | |
| | Rayon + Acetate | | | Noncellulosic (except olefin) | | | Total | | Raw Cotton | | Raw Wool | | Raw Silk | | Grand Total | |
Year	Yarn	Staple	Total	Yarn	Staple	Total										
1966	3,030	4,334	7,364	2,815	2,412	5,227	12,591	32	23,849	59	3,424	9	72	—	39,936	100
1967	2,968	4,329	7,297	3,147	2,866	6,013	13,310	33	23,565	58	3,470	9	75	—	40,420	100
1968	3,133	4,647	7,780	4,038	3,851	7,889	15,669	35	26,050	57	3,571	8	82	—	45,372	100
1969	3,142	4,694	7,836	4,673	4,534	9,207	17,043	37	25,057	55	3,543	8	86	—	45,729	100
1970	3,067	4,498	7,565	5,206	5,145	10,351	17,916	38	25,060	54	3,508	8	90	—	46,574	100
1971	3,084	4,530	7,614	6,297	6,034	12,331	19,945	39	27,363	54	3,430	7	88	—	50,826	100
1972	2,961	4,872	7,833	7,068	6,922	13,990	21,823	41	28,508	53	3,250	6	88	—	53,669	100
1973	3,012	5,071	8,083	8,378	8,309	16,687	24,770	44	28,649	50	3,228	6	87	—	56,734	100

SOURCE: *Textile Organon*, **45**, No. 6 (June 1974), p. 65.

extent the listing of fiber productions in terms of pounds of fiber can be deceiving. The weights of the synthetic fibers when expressed as specific gravity are much lower than those of the natural fibers. Therefore, equivalent yarn diameter and fabric covering power are provided by less weight of fiber—the synthetics actually go farther per pound. Thus, in nylon tire cord, 1 pound of fiber replaces almost 2 pounds of cotton; 1 pound of acrylic

Table 4-14   Uncategorized Fibers

Fiber	Company
Algil (polyacrylonitrile/styrene)	Polymers
Basic (carbon)	Basic Carbon
Bristrand (polyvinyl chloride/acetate)	Polymers
Fiber Frax (alumina-silica ceramic)	Carborundum
National (carbon)	Union Carbide
Polyfiber (polystyrene)	Dow Corning
Shalon (polystyrene)	Polymers
Teflon (polytetrafluoroethylene)	du Pont
Tipersul (fibrous potassium titanate)	du Pont

staple, knitting yarn, can replace nearly 1½ pounds of wool according to W. H. Poisson.[17] Since 1945 the volume of the world production of synthetic fiber has been increasing at an average rate of 23 per cent (see Figure 4–17). The significance of this development upon our chemical industry is impressive; it is estimated that this industry consumes daily between 20,000 and 25,000 tons of chemicals and monomers. Manufacturers are deeply concerned with the ever-increasing problems of pollution, especially of air and water, as refuse passes into the atmosphere and streams at an increasing rate.

MAN-MADE FIBER IMPORTS AND EXPORTS

In Table 4–15 the United States imports and exports of man-made fibers and products are given in various categories. In seven of the last ten years, our imports have exceeded our exports, thus producing a negative balance of trade. However, in 1973, exports of man-made fiber and products surpassed imports, resulting in a positive export balance. This has been a welcome change to textile manufacturers. Over the last five years the United States has exported an average of 9 per cent of its production of man-made fiber and products. Imports for the same period have averaged about 12 per cent.

[17] W. H. Poisson, *American Dyestuff Reporter*, **58**, No. 4 (April 1970), pp. 40–47, 66.

Table 4-15   United States Imports and Exports of Man-Made Fiber and Products
(millions of pounds)

Year	Fibers and Yarns		Fabrics		Apparel		Total		Export Balance
	Imports	Exports	Imports	Exports	Imports	Exports	Imports	Exports	
1964	159.2	162.1	20.7	56.4	28.1	58.5	208.0	277.0	69.0
1965	159.3	128.1	34.9	80.8	44.1	55.1	238.3	264.0	25.7
1966	212.6	150.0	55.5	85.5	66.7	61.9	334.8	297.4	− 37.4
1967	196.2	168.9	49.1	86.4	88.5	52.4	333.8	307.7	− 26.1
1968	293.2	222.7	65.9	85.1	106.5	43.9	465.6	351.7	−113.9
1969	215.4	261.5	77.7	95.1	179.8	51.1	472.9	407.7	− 65.2
1970	285.0	313.5	105.8	96.2	223.5	50.9	614.3	460.6	−153.7
1971	451.2	333.7	153.2	89.5	297.9	57.2	902.3	480.4	−421.9
1972	439.3	384.1	151.5	103.3	329.0	74.3	919.8	561.7	−358.1
1973	367.5	652.0	138.3	167.7	324.6	118.5	830.4	938.2	107.8

SOURCE: *Textile Organon.*

Table 4-16 *United States Imports of Man-made Fiber and Products from Major Sources*

(per cent of total imports)

Country	1969	1970	1971	1972	1973
			Fibers and Yarns		
West Germany	27.2	36.6	28.2	30.1	28.8
Japan	17.0	15.4	23.7	17.1	16.1
United Kingdom	16.7	12.8	15.1	15.1	13.8
Italy	8.2	5.8	5.6	6.0	7.5
France	8.2	6.8	3.7	5.8	6.1
Canada	4.1	4.3	5.0	4.7	6.8
Total	81.4	78.7	81.3	78.7	74.1
			Woven Fabrics		
Japan	72.5	72.5	50.2	47.1	48.9
Belgium	4.0	3.0	13.7	13.2	12.9
Canada	1.5	1.3	7.3	12.2	11.3
Italy	3.5	4.5	5.5	5.0	7.7
France	2.4	2.4	1.7	1.7	2.7
Total	83.9	83.7	78.4	79.2	83.5

Table 4-16 (continued)

Knit Fabrics

Japan	42.4	46.3	39.5	31.7	32.2
United Kingdom	13.7	22.0	19.9	21.2	22.2
West Germany	5.6	6.8	16.5	12.8	10.9
Ireland	14.8	5.5	2.3	4.9	10.1
Israel	1.0	3.6	5.9	6.4	8.0
Total	77.5	84.2	84.1	77.0	83.4

Apparel

Taiwan	23.1	27.0	33.5	28.0	24.4
Korea, Republic of	22.2	21.0	22.4	23.0	19.1
Hong Kong	15.5	16.4	15.5	14.6	12.0
Japan	25.5	21.7	16.7	14.8	11.3
Total	86.3	86.1	88.1	80.4	66.8

SOURCE: Calculated from data in *Textile Organon*, 45, No. 4 (April 1974) p. 44.

Table 4–16 shows the major countries that serve as import sources for man-made fiber and products. It can be seen that, in 1973, six countries furnished about three-quarters of the fibers and yarns imported by the United States. West Germany, Japan, and the United Kingdom have been the major sources for the past five years. Japan has been our major supplier of imported, woven, man-made fiber fabrics for several years, but Belgium and Canada are becoming more important suppliers. High proportions of knit fabrics of man-made fibers have also been imported from Japan and the United Kingdom. However, several other countries are beginning to contribute significant amounts.

Imports of apparel products of man-made fibers have mostly come from four Asian countries. Japan was the largest supplier in 1969, but, since that time, Taiwan has become the largest. Lower labor costs in the Asian countries have contributed to their good competitive position in supplying apparel products in the lower price ranges. Increasing costs for labor and raw materials in the Asian countries are beginning to narrow the gap.

THE SEARCH FOR NEW POLYMERS

Financially successful new fibers and fabrics do not just happen. Their introduction into the trade and their ultimate acceptance by the public must be gauged in advance through a number of research operations. It is not enough to have a new polymer capable of fiber formation unless it can be produced economically and for numerous end-use applications. The ability of a new product to satisfy consumer wants or needs must be gauged by a research study of available materials and their possible shortcomings compared with the properties of the new product. Sometimes a need will be clearly indicated from the preliminary study of the service performances of available products. Then they can be compared with consumer requirements for specific uses and the degree of lasting satisfaction shown by these materials can be evaluated as demonstrated in trends in consumer-use changes and in the clear-cut interest of the public in the product by repeated buying. At other times, it may be clearly indicated that there is no available fiber or fabric ideally suited for some new climatic environment or wear exposure, in which case a potential market for the new product can be anticipated. Does this new fiber seem to fulfill its purpose, or with further research and development will it promise a better material or one that will be improved by special finishing?

Research into Consumer Acceptance of New Fibers

Research is systematic investigation conducted for the purpose of discovering new facts. Practitioners of the science customarily accent the second syllable. The public at large, more generally, accents the first. If one wishes to be exact insofar as the techniques of investigation are concerned, each pronunciation is applicable to different general procedures. It is re*search* of the unknown that is generally carried out by scientists; at some point of the development of any new product, *re*search is also needed, for this is the *re*search or the review and more thorough study of everything that has previously been done in a particular field (including a study of patents and other technical details) that might interfere with the completion of the new product.

For a new fiber to find its significant place in the market and to become economically profitable, still other kinds of research are called for. There is an old saying, "Build a better mousetrap and the world will find a way to your door." This is not true in a technological society; now a better mousetrap or a better fiber must go more than halfway to meet its customers. Having researched and produced a textile fiber, there remain several further research procedures before the fiber can be introduced into the market:

1. Physical and chemical properties of the fiber.
2. Unique points of advantage or disadvantage to the fiber in use.
3. End-use possibilities as suggested by the properties.
4. Cost of production.
5. Hazards and cost involved to avoid polluting the environment.

Market Research Procedures—Problem of Distribution

1. Survey the market capacity in the end-use applications suggested by the properties of the fiber.
2. Study the competition in similar fibers.
3. Discover the potential size of the market.
4. Examine the profit potential in the several suggested markets.
5. Study the potential value of a test-market procedure and sales methods.

Consumer Research—Problem of Acceptance

1. Study the price structure within the selected market.
2. Study the potential size of the market.
3. Discover the type of sales appeal and the stores best suited to this product.
4. Study the properties wanted by consumers.
5. Know the age and income brackets of principal consumers.

Advertising—Problems of Sales Promotion

The most experienced commercial media seek the general sales promotion plan best suited to the selected end-use items, utilizing any particular advantages possessed by a new fiber, and selecting the most appropriate advertising messages for the market.

A company with an aggressive policy will constantly look for other end-use applications for a fiber and will study its compatibility with other materials, possibly in blends, in which the advantages of each component will be utilized further. It has been interesting to note through the development of the man-made fibers how many different approaches have been made in initial promotion efforts. Very early in a promotion, a company must decide whether the fiber is to be identified with a proprietary name or sold under its generic family classification. Once the end-use items have become fairly well established in the market, it is time for aggressive programs on labeling and consumer information to demonstrate the position in the market that this fiber holds and the reasons for its influence. At all times any peculiar properties that may enhance or limit its acceptance by the consumer should be disclosed. This is particularly true in the servicing of the end-use product —that is, should the clothing item be washed and, if so, under what conditions? Is it necessary that it be dry-cleaned?

The production of good fibers is becoming increasingly costly and a new product will have long-established competition filling many existing needs satisfactorily.

CHAPTER **FIVE**

Yarns: The Bones and Sinews of Textiles

YARN STRUCTURE

The official definition of a yarn was agreed upon by a committee on textile materials of ASTM; a yarn is "a generic term for the continuous strand of textile fiber filaments or material in a form suitable for knitting, weaving, or otherwise intertwining to form a textile fabric." [1] Yarns occur in the following forms:

1. A number of short fibers twisted together to form a staple yarn.
2. A number of long filaments laid together without twist (O-twist yarn).
3. A number of filaments laid together with more or less twist.
4. A single filament with or without twist (a monofilament).
5. A strip of material such as paper, cellophane, or metal foil with or without twist.

In order better to understand the properties of yarns and the fabrics made from them, a brief de-

[1] *Standard Definitions of Terms Relating to Textile Materials* (1967), ASTM.

191

scription will be given as to the methods by which the more important groups of fibers are formed into yarns. This will explain why some of the physical properties characteristic of the fibers tend to lose their identities in the fabrics and garments made from them. The chemical properties, on the other hand, might be expected to persist regardless of the physical form in which the fiber is found in a garment or in woven furniture coverings.

Formation of Cotton Yarns

Spinning cotton yarn includes all the processing required to prepare and clean the fibers from the time the bale is opened to the twisting of the yarn in its preparation for the textile loom as a warp yarn or as a filling or weft.

    1. *Opening and blending.*   Cotton fibers of similar grade from a number of bales of ginned cotton are placed in a machine called a blending feeder in which the masses are loosened and thoroughly mixed.

    2. *Picking and breaking.*   A series of machines that thoroughly fluff

Figure 5-1 Cotton halfway through the breaker picker. The conical fingers, together with air circulation, open and clean the fibers. (Courtesy of Pepperell Manufacturing Company)

these masses of cotton fibers cause remaining impurities, such as dirt, seed, shells, leaves, and stems, to fall out; the cotton emerges from these machines as a loose, formless roll called a lap or picker lap. (See Figure 5–1.)

3. *Carding.* The picker lap, in the form of a loose roll, is unrolled and drawn onto a revolving cylinder that is covered with fine hooks or wire bristles to pull the fibers in one direction and separate any that are entangled. The cotton then emerges as a thin film that is then drawn into a funnel-shaped opening from which it emerges as a ropelike strand called the sliver. It is the **sliver** that is further narrowed and twisted to form the coarser-grade cotton fabrics.

4. *Combing.* The comb is a more refined form of card, producing a more parallel mass of cotton fibers; in this machine, the shorter fibers that may be present generally fall out. These are referred to as the **noils** and may amount to as much as 13 per cent of the fiber content. The remaining long fibers are then combed into a comb sliver.

5. *Drawing.* The drawing operation blends the slivers from either the comb or card by working several slivers together and pulling them out on what is called the drawing frame. The **drawing frame** reduces the numerous

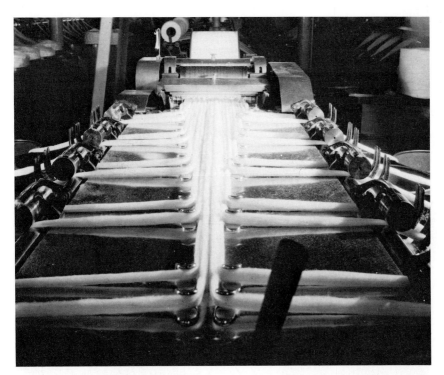

Figure 5-2 Twenty large cotton threads emerge from cans and are gathered into the doubling machine at the rear to be combined into a wide blanket. (Courtesy of Pepperell Manufacturing Company)

slivers to a single one of about the same diameter as the individual components.

6. *Roving.* The combined sliver is taken to the **slubber**, the first of several machines called roving frames. Here the cotton is given a very slight twist, which causes the strand to become longer and finer. For coarse yarns, only one slubber is used; but for fine yarns, three or more are used (Figures 5–2 and 5–3). These finer strands are referred to as roving.

7. *Spinning.* Spinning is a continuation of roving; on the spinning frame many spools containing rovings pass through the ring-spinning mechanism, which further draws and twists the cotton into a yarn of the required size and twist. On this machine, the cotton is wound onto bobbins preparatory to the weaving operation (Figure 5–4).

Classification of Cotton Yarns

The **classification** of yarns is based on thickness; another way of expressing it would be in terms of relative fineness. By this method, numbers are assigned to express the fineness of the yarn, the number being the number of

Figure 5-3 Cotton roving. (Courtesy of Pepperell Manufacturing Company)

Figure 5-4 Film of fibers shaved off the roll and then gathered into a large roving to the left. (Courtesy of Pepperell Manufacturing Company)

hanks or strands of cotton, 840 yards long, required to weigh 1 pound; thus, if one had an 840-yard hank of yarn, which weighed 1 pound, one would call this a number 1 or a 1's cotton. Five's cotton would be one-fifth the diameter or thickness of 1's, because it would take five of these hanks, or a total of 4200 yards to weigh 1 pound. One of the most widely used grades or classes of cotton yarns is the 30's, which indicates 25,200 yards to the pound. If these are single yarns, the designations for 5's, 10's, or 30's are, respectively, 5/1, 10/1, and 30/1. If these were two-ply yarns of the same size, the number of the ply would appear below the slanting line: 5/2, 20/2, 30/2. In the case of ply yarns, however, the size or classification depends on the number of plies as well as on the fineness of the individual yarns making up the ply. For example, if two 10's single yarns are twisted to form a two-ply yarn, it would be described as 10/2; however, in total diameter, it would be equivalent in size to a 5/1 yarn, because each of the 10's single would weigh 1 pound for 10 hanks; combining these doubles the weight of the yarn to the equivalent size of a single 5's, or 5/1 (Figures 5–5 and 5–6).

***Figure* 5-5** A section of rope, or tow, in the process of becoming staple from man-made textile fiber. Each tiny thread is a length of continuous multifilament yarn, each thread being made up of many filaments. (Courtesy of E. I. du Pont de Nemours & Co.)

Cotton Spinning Methods

Several types of spinning frames are used under the **cotton system**. In any case, a fine roving, or loose plait, of cotton is made into a satisfactory yarn for weaving. Generally, the minimum practical length for cotton fiber to spin into a satisfactory yarn is ⅞ - to about 1½ inches.

The **American system** is a modified cotton system frame that has been developed to use heavier weights and larger rolls in order to produce not only cotton yarns but also worsted yarns of wool. With this, it is also possible to spin fibers from longer staple cotton blended with other fibers up to about 5 inches in length. Most staple yarn fabrics today are spun on this type of equipment.

These staple yarns must go through the preliminary stages of mixing, carding, drawing, and roving in order to produce a uniform product season after season of yarns of satisfactory characteristics for the end-use product (Figure 5–7). The man-made fibers, being mechanically extruded are, of course, more uniform in their exterior structure than are any of the natural fibers, so one need not worry about thick or thin spots or other defacing irregularities that would show up in the fabric. The American system also

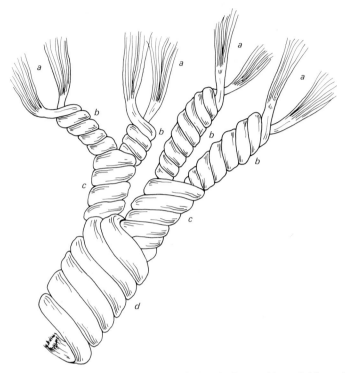

Figure 5-6 Yarn structure: (*a*) fibers; (*b*) single(s); (*c*) ply yarn(s); and (*d*) cord yarn(s).

enables the operators to use fibers of varying degrees of coarseness to give special textures. Time and again, it will be noted that at many stages in production, even of the man-made fibers and filaments, the blending operation is used to ensure uniformity of quality (see Figure 5–8).

Wool Yarn Systems

Soft-textured fabrics, such as dress goods, blankets, and materials for robes and flannels, use woolen spun yarns, as described in Chapter Eight. In general, fibers of approximately the same degree of fineness and length will be the most compatible and will be spun into the most uniform yarn. In Table 5–1 the uniformity of wool fibers is compared with synthetics of equivalent fineness.

Although the numbering systems have similar figures for wool and cotton (40's for wool and 40's for cotton, for example), the units are not the same. The woolen system figure refers to the number of 560-yard hanks of wool

Figure 5-7 Staple from man-made textile fibers after the uniformly cut lengths have been fluffed. (Courtesy of E. I. du Pont de Nemours & Co.)

Table 5-1   *Wool Fineness and Synthetic Fiber Denier*

Blood	English Number	Synthetic Fiber Fineness Approximate Denier
Fine	70's	4
Fine	64's	4.5
½	60's	6
⅜	56's	7.5
¼	50's	9

SOURCE: Russell L. Brown, in J. J. Press, ed., *Man-made Textile Encyclopedia* (New York: Wiley & Sons, Inc., 1959), p. 199.

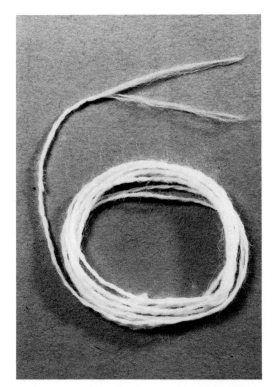

Figure 5-8 Spun yarns from staple—whether cotton, wool, any natural or man-made fiber—are bulky and fuzzy compared with continuous filament yarn, which is smooth. Sweaters and suitings are made from spun yarns, which are made from staple. Women's full-length hosiery and lingerie fabrics are knitted and woven from continuous filament yarn. (Courtesy of E. I. du Pont de Nemours & Co.)

yarn to weigh 1 pound; in the cotton grading system, the number 40's refer to the number of hanks of 840 yards of yarn to weigh 1 pound.

It is imperative that, in the case of blends of fibers, the carding operation laying the fibers parallel be fully as important as in the case of a yarn made from all natural fibers. The mixing of the two must be thorough for a uniform yarn. Sometimes this mixing is difficult because the wool fiber has a natural crimp and is more resilient than the man-made fibers; thus, the wool tends to wrap itself around the nearby fibers of synthetic or man-made origin. If this happens, the yarn assumes a cord effect with the stronger, straighter fibers of the synthetic in the center and with the wool fibers wrapped around them. Such complications will affect the uniformity of the dyeing operations, the appearance of the pattern and the durability of the fabric.

The Worsted System

In the worsted system, the fibers are generally longer (from 2 to 7 inches) than in the woolen system, and the combing and twisting are more extensive. Although this spinning method was originally intended for worsted fabrics of wool, it is now used for many other fibers, alone or in blends with one another or with wool.

The Spinning Operation

Whether the yarn is from a single fiber type or a blend, an intimate mixture is desired in the yarn itself. Accordingly, several combed slivers, possibly as many as 6 to 10, are fed into the machine together in order to bring about further blending and greater uniformity in the final product. Rollers rotating at different speeds draw out the single strand formed from the several slivers and give it a degree of stretching. This operation makes the roving thinner and thinner; when this very thin strand is put on the spinning frame, it is given a slight twist, enough to hold the fibers together. From the spinning frame, the yarns pass onto the bobbins, spools, or other kinds of holders for marketing.

These yarns can then be processed further for the particular purpose they are to fulfill in the weaving operation—whether they are meant to be used for filling yarns or for warp yarns.

CONTINUOUS FILAMENT YARNS

These yarns have been by-passed thus far because they do not require any of the mechanical operations prior to the spinning frame. The procedure to produce the desired yarn size is called throwing. Thus, **throwing** includes all the elements of drying, spinning, and winding. The continuous filament yarns are then wound onto the holders on which they are to be used or marketed, as shown in Figure 5–9. A lubricant may be added if the yarn is to be a warp yarn; some filling yarns similarly are lubricated. It is common practice to treat synthetic fibers with an antistatic agent to reduce the flying about of yarns and fiber ends during the weaving operation. Generally, too, synthetic fibers, whether spun or filament, are more easily handled in a relatively high humidity condition in which the static electrical effects are reduced. Warp yarns sometimes need extra strength and firmness; these properties are given by a sizing agent, such as a synthetic or natural gum, or by a soap or starch.

YARN NOMENCLATURE AND MEASUREMENT

Yarn Twist

Yarns are twisted either clockwise or counterclockwise; there are designated as S and Z twist, respectively (see Figures 5–10 and 5–11). It will be noted that the slant of the stem of the letter corresponds to the direction of twist in the yarn. As a general rule, warp yarns are given a higher twist because they must withstand the stresses of weaving and be as free of friction as possible so that the shuttle can be passed through the shed easily and without binding.

Figure 5-9 Celanese yarns are shipped to weaving mill customers on merchandise or section beams (foreground), which weigh approximately 800 pounds when full. More than 700 individual bobbins of yarn feed onto the same beam (machine in center), which, when full, is wrapped in kraft paper and transported by an automatic hoist to the shipping platform. (Courtesy of Celanese Corporation of America)

The filling yarns are given varied degrees of twist depending on the characteristics of the cloth to be woven. If the surface is to be lustrous, as in the case of satins and some brocades, there may be almost no twist. Low twist of the filling is also desirable in fabrics in which the surface is to be raised, such as in napped blankets and flannels. On the other hand, extremely high twist, great enough to cause distortion and knotting of the filling yarns, is characteristic of many crepes. Generally, the yarns in both warp and filling are given a relatively high twist, as in the case of worsted fabrics from wool yarns; woolen fabrics have a low twist in both directions.

Yarn Classification

When fibers have been twisted together to form a yarn, such a yarn is called a single-ply or usually a singles yarn. It may be a monofilament or it may be a cluster of fibers with little or no twist or with a tight twist. Whatever twist is present is always in one direction, either S or Z. Often yarns are made up of more than one twisted unit or **ply**. When untwisted, the individual plies

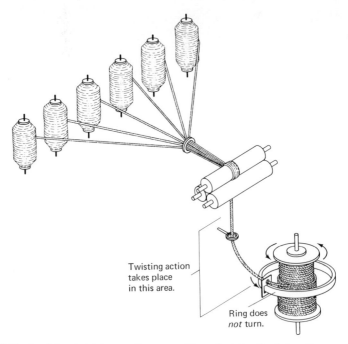

Twisting action
takes place
in this area.

Ring does
not turn.

Figure 5-10 Applying twist to a cotton yarn. The principle of twisting illustrated is the same as that used in spinning, except that the rolls do no drafting. The purpose of the rolls is to grip the multiple strands of single-ply yarn and feed them at a controlled rate. All three rolls turn at the same rate of speed. The speed of the rolls is adjusted to feed out the yarns at a rate that will give time for the spindle and traveler to insert the desired amount of twist before it gets past the twisting area, which is between the rolls and the bobbin. (Courtesy of Bibb Manufacturing Company)

separate into singles, which, in turn, can be untwisted to form fibers. If two or more plies are twisted together, the unit formed is called a **cord**. Generally, textile fabrics for wearing apparel are of singles. Ply yarns are used in heavy fabrics for work clothing and for industrial fabrics in which great durability is required. They are also used for some sheers, such as voiles, in which the yarns are so fine that a ply is required to give greater strength per unit of cross section. Similarly, cord yarns are used in extra-heavy industrial fabrics, such as are used for heavy belting material for conveyors or for automobile tire use, and, as a contrast, for ultrafine sheer materials.

Yarn Uniformity

Uniformity in a yarn can be evaluated either by its physical appearance and texture—that is, whether it is uniform throughout its length or whether it is

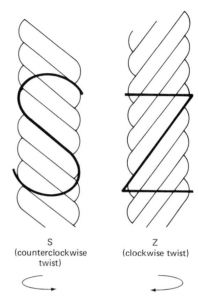

S
(counterclockwise
twist)

Z
(clockwise twist)

Figure 5-11 Yarn twists S and Z.

Figure 5-12 Fine denier Taslan textured nylon yarns, showing the uniformity of Taslan yarns, both in yarn size and loose fiber density. (Courtesy of Chemstrand Corporation)

characterized by irregularities, surface effects, and color variations—or by its composition—that is, the uniformity of the individual fibers in size, shape, or identity (see Figure 5–12).

Generally, the very uniform yarn is called a simple yarn and is characterized by uniform twist throughout its length, by a very uniform diameter, and by the fact that only one type of fiber is used customarily. A blended yarn may have two or more different kinds of fiber blended together in the same color; it may be cross-dyed, with each fiber being a different color; or one fiber may be colored while the other is left white.

Novelty yarns are those of complex or irregular structure. Some of these are singles yarns in which are formed neps or small tangles of fibers (usually immature cotton fibers); thick areas, such as slubs; or complex effects, such as loops and curls, as in bouclé. There are also the spiral yarns; covered, coated, or striped yarns; ratiné; and yarns with other irregular configurations (Figure 5–13). In general, the purpose of these novelty yarns is to give either the woven or knitted fabric an irregular surface appearance that will impart a three-dimensional effect to it and thus make it more interesting. It has been shown that yarns can vary greatly in their diameter, or fineness. They can vary also in their compactness, which perhaps may be better stated as their linear density—that is, roughly their weight per unit of length.

Figure 5-13 Twisting ply yarns. The machine in this picture is used to put a twist in a 2-ply yarn made from two kinds of singles. (Courtesy of Agricultural Research Service, Western Utilization Research & Development Division)

Yarn Numbering

The historical development, tradition, and habit of each textile fiber has brought along its own yarn number system, which is still used in most mills. Thus, we have one system based on the weight per unit of length, and another based on the length per unit of weight. To complicate things still further, the units of weight and of length vary between fibers.

The system using weight per unit of length is a **direct system**. This is the one used traditionally for silk and some jute fibers and has been carried over into all man-made fibers in both the filament and spun yarns. These numbers are based on the denier system—that is, the number of grams (deniers) weighed by 9000 meters of yarn. (For convenience in measuring and weighting, both the weight and length are commonly divided by 20. Under this system, denier is the number of 0.05-gram that a 450-meter length of yarn weighs.) As the yarn becomes coarser, or greater in diameter, the number increases; thus, denier is a direct measure.

The length per unit weight is an **indirect system** in which the number designation decreases as the diameter of the yarn becomes greater. This system, with different units used for wool, cotton, linen, glass, and asbestos, is based on the number of units of constant yardage (but with the constant varying, depending on the fiber) required to weigh 1 pound.

Fiber	Number to Weigh 1 pound
Cotton and spun silk	840-yd hanks
Linen and woolen yarns	300-yd hanks
Worsted	560-yd hanks
Glass	100-yd hanks
Asbestos	100-yd cuts

It is not to be wondered at, therefore, that laboratories and the several technical societies are interested in a common system applicable to all fibers. Such a system, being promoted actively by ASTM, is the TEX system, in which the yarn numbers for all fibers are the weight in grams of 1000 meters of yarn. This is being applied gradually in this country and abroad, but mill men, steeped in tradition, have been slow to respond to a more uniform system.

TEXTURED YARNS

As a matter of convenience, two types of so-called texturized yarns are grouped together: **bulk yarns** and **stretch yarns**. Although any thermoplastic or heat-set yarn or fiber can be used, the early texturized yarns commonly were of nylon because (1) nylon is produced in both filament and staple form in a very wide variety of deniers; (2) it is the strongest of the synthetic fibers in commercial production with a relatively high softening temperature; and (3) there are more commercial producers of nylon than of any other manufactured fiber. (See Table 5–2.) I. A. Brunet predicts, however, that by 1977 polyester will represent 80 per cent of the textured yarn market.[2]

Table 5-2 Percentage of Manufacturers Using Certain Polymers in Textured Yarns

Nylon	59
Polyester	40
Acetate	22
Triacetate	19
Olefin	10
Rayon	3
Acrylics	2
Polyamide/polyester	1
Triacetate/nylon	1
Glass	1

SOURCE: Courtesy of R. Jolly, *Modern Textiles Magazine*, **43**, No. 7 (July 1968).

Bulk yarns are generally continuous filament yarns that have been crimped or repeatedly folded back and forth on themselves in order to give greater bulk per unit length of the yarn after modification. They are stretchable to the limit of the crimping or folding.

Stretch yarns are usually of spun yarns and have been looped or coiled. They have considerably higher elongation than the bulk yarns and are used in garments such as sweaters and other knitted articles. Their growth has been phenomenal, from approximately 2 million pounds in 1950, to 5 million pounds in 1954, to 30 million pounds in 1958, to 45 million pounds of nylon in 1960, to 200 million pounds in 1968, to 300 million pounds in 1971. (See Figure 5–14.)

Helanca was the first of the commercial yarns of bulk nature to be introduced into the United States. Coming from Switzerland in 1950, it became important primarily in stretch socks. This promotion made it possible for a manufacturer to knit but two sizes, large and small. The stretchiness, bulk, and softness of the yarn gave comfort to all who wore them. It proved an aid in the inventory of the retail establishment. It is made by a twist, heat-set, and untwist operation. Usually, the first twist is tighter than the final twist.

[2] "Texturing Equipment Demand," *Modern Textiles*, **54**, No. 7 (July 1973), p. 18.

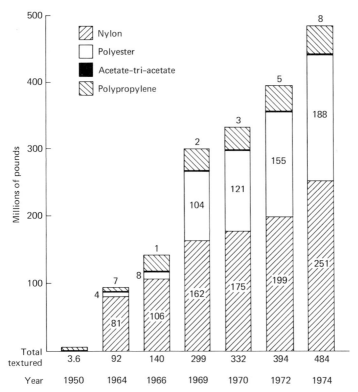

Figure 5-14   United States textured yarn production. (Excludes textured yarns for carpet and upholstery.) (Courtesy of *America's Textile Reporter*)

Thus, when heat-set and then untwisted and then retwisted part way, the filaments kink up and snarl. The wear resistance and strength of nylon, together with its low moisture regain, assure good durability and satisfactory washing. These high-bulk yarns are relatively free from pilling; however, there is some tendency for them to pick up lint and dust through electrostatic attraction.

Agilon is a curled-type static or nontorque stretch yarn developed by Deering-Milliken Research Corporation. The continuous filament yarn is heated just to the softening point and is then rubbed along a knife edge; this deforms the filaments by giving them a slightly flat surface plane, replacing a small arc of the circumference. This flat plane twists slightly around the fiber, causing it to spiral (somewhat the same principle as drawing a knife edge along the flat side of a ribbon in order to curl it in gift wrapping). Sometimes a monofilament yarn is used instead of the multifilament. In either case, the yarn is suitable for seamless full-fashioned stockings, sweaters, knitted outer wear, underwear, and even for carpets; it is now a strong market force. **Helanca NT** (nontorque) stretch yarn can be given a false twist on a machine to give a single yarn without distortion. These are widely used in sweaters and underwear. **Chadalon** and **Shape 2-U** are other curled-type yarns.

Ban-lon and **Textralized** are products of the Joseph Bancroft and Sons Company. Other firms have been licensed to produce these yarns on a quality-control basis. Although nylon is the principal fiber used for Ban-lon and Textralized, there is considerable variation in the types of nylon and their denier; in other words, 30- to 200-denier find practical use in these yarns, and often they are three- to five-ply in order to prevent broken ends. The various steps follow:

1. Crimping occurs when the yarn is compressed into a metal stuffer box, causing the individual filaments to fold or bend at a sharp angle; crimping also occurs when the yarns are heat-set during compression.
2. The yarns are then cleared of broken filaments or any imperfections.
3. Slight lubricating aids are used in the process of fabrication.
4. After the fibers have been plied and twisted, the textured yarn is lubricated and wound on cones.

Some of the finer denier yarns have been named **Textralized**; for others, Ban-lon is still used. The characteristic figure for these yarns is a zigzag crimp, providing unusually soft hand, high bulk, an increase of 200 to 300 per cent in volume, sufficient elasticity to permit comfortable fit, and an increased moisture absorption for additional comfort.

Super-Loft and **Fluflon** are so-called false-twist methods of producing a bulk- and stretch-type yarn. In the Super-Loft, the thermoplastic yarn is taken from the package, twisted, heat-set with direct contact heat, untwisted, and then taken up again on a cone in loose form for further processing. (Various bulked yarn fibers are shown in Figure 5–15.) The use of radiant heat in Fluflon at a constant tension during heating is the principal difference. There may, however, be some variability among different packages of yarns produced by this method because of slight differences in the amount of twist, the temperature of setting, and the amount of tension applied. Thus, these yarns are sometimes found to be stiff; at other times they are soft and bulky. Additional treatment can be given, under controlled temperature and heating time, with the tension modified, to remove some of the stretch previously put in the Super-Loft and Fluflon yarns without losing their bulk. The yarn so modified by one producer to give high bulk as the primary characteristic is known as **Saaba.** These yarns are particularly good for knitted outer wear, swim wear, hosiery, warp-knit fabrics, industrial fabrics, webbings, braids, and girdles.

Spunize is another bulky yarn developed by the stuffer-box technique to induce crimp in the yarn, utilizing heat setting in an autoclave. It is very often applied to filaments of heavy denier; these bulky yarns are excellent for rugs, carpets, and upholstery fabrics.

Taslan has a characteristic loop structure; the technique for its formation can be applied to any continuous filament—that is, the filament need not be thermoplastic. It is produced in a more random manner by feeding nylon, polyester, viscose, or other filaments through a spinneret into a turbulent air jet. The strand of filament is fed out at a rate faster than it is taken up on the rolls; thus, there are loose loops and curls formed in the individual filaments as they flow out into a bulky mass of loose fiber instead of remaining close together in a conventional type of multifilament yarn. As these yarns are wound on the pickup rolls, many little loops are left loose both inside and outside the yarn. Possibly 20 per cent of the yarn length is lost by this bulking; but the volume of the yarn increases anywhere from 50 to 100 per cent, depending on the jet force and the speed of take-up. Taslan yarns do not stretch but retain a permanent bulk. American Enka Corporation has a similar yarn called Skyloft.

Tycora is a yarn from the Textured Yarn Company; the name designates the source of manufacture but not the method, because Tycora's producers utilize a wide variety of procedures to produce yarns of a bulking or stretching nature.

A newer method of producing textured yarns is the knit-deknit method. A thermoplastic filament yarn is prepared with a near-zero twist, it is loosely knitted into a fabric with a plain knitted structure, and the loops are heat-set and then unraveled. The set configuration of the loops now appears as kinked strands, which are loosely twisted into a lofty, crimped yarn.

TWINNED FIBERS

Fiber Joining

Having created such a number of new-fiber polymer families by synthetic organic chemistry and having modified individual fibers for various properties, it was natural for chemists to explore the intimate mixture of two or more polymers into a single fiber in order to discover unusual properties.

One example of this approach is du Pont's Cantrece nylon. In this filament, two different nylons are spun side-by-side through a single orifice to form a **bicomponent** fiber. The two nylons have different shrinkages and develop a new structure during the finishing operation. It is bulkier and more crimped than either component alone and is used for ladies' hosiery. In this bicomponent fiber, each element appears to be composed of equal amounts of each nylon type. When this fiber is drawn, or subjected, to steam—after it has been woven or knitted into a fabric—one of the nylons shrinks much more than the other causing the filament to crimp. The amount of this distortion depends on the tautness of the filaments in the fabric. As an example of this relaxation to shape, a brief description of knitting is in order.

The knitting of hosiery made of Cantrece differs only slightly from that commonly associated with nylon 66. The principal differences follow:

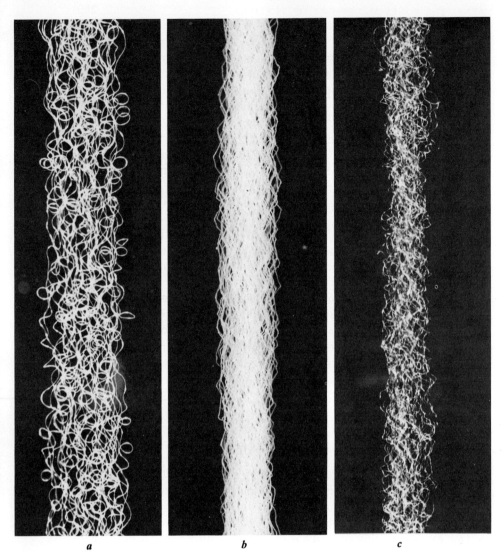

Figure 5-15 Various bulked yarns: (*a*) Superloft, 70 denier nylon stretch yarn; (*b*) Spunize; (*c*) Saaba; (*d*) Agilon, monofilament stretch yarn; (*e*) Whitin, 70 denier 2-ply nylon;

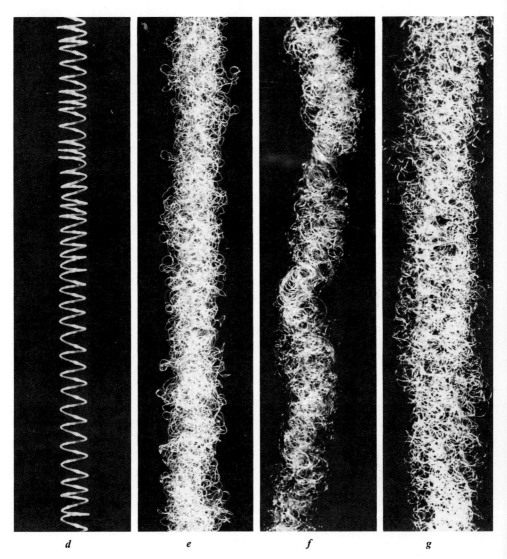

| d | e | f | g |

(f) Agilon-crimped type; and (g) Agilon-stabilized type. (Courtesy of Chemstrand Corporation)

1. Because Cantrece is a stretchable yarn under tensions as low as 0.7 gpd, the knitting must be carried out at low tensions.
2. Cantrece stockings are steam-treated after looping in order to avoid stretch distortion of the yarn during the knitting operation.
3. When steamed in a relaxed state, the yarns crimp into the helical configuration.
4. The final crimping limits are reached by scouring the whole hose at a boil and then cooling it to the preferred dyeing temperature, generally 160°F.
5. No resin finishes are applied because, contrary to the properties wanted in other nylon hose, Cantrece must be left free to stretch and yield. Like other nylon stockings, Cantrece is boarded to size in order to set the stitch and give the desired leg shape.

One might judge from the name Touch that this new fiber from Allied Chemical Corporation has some unusual tactile properties. This new modified nylon 6, which closely resembles Qiana in texture and feel, is described as having a "crisp, dry, silklike" hand.

Another filament-type has two different fiber constituents, or families, in

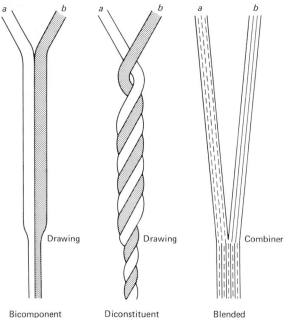

Bicomponent
Cantrece—two
types of nylon

Diconstituent
Source—polyamide
and polyester

Blended
Arnel (*a*) plus
nylon (*b*)

Figure 5-16
Twinned fibers.

a single strand (Figure 5–16). This is a **biconstituent** fiber—one polymer is dispersed through the matrix or body of the other. One of these, Source (p. 179), produced by Allied Chemical Corporation, has 70 per cent by weight polyamide in the matrix and 30 per cent polyester. In one variant, the minor constituent may be water or solution-soluble and can be leached out to give new properties.

A combined filament yarn corresponds to the blending of two fibers in a single yarn. In this case, a group of filaments of nylon and a group of Arnel filaments have been used by the Celanese Corporation. This method is limitless in its variety of combinations whereby two extruded fibers can be brought together in a combiner to form a yarn.

In other respects, its properties are different from the usual nylon in that it is said to have moderate water absorption, less static charge, and some loft in the yarns without requiring texturizing.

STRETCHABLE TEXTURED COTTON YARNS

Cotton stretch yarns are a fairly recent development intended to help cotton hold its place in bulky or stretchy outer garments. Several research teams at the Southern Regional Research Laboratory of the U.S. Department of Agriculture have been engaged in these researches. Three principal methods have come on the market: (1) using cross linking to set the yarns in a coiled or crimped position; (2) using heat-setting yarns that have been given thermoplastic properties by chemical modification of the cellulose molecule; and (3) slack mercerizing to cause shrinkage.

The same type of cross-linking resins used to give cotton the wash-and-wear property can be used for the stretch result. In one process, the back-twist method, tightly twisted plied yarns are treated with a resin solution. They are then dried and heat cured, after which they are untwisted and relaxed. In the relaxed state, the treated yarns tend to return to the twisted state, forming a mass of twisted helical coils. When knitted or woven in this state, the yarn has stretch and bulkiness. Another method using resins is the false-twist method; a plied yarn is (1) twisted in one direction, (2) passed through a trough containing a resin solution, (3) squeezed, (4) passed through a heater onto a false-twist spindle (5) twisted in the opposite direction, (6) cured, and (7) restored on another spindle assembly to its original twist, thus producing a bulky, stretchy yarn.

Chemical modifications of cellulose can produce derivatives that can be heat-set by the usual commercial processes. Ethers and esters can be used and the yarns are given the proper degree of bulkiness by either the false-twist or back-twist techniques utilized in the resin treatment previously mentioned.

The cheapest method for producing stretch cotton yarn is the slack mercerization method. The cotton fabric is treated with a 23 to 30 per cent caustic soda solution at a mild temperature and under a complete state of relaxation. This method is being used widely by manufacturers of stretch bandages and diapers.

FUTURE TRENDS IN TEXTURED YARNS

A number of investigators have studied the recent history of textured yarns and the present market. They have also conjectured about the future of this type of lofty, bulky, warm textile product and its stretching characteristics. From a market of 150 million pounds in 1967, it was anticipated that in 1969 the market will be approximately 240 million pounds. By the end of 1970, this was expected to rise to 275 million and by 1971, to close to 325 million pounds. These projections were based upon the present market and the ever-increasing demand for this type of yarn. A contributing factor to this increase was that, in addition to the knit goods market, the woven fabric trade showed considerable interest in texturized yarns. The fabrics using them extend from crepes to twills and even to broadcloth. Other textile products, such as durable-press denim and other uniform materials will also utilize these yarns.

The greater variety of yarn fiber is being made available with variations within the yarn of fibers with different deniers and cross sections, as well as through blending two or more types of fibers in the same bulk yarn. The August 1969 issue of *Modern Textiles Magazine* includes a list of textured yarn processes in the United States that contains the names of 54 textile firms making textured yarns—some making one type, but others, 10 to 12. The false-twist process appears to be the most widely used with knit-deknit second. In Figure 5–17 the sketches are illustrative of the principal methods of forming these yarns.

As in the case of all new developments in textiles, for a period of time users are content with the materials available. Thus, for a considerable period of time, even in the case of textured yarns, the throwsters were content to use the available filaments and then vary the characteristics of the yarn by the severity of treatment. The apparel manufacturers and consumers began to ask for certain refinements, such as a change of luster, perhaps brighter or more dull; a silky look and feel; a crisp hand or a softer one; and even variations of color within a yarn. These changes then became objectives for the throwster to meet. Finer denier filaments provide yarns with a softer feel; however, the reverse is also true: a heavier denier yarn will give one with a crisper texture. In the discussion on yarns, it was shown that multi-lobal filament cross sections prevent the close packing that round cross-section filaments allow. Thus, yarns can be varied in their loft by using combinations of cross sections. The filaments themselves can be spun bright or delustered, and these two extremes can be used to give a wide variation

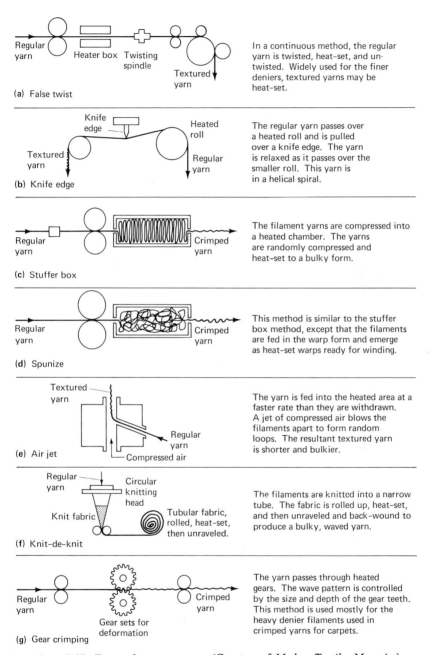

(a) False twist

In a continuous method, the regular yarn is twisted, heat–set, and un-twisted. Widely used for the finer deniers, textured yarns may be heat–set.

(b) Knife edge

The regular yarn passes over a heated roll and is pulled over a knife edge. The yarn is relaxed as it passes over the smaller roll. This yarn is in a helical spiral.

(c) Stuffer box

The filament yarns are compressed into a heated chamber. The yarns are randomly compressed and heat–set to a bulky form.

(d) Spunize

This method is similar to the stuffer box method, except that the filaments are fed in the warp form and emerge as heat-set warps ready for winding.

(e) Air jet

The yarn is fed into the heated area at a faster rate than they are withdrawn. A jet of compressed air blows the filaments apart to form random loops. The resultant textured yarn is shorter and bulkier.

(f) Knit-de-knit

The filaments are knitted into a narrow tube. The fabric is rolled up, heat-set, and then unraveled and back-wound to produce a bulky, waved yarn.

(g) Gear crimping

The yarn passes through heated gears. The wave pattern is controlled by the size and depth of the gear teeth. This method is used mostly for the heavy denier filaments used in crimped yarns for carpets.

Figure 5-17 Textured yarn processes. (Courtesy of *Modern Textiles Magazine*)

215

in yarn brightness. Polyester and nylon or acetate and polyester are examples of combinations of filaments.

PAPER YARNS

In the late 1960s a number of novelty fabrics knitted or woven out of paper yarns were introduced for wearing apparel. Generally, however, use of this type of yarn is confined to hats and bags; shopping bags; hat bodies; and some disposable curtains and draperies. Such yarns are actually made of a high-grade paper that is light in weight and of uniform composition. The paper is cut in slices ⅛- or ½-inch wide, and these tiny ribbons are tightly twisted to form the yarn. For industrial applications, ½-inch ribbon of moderate twist is used. The fabrics out of which many automobile seat covers were made prior to the introduction of nylon, saran, and other manufactured fibers were of paper yarns. Industrially, the yarns have been used in bags for fruits and vegetables, and as a cheap covering sheet for banks of soil and freshly tilled ground to protect the soil from erosion. In 1962, imitation burlap was produced in many bright colors using paper yarn instead of genuine jute for girls' shirts.

CHAPTER

Fabric Constructions

THE BASIC WEAVES

Weaving is the process of forming a fabric by interlacing two sets of yarns at right angles by means of a loom (Figure 6–1). The weaving operation requires a rigid support to which are attached the yarns that form the vertical or lengthwise grain of the fabric. These are the **warp** yarns. There must also be a method or mechanism by which the crosswise yarns are interlaced with the warp. In primitive weaving, these cross yarns—generally referred to as **filling** yarns or **picks**—were passed over a warp yarn or group of warp yarns and then under the next by the fingers of the weaver; a needle or some other sharp tool was used by which the warp yarns were slightly raised or lowered.

In the mechanical weaving operation, a conventional loom has two or more rigid cross members called the harnesses. Each **harness** is a frame holding a series of wires, each having a needle eye and referred to as a **heddle.** This frame is raised or lowered by mechanical action, carrying only those warp yarns affixed to it. Thus, in a simple loom, two harnesses are used, forming a plain weave— that is, with the filling yarns going over and under alternate warp yarns throughout the width of the fabric—one harness for the even-numbered yarns, the other for the odd numbered. This raising and lowering is called shedding, perhaps because the

217

Figure 6-1 Modern textile loom for broad woven fabrics. Looms are available to weave fabrics as wide as 70 feet or as narrow as $\frac{1}{4}$ inch. (Courtesy of Crompton and Knowles Corporation)

harness in the raised position makes the series of warps look something like the slanting roof of a shed. Filling yarns are shot through from one side to the other and back again by means of a shuttle. This is of wood or metal, travels back and forth at great speed, and is extremely noisy. Some new shuttleless looms are said to pass as many as 500 picks per minute, about three times the rate of conventional looms. These employ a jet of air or water to carry the filling yarn and are noise free. Another type has a rapier-like metal rod to carry the yarn through the shed. After a filling yarn has been passed through, another frame, called the reed, which consists of wires set vertically in the spaces between each pair of warp yarns, moves forward and presses the new filling yarn firmly against those already woven in. This produces a compact fabric. When the desired yardage of fabric, called gray goods, has been woven, the cloth is wound onto a roll called the merchandise beam. The weaving operation then is continued with the length of warp yarns still left on the warp beam, or additional lengths of warp yarns are tied to those on the beam. (See Figure 6–2.)

The examination of any finished fabric will show that the edges are more compact than the fabric used in making garments or other articles. This

Figure 6-2 Celanese yarns.

compact edge is called the selvage. It is usually made with heavier or more closely packed warp yarns in order to give strength to the edge of the material and to prevent it from raveling. The width of the **selvage** varies, depending upon the weight of the goods and the end-use of the fabric. In synthetic fiber fabrics, the selvages can be strengthened further by means of a hot iron; this causes some degree of fusing of the yarns along both sides of the fabric.

THE COUNT OF FABRICS

In some fabrics the size, or diameter, of the yarn used in the warp and in the filling is the same, but it is common for the warp to have more yarns to the inch than the filling because the weaving operation itself imposes more stress on the warp yarns. One has only to compare the density of a percale sheeting with the open structure of a voile to see the different degrees of compactness that can be achieved even on a simple loom (Figure 6–3). It is logical to expect better service from a more closely and firmly woven fabric than from one that is extremely open in texture. This close weave is measured by the **count** of the cloth, which is the number of warps and fillings to the square inch. The count is customarily made with the help of a small pocket magnifying glass, called a pick glass, which has beneath it an exact square of ½-inch or 1-inch sides and is marked off in sixteenths of an inch, similar to the markings on a ruler. Because this glass was first used in the linen industry, it is sometimes referred to as a **linen tester.** If the cloth is fairly open, it is very easy to set one edge of the opening in the base against a warp yarn and then

Figure 6-3 More than 700 bobbins of Celanese yarn, all to be wound on the same warp or merchandise beam, are used in this creeling operation. Each of the 700 ends or threads is fed to an assigned position on the beam, which is then wrapped for delivery to customers. An electric stop-motion device halts the operation if a single strand of yarn breaks. (Celanese Corpor- of America)

to count the number of warp yarns in a quarter of an inch and multiply by four to give the full count per inch, or preferably, to count clear across the 1-inch span; this process should then be repeated with the filling yarns. The count is expressed as 60 × 40 if the warp yarns count is 60 and the filling yarns is 40—the warp count is always given first. If the fabric structure is made obscure either because of a more compact weave or the finish process, it is sometimes simpler to pull out a few yarns from the warp and a few from the filling, leaving a short fringe along two sides, the ends of which can then be counted under the glass with the aid of a pin or textile pick to separate the fringe for better visibility.

If the count is the same in both warp and filling, it is said to be square count as in 80-square print cloth. Muslin sheeting standards call for two counts, or types, type 128 and type 140. These figures refer to the total warp and filling threads in a square inch of the muslin. These fabrics have their greatest durability when they are evenly balanced—that is, with a 64-square count for type 128 and a 70-square count for type 140. Generally, however, there will be more warp threads than filling threads. The differences may be of the order of 10 per cent or slightly more. Thus, a 77 × 63 count muslin sheet could be called a type 140, but it would not be as strong a fabric in the filling direction as in the warp. It must be remembered that, from the practical point of view, the greater stress or pull on a bed sheet is in the warp direction, both during the weaving operation and in placing the sheet on the bed. Before the adoption of these standards, very cheap bed sheets could be found with counts as low as 50-square, the openings being filled in with clay, starch, or some other inert material to give the appearance of a lustrous, compact sheeting—until the first laundering.

One of the hazards of using low-count fabrics in wearing apparel is the tendency of the material to ravel at the seams. More compact and firm cloths are more resistant to this raveling, especially in the case of the man-made and synthetic fibers, which are generally more slippery than the natural fibers because of their smooth outer surfaces.

BALANCE OF THE FABRIC STRUCTURE

The proportion of warp threads to filling threads decides the **balance** of a fabric (Figure 6–4). Generally, a cloth is considered to be in balance or to have good balance if there is not more than a 10-yarn difference between the two. We refer again to the case of the 77 × 63 count type 140 muslin sheet. This would not have good balance; however, a 75 × 65 would be reasonably good. Similarly, a gauze with a count of 28 × 24 is in good balance, but one of 34 × 18 would be poor. If there are insufficient filling threads to give a firm structure, shifting and slippage may occur.

Figure 6-4 Setting up the warp beam from several hundred spools of cotton yarn. (Courtesy of Burlington Industries, Inc.)

A cloth can also be out of balance if the yarns in one direction are much heavier than those in the other. For example, in a print cloth of 80-square, the warp yarns might be much finer than the filling, and the fabric would actually be unbalanced as far as durability is concerned. On the other hand, one might have a cotton broadcloth of what seemed to be a count far off balance, such as 144 × 72. In this case, if the filling yarns are about twice the diameter of the warp yarns, we could have a dense, compact fabric having a rigid surface effect and it would be in balance. It could be expected to be serviceable unless the effect of wear and ironing were to weaken the thinner warps as they passed over the heavier fillings.

A loom is shown in Figure 6–5; warp threads being fed from the beam to the loom are shown in Figure 6–6.

TEN IMPORTANT TYPES OF WOVEN STRUCTURE

It is in the weave and the method in which the filling yarns are enmeshed with the warp yarns that man has his first opportunity to develop novelty

Figure 6-5 The loom. (Courtesy of The Wool Bureau)

and distinction in the appearance of a cloth. Weaves are named in accordance with the design followed in interlacing these yarns. The more important weaves to be discussed are

1. Plain	5. Jacquard
2. Twill	6. Dobby
3. Satin	7. Leno or gauze
4. Pile	8. Applied patterns: swivel, lappet, and clipped-spot

The first three are the fundamental, or ABC weaves; the middle four are pattern weaves; and the last three provide embroidered effects.

Figure 6-6 Warp threads being fed from the beam (foreground) to the loom. The metal strips (foreground) are elements of the automatic stop-device, which halts the loom when a thread breaks. (Courtesy of Pepperell Manufacturing Company)

Plain Weave

The plain weave is the most common of the woven constructions and accounts for about 80 per cent of all woven goods (see Table 6–1). In the plain weave, the filling passes over one warp yarn, under the next, over the third, under the fourth, and so on across the fabric (see Figure 6–7). On the return trip, the shuttle carries the filling over each yarn previously passed under. In Figure 6–8 the plain weave is shown in both fabric sketch and paper-pattern styles. It is sometimes referred to as the taffeta, tabby, or cotton weave and is the major construction in much of the clothing referred to in Chapter Six.

Table 6-1   Variety of Fabrics in Plain Weave *

Cotton	Linen	Woolens and Worsteds	Silk and Man-made Fibers
Balloon cloths	Airplane linen	Albatross	Bengaline†
Batiste	Art and pillowcase	Balmacaan	Broadcloth
Bengaline	linen	Broadcloths‡	Canton crepe
Broadcloth	Butcher's linen	Challis	Chiffon
Buckram	Cambric	Flannel	Crepe de chine
Bunting	Crash	Georgette	Faille
Calico	Dress linen	Homespun	Flat crepe
Cambric	Handkerchief linen	Nun's veiling	Georgette
Canvas	Toweling	Some tweeds	Habutai
Chambray			Mogadore
Cheesecloth			Moiré
Chintz			Ninon
Crash			Organza
Cretonne			Pongee
Dimity†			Pucker prints
Faille			Shantung
Flannel			Some plaids
Gingham			Taffeta
Lawn			Voile
Muslin			
Nainsook			
Organdy			
Oxford†			
Percale			
Poplin			
Scrim			
Sheeting			
Tarlatan			
Voile			

* In modern textile fabrics, the plain weave as well as others can be used for any fiber, natural or man-made.
† Variations in texture.
‡ Mostly twill to give good napping.

Variations for Surface Interest

The plain weave lacks interest in texture and appearance even when the warp and filling yarns are of different colors (see Table 6–2). Unbalanced fabrics are often made in order to produce materials of greater attractiveness and

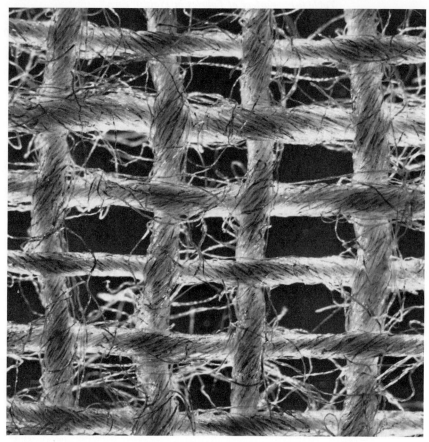

Figure 6-7 Plain weave, single-ply cotton gauze for diapers (highly magnified). (Courtesy of Chicopee Manufacturing Company)

with greater consumer appeal. Vertical ribs appearing at regular intervals can be produced in the plain weave by using a much heavier warp yarn at regular intervals across the harness of the loom. A rib or heavy stripe such as in striped dimity or corded madras, can be produced with a periodic heavy warp yarn constrasting with a succession of fine warp yarns. Heavier ribs and cords in the filling direction can be produced in fabrics such as dimity, faille, bengaline, and certain broadcloths. Heavy yarns can be inserted in both directions to create cross-bar effects. It must be kept in mind that the surface fibers of the fine yarns resting across the top surface of a heavy rib yarn reduce the durability of such fabrics, especially in resisting abrasion which may cause the cutting action of one yarn against another in deliberately unbalanced fabrics.

Oxford cloth, used for men's shirtings and dress fabrics, represents

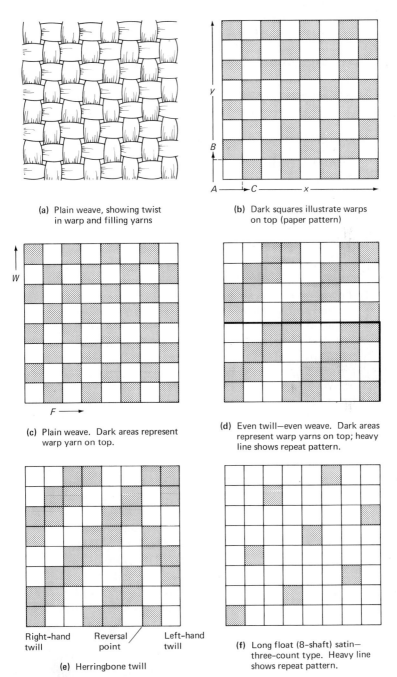

(a) Plain weave, showing twist in warp and filling yarns

(b) Dark squares illustrate warps on top (paper pattern)

(c) Plain weave. Dark areas represent warp yarn on top.

(d) Even twill—even weave. Dark areas represent warp yarns on top; heavy line shows repeat pattern.

Right-hand twill   Reversal point   Left-hand twill

(e) Herringbone twill

(f) Long float (8-shaft) satin—three-count type. Heavy line shows repeat pattern.

Figure 6-8   (a), (b), and (c): plain weave; (d) and (e): twill weave; and (f) satin weave.

another method of creating surface interest in the square weave. One type of Oxford cloth common to men's shirtings is called a 2 × 1 basket weave. In such a fabric, a single heavy filling yarn passes alternately over and under two warp yarns, each of which is one half of the diameter of the filling yarn. If this size ratio is not exact, the fabric will develop an oblong rather than a square effect. This basket weave can be extended to cover other geometrical

Table 6-2   *Advantages and Disadvantages of Plain Weave*

Advantages

Washes easily
Generally serviceable
Easy to dry-clean
Comfortable
Shows off color and patterned prints well
Generally becoming
Usually inexpensive because of ease of weaving

Disadvantages

Loose weaves may shrink
Loosely woven, slippery yarns will shift
Seams may be pulled out of loosely woven, slippery yarns
Fabrics may become monotonous because of lack of surface
   interest

combinations of yarns. For example, a 3 × 2 basket weave (a common dress material of Oxford cloth) has two fillings passing over and under three warps. An interesting fabric of long-standing popularity as a drapery material is monk's cloth. This is available in several different weights of basket-weave construction, varying from 2 × 2 to 4 × 4 and even 8 × 8 combinations in which two fillings pass alternately over two yarns in the first fabric, four fillings over and under four warps in the second, and eight fillings over and under eight warps in the third. Monk's cloth is an open-weave fabric; hence, it is likely to shrink in washing, and it will ravel at the seams unless it is reinforced very carefully. This kind of fabric in a synthetic fiber will scuff up and pill badly when abraded or rubbed.

The plain weave lends itself to other textural and appearance effects by the use of random heavy yarns combined with fines, or with yarns deliberately made thick and thin, or with heavy slubs, as characterized by some of our coarser linen fabrics and dress fabrics of shantung silk. Reference to thick and thin yarns was made in our discussion on yarns. Variations in twist are characteristic of these slubbed yarns and other novelties. Texturized yarns, stretch yarns, and tightly twisted yarns producing a crimped or a crepe effect are all modifications deliberately introduced in order to give style and interesting texture to a fabric.

Other modifications already briefly referred to can be achieved by using two colored filling yarns in combination with white warps or vice versa, or by introducing combinations of colors in one or both directions. Similarly, unusual effects can be achieved by the use of different fibers in the yarns of the two directions. Combinations of natural fibers with synthetics or with rayon and acetate are very common. Indeed, several of our most popular crepes for women's blouses—alpaca and ratiné—are actually combinations of rayon and acetate yarns plied together (twisted together) to produce a heavier yarn with interesting variations (shiny viscose yarns are contrasted against the dulled acetate). The use of luster adds to the attractiveness of textiles and is, of course, highlighted through the use of metal yarns (p. 121), or of heavy monofilament yarns, of a shiny synthetic contrasted with less lustrous yarns in the other direction.

Variations can be created by the method of finishing (reference to these will be made in Chapter Seven), but it is at once evident that even the basic mechanical processes for the removal of short fibers from the somewhat dull and lifeless-looking cotton gray goods, followed by bleaching, mercerizing, and pressing, will enhance the brightness and uniformity of the material, making it a much more saleable piece of goods. A three-dimensional, or puffy, effect can be given this same piece of material if it is printed with a strong alkali, such as is used in mercerizing, thus producing a shrinking and lustering in the printed areas. Some seersuckers are created by this method. Twinned yarns (p. 211) produce interesting and permanent textures.

Twill Weave

The outstanding characteristic of the **twill** weave is a woven diagonal pattern that gives fabrics an interesting surface appearance. The twill weave is extremely durable in both abrasion resistance and breaking strength.

Virtually all textile fibers are found in fabrics of twill-weave construction (see Table 6–3).

The diagonal lines in twills are often referred to as **wales.** They are formed by interlacing the warp and filling threads as shown in Figure 6–9, which illustrates a right-hand twill in which the diagonals extend from the lower left to the upper right-hand corner of the illustration. In left-hand twills the wales pass from the upper left to the lower right-hand direction of the cloth. The modification of the twill construction in which the wales appear to run in both directions is called a herringbone twill, a very popular suiting fabric in wool worsted for men and women (Figure 6–10). In an even twill, the filling yarns pass under and over the same number of warp yarns, that is, under two, over two, or under three, over three, and so on.

These are identified by having the wale or raised diagonal of the same width as the valley or identation line on the face of the cloth. In uneven twills, the filling yarns pass under two, over three, under two, over three, and so on, or they can be a combination of under one, over two, under one, over two. In coarser, uneven twill, longer floats—or lengths of yarn passing over the warp—can be used. In order to understand more clearly the way in which

Table 6-3   Typical Twills from Various Fibers

Cotton	Linen	Woolens and Worsteds	Silk and Man-made Fibers
Canton flannel	Tickings	Cassimere	Foulards
Denims	Towelings	Cavalry twill	Gabardines
Doeskins		Checks	Novelty goods
Drills		Cheviot	Plaid cloths
Gabardine		Covert	Serges
Galatea		Doeskin	Surah
Institutional fabrics		Elastique	
Jeans		Flannel	
Linings		Gabardine	
Ticking		Novelty dress materials	
Twill cloth		Serge	
Uniform goods			

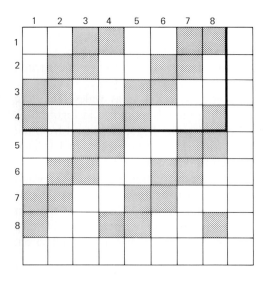

Figure 6-9 Right-hand even twill. The heavy line shows the *first* repeat of the pattern.

twills are formed, consider the even right-hand twill, the paper-designed pattern in Figure 6–9, as representing a small section of eight warp and eight filling yarns; let us number the warps one to eight inclusive as well as the rows of filling yarns. The warp shed used to form such a twill would be set up to lift alternate pairs of warp yarns to permit the shuttle carrying the filling yarn to pass under the warps in the following order:

1. Top row: warps three and four, seven and eight
2. Second row: warps seven and six, three and two
3. Third row: warps one and two, five and six
4. Fourth row: warps eight and five, four and one
5. Fifth row: repeat the first-row order

It is evident that it takes four rows, or picks, to complete a design of this even twill. Thus, four series of warp combinations must be lifted and four harnesses will be used on the loom. The fabric is, therefore, called a four-shaft twill. The **shaft number** is quickly determined by adding together the number of warp yarns the filling goes over and under in forming the summit of one ridge and one valley for a single unit in the twill construction. In this case, the filling went over two and under two for a total of four.

HERRINGBONE TWILL   In the herringbone pattern, the twill runs in both directions in the cloth; however, in Figure 6–10 the pattern for an even her-

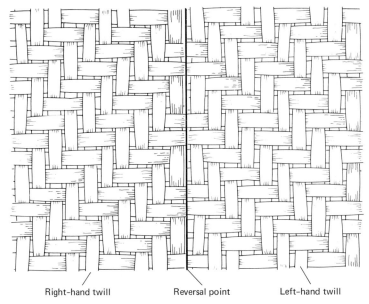

Right-hand twill   Reversal point   Left-hand twill

Figure 6-10   Herringbone twill.

ringbone weave is shown in which the herringbone is a right-hand twill for a certain distance and then reverses and becomes a left-hand twill. The effect resembles the backbone of a fish, as the name implies. In order to create this reversal, there must be a variation in the weave at the apex or point of the inverted **V** in order to reverse the wale direction. In the fabric portrayed, the two over two, the pattern is broken at this apex by passing under one warp, over the next, then under two, over two, under two, and so on, to change the direction from lower left to upper right into a ridge running from upper left to lower right. Intricate geometrical designs can be made in twills, forming diamonds and other figures in some fine suiting cheviots. Changing the twist, modifying the thickness of the yarn, and using combinations of dyed warp and filling yarns produce many of the novelty effects that make the twill weave so popular.

PROPERTIES OF TWILLS   The general characteristic of twills is their density. These fabrics are generally closer in texture than plain weaves; thus, they are heavier in weight and are stronger. The twill weave may be referred to as the backbone fabric construction for men's outer clothing and for uniform fabrics in which extreme durability is one of the most important considerations. They require more intricate loom setting or shedding, which adds somewhat to the cost; also, they are heavier, having a greater weight of actual textile fiber per square yard than the usual plain weave.

SATIN WEAVE   The characteristic of the **satin weave** is the apparent absence of surface pattern. This is accomplished by having long floats passing over several yarns before interlacing with a single cross yarn, followed by another long float. These floats may be from 4 to as many as 12 yarn crossings long. In fact, the satin or sateen weave is a highly unbalanced twill designed to emphasize the shine and smoothness of silk, rayon, acetate, mercerized cotton, and the lustrous synthetics, and to give the illusion of a perfectly smooth, shiny-surfaced material without any pattern.

In **satins**, the long floats on the right side of the material are the warp direction. Thus, the fabric feels more slippery when rubbed in the lengthwise direction. On the reverse side of the fabric, the floats would then be predominantly in the filling direction. If on the right side of the fabric the filling direction shows the predominance of floats, and its slipperiness is the direction of the width, the fabric is called sateen. Generally, in **sateen**, the floats are shorter than in satin.

Figures 6–11 and 6–12 show the typical interlacings for short- and long-float satin weaves, respectively.

The smooth, lustrous, dense appearance of satins suggests reasonably good service in use. However, the long floats are subject to damage from abrasion or rubbing, and the longer the float the more easily the surface can be scarred by the cutting or chafing of the floating fibers. The short-float fabrics are more durable than the long, but they do not have the luster or

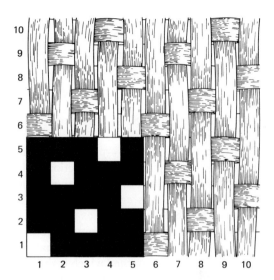

Figure 6-11   Short-float satin. Warp-face satin; 5-harness base (or counter) of 2 showing the first repeat as a paper pattern, the rest with sketches of woven yarns.

brilliance. These fabrics make excellent materials for coat linings because they allow the garment to be slipped on and off easily. They generally shed dirt well, but spots and stains are as visible as smudges on a mirror.

The complexity of the harness setup of the loom for long-float satins adds considerably to the cost of production. For example, in a sateen in which the filling passes over 4 and under 1 warp, five shafts are required $(1 + 4 = 5)$; and in a 12-float satin, the filling would be under 12 and over 1, requiring thirteen shafts.

Modifications in twist will provide variety in surface appearance. A high-sheen satin is produced when the warp yarns are very low in twist. A more tightly twisted warp in a shorter float fabric would produce a softer luster. Combinations of tightly twisted filling with loosely twisted warps will pro-

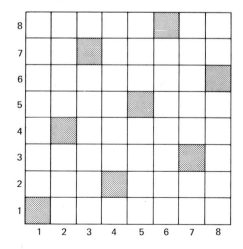

Figure 6-12   Long-float (8-shaft) satin showing first repeat. Eight-harness, base of 3 (7-over, 1-under). No. 1 filling is up. The next filling, in row 2, if the base or counter is 3, would be over the third warp to the right, or no. 4; in the third row, again 3 to the right, or no. 7. In row 4, the repeat boundary requires the use of warp no. 2 (1 to the right to the boundary, then to the extreme left and 2 more to the right. The construction continues for the full 8-yarn pattern with the filling being over the third-warp yarn in each successive row from the bottom (no. 1) to the top row (no. 8).

duce crepe-backed satins called satin crepe. Combinations of fibers can be used—for example, a silk warp on the face, rayon or cotton on the back. Nylon and other synthetics can also be used in these various satin constructions for novelty effects.

THE IDENTIFICATION OF FABRICS

The three basic weaves—plain, twill, and satin—are relatively easy to identify as to warp and filling direction and for right and wrong faces for the purpose of using them as fabrics for garments. In the fabrics department of a store, of course, it is easy to determine the direction of warp and filling because the whole bolt can be examined or the selvage can be seen in a small sample. The warp yarns, of course, are parallel with the selvage. If, on the other hand, the customer has but a small sample, it is sometimes difficult to know which is the warp and which is the filling.

Because the warp, or lengthwise direction, must withstand the greater amount of pulling during manufacturing and processing, and because most of the pull in garment use is also in the length direction, the warp usually has more yarns than does the filling in a sample of material. Therefore, in plain weaves, the higher count generally indicates the warp. In the case of a square-count cloth, such as the common 80-square print, the strength of the yarns is the best indication. This can be estimated by raveling out a few yarns from each direction; then by giving them a pull between the fingers, the stronger direction can be ascertained. This usually will be the warp. In basket weaves, the warp is the more tightly twisted yarn. In unbalanced fabrics, particularly those with a large yarn in one direction and numerous finer yarns in the other, the warp will be in the direction of the finer yarns and the bulkier crosswise yarn will be the filling. In the case of other novelties in plain weave, such as the thick and thin or the nubby yarns of pongee and shantung, the irregular yarns are usually the filling. The pattern, if any, is generally in the warp direction. Usually, the filling yarns will be wavier when raveled back for inspection.

Identifying the Right Face of a Fabric

In using a piece of cloth, it is, of course, customary to have the right face outside. However, wool fabrics are generally folded or rolled on a bolt with the back surface on the outside to protect the face against accidental soiling and abrading. In the case of a small sample, it is sometimes difficult to tell which is the right and which is the wrong side of the material. Generally, the brighter, shinier surface will be the right side, the one intended to be seen. If the weave characteristics are more distinct and the pattern more attractive on one side than the other, then the more attractive face is the right side. It is usually much simpler to determine this in the case of prints, because the print will be more vivid and clearer on the right side of the material. Some woolens and wool-synthetic fiber combinations in suitings and coatings are napped on one face. This is usually the right side, the side to be exposed to the onlooker. Although the wale is more distinct on the right side, twill weaves are sometimes more obscure. If the small sample is held in such a way that the wales run either from lower left to upper right or from upper left to lower right, the warp yarns will then be in the vertical direction and the filling yarns in the horizontal direction. The warp yarns will probably be more tightly twisted (if there really is a difference in twist), and when yarns are pulled out in either direction, those that stay straighter and show the least amount of waviness will be the warp yarns that have been made more rigid by stresses imposed on them.

With the very smooth, lustrous fabric characteristics of the satin weave, it is easy to determine the direction of the floats, and knowing this and the identity of the fiber, the conclusion can be reached as to which is the right side. For example, if the fabric is of silk, rayon, acetate, or synthetics alone or in combination, the weave is a satin and the floats are in the warp direction. If the fabric is all cotton, the float is usually the filling in the sateen construction. There is one exception, however, and that is in the all-cotton material farmers' satin that is used for coat linings. This is a warp-float cotton.

NOVELTY WEAVES

Novelty weaves provide texture, pattern, or surface interest not found in the basic weaves previously described. In some cases, special attachments are used on the conventional harness loom to produce fancy fabrics with a woven-in pattern. Special looms and weaving operations are required for more intricate fabrics, including rugs and carpetings, velvets, patterned brocades, and even for such end-use products as terry towels and bird's-eye diaper cloths.

Jacquard and Other Pattern Weaves

Everyone marvels at the beautiful and often intricate patterns woven into the finest of linen table **damasks**. Similarly, the delicately and precisely colored patterns woven into upholstery damasks of silk or synthetic fibers, the beautiful brocades, and the intricate colorings in rugs are all beyond the capacity of the conventional harness loom. If the pattern is especially complicated or if the **repeat** is large—that is, greater than about 16 picks along the length of the goods—a Jacquard loom is used. A less expensive dobby loom may be used for the shorter repeats. In the Jacquard loom, the control is not of groups of warp yarns but of the movement of each individual yarn. (See Figure 6–13.)

There is no standard Jacquard weave, for this loom is capable of weaving plain, twill, satin, and combinations, because of the control of the individual warps. It was invented by a Frenchman, Joseph Marie Jacquard, in 1801 to produce by mechanical means the pictorial effects of hand-woven Flemish tapestries. The term **Jacquard** refers to the method of weaving some of the most intricately patterned apparel fabrics.

It often requires months to set up a Jacquard loom for a particularly elaborate pattern. The pattern is first sketched and all the colors decided upon. The sketch is then transferred to the conventional point-paper pattern. However, instead of setting up the warps in the colors desired along a harness beam, a series of paper-pattern punch cards or tapes is prepared. There is a punch card for every filling yarn to be used in each repeat; and on each card, there is a space for a punch hole to be inserted for each warp yarn across the width of the loom. A hole is punched in the appropriate place on each card for every warp yarn that is to be raised when the filling yarn is shot through. Each warp yarn to be passed over by that pick has its pattern spot on the card unpunched. In a sense, then, each of these paper-pattern cards activates the

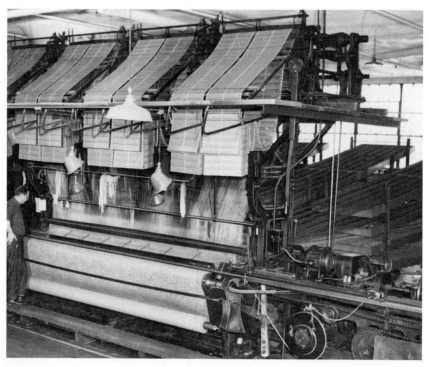

Figure 6-13   Jacquard loom. (Courtesy of Mohawk Mills and the Hoover Company)

warps to be raised in a fashion similar to the old-fashioned pianola record, on which holes were punched in a paper roll to cause certain piano keys to respond.

It is obvious why this setting-up operation is laborious—the repeat may have as many as 4000 or 5000 picks. This means 4000 or 5000 cards, and the fabric width may be such that 5000 ends are used. For each of these, there must be an identical possible hole position on every card. These cards are then laced together in order, and they pass successively over a long oblong cylinder near the top of the loom. Each warp yarn is threaded through an eye at the lower end of a fine steel wire that hangs by a cord, the upper end of which is attached to a horizontal wire called a needle. Thus, there is a needle for each of the warp yarns. When a shed is to be formed, all the needles press forward against the card that is in place. Those needles opposite the holes in the card press through, and the pull on these cords lifts the wires and thus raises the warps to form a shed through which the shuttle passes. The oblong cylinder then makes its next turn, placing the second card in position as the first one drops down. The operation is then repeated with another set of warps forming the shed until the pattern or repeat has been completed. When the cards have all been used once, they are repositioned for the next repeat of the pattern. Some Jacquard looms weave the pattern on the down face of the fabric in the loom; in this operation, the shed is formed by a down-thrust of the wires.

The motion of the loom is slow compared with the ordinary harness type, and the price of the fabric produced is necessarily high. Every attempt is made at economy through the reuse of old pattern cards. Indeed, some of the patterns now being used in fine table damask are similar to those of heirloom pieces. If a pattern is a staple that can be used again and again, great savings are effected by simply tying a new set of warp yarns onto the old—in a sense, the patterned goods will be virtually endless because the cards are used many times. In fine damask, the design stands out clearly, because it is often a sateen figure with long floats in the filling direction contrasted against a background fabric having a satin weave with the luster in the warp at a 90° angle to the design.

The Dobby Weave

The dobby attachment can be put on a harness loom to weave small designs. Strips of wood take the place of the cards of the Jacquard loom. These strips are plaited together in a chain, and in each strip of wood, pegs are inserted to indicate the pattern. There is a strip of wood for each pick in the design or repeat, and there is a peg position for each warp to be lifted to form the shed with any pick—16 being the most common repeat. One of the most common fabrics produced by this method is the bird's-eye weave in diaper cloth. The dobby attachment can control about 25 harnesses, but the complexity of the controls limits the frequency of repeat, usually to not more than 16 rows. There is a similar limitation in an American device called the hand-motion attachment, which is referred to also as the dobby weave.

Huck toweling, honeycomb, and waffle cloth are other textures introduced by the dobby method. In men's suitings, the so-called sharkskin, which has much the same figure as bird's-eye, is a dobby-weave product. Small figures on men's shirtings and dress goods, such as the figured madras or the "white-on-white" patterns, are also dobby products.

The Leno Weave

The **leno** or **doup** weave produces a plain, lacelike, open-construction gauze; marquisette curtains are generally made by the leno weave (Figure 6–14). It is produced by a special attachment that crosses adjacent warp yarns over each other during each passage of the shuttle while the filling passes through the eye formed by the twist. In some marquisettes, the two warps are in equal tension, and the loop then is fairly round; in other constructions, one is kept taut while the other is twisted around it, producing what is known as the gauze construction. It must be distinguished, however, from the plain-weave gauze that is used in bandaging and as an interliner. The leno weave is more resistant to the shifting or sliding of yarn under tension than is a plain weave in a similarly thin fabric. Many different man-made fibers are used in this construction. Examples include curtains of nylon, polyester, acrylic, glass, and rayon. Mosquito netting used so widely in the tropics is also of a leno weave. Some nettings have occasional heavy yarns inserted in order to give greater strength. They are usually heavily sized so

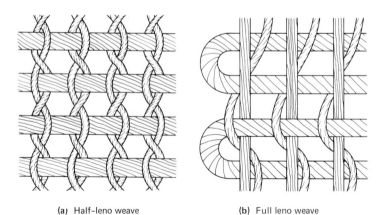

(a) Half-leno weave   (b) Full leno weave

Figure 6-14   The leno weave.

that the netting will stay firmly and stiffly in position and not sag down over the sleeper. **Sizing**, although primarily a finishing process to stiffen and strengthen yarns by adding gums, waxes, or starches, also helps prevent soiling and reduces the tendency of mildew growth in extremely humid conditions.

APPLIED PATTERNS OR STRUCTURAL DESIGN

Although more and more of the fabrics resembling dotted swiss and other small tufted figures are being applied by means of loose flock fibers glued to the surface of the fabric, there are still some fabrics in which a simulated embroidery is actually woven into the cloth. Some of these ornamental effects are the swivel, lappet, clipped-spot, and Schiffli designs. The characteristics of these designs are that the yarns are not an integral part of the ground fabric, and, unlike the pattern figures in the Jacquard or dobby-woven goods, which are permanent, these embroidered effects can be pulled out simply by pulling on an end of the figure on the reverse side of the cloth.

SWIVEL DESIGN   The swivel design uses extra filling shuttles that weave small geometrical designs into the base fabric such as the figured dot in a marquisette and in the fine-quality dotted swiss imported from Europe.

CLIPPED-SPOT DESIGN   The **clipped spot**, an embroiderylike design, also uses an extra filling yarn. The filling yarn extends across the back of the goods. This surplus is generally cut away or clipped by shearing knives, although unclipped patterns are produced also. The eyelash-type patterns have an extra warp yarn.

LAPPET DESIGN   The **lappet** has an extra set of yarns in the warp direction. These are threaded through needles in front of the reed and are moved from side to side to engage with the filling yarns to form a pattern in the woven cloth. These designs are of one continuous yarn and are not clipped on the reverse side.

SCHIFFLI DESIGN   The **schiffli** machine was developed in St. Gall in Switzerland. The word means "little boat," and, indeed, the shuttle somewhat resembles one. This shuttle produces lace or embroidery in widths of up to 15 yards on any kind of fine material, such as batiste, lawn, or organdy. It makes a machine embroidery resembling handwork. The design is controlled by cards similar to those used in the Jacquard loom, but the machine applying the lacy embroidery to finished goods has from 682 to 1020 needles capable of producing intricate appliqués on lingerie fabric and on other fine textile products. Although the products from this machine closely resemble lace, it is not a lace machine; hence, it is more properly described as producing an ornamental effect by an applied design and not as a fabric-construction method.

PILE WEAVES

A fabric having one face with a soft, clipped fiber to give a "furry" feel is called a pile weave. These fiber ends are referred to as **pile**. The term **pile woven** also refers to fabrics having one or both faces covered with loops of pile yarns, such as in twist carpets and in terry toweling. Carpets, of course, have the loops on one face while towels generally have them on both. The twill weave is often used as the basic structure for these pile-type materials. However, extra yarns can be woven to form loops that, in turn, are cut—as in the case of pile-surfaced carpets—or uncut—as in twist or loop-weave carpets.

Resembling these weaves are the tufted fabrics p. 245) formed by tufting or needle punching the pile yarns through a base fabric.

There are five common methods of weaving pile fabrics:

1. *Filling pile method.* This method often is used for such wearing apparel fabrics as corduroy, plushes, and velveteens.

2. *Double-cloth method.* This method is used for such wearing apparel fabrics as transparent velvets and millinery velvet. It is applicable also to some types of fabrics used for blankets.

3. *Terry-weave method.* This method is used for fabrics for terry cloth towels and for bathroom and some cotton throw rugs.

4. *Wire method.* This method is applied to such fine fabrics as velvets for wearing apparel or for upholstery plush fabrics and for such heavier fabric structures as carpets and rugs. Frieze, a fabric rather widely used for upholstery material for many years, but not now particularly high style, is made by this method.

5. *Rug method.* This method incorporates several techniques and has several applications, including hooked rugs and chenilles.

Filling Pile Method

The filling pile method requires extra filling yarns that float over 4 to 5 warp yarns. These floating yarns are cut accurately in the center so that the ends are even in height over the entire surface of the fabric. Sometimes a clipping, or evening, process with rapidly revolving sharp-edged knife blades is necessary to make the surface perfectly smooth. Corduroy is characterized by having vertical stripes, formed by the raised, cut pile, the full length of the goods. This raised figure is called a wale. Alternate extra filling yarns are not cut, and so the fabric shows the series of ridges and canyons characteristic of the corduroy structure. Corduroys vary in fineness from so-called wide **wales**, with 5 wales or fluffy ridges to the inch, down to pinwale corduroys in which there may be as many as 23 wales to the inch. Corduroys can further be described as V- or W-loop construction. Figure 6–15 shows that

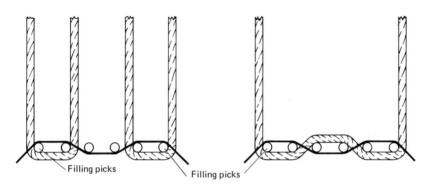

   (a) V–corduroy; under filling once only   (b) W–corduroy; under filling, over filling, and
                                                                      then under

Figure 6-15   Corduroy constructions.

the V-construction corduroy has the cut pile loop held under only one warp yarn, whereas the W-construction corduroy has the loop passing under one, over one, and under a third warp. The second construction is a much more durable structure.

     Velveteen has an all-over pile construction, and plush fabrics for upholstery or for apparel also have the texture of an overall naplike effect. These fabrics, including corduroy, are very resistant to wear against the pile-loop ends—that is, on the right side of the fabric. However, moderate rubbing very often pulls the pile loops through from the back; thus, corduroys and velvets can become totally denuded of their pile when severely abraded on the wrong side (when the loops are pulled out).

Double-cloth Weave

As the name implies, this construction produces two layers of cloth woven face to face, using two sets of warps and two sets of fillings, each pair of which forms one of the fabric layers. An extra set of warp yarns binds these two together. The individual cloths can be woven in any of the conventional plain weaves. In Figure 6–16 the method of construction of such a **double cloth** is shown. The figure shows that two shuttles are required, one for each

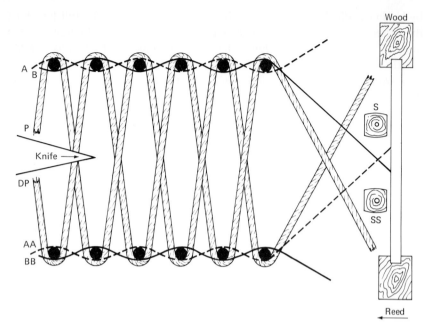

Figure 6-16 Double cloth construction. A and B: ground yarns of the top fabric, woven face down; AA and BB: ground yarns of the lower cloth; P and PP: pile-forming warps interlacing both cloths and cut by knife; S and SS: shuttles working simultaneously; and ● : filling picks.

After the passage of the shuttles, the reed advances to press or compact the newly formed pile loop against those previously woven.

of the two cloths. The filling threads attached to each are woven into their respective warps. The extra binder yarn holding the two fabrics together may be cut apart later with a sharp knife; the ends projecting on the right face of each layer then will make up the pile surface. This method is used for delicate transparent velvets and for velvet and warp-pile velveteen fabrics for the hat industry.

Not all double-cloth fabrics are cut apart for pile weaves. This method is widely used to construct reversible coating material, one surface of which will be a plain fabric while the other is a gay plaid or patterned material. Heavier double-cloth constructions are found among meltons, kerseys, bouclés, and webbings.

Terry Weave

The terry weave can be carried out on a conventional loom with four harnesses: two for warp yarns that are held taut and make up the ground, or base fabric structure; and two to carry warp yarns that are allowed to relax by having the tension released at intervals (at which time they are pushed forward by the reed, thus forming the loops). They are then caught and held in position by the filling yarns that are shot through a shed made of the taut ground-fabric warps. In one common terry construction, the pile or loop warps are raised in the first shed through which two fillings are shot; when the loop warps are lowered and the third filling has been shot through, all three are battened back together, thus sealing the loops. This is known as three-pick terry because three picks—two under and one over—constitute the basic unit. A characteristic of terry is that the loops are generally alternating, first on one face, then on the other. Variations in figures are possible by weaving terry fabrics on dobby and Jacquard looms to form patterns. In most terry fabrics, water absorption is one of the principal characteristics desired; therefore, the warp yarns used in the terry loops are generally of low twist to permit as much water absorption as possible.

Wire Method

The wire method for constructing pile fabrics uses an extra warp to form the yarns. As in the case of terry, one set of warps interlaces with the filling to form the ground or basic fabric. This can be a plain weave or a twill (Figure 6–17). The other set of yarns forms the pile. When the harness carrying the pile-warp yarns is raised to form the shed, instead of a shuttle bearing a filling yarn being shot through, a wire is inserted. The diameter of the wire determines the height of the pile. When the harness is lowered, the pile-warp yarns wrap over this wire, and the loop is held in place by the filling yarns battened against the base of the wire on either side. The wire is then withdrawn; the ground fabric is woven for a number of fillings or picks to hold the loops before another loop is formed and so forth through the length of the fabric. If it is a cut pile, the wire used has a sharp knife at its end. When

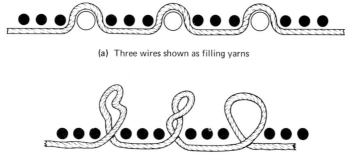

(a) Three wires shown as filling yarns

(b) Two wires withdrawn and battened down. The third loop is not yet battened in position by the reed.

Figure 6-17 The wire method for constructing pile fabrics.

the wire is withdrawn, this knife cuts each loop across the width of the goods. In order to obtain absolutely even pile height over the whole length of fabric, it is sheared with a device something like an electric razor. If the pile is to be of loop or uncut type, then, of course, the smooth wire is withdrawn, leaving the loops intact.

Rug Method

The rug method of forming pile fabrics depends on the type of rug. The quality of the fabric produced varies from velvets woven on the conventional loom with a cut pile of wool or synthetic fiber on a base fabric of jute and cotton to chenilles. Broadlooms (p. 398) are special products and such intricately patterned types as Axminsters and Wiltons generally are woven on Jacquard looms. About 90 per cent of all carpets and rugs today are made by tufting instead of traditional weaving methods (pp. 402–404).

Characteristics of Pile Fabrics

In the case of cut cotton piles, the primary esthetic qualities are softness to the touch and richness and warmth of color without luster or shininess. To aid in achieving dullness in wearing apparel, it is customary to cut the fabric so that the pile runs in the vertical direction. Thus, the wearer looks downward into the depth of the fabric, and the richness of color is emphasized without luster. In this position, also, any friction or rubbing tends to be against the lay of the pile fibers, and matting is reduced. Most cut-pile fabrics are subject to spots and stains that produce shiny marks where the pile may be flattened by the staining liquid as it dries. The garment can be steamed to remove these unsightly spots after the staining material has been removed by conventional methods. Pile is greatly improved in appearance and service life by frequent brushing with a soft brush, working first against the lay of the pile and then parallel to it. These fabrics are very sensitive to wear and abrasion on the inner surface, because the cut pile can be plucked and pulled through by catching the loop where it is interlaced with the filling yarn.

The principal functional role of pile-woven apparel is warmth. This results from the entrapment of air in the loose fiber pile or in the loops. Double-layer fabrics either from double weaving or from double knits also entrap dead air for warmth.

Pile Fabrics for Household Decoration

Pile fabrics for household decoration—such as in upholstery coverings (frieze, for example) or for carpets and rugs used in finishing interiors—

depend very largely on the quality of their construction for durability. Again, one of the primary considerations is wear. Rubbing on the face of such fabrics usually does not seriously damage them. There is a tendency, however, for cut-pile carpets and rugs in fibers other than wool to show traffic lanes where the fiber ends are flattened out under prolonged compression. Staple fibers of nylon, polyester, acrylic, and saran can be given a permanent crimp before spinning, and when the denier is heavy enough, these fibers also are quite resilient under compression. Textured filament yarns are often used. Wool has a greater resiliency, and these fibers will come erect more readily. It is primarily because of this traffic-lane problem that most of the synthetic fiber carpets are in uncut pile or loop construction, which does not crush down as readily as cut pile.

TUFTED FABRICS

One of the fastest-growing branches of the textile industry is that of processing fabrics for bedspreads, blankets, and carpets by new high-speed tufting machinery. It is done by punching extra yarns into a ground or base fabric that can be anything from a thin cotton scrim to jute, heavy nylon duck, and even polyurethane foam reinforced with embedded nylon scrim and other fibers. Any choice of ground material and pile fibers can be made—rayon, nylon, polyester, cotton, wool, or acrylics—depending on the end-use. Man-made fibers were found by the U.S. Department of Commerce to account for 85 per cent of the 1965 production of tufted fabrics. In 1972, the carpet industry used the following quantities of fibers in face yarns:

Fiber	Millions of Pounds
Nylon	989
Polyester	189
Acrylics and modacrylic	120
Other man-made fibers	97
Cotton and wool	45

SOURCE: *Textile Organon,* **45**, No. 11 (Nov. 1973), pp. 164–65.

This is a revolutionary change from the cottage and handcraft tufting of spreads and carpets. The machine control of the industry began in the 1930s. The new machines insert the tufts or pile by means of a series of needles, all of which descend at once, passing through the horizontal base fabric. As the needles retreat, a hook holds the loop in place beneath the fabric. The pile can be left as a top-surface loop or it can be cut. Loop and pile height can be varied for textural effects. A blanket can be constructed in 2 minutes, a 9 × 12 carpet in 4 minutes. A Jacquard loom would take more than an hour. This speed enables the producer to sell these products more cheaply.

KNITTED FABRICS

Knitted cloth has a series of interlocked loops as its basic structure. Garments made of knitted cloth are, therefore, elastic. They yield more to body movements than the rigid interlaced woven yarns because the loops can be extended either lengthwise or widthwise, depending on the direction of stress. Close-fitting clothing such as lingerie, hosiery, sweaters, leotards, panty hose, and ski pants adapt themselves to the changing shape of the moving body. Other advantages with these fabrics are greater freedom from wrinkles, increased porosity, freer air movement, greater moisture absorbency and, in general, improved comfort. This construction is now applied also to outer wear, such as in topcoat and suit material, because (1) commercial knitting is a more rapid process than weaving, (2) the time and labor cost of fabric making is lower, and (3) yarn mobility and its effect on wearing comfort can be used to advantage.

Knitting Progress

The first knitting machine was invented in 1589 by the Reverend William Lee of Nottinghamshire, England, to knit full-fashioned stockings. Since that time, there has been constant improvement in the art of knitting, and countless inventions have been patented. Tricot knits and double knits have contributed to comfort in apparel today. A sensational new invention is a computerized knitting machine developed in England that can complete a knitted garment, fully fashioned, at the rate of one every 52 minutes, and these can sell at moderate prices. The term **cybernetics** has been applied to this new science of computerization. The desired knitting pattern is put on tapes that are then scanned so that the electrical impulses set the program or sequence of knitting, course by course. A beam of light scans the tape, and where a hole appears, the beam activates a photocell that controls the needle to be used to knit a stitch. The gauge can vary from 8 to 16 needles per inch, with the probability that the number will be doubled within a few years.

Knitting Methods

There are two basic types of knit construction, but each has several modifications. Although **warp knitting** is becoming increasingly popular, by far the greater volume of knit goods is of the **filling**-knit (formerly called weft) construction. Two types of filling knits are better known as **circular** and **flat** knits, respectively. The essential difference between warp knitting and filling knitting is that hundreds of parallel yarns can be used in warp knits, each carried by a separate needle in a vertical direction and all looping at the same time to produce a flat fabric. Filling knitting is similar to hand knitting and knits the yarn in a crosswise direction. Modern equipment permits a number of yarns from separate feeds to form rows simultaneously to produce a tubular fabric. This is circular knitting. For example, in sweaters, as many as 84 yarns can be used and 84 courses can be knitted at once. The diagrams may appear complex at first, but further study will emphasize the essential differences between them.

Circular-knit nylon hosiery, and most sweaters, bathing suits, and undershirts, are examples of filling knit items, which are formed in a continuous tube. Usually, except in hosiery, the tube is split open and then cut into the pieces from which the article is to be assembled.

The weft-knit fabrics formed by flat machine knitting are generally known as full-fashioned. In this construction, yarns travel back and forth, and the lengthwise edges are narrow selvages. It is a slower method of construction but permits the accurate garment dimension characterized in the shaping of full-fashioned hosiery and full-fashioned sweaters. The time required to knit this fabric and the demands for an accurate fit by this method are the factors that cause its higher price. This structure is made also in hand knitting. The **flat machine** must not be confused with flat or warp knit, which is a texture imparted by multineedles in the warp direction. (See Figures 6–18 and 6–19.)

Each of these constructions permits the production of numerous surface textures, depending on the yarn, type of stitch, and kind of finish.

Common Types of Knitting

Among the various stitches to be found in garments are the full-range of knitted constructions from the simplest, the jersey stitch, to the more com-

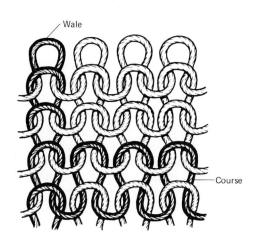

Figure 6-18 A wale (vertical row) and a course (horizontal loop row) in a plain-knit fabric.

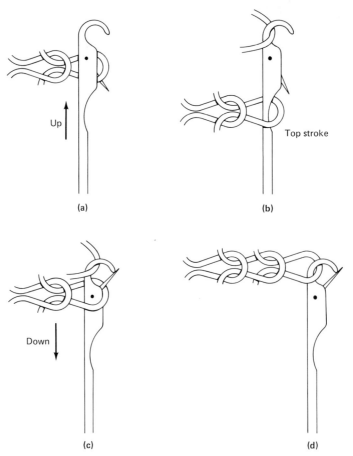

Up

Top stroke

(a)   (b)

Down

(c)   (d)

Figure 6-19   How the latch needle forms a loop.

plex lacy knit structures, such as Raschel, which are accomplished on eight widely used knitting-machine systems.

1. *Jersey flat knit.* This flat-bed filling knit machine is used for full-fashioned knit fabrics, such as sweaters, body hose, ski wear, and other comfortable apparel. A single yarn is fed at one time as in hand knitting. The mechanism feeding the yarn moves back and forth, and the yarn is engaged by a succession of needles, the number of which determine the width of the piece to be knit (Figure 6–20). By putting in more needles or by removing surplus needles the width of the article can be altered. In hand knitting, the edges tend to curl until the garment is assembled by stitching the various sections together. The heavy, bulky type of sweaters are among the most popular articles made by this method. The same technique on special flat

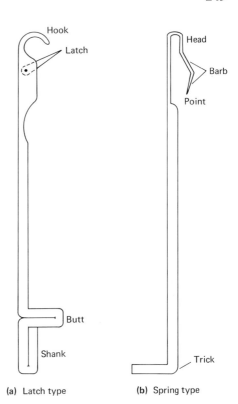

Figure 6-20 Commercial knitting needles.　(a) Latch type　(b) Spring type

equipment is used in making women's full-fashioned hose. Good fit, comfort, and freedom from waste material, resulting from cutting circular-knit fabrics to fashion the garment, contribute to the continued popularity of this method, despite its somewhat higher price due to the slowness of operation.

2. *Jersey circular knit.* This knitting machine produces articles sold in high volume, such as circular-knit hosiery and underwear. The machine is characterized as being the "workhorse" of the industry. More than 100 million pounds of men's undershirts were produced in 1968, the highest poundage production of any item of men's apparel. Approximately the same poundage in women's sweaters was produced, 28 per cent of all of the poundage of women's apparel. Jersey circular knit accounts for a vast amount of the textile production of striped jerseys, of velours, of pile fabrics, of jersey fabric for bonding fabrics for apparel, and of women's seamless hosiery.

A special jersey construction is used to produce **double knits** on a circular machine. V. J. Lombardi[1] describes the fabric as being knitted on two sets of needles in which the two sides of the cloth are interlocked. Generally, for

---

[1] V. J. Lombardi, "The Expanding World of Circular Knitting," *Modern Textiles Magazine,* **42**, No. 9 (Sept. 1961), pp. 62–63.

outer wear and especially for men's apparel, this heavy cloth has a fine-ribbed outer surface and a fine bird's-eye or geometrical pattern on the reverse. These fabrics do not curl at the edges as do conventional jerseys and are much more dimensionally stable. They are discussed further under men's apparel, p. 249.

The great advantage here is speed of production; and with the greatly expanded pattern variety it is entering into the men's suiting industry. Another interesting application is in wall coverings and draperies.

3. *Rib flat knit.* This flat-bed machine uses two needle beds, and the carriage carrying the yarn can be made to switch from one bed to the other to make a variety of stitches, even to lacy openwork. In another adaptation, two stitches can be taken every sixth needle to produce an elastic cuff; in knitting a full-fashioned sweater, the body can be knit with perhaps 100 stitches over a given length with 120 stitches over the same area for the cuffs. This machine is used primarily for making collars, cuffs, and trimmings. The machine can knit patterns and do cable stitches, turtle-neck collars, plackets, and other garment portions. The garments are shaped to fit and they result in no waste.

4. *Rib circular knit.* The principal application of this machine is in the popular double knits that are an important skirt and suiting market for women's wear; the machine produces most of the knit fabrics for men's outer wear. It is the highest speed machine knitting tubular goods and can produce a fairly wide range of simple patterns. The growth of this type of machine is illustrated by the fact that from an estimated 1100 machines in 1962, the number in 1968 was 4200; and it was estimated to be 9000 in 1970. As in other circular- or warp-knit machines, the fabric can be cut to shape for tailoring; it does not run, but a relatively high amount of wastage, sometimes as high as 20 per cent, results from the trimmed portions.

5. *Purl flat knit.* In this machine, the yarn is fed from the left, producing the typical round stitch produced by purling in hand knitting. This machine is used mostly in the production of sweaters, such as pullovers and cardigans. Fancy knits can be produced in interesting patterns because the machine can transfer the stitches from one needle to another (Figure 6–21). In some sweaters with a pattern front and a plain back, the front is knit on this full-fashioned machine and a circular knit is used in the back; the two are then pieced down the sides. It is a slow process, and the products, therefore, are high priced.

6. *Purl circular knit.* As in the case of the other circular machine, the pattern is the same on both faces. The principal difference in this machine from the purl flat operation is that the needle bed is set up in a circular shape instead of being flat, but the yarn is fed back and forth on the same needle to produce the fabric (Figure 6–22). It is a more rapid operation than the purl flat operation and produces Jacquard patterns in sweaters. The widest application of this machine is in men's sports socks and in high-volume sweaters.

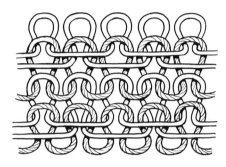

Figure 6-21 Purl or link and link stitch (same pattern on both sides).

Figure 6-22 A circular knit of run-resistant type.

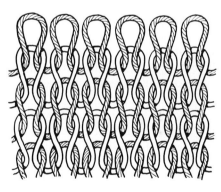

Figure 6-23 The tricot stitch.

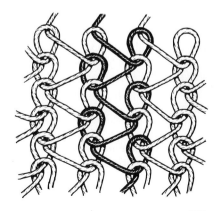

Figure 6-24 A warp knit of run-resistant construction.

Warp Knits

1. *Tricot knit.* Tricot is an example of a warp-knit machine in which the fabric is produced on a flat surface. Tricot has long been identified with the lingerie industry. A guide bar controls the movement of the warp yarns around the needles. The simplest tricot is known as two-bar (see Figure 6–23); its warp yarn is guided from one horizontal row or course to another in a zigzag fashion producing a fabric that will not run when broken. Multibar machines can be used that produce a more intricate meshing for ornamental effects. Thus far, the principal application has been in fine yarns of filament nature, but currently there is experimentation in spun yarns. The tricot knit is regarded as one of the most foolproof methods of machine knitting, requiring less supervision than any of the other types. The main end-uses, as of 1971, according to *American Fabrics,* were for lingerie, 32 per cent; bonding and laminating fabrics, 24 per cent; nightwear and lounge wear, 17 per cent; uniforms, 3 per cent; women's dresses and blouses, 10 per cent; men's shirts, other outer wear, automotive, and industrial, all under 3 per cent.[2] Total production was about 105 million pounds in 1960; by 1975, production is expected to reach 450 million pounds, with much of it going into bonding and into textured yarns for outer wear. Acetate, nylon, and polyester fibers are the principal ones used in these fabrics.

2. *Raschel warp knit.* In this machine multiple bars, as many as 48 are used to produce a great variety of fabric textures from rigid, close-knit to filmy, lacy materials. In texture, they may be of stretch nature, or rigid, firm laces, depending on the texture of the yarn used and the arrangement of the pattern bars (Figure 6–24). One of the major applications is in producing the firm, elasticized fabric called Power Knit, which is the support-textile part of foundation garments. It is a fast and inexpensive way to produce fine laces for lingerie, bridal wear, and for curtains. It is a complex machine requiring careful programming and care. Thus, the fabrics are on the expensive side. On the other hand, its versatility and design are almost infinite and make it very important to the men's garment industry. It has been used in some pile fabrics because it distributes all of the pile yarn to the face of the fabric; in normal construction, either by weaving or by tufting, a percentage of each pile tuft is embodied in the base fabric.

3. *Milanese.* In this machine two sets of yarns are used, one moves from left to right, the other from right to left; a diamond effect results where the yarns cross. The pattern resembles tricot. It is used most commonly in lingerie.

COMBINING FIBERS   Thus far, the combination of fibers in knitting yarns has been mentioned only briefly. There are several ways of combining fibers

[2] *American Fabrics,* No. 91 (Fall 1971), p. 65.

in yarns to produce different effects or to provide a cheaper or a stronger product. These fibers can differ in identity, size, grade, or color.

The mixed yarn is produced by one, or by a combination of two or more, of the following methods:

1. Before spinning, the fibers are mixed, or blended, together. This method is useful for mixing two or more dyeings of the same fiber; for combining short wool fibers with cotton, polyester, other synthetics, staple rayon, or silk; for combining various grades of wool fibers; or for combining rarer fibers, such as cashmere or camel hair, with wool. Fine fur fibers can be mixed with wool for very soft yarn.

2. Spinning each kind or color of fiber into an individual yarn permits the combining of different yarns into a single yarn or strand.

   a. The individual yarns may be twisted into ply yarns.
   b. Several different yarns may be knitted together as a unit, but without twisting or definitely joining them together before knitting.
   c. One yarn may be wound around another, as in core yarns, metal yarns, rubber yarns, bouclé, and other novelties, including spandex fibers.

Several methods of combination may be employed during the knitting operation:

   a. Yarns from several hanks, or containers, called multiple feed may be used.
   b. Double knitting and tuck stitches may be used to throw a desired yarn on the outer surface.
   c. Plating is a method in which a desired yarn is thrown to the face surface of the fabric and another yarn is thrown to the back. Almost any desired combination of yarns can be used. One widely applied technique in men's rayon and nylon hosiery is to throw the nylon onto the outer surface at wear areas, such as heels or toes. Some low-priced hose are actually such a plated fabric.

Knitting Fineness

The degree of fineness of a knitted cloth cannot be expressed in terms of yarns per inch. Instead, there is a count of the number of loops, or wales, per unit of space. The fineness is expressed as the gauge of the knitted article, although only in hosiery is the gauge generally given on labels or printed on the article. The openness or compactness of the knitted article is usually expressed in terms of gauge, and the number refers to the number of wales (vertical loop rows) or of needles used in 1½ inches of space in the needle bar (for full-fashioned) or cylinder (for circular knit). The thickness or width of the needle is dependent largely on the size of the yarn being processed. Thus, in sweaters, generally 15- to 20-gauge would be as fine as the yarns could accommodate. In knitting nylon hosiery, 60-gauge is one of the standard constructions. This means there would be 60 needles used in 1.5 inches of needle bar, which is 14 inches wide for a full-fashioned stocking. **Needle count** is two thirds of the gauge value; some manufacturers refer to gauge in terms of number of needles per inch: 45-gauge—that is, 45 wales for 1.5 inches—would be equivalent to 30 needles per inch. Thus, 51-gauge, 60-gauge, and 72-gauge are increasing degrees of fineness in nylon hose of the full-fashioned flat-type. In circular-knit hosiery, it is customary to express the fineness in terms of the total number of needles used in knitting such hose. Circular-knit hosiery knitted with 400 needles has the same wale count as 51-gauge. Since 1949, the Federal Trade Commission has permitted the term *gauge* to be applied to circular-knit hosiery. However, the label must indicate, by the equally conspicuous words *circular knit, no seam,* or *seamless,* that the hosiery is not full-fashioned.

KNITTING UNDERWEAR   A commercial knitting machine now used in the knitted underwear industry may use as many as 1600 needles, each of which forms 2000 stitches per minute. The machine is fed by anywhere from 8 to 148 cones, each of them carrying a yarn to the machine at the rate of 700 feet per minute; thus, the fabric is formed by knitting at a vastly greater rate of speed than by any method of weaving. Most underwear is circular knit, by which a long continuous tube is formed—the width being regulated by the size of the cylinder of the machine. This may vary from 12 to 24 inches, depending on the size of the garment to be made. The smaller-diameter machines are being used for the manufacture of infants' clothing. In the latch-needle machine, the yarn is caught on the hook end to make a loop, the latch then pushes back and permits the finished loop to fall away. In the spring-needle machine, the hook makes a close, firm loop, characteristic of the flat-knit goods. The term as used here refers to the lack of loft and absence of visible raised ribs; it is not to be confused with the flat-knit goods formed by the flat-knitting machines. The fineness of the fabric depends upon the coarseness or fineness of the individual needles used.

No details as to bleaching, dyeing, cross-dyeing, printing, preshrinkage, moisture repellency, moth repellency, or other routine textile-finishing processes will be elaborated on here because they are discussed in Chapter Seven, which deals with the finishing of textiles.

Nylon Hosiery

The degree to which nylon has taken over the women's hosiery business was first shown by the production statistics for 1970, which showed the use of approximately 62.9 million pounds of nylon hose, including panty hose. This was 99.7 per cent of all man-made fibers used for women's hosiery. In 1970, women's hosiery totaled 124,023,000 dozen pairs. (See Table 6–4.) The American woman, teenager and adult, uses approximately 30 pairs of nylon hosiery each year. Full-fashioned hosiery is knit flat with loops added or dropped at various points in order to shape the hosiery leg accurately. The stocking then is sewn up the back, giving the characteristic back seam and the small gatherings, or fashion marks, indicating where changes in the number of needles or loops have taken place on each side of the back seam. For shaping, there are narrowings near the knee and again at the ankle. A faster and cheaper way of knitting is made possible by the fact that nylon can be boarded (heat-set) to accurate size and shape; thus, a continuous tube of knit nylon can be shaped to fit the leg smoothly. This circular knit (p. 247) lacks a back seam, but an imitation seam can be put in to resemble the full-fashioned hose. Variations in the knitted structure produce mesh hose, which will not run when a yarn is broken. One of the criticisms of man-made fibers is their luster or brightness; often consumers prefer to have such fabrics made duller. Nevertheless, a demand has developed for some special fabrics—one of which might be called **sparkling nylon**—in which the physical shape of the yarn is made more reflective by manipulation, and the surface appears to gleam with light from many sources. Some of these fabrics, used in hose, have a gold reflective tone; others are brilliant blacks or luminous pastels, in addition to the more conventional colors. Stretch nylons, utilizing stretched yarns that are allowed to relax into a looped and kinked structure, can be pulled to four times their length and will return to their original shape. These, and Cantrece hosiery (p. 211), do not bind or cause discomfort to the leg of the wearer.

Foreign researchers interested in the effects of extremely high-frequency waves in the ultrasonic region on various chemicals and polymers, have created fundamental changes in the nylon molecules. The Berkshire Knitting Mills of Reading, Pennsylvania, has licensed this **sonochemicals process**, and the hosiery produced has been found to possess some very unusual properties, including a closer adherence to the leg in motion, a greater degree of comfort in temperature extremes (that is in winter and in summer), and more porosity and softness.

It is clear that if a customer simply goes into a store and orders nylon stockings, she is overlooking the opportunity to enjoy the benefits of many of these researches. The nylon stocking, especially, the self-shaping Cantrece or Agilon stocking, may show properties unique in the experience of the average consumer.

The degree to which circular-knit construction has seized virtually the entire women's hosiery market from the full-fashioned variety was demonstrated in Table 6–4. From 16,673 dozen pairs or 22.9 per cent of the market in 1962, the full-fashioned fell to only 137 dozen pairs or 0.1 per cent in 1972. During this 10-year period, the market of women's hosiery rose by one-third. The better full-fashioned hosiery selling for around $2.50 a

Table 6-4 Annual Production of Women's Hosiery, by Types, 1962-1972

(dozens of pairs in thousands)

	1972	1971	1970	1969	1968	1967	1966	1965	1964	1963	1962
Total, all types*	227,901	210,893	244,051	241,414	220,285	230,309	218,137	198,244	189,215	178,012	172,557
Women's total	97,805	92,369	124,023	126,877	121,463	119,159	105,048	92,323	89,900	75,979	72,674
Women's full-fashioned	137	154	370	374	691	1,346	2,867	4,346	6,995	10,495	16,673
Women's seamless—											
total	97,668	92,215	123,653	126,503	120,772	117,813	102,181	87,977	76,905	65,484	56,001
Seamless, full length	16,993	27,225	35,849	68,112	103,079	117,813	102,181	87,977	76,905	65,484	56,001
Panty hose	80,675	64,990	87,804	58,391	16,893						

SOURCE: *Textile Organon*, **44**, No. 7 (July 1973), p. 105.
* Includes women's, men's, children's, and infants' hosiery.

pair and upward must compete with the circular-knit hose that is available at $0.50 to $1.00 in almost any supermarket. It is not surprising that the cheaper, faster-produced circular knit is the popular item. Price, along with poorer durability and fit, accounts for the high-consumption rate; the price of circular knits almost classifies them as semidisposable apparel items.

Another interesting statistic in this table shows that panty hose, not even charted prior to 1968, had more than a fourfold increase by 1972.

Formelle Nylon Hosiery

The use of the heavier-textured nylon yarns in form-fitting knitwear articles, such as in panty hose, has been marked by some consumer complaints about the eventual stretching and wrinkling of the panty hose after use. The terms *sag* and *bag* have been used in the wording of these complaints. **Formelle** yarn, patented by the Rohm and Haas Company, is said to resist this stretchiness—which has been attributed to the high temperature required to dye these articles in the many bold and deep colors required by fashion. This new yarn is colored prior to knitting; therefore, it resists any stretching after it has been knitted.[3]

Knitted Pile Fabrics

The introduction of durable, nonwater-absorbent synthetic fibers, intrigued the manufacturers of outer coats, especially for women. The fibers could be made to resemble fur. In recent years, more of these fabrics have been formed by the knitting procedure than by the earlier weaving methods.

These simulated fur garments have grown rapidly in importance since 1955. In that year, 750 thousand coats of this type were produced; in 1970, more than one million units utilizing some 6 million pounds of synthetic fiber were produced by ten different mills. Most of these coats are produced from acrylic and modacrylic mixtures, usually 65 per cent Orlon and 35 per cent Dynel. Other acrylics, such as Acrilan, Creslan, and Zefran, have also been used. Knitted fabric has been found to be more comfortable and to have a more natural drape than coat bodies of woven structures; Dynel is added to reduce the hazard of flammability in these dense pile textiles. The construction of these fabrics is a complicated and relatively slow procedure.

In the conventional machine, the pile sliver is fed into the knitting cylinder and is locked in by a jersey construction using a heavier base yarn. The mixed staples used to form the pile—that is, the blend of Orlon acrylic and Dynel modacrylic, or other fiber combinations—are carded; the sliver is placed on

---

[3] *American Dyestuff Reporter*, **59**, No. 12 (Dec. 1970), p. 50.

the feed roll, which is taken by the worker, who places it on the main carding cylinder to be straightened. As the knitting operation begins, the knitting needles seize the staple in the small hooks near the needle head, and as the knitting operation proceeds, this staple is firmly caught into the jersey base, where it is locked into place by the yarn structure. The depth of the pile is determined by the length of the staple selected for the fabric and the pile may be sheared to make it absolutely even in height. Machine production is at the rate of about 5 yards per hour. If the sheared fabric is ¾-inch staple, the weight of imitation fur is approximately ⅝-pound per square yard. In order to simulate more closely the beauty and luster of natural furs, these coat materials must go through the following steps:

1. *Heat setting.* The cloth is shrunk lengthwise to a stable position and the diameter of the individual fibers is expanded.
2. *Tigering.* The purpose of tigering, which is a heavy brushing operation with wire brushes, is to ease out any loose fibers from the staple that may not have been completely held in place by the knitting operation.
3. *Rough shearing.* The height of the pile is carefully regulated in a mowing-type operation.
4. *Electrifying.* An electrically heated cylinder, on the surface of which are a series of polishing helixes or grooves, polishes and adds high luster to the pile in a combing operation.
5. *Wet application.* This step is intended to increase the luster of the fibers.

In wet application with acrylic-modacrylic mixtures, alcohol and water can be used. If the imitation fur contains quantities of wool, then acetic acid, formaldehyde, and alcohol and water may be used. In the case of wool, one of the objectives is to remove crimp so that the fibers will stay at a uniform height throughout the wear life of the garment. Following this, there is a second **electrifying** and a second and final **shearing operation**.

Fibers of Knitted Apparel

Despite the new shuttleless looms and their greatly accelerated rate of weaving, it appears that the further growth of knitted apparel is almost unlimited. Knitted fabrics do have certain basic disadvantages, including stretching or shrinking, runners, and missed stitches in some types of stitch.

Occasionally, a knitted fabric will show horizontal lines that may be darker or lighter than the rest of the fabric. This is noted especially in patterned knits, in which the line may appear through the repeat pattern. Technically, this is known as **barre.** Sometimes these lines appear as thicker or thinner yarns. This may result from uneven tension of the yarn prior to dyeing, from differences in the absorbency of the fabric during dyeing, to a difference in tightness of twist, or to temperature differences. The most prominent fibers used in knits are shown in Table 6–5.

Knits for Fashion Change

The acceleration of fashion change and the increased demand on the fabric manufacturer that he produce more and more unusual and different textile constructions have aided greatly in the advance of knits as compared with woven fabrics. In recent years, apparel manufacturers have been called on to produce four or five lines a year as compared with the two seasonal lines formerly shown to the public. To produce a new fabric construction may take a weaver between 6 and 12 months, but a new knitted fashion can be produced in 60 days. Most of today's consumers recognize that the knitted

Table 6-5 Fibers Used in Knits, 1972 Projected

(millions of pounds)

	Apparel		Home		Industrial		Total	
	1968	1972	1968	1972	1968	1972	1968	1972
Cotton	547	560	23	25	35	50	605	635
Nylon	264	351	5	7	6	12	275	404
Acetate	213	289	—	—	—	—	213	289
Acrylic	211	470	3	5	—	—	210	475
Wool	113	105	2	3	—	—	115	108
Polyester	70	179	—	25	2	12	72	216
Rayon	23	25	5	6	—	—	28	31
	1441	1979	38	71	43	74	1559	2158

SOURCE: *American Fabrics*, No. 68 (Summer 1969), p. 109.

structure is no longer characteristic only of hosiery, lingerie, and sweaters. Modern knitters produce fine silky fabrics for blouses, shirts, and dresses; in bulky yarns, there are stretch pants, sweaters, and ski wear; and double-knit fabrics are extremely popular in suits and coats for both men and women. Knitted fabrics have a greater extensibility. Knits fit more comfortably, and they are usually more resistant to wrinkling; thus, they are as much at home in dress fabrics today as in casual garments.

In the discussion of yarn construction, reference was made to the bulk yarns, the textured effect. This was a boon to the miniskirt market of recent memory. Long hose and body hose have been in great demand for the light weight and comfort in wear that results from fabric breathability. Knitting

yarns, both textured and untextured, have been used widely in athletic garb—
even for heavy football shirts.

Open-knit apparel is now possible as a result of fabric bonding. Thus, a
garment can have an open jersey knit outer surface and be bonded to tricot
for comfort while giving the appearance of being a double knit.

In addition to the time required to set up and develop a new pattern in
knits as compared with woven fabrics, the speed of operation is greatly in
favor of the knitting equipment. A circular-knit jersey machine can produce
a yard of fabric 44 inches wide in about a minute. A loom will often produce
no more than 5 inches of fabric per minute. Some of this differential is being
canceled out now with the high-speed looms, especially the water-jet and
air-jet types. These have been in the experimental stage in the United States
for several years, but some types are now in commercial use.

Forecasting Knitted Production

The inherent advantages of the knitted structure over that of woven fabrics
for apparel has resulted in the enormous growth shown in Figure 6–25. This
has been extrapolated to the year 1975, assuming that the rate of con-

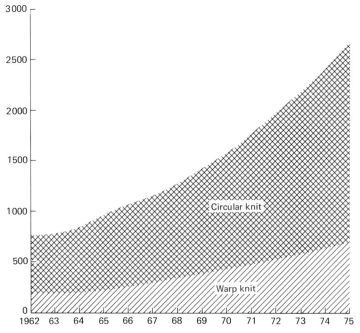

Figure 6-25 Fiber consumption in domestic production of circular knit versus warp knit
apparel fabrics (millions of pounds). [*Modern Textiles Magazine*, **45**, No. 4 (April 1970), p.21]

sumption will remain the same. Production figures for knit versus woven apparel are given in Table 6–6, and for U.S. knit production in 1969–1970 in Table 6–7.

In reviewing the status of the knitted structure, it should be noted that knitting is a simpler, more efficient, and more rapid method of converting yarns into final textile structures for apparel than is weaving. In addition to this, the knitted structures have some functional properties superior to those of wovens, such as greater air porosity; greater elasticity and stretchiness; and more resistance to wrinkling. Therefore, they are easily packed and do not require pressing and freshening before sales display. Knitted fabrics generally hang more gracefully and, because of their superior stretchiness, follow the contour of the figure in a more flattering manner. More sophisticated knitting equipment, such as Raschel equipment, permits a greater variation in fabric pattern and should a knitted structure require excess stiffness or rigidity, this can be given by means of an adherent underlayer fabric. In Figure 6–26 it is forecast that by 1975 knits will account for 52.2 per cent of all apparel-fiber consumption, a consumption of 2.6 billion pounds at an acceleration rate of 11.1 per cent. This contrasts with an annual increase of 4.2 per cent for all apparel fibers, for a total of 5 billion pounds of fiber.

As is indicated elsewhere in this chapter, there will be an enormous growth in the production of circular knits. The differential between warp knit and circular knit shows the circular to account for 3.5 times the volume of warp knits, with approximately 169 million pounds of warp knit and 596 million pounds of circular knit in 1963. By 1975, it is estimated that the

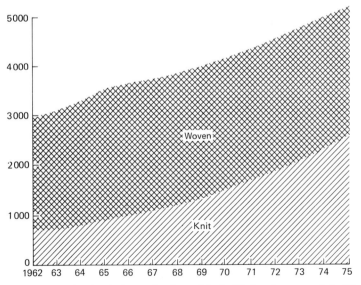

Figure 6-26 Growth in domestic production of knit fabrics for apparel (millions of pounds). [*Modern Textiles Magazine*, **45**, No. 4 (April 1970), p.20]

Table 6-6 Knits Versus Wovens in Apparel

(millions of pounds)

Fiber	Warp Knits				Circular Knits				Wovens			
	1969	1971	1976*	1981*	1969	1971	1976*	1981*	1969	1971	1976*	1981*
Acetate	180	220	235	250	30	45	55	55	175	135	135	135
Rayon	7	5	5	20	20	15	20	20	340	350	420	440
Nylon	133	160	220	275	170	145	120	120	55	65	50	60
Polyester	18	60	225	400	130	400	750	1000	540	625	950	1300
Acrylic	8	10	10	20	200	200	225	250	55	50	75	100
Cotton	10	15	20	40	475	475	500	525	1100	1000	1100	1100
Wool	0	0	0	0	87	85	70	50	285	285	270	250
Total	356	470	715	1005	1112	1365	1740	2020	2550	2510	3000	3385

SOURCE: *American Fabrics*, No. 91 (Fall 1971), p. 36.
* 1976 and 1981 figures estimated.

262

Table 6-7   United States Knit Production for Apparel, 1969–1970

(millions of pounds)

Men's and Boys' Wear		Women's, Misses', and Children's Wear	
Underwear and night wear	190	Underwear, night wear, foundations	229
Sweaters	51	Sweaters	70
Sport and dress shirts	151	Blouses and shirts	44
Hosiery	91	Full-length hosiery	78
		Anklets and socks	31
Gloves, mittens, headwear	19	Gloves, mittens, headwear	6
Swim wear	2	Swim wear	8
Tailored clothing	19	Dresses and suits (including pants suits)	270
Washable service apparel	1	Washable service apparel	12
Athletic uniforms	59	Apparel lace	13
	583	Coats and jackets	3
		Sportswear	81
			845

SOURCE: *American Fabrics*, No. 91 (Fall 1971), pp. 38–39.

circular knits will account for 38.7 per cent of the fiber consumption in apparel fabric, while warp knits will account for 13.5 per cent. It is felt that the full-fashioned warp-knit intimate-apparel fabric has about reached its saturation point and its only growth from now on will be in terms of a higher population of wearers. Double-knit and circular-knit fabrics have also shown a phenomenal growth.

In view of the continued interest of the public in ease-of-care fabrics of all kinds—they bring relief from ironing due to wrinkling—the manufactured fibers will continue to predominate not only in lingerie and intimate attire but in apparel for outer wear. The textured yarns for ski wear, sweaters, swim wear, and recreation clothing in general will continue to be important and virtually all these are of the manufactured yarns. These forecasts are probably optimistic because they fail to take into account some of the realities of caring for knitted fabrics.

All knitted structures shrink. The tendency to shrink is less, of course, in the manufactured fibers than in the natural fibers (cotton and wool) or in the man-made cellulosics. Generally, knitted apparel whether undershirt, swim suit, slacks, socks, or sweater, unless it has been boarded to size, will be longer when first taken from the box than at any time after wear. One advantage of knitted structures is their ability to adapt themselves to body shape and dimension. Thus, they are stretched in the width when worn. This action alone tends to work the garment upward—because the stress in the length-wise direction is minimal. When washed and the fibers or yarns are allowed to relax, they generally relax in the new configuration, or close to it, with the result that with each wearing and washing the garment tends eventually to achieve a greater dimension in width while the length is proportionately shortened. This is an intolerable situation for such apparel as knitted slacks. During World War II when every effort was being made to conserve the consumer's dollar and to encourage him to buy as carefully as possible, signs in most stores warned that one should purchase knitted underwear, T-shirts, socks, and other knitted merchandise at least two sizes larger than that actually worn in order to compensate for shrinkage (most of this referred to the natural shrinkage of knitted cotton). In this day of durable-press, it is likely that consumers are less critical of shrinkage of apparel of all kinds than they were formerly because shrinkage is delayed in its occurrence as a result of finishing.

Undoubtedly, some of the growth forecast for knitted fabrics during the next five years is in anticipation that more of these goods will be going into men's wear—that is, into outer apparel, such as suitings, sports jackets, slacks, and trousers. The men's apparel industry does not prepare for as many changes in style during the year as in the case with women's apparel. In other words, it is a more static industry as far as inventory is concerned. Generally, these manufacturers, being much larger and cutting much greater thicknesses of goods, must necessarily be more conservative. Certain characteristics of knitted fabrics do not make them as suitable for men's wear as the more firmly woven fabrics with which cutters are familiar. Knits tend to roll at the edges; furthermore, a poor stitching job is likely to leave an opening that may run. Just at this time, the variety of woven fabrics seems to be at a new high in textures, colors, and other esthetic features; this, in itself, makes the success of an entirely new texture somewhat more problematical for some cutters. In the men's apparel industry, particularly in suits and coats, the same quality fabric may be used in suits selling at approximately $50 to $60 as are found in garments retailing at more than $100. The great difference in price lies in the amount of hand tailoring done on the garment. The lower-priced suits are essentially machine-stitched—with the exception perhaps of the lapels and shoulders, and even these are now often stitched by machine. Then, as the price goes up, the proportion of hand sewing increases; thus, both the cutting and sewing operations in the case of men's apparel may interfere with the rapid adoption of knits.

Three functional characteristics of knits militate against their suitability for all-weather outer wear. One of these factors is the problem of snagging and running—although, admittedly, in the heavy fabrics used for this kind of garment, the yarns are strong enough to withstand considerable snagging and pulling. The second factor ties in with the stretchiness of the yarns. This stretch, which gives comfort and ease of movement to the body, and the relative size of the openings between yarns and the loops promise poorer water repellency. The openings are just too large and there is too much shifting of position of yarn surfaces in the loops to promise any high degree of water repellency in the fabric. Earlier in this chapter, comfort was mentioned as being one of the great advantages of knits in comparison with woven fabrics. It must be remembered that this observation was based on articles of apparel in contact with the skin. Comfort depended on ventilation whereby body moisture and body heat could be conducted away in warm weather and the garment would remain comfortable in cold, damp weather as long as there was an air-impermeable, or at least a tightly woven, exterior fabric to prevent too much ventilation through the clothing assembly. This feature would be lacking in the case of a knitted outer-wear article. It would not be in a position of increasing air circulation near the body in relatively warm weather and in cold weather or in the presence of wind; it would permit a too-easy entry of chilly exterior air. It is apparent, therefore, that to expect all-weather protection from knitted outer wear is unlikely to be satisfactory; knitted outer-wear fabrics will be admirably suited to appearance and ease of wear, but not for utility in weather extremes.

Deep Pile Knitted Fabrics

One of the most dramatic growths in textile-construction development has been in the deep pile knitted fabrics. According to G. T. Elmes and G. B. Wilkinson, the United States production increased to 90 million linear yards in 1968, a figure double that in 1962; it is anticipated that this will again double by 1975.[4] These deep pile fabrics show the expanded demand for the furry look not only in the high-fashion simulated animal furs for outer wear, but also in furry shell fabrics for men's wear, in home furnishings in floor and wall coverings, and in linings for gloves and boots. Certain modifications, such as crimping and crushing, add surface interest and can actually simulate the curly structure of Persian Lamb and other wavy textures. It is to be noted that manufacturers forecast a more rapid expansion of polyesters in this field, from 6 per cent in 1968 to approximately 20 per cent in 1973. However, the acrylics will still be the predominant fiber. The principal advantage of polyester is its resilience; it avoids the matting and packing down of fibers under heavy loads. It also requires less care and has a more luxurious pile.

It may well be that these furlike fabrics will provide the method by which some of the more scarce fur-bearing animals will be protected from complete obliteration. In the late 1960s the fur of spotted cats became popular among the very wealthy. But these species are facing extinction all over the world. A voice of fashion speaking on television in January 1971 called attention to the fact that the current most popular fur was that of the fisher, an animal of

---

[4] G. T. Elmes and G. B. Wilkinson, "Knitted Pile Fabrics Progress," *Knitting Times,* **39**, No. 43 (Oct. 19, 1970).

the weasel family obtainable only by trapping, whose native habitat was Canada. The voice then went on to say that in 1971 only about 20 coats would be produced and that these coats would sell for between $10,000 and $14,000. The voice then cheerfully added that only enough fishers can be found each year to supply this quantity. The fisher is not yet on the list of endangered species to be protected. It may be that the only natural furs that can be worn without the stigma of destruction will be those of species that can be successfully reared in captivity. These can then be harvested for pelts each year.

NONWOVEN TEXTILES

The 1971 *ASTM Book of Standards* gives the following definitions (D123–71 Standard Definitions of Terms Relating to Textile Materials):

> Fabric, nonwoven—A textile structure produced by bonding or interlocking of fibers, or both, accomplished by mechanical, chemical, or solvent means and combinations thereof. (See also ASTM D2646.)

Note: The term does not include paper, or fabrics that are woven, knitted, or tufted, or those made by wool or other felting processes.

> 3.2 Fabric, nonwoven—A planar structure produced by the bonding or interlocking of textile fibers or both, normally accomplished by mechanical work, thermal treatments, chemical or solvent action, or combinations thereof. (ASTM D2646-69).

The nonwoven fabrics, although they include felts, are described in the following manner:

1. *Nonwoven textiles* of ½- to 5-inch fibers are formed into a dry web by one of several methods and made to adhere tightly. This group offers the greatest potential commercial value and variation.
2. *Wool-blend felts* are made from the same fiber lengths but depend on wool or other animal hair to bind together two or more thin sheets.
3. *Needled and shrunk felts* use a mixture of nonshrinkable and shrinkable fibers that can be made to move about by chemical or heat applications until a web is formed. They are then needled or stitched one web layer to another and made to shrink to the desired firmness.
4. *Papers* are made from very short fibers by a wet process, followed by chemical bonding to a firm mass.
5. *Battings* are low-density dry fiber masses that can be bonded.

Nonwoven fabrics are defined by Committee D-13 of the ASTM as follows: "Nonwoven fabrics are a structure of fibers held together with a bonding material." The actual material can be applied to the fiber mat by a painting, spraying, coating, or printing operation.

Major producers of these textiles are the following: the American Felt Company, Star Woolen Company, Pellon Corporation, Visking Corporation, Minnesota Mining and Manufacturing Company, Avondale Mills, Raybestos-Manhattan, Inc., C. H. Dexter and Sons, and Chicopee Manufacturing Company.

A few years ago, there was an exciting flurry of what the trade called paper dresses; most of these actually were nonwovens. As in many other fads, the public interest lagged rather soon, but there is no reason to suppose that nonwoven dresses will not reappear in a much healthier and more fully technically developed and improved form. To some extent, this paper-dress market dropped off as a result of widespread interest in the protection of textile items from fire. Critics of these products and some fire marshals condemned the materials without testing as being hazardous to the wearer, despite the fact that practically all of them had been given a fire-retardant finish that would remain on the nonwoven material until it was washed. In other words, the only hazard of fire came about after such a garment had been exposed to soap and water.

Nonwoven Formation

Today there are no fewer than seven different methods by which the small fibers in nonwovens have been bonded together to form the fabric. These categories are resin bonding, spun bonding, wet bonding, mechanical bonding, scrim and yarn bonding (laminated), chemical bonding, and extrusion bonding.

There is no more simple method than resin bonding, in which the **lap**, or layer of fibers, is joined together with a bonding material having a nitrile or acrylate resin as its base.

Spun bonding can be defined as a web structure of randomly oriented, continuous filament thermoplastic fibers bonded at crossover points by a thermal treatment.

Wet bonding can be compared with the formation of paper. It involves the formation of a sheet by a paper machine to produce a paperlike fabric. This is the source of most disposable items, in which long staple fibers are mixed with a kraft-type paper pulp to produce the textile product.

Mechanical bonding involves the fiber slant-locker machine, which interlocks adjacent fibers to form a textile structure. These products are principally identified by the end-use item, which is a nonwoven-type, indoor-outdoor carpeting.

In scrim or yarn bonding, a yarn of one type is laid down over another in a definite pattern. The two are then heat-bonded at the crossover points, after which a structure of either textile or paper is adhered to it for the production of a nonwoven fabric. Obviously, one or both of the fibers used would be thermoplastic. In one important product the nonwoven scrim is laid down and two sheets of tissue stock are laminated to it.

In chemical bonding, we have a product defined as a chemical orientation of fibers laid randomly by means of a salt bath. This is a rather limited usage, applicable at present to individually packaged wash towels.

The newest method is that of extrusion bonding, which is defined as the orientation of extruded sheet to form a textile structure through fibrillation. By this method, a plastic sheet of certain types of polymers is turned into a mass of textile fibers all totally interconnected, thus providing a vast number of openings of random shape and size—a sort of honeycombed fiber mass with an infinite number of crossover connections.

Machine-stitch-bonding Process

This machine provides a web of nonwoven fabric with extra strength by knitted reinforcement. A variety of knitting stitches are used depending on the end-use of the fabric and the degree of pliability and drapeability required. Generally, a nylon monofilament thread is used. The machine was invented in Czechoslovakia and has been utilized to make outer wear fabrics from webs containing a certain content of woolen fibers, usually reprocessed or reused. Most of the conventional finishes can be applied to improve dimensional stability, smoothness, water repellency, and bleaching and dyeing properties. It is the belief of textile engineers that the capabilities of the process have scarcely been touched and that pile fabrics, novelty weaves, foam-backed fabrics, and many others can be similarly reinforced for new textures.[5]

Industries Concerned with Nonwovens

An examination of the list of manufacturers of nonwoven fabrics would show that three separate industries are interested in the manufacturing of this product: namely, the producers of synthetic fibers, the paper manufacturers, and the textile industry. It is not surprising that the product of each of these industries is made by different techniques, each one using some modification of its traditional production methods. Thus, the producers of synthetic fibers as continuous filament yarns collect these filaments as a random web, rather than as a collection of continuous filament to be spun into a yarn. The random web is thermally bonded into a sheet form. This process most commonly utilizes such thermoplastic polymers as those entering into nylons, polyesters,

[5] "Stitch-bonding with the Machine Unit," *Modern Textiles Magazine*, **47**, No. 7 (July 1966), pp. 30–35.

and polyolefins. Because this intricate mass is made up of continuous filaments and requires no binder, the sheets are exceptionally strong in both machine (length) and width (cross) directions.

The paper manufacturing industry, as expected, uses a modification of the conventional paper mat lying methods. Short fibers are used and these may be (1) natural fibers, such as cotton, flax, wool, or wood pulp; (2) a mixture of natural and man-made fibers; or (3) man-made fibers entirely. This is a wet-laid process and the paperlike mat can be reinforced by means of scrim, yarns, or resins. Their strength is usually low, but a high-strength product can be produced by laminating these thin tissuelike fabrics to the reinforcing fabric, such as scrim.

The textile industry uses a dry-laid system with fibers as long as 1 to 3 inches. Natural fibers, rayons or acetates, or manufactured fibers can be used, individually or in combinations. These fibers are laid in a random sheet, either mechanically or by allowing them to fall from an airborne mass. The sheet is bonded into a firm structure and may be flat, lofted, or napped by use of electrostatic controls. Bonding, or reinforcing, may result simply from the physical entanglement, as in a felt or a fusible fiber or adhesive; resin may be used to set the fibers; or a needle-punched nonwoven technique may be employed for high strength.

John J. Roden and Frank Y. Johnson[6] indicate the three extreme fiber formations to be found in the nonwovens—that is, completely parallel, ideally cross-laid at 90° angles, and completely randomized. These are illustrated in Figure 6–27. It is obvious that any nonwoven fabric in these idealized constructions, or in any combinations thereof, will have the greater strength under tension in the direction in which the greater number of fibers lie; that is, the parallel construction will have the greater strength in the lengthwise or machine direction and virtually none in the cross direction where there are no fiber lengths existing. The cross laid, on the other hand, might ideally have equal tensile strength in both directions, but, of course, with lengthwise strength proportional or roughly proportional to the number of fibers in that direction. The fabrics with random orientation would be expected to have uniform strength in all directions, not only at direct pulls from lengthwise and widthwise directions but at those various angles between. Nonwoven fabrics, in general, have poor draping qualities compared with those of woven or knitted structures because of the restriction of fiber movement in the fabric. In the nonwovens, the drape will be affected by the frequency of bonds in the individual fibers—that is, the length of fiber between successive bonded sites of one fiber with others and with the rigidity or firmness of the bond itself (Figure 6–28). For example, because the straight line is the shortest distance between two points, a straight fiber bonded at two points, for example, 1 millimeter apart, would be more rigid

6 John J. Roden and Frank Y. Johnson, "Non-wovens," *Bulletin of the Southern Research Institute*, Birmingham, Alabama (1970), pp. 13–16.

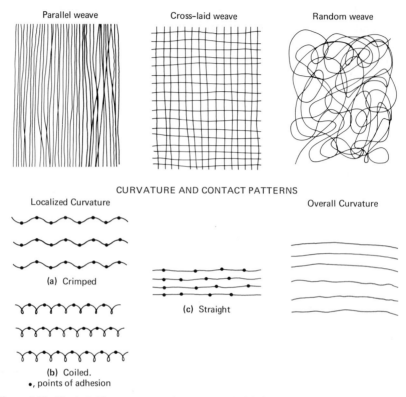

Figure 6-27 Typical fiber geometry for nonwoven fabric structure. (*Bulletin*, Southern Research Institute)

and less drapeable or curvable than a crimped fiber or a coiled fiber bonded at the same two points. This extra length of fiber (the curl) between bonds would permit more freedom of movement. This crimping structure is sometimes referred to as localized curvature. In the random-laid structures, there has been no attempt to eliminate curvature—which may be an over-all curvature. However, within the short distances between points of adhesion or bonding, these fibers generally lie fairly straight; thus, they have poorer draping qualities than do those of the more paralleled structures (Figure 6–29). On the other hand, it is seen that their over-all strength in every direction is superior to the oriented structures.

Bonding Methods

Three principal bonding methods are used: resin bonding, thermoplastic fiber bonding, and stitch-through bonding. Combinations of these methods

Figure 6-28 Graduation caps and gowns made from nonwoven fabrics. (Courtesy of the Kendall Company)

are also used. To confuse one still further, most of the resins used are thermoplastic and are used either as a coating or as an impregnation material.

In the resin **bonding method**, the manner of resin application depends on the end-use and may be a bath, spray, or paint. The web is then dried and heat-cured at temperatures of 200 to 400°F, depending on the materials used.

In thermoplastic **fiber bonding**, a small percentage of a thermoplastic fiber is added to the higher melting, or nonthermoplastic, web materials. When such a web is **calendered**, or pressed by passage between hot rolls, the lower-melting fibers, generally 10 to 30 per cent by weight of the fabric, seal themselves into the web structure. The newest fibers being used are the acrylics, for they give webs of high strength and durability, some limited washability and reuse, good light fastness, and fair solvent resistance.

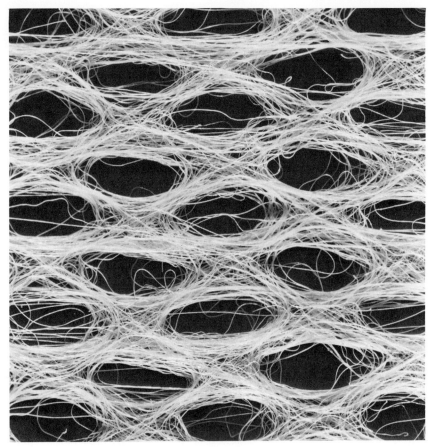

Figure 6-29 Keybak nonwoven fabric (X20). (Courtesy of Chicopee Manufacturing Company)

In the **stitch-through** operation, the layered webs are basted together. A thermoplastic thread would respond to heat treatment by shrinking as it softened to give a more compact structure.

Properties

Among the important properties associated with the nonwoven fabrics are that they are opaque and moisture-absorbent, can be produced in a variety of densities and textures, are porous to air, and controllable to shrinkage limits, have no threads or yarns to be distorted, will not ravel, and have a surface range from smooth to spongy. As a class, however, they have a lower tear strength than woven fabrics, do not have as high a tensile strength, and have a limited resistance to abrasion.

Some of the characteristics noted in nonwovens of various fibers follow:

1. Cotton (unbleached) gives good wet strength and opacity, but the color may not be clear; bleached cotton is more expensive than rayon but gives good color, opacity, and strength.
2. Rayon (viscose) gives excellent whiteness and good dry strength, but is water-sensitive; the fabric has a papery feel.
3. Acetate is equal to viscose in color and opacity and has a less papery feel.
4. Nylon is excellent in color and strength and has good resilience; however, it is expensive and has poor opacity.
5. Wool gives good hand and drape, high bulk, and good resilience, but has low strength.
6. Glass fibers have high strength, but adhesion is poor.
7. Other fibers, it is reasonable to assume, will be tried from time to time, and any one may be found to be superior for certain types of webs.

Applications

Products made of nonwovens were initially introduced as semidisposable items, and that still is one of the objectives in their use. (See Table 6–8.) The products should then be less expensive than a conventional fabric. This relatively new use, however, is not to be supplied with waste or scrap fibers. Quality nonwovens require fibers as good and as clean as those for other textile formations. The fiber use in nonwovens by type is listed in Table 6–9.

MEDICAL AND SANITARY   In the following items, nonwovens have already been found to be highly desirable:

Bandages
Bed pads and sheets
Bibs
Covers for tables, trays, and dressers
Dressings
Tissues

They also go into nurses' caps, gowns, and aprons; patients' gowns; and into washcloths and hand towels.

An unanticipated problem has arisen in the use of these nonwoven

Table 6-8   End-use Consumption of Nonwovens

(millions of pounds)

	1969	1974*
Apparel	37	78
Interlining	10	16
Casual wear†	1	9
Protective garments	3	19
Apparel batting	23	34
Sanitary/medical	90	131
Bandages	68	79
Diapers†	22	52
Household	121	286
Carpeting (excluding padding)	49	95
Carpet backing	31	75
Blankets	17	28
Furniture and bedding	20	58
Linens, hospital drapes, etc.†	4	30
Industrial	67	132
Filters	21	48
Wiping cloths, etc.	6	13
Coated fabrics,	13	26
Miscellaneous		
(abrasives, tapes, etc.)	27	45
	315	627

SOURCE: *American Dyestuff Reporter*, **60** (March 1971), p. 67.
* Projected.
† Including Wood Pulp and/or Paper.

materials in hospitals and other institutions: the problem of disposal. City ordinances against air pollution have, in many cases, prevented the burning of these waste materials, and their accumulation and hauling away create additional problems.

APPAREL   Rather wide use, especially when traveling, is made of apparel in disposable materials. Among these are diapers, face cloths, and bibs. Semidisposable garments, those that may be washed once or twice such as underwear, blouses, collars, and shirts have not yet appealed to the public. Moreover, travel-convenient items such as packaged swim wear available at

Table 6-9   Fiber Use in Nonwovens by Type

(millions of pounds)

	1969	1974*
Acetate	8	5
Cotton	70	53
Nylon	13	31
Polyester	36	83
Polypropylene	71	180
Rayon	83	169
Other (acrylic, modacrylic, wool etc.)	7	11
	288	532
Wood, pulp/paper	27	95
	315	627

SOURCES *American Dyestuff Reporter*, **60** (March 1971), p. 67.
* Predicted.

public pools are liked; stiff interlining materials are popular in girls' dresses and in many apparel items. Additional popular uses are

Aprons and bibs	Caps and sport hats
Facings	Paddings
Findings in garment	Packaged swim wear
construction	Work clothes
Graduation garb	

HOME FURNISHINGS   Many uses are found for nonwoven fabrics in varieties of weight, texture, and degrees of stiffness. For the most part, the products are disposable after one use, although their length of service may vary from a few minutes for a disposable dishcloth to a year or more for draperies or glass curtains in a summer cottage.

Dishcloths	Doilies
Draperies	Pads
Dustcloths	Placemats
Sheeting	Tissues
Napkins	Towels
Tablecloths	Window shades
Cleaner bags	Curtains
Shelfcovers	

INDUSTRIAL   Fabrics for industry do affect the home; the tea bag, for example, is made of a nonwoven fabric. Polishing and wiping cloths of nonwovens are superior to the pickup apparel scraps homemakers use. Industry uses nonwovens for

Filters of all kinds
Backing fabrics
Wrapping materials
Insulation
Laminated products
Packaging

When nonwoven fabrics are as soft and pliable as woven or knit goods, their market in protective clothing of a semidisposable type will grow. The new synthetics, with their chemical resistance, could make much cheaper laboratory coats and aprons. However, the factors of comfort and mobility require roomy sleeves and armholes. These, in turn, can cause accidents, such as catching apparatus with a sleeve cuff or, in industry, having a too-roomy garment caught in moving machinery.

One of the newer and more interesting textures available in nonwoven textiles is called **Vellux**, patented by the West Point Pepperell Company. A lightweight blanket, the fabric consists of a core of polyethylene foam to which a nylon flock is applied by electrostatic forces to create a velvetlike surface. This material, which feels soft to the touch, is machine washable. It is dimensionally stable and resistant to matting or pilling. It is sufficiently durable to be used for home furnishings, footwear, children's toys; and even for apparel.

Market Scope

In Table 6–8 the projected consumer-use market for nonwoven textile materials is shown. The growth in apparel is expected to be moderate, about 50 per cent, between 1969 and 1974. In this use, the nonwoven product is generally a part of a garment and therefore is not freely disposable. The only disposable items are the protective garments, which have about a 500 per cent increase estimate. In sanitary and medical usage, household items, and industrial textile products, the estimate is a doubling of the 1969 market by 1974. Many of these fields are for truly disposable fabrics; others, such as carpet backings, may increase as a result of new techniques in manufacture and a widening market for lower-cost products.

The Future of Nonwovens

Nonwoven textile fabrics, such as paper, are structureless to the eye. This means that the fibers of which they are composed lie in such random distribution and are individually so short that they are not visibly discernible. The original concept of the use for this kind of material was as a disposable— that is, single-use textiles to replace paper towels, throw-away diapers, dusting cloths, and similar items.

Research has led to nonwoven textiles with a wide variety of textures, weights, thicknesses, and physical and chemical properties. This has led to acid-resistant materials for laboratory aprons, coverall jackets, and coats. Some fabrics as light as 3 ounces per square yard, having a tensile strength as high as 50 pounds, would have repeated use applications. The number of uses to be expected depends on the severity of wear and the length of time the article can be used before it becomes too soiled. As yet none of these temporary fabrics has been found to be satisfactorily washable or cleanable for apparel. One of the more rigorous demands such fabrics have been called upon to meet is in packaged bathing trunks and bathing suits to be available at low cost to travelers patronizing public pools. These could be worn several times, but neither the fabric nor the color would be affected by chlorine bleach.

Nonwovens have, as yet, scarcely ventured into some of the applications that promise the greatest potential sales volumes. Probably the largest potential user would be the hotel and motel business, in which nonwoven bedding, towels, and other washable items could be replaced by semidisposable materials. When surface textures have been improved to compare with fine muslin or percale, even a one-night use of such fabrics for linen replacements by nonwovens could compare favorably with the ever-increasing cost of laundering, pressing, storage, and redistribution. Hospitals are using an increasing volume and variety in this field: bandages, wrappings and tapes, surgical garb, and other end-use products. The first great use for nonwovens was in sanitary napkins as inner layer separators. This industry alone uses approximately 3 billion yards of nonwovens each year. Research in nonwovens for the disposable diaper has resulted in the development of a flushable nonwoven fabric that is biodegradable (the textile material is completely disintegrated by bacteria in the water) and is, thus, completely disposable. These compare, on a cost basis, with the expense of diaper service. This is a potential multimillion dollar business. In the 1970s some college seniors graduated in gowns made of a disposable nonwoven material and wore a stiffened nonwoven cap.

The transportation industry, such as the airlines and buses, uses linenlike nonwoven fabrics for headrests at an annual saving of approximately $3600 per year per vehicle. Many hospitals are using prepacked sterilized operation assemblies for specific operations that include catheters, hypodermic needles, clamps, and other appliances, and the necessary pads, towels, and textile products a surgeon requires. After use the complete unit can be thrown away. The cost of these kits is nominal and in the long run may be cheaper and safer than filling the surgeon's order from stock shelves.

LAYERED CONSTRUCTIONS

We have seen that a system of intertwining individual yarns is involved in weaving and in knitting. There are limits as to the speed with which the filling yarns can be shot back and forth through the warp shed to produce a woven fabric or the loops to be caught with one another by the knitting needles.

Stitching

Some newly invented mechanical devices permit the simultaneous stitching through by many needles to form a fabric from two or more layers of textile fibers in the shape of loose yarns or of nonwoven weblike layers.

Several of these high-speed production methods, which are somewhat analogous to weaving, appear in Table 6–10:

Table 6-10   Stitch-thru Constructions

Trade Names	Country of Origin	Speed over Regular Loom	Technique
Malimo	East Germany	20	Filling yarns and warp yarns stitched together by thread
Malipol	East Germany	20	Stitches pile loops into backing fabric or nonwoven
Maliwatt	East Germany	20	Stitches a base of nonwovens
Malifil	East Germany	20	Stitches a thread structure around a loose roving
Kraftmatic	England	30	Similar to the Mali technique but produces conventional fabrics—Terrytuft and pile types

Stitch-thru Fabrics

The term **stitch-thru** was coined to describe methods by which fabrics could be created by passing a threaded needle from one side of a structure to the other causing interconnected loops to be formed that would stabilize the structure sufficiently so it could be called a fabric. There is a separate classification for tufting equipment that is similar in some respects but produces heavier fabrics, the tufted face of which is designed to provide pattern and durability under wear.

This stitch-thru technology includes four basic constructions. The first of these, the **Malimo** method, consists of laying down a loose mat of filling yarns and then placing a layer of warp yarns over it, but without any meshing. These two sheets are held firmly and a third yarn binds the two together by a stitch somewhat resembling the tricot knit. The resulting fabric closely resembles a woven material.

The second procedure, which includes such trade names as Singer, Lokloop Malipol, Kraftmatic, and Mali-mo-pol, stitches a pile into a base fabric, producing a terrylike pile on one face or on both. The base fabric is fed into the machine and the loops of pile are then stitched through at a rate as high as 1200 stitches per minute.

The third method is the **Maliwatt** or the **Arachne**, in which the procedure is to stitch a yarn through a loose fiber batting to form a fabric. This produces a fabric with a loose fiber base, converted into a tight fabric by means of a sewing yarn. The physical properties of the resultant fabric depend on the type of stitch used in the sewing process; it influences softness of texture, drapeability, and stretchability. The speed is in excess of 120 yards of fabric per hour.

The fourth method, of which **Arabeva**, **Malifleece**, and **Voltex** are examples, stitches a fibrous batting together without using another yarn. In other words, a stitching needle seizes a group of fibers on one side of the batt, pulls them into a loop on the other side of the fabric, and locks them with a previously formed loop. The important distinction is that here the batting is held together only by fibers, without the use of an external yarn system.

By the same system of stitching together several layers of base materials, it is possible to apply the construction of nonwovens of various weights and types. These can be placed in layers and tricot-stitched to form fabrics for industrial use, interlinings, interfacings, base fabrics for resin coating, imitation leather, and for some apparel items. Conventional fabrics, either woven or knitted, can be stitched with very loose tricot loops that can form a pile face on one or both sides of the base cloth to resemble a terry pile.

If the high-speed Malimo devices produce cloth as acceptable to the consumer in the United States as to the consumer in East Germany, they may be producing 30 per cent of the world's fabrics in 20 years, according to some optimistic observers. The devices are being used experimentally in the United States and 22 other countries. A single **Mali** unit produces on an average the same yardage per unit of time as 20 conventional looms and can be used in continuous installations including fabric formation, finishing, dyeing, drying, and packaging.

Laminated Fabrics

Laminated fabrics often are called bonded fabrics because two or more layers are bonded, or are adhesively bound, together into laminated structures. In this way, they resemble laminated wood, or plywood.

The adhesion of certain resins to fabrics appears in textile finishing by chemical means and by chemical bonding through some physical process, such as in the application of heat or the use of an adhesive. It is a fast-growing textile market. Polyvinyl chloride and polyurethane foams are the fastest growing polymers in this field. The laminated fabrics are being used for luggage, upholstery, and footwear. They are also serving as insulating materials for cold-weather apparel, scatter rugs, and display materials.

There are five main methods by which the fabric is coated with a polymeric material, either a plastic, a resin sheet, or a foam.

1. The coating paste is spread directly on the base fabric, which is then cured at a proper temperature.
2. The polymer sheet, or foam laminate material, is calendered and is then laminated to the base fabric by the use of heat.
3. A film of the polymer is cast onto an intermediary surface, such as a sheet of release paper; the film is then cured and it is laminated on the base fabric utilizing a liquid solvent to effect the union.
4. The polymer film is extruded onto a fabric and is laminated by extreme heat.
5. The thermoplastic material is softened between heated rollers and this film is transferred onto the fabric. This method is used primarily on nonwoven textiles or on papers, but is not used extensively on woven fabrics at present.

These bonding techniques have contributed to the rapid growth of knitted fabrics, especially tricot. As recently as 1962, only 50 million yards of bonded fabric were being produced. This increased to 400 million yards in 1967, and it is forecast that the volume will reach a billion yards in the early 1970s. This technique of fabric construction enables a knitted fabric to have a firm, durable construction. The texture of the final fabric depends on the bonding technique used. A foam bond provides a stiff, firm fabric, whereas adhesive bonding enables the fabric to have a soft, easy drape or "flowing silhouette." Standards are under development for additional testing methods for the evaluation of the durability of these types of apparel, more accurately described as laminated fabrics. The separation of fabrics at the laminating layer may result from dry-cleaning, from washing, or simply from a mechanical pull if the process has not been completely carried out.

Early producers of these fabrics such as **Celabond**, from the Celanese Corporation; **Certifab**, from Collins-Aikman; **Coin** from Coin International; **FLA**, from the Fabrics Laminated Association, and the Tricot Institute's method, called TI, have their own standards of performance. These producers are all members of a committee currently engaged in the setting up of test methods and standards of performance.

In most cases, these companies license others to produce laminated fabrics by their patented methods. They are, however, concerned with the quality-control program to see that products bearing their trademark conform to and maintain their standards.

Chemstitch

Chemstitch is a novelty fabric produced by a patented bonding process that results in a sculptured surface effect, showing any desired pattern, not only on plain surfaced fabrics but also on velvets. The fabric is bonded to a layer of resilient material, such as polyester fiber-filled batting or a polyurethane foam. The design is then printed on this cloth with a special chemical that, when cured, transfers the pattern as a sculptured effect on the fabric. These fabrics are largely confined to high-fashion merchandise.

Foam Bonding

One of the earliest processes for applying a foam laminate or layer to a textile material was by means of flame played on the foam. This could be used on both surfaces of a foam layer so that fabric could be affixed to both sides. Initially, this caused some problems in sewing because of needle friction. Foam bonding is a quick, easy method; by the use of lubricants of a silicone-coating nature, the problem of friction can largely be overcome. These materials develop full strength almost immediately, and the resultant multilayer fabric can be tested quickly for foam adhesion.

Another bonding method, the fusible system, involves the application of heat to a thermoplastic resin to form a liquid on each face. The resin, having low viscosity, will flow into the fabric on both faces resulting in a close bond between the two. One advantage of this process is that the union of the face fabric, the resin adhesive, and the backing fabric need not be immediate. It can take place after the three-part assembly has been made into a sandwich form, which can actually be placed over a mold or shaper, with heat, and then applied to give a durable shaped article. The choice among the wide variety of thermoplastic resins for the sandwich layer is dictated to some extent by the nature of the two face fabrics. Typical of combinations made possible by this process are those with a print cloth face and a bonded web backing, tobacco cloth with a saturation-bonded web, sheetings with apertured webs, rayon-cotton blends with a felt backing, or a canvas face with needle-punched nonwoven fabric in the backing. Another advantage of this system is that the adhesive layer itself can be noncontinuous—that is, it can be applied in random areas. For this purpose, the thermoplastic resin is sprayed onto the back of the face fabric or onto the nonwoven base. When heated, the adhesion is in spots rather than in a moisture-vapor-impermeable layer uniformly spread between the two fabrics.

In any bonding procedure using heat, the workers must be protected from the products of the decomposition. The amount of permissible decomposition for a good bond must be carefully controlled in order to retain the greater part of the foam intact for a durable sandwich. In Europe, there has been some use made of a hot, melted adhesive of polyamide in a powdered state. A very small amount, approximately 10 grams per square yard, is required to give a strip peel test in excess of 2 pounds per inch.

There is also a coated-fabric type of bonding in which the fabric is coated with a thermoplastic adhesive that is sprayed onto the material. Samples of this type of product are found in air-permeable inner facings for lapels of suits, backing materials, flannels, nonwovens, and interlinings. Usually, the spraying technique is used to produce a noncontinuous layer. In other words, the adhesive is at random. In any hot-melt adhesive process, the bond must remain unchanged during the lifetime of the apparel under normal conditions and cleaning. It must not age, for this would result in a greatly reduced peel strength after a period of time. It should not discolor either.

A third method of effecting bonded structures is by means of a soluble adhesive system such as that of a urethane base. This method permits much greater latitude in texture, even to the use of extremely stretchy and bulky fabrics through knitting. Finer knitted textiles such as tricot and jersey can be laminated without the addition of excessive weight or stiffening. The developing variety of textile fibers, textile finishes, and of end-uses (such as in children's wear) have brought about an increased use of this type of adhesive.

Problems with Laminated Fabrics

A bonded fabric is only as serviceable as its weakest link; therefore, the effectiveness and permanence of the adhesion between the layers of the fabric and the foam layer affect the durability of the fabric in use. The International Fabricare Institute has found four principal complaints concerning this method. The data for 1967, 1968, and 1969 are shown in Table 6–11. The parenthesized figures show the rank or order of a particular complaint among all of the textile problems reported by the member cleaners. Thus, in 1967, the principal cause of damage to textiles as met by the dry cleaner was in the shrinkage of one layer or the other of the bonded fabric. By 1969, the number of complaints had been reduced by 50 per cent for this cause of damage and was fifth in order. The blistering or separation of bondings, much of which was edge failure, remained fairly constant; and in 1969, it was the third principal cause of complaint. Foam-laminate deterioration was an indication of chemical failure, such as oxidation; the fourth cause was discoloration, usually a yellowing of a white or cream-colored foam.

Table 6-11   Bonded Fabrics Problems—Comparison of Three Years

	1967		1968		1969	
Type of Complaint	*Rank*	*No.*	*Rank*	*No.*	*Rank*	*No.*
Shrinkage—bonded fabrics	(1)	1572	(3)	1344	(5)	858
Blistering or separation of bondeds	(5)	950	(6)	940	(3)	922
Foam-laminate deterioration	(11)	447	(9)	503	(10)	434
Foam-laminate yellowing	(17)	234	(13)	270	(14)	245

SOURCE: International Fabricare Institute.

The L–22 standard is the set standard of quality for this type of merchandise. These foam laminates are being widely used for table mats and in upholstery materials, and it is here that some of the shrinkage complaints result. It was assumed that the foam layer would stabilize the dimension of the outer fabric, but the reverse has been the case. If the outer fabric had any tendency to shrink or stretch, the foam laminate yielded to these distortions.

Finishing and Coloring Fabrics

ROLE OF THE CONVERTER

When a fabric emerges from the mill or processing plant in which it was woven, knitted, or matted, it is distinctly unappealing in color, texture, and even in dimension. Fabrics in this stage of production are termed **gray goods** (or greige). They must now be converted into fabrics acceptable to the apparel manufacturer and to the public. Responsibility for this rests on the shoulders of the **converter**. It is his responsibility to give the fabric the desired softness or stiffness, luster or dullness, or other esthetic features in addition to color and design. He is responsible for any kind of service or functional finishes the end-use product may require of the textile, including such properties as fire resistance, water repellency or absorbency, ease of care, and other desired features. The converter performs his duties in one of three general capacities. (1) He may actually own the goods and process them for sale to the apparel manufacturing customer. (2) He may be a service agent to whom apparel manufacturers and other textile producers send their goods to be processed according to specifications and at a certain price. (3) The method of operation may be that of a large integrated mill that serves all the way from fiber production through finished fabric, or even through the manufacture of certain staple garments.

It is apparent that the finisher is a man who creates first the customer appeal or the esthetic properties of the textile product and then the service requirements, such as the specified functional finishes. The various fibers require modifications in finishing methods, depending on the physical and chemical nature of these fibers. With the addition of so many new fiber families, and particularly with the blending of two or more of them in a single yarn, or the combining of yarns of different types to produce a combination fabric, the job of the finisher has become very complicated. Beyond the simple breakdown of the two classifications, esthetic and functional— that is, customer and consumer wants—he is also responsible for the satisfactory behavior of the finished goods under today's more critical ease-of-care conditions. These have progressed from the ordinary laundry procedures our mothers followed through easy care, to wash-and-wear, through durable-press, to spot-and-stain release finishes.

Americans tend more and more to require tailor-made characteristics in their apparel. It is to meet these changing conditions that the converter is called upon to exercise his research facilities and ingenuity.

The converter and dyer of tomorrow may find himself facing more and more new problems connected not only with new materials—by way of fiber blends coming on the market—but also with new requirements that the fabric producer and the manufacturer of the textile product will intend to meet in anticipation of new levels of consumer expectation. The criteria to be met if the fabric were destined for style apparel would show little demand for durability—nor might the price be a primary concern. On the other hand, the fabric might be intended for a market in which durability and price were of great importance. Preferably, the converter would have dyeing and finishing equipment to satisfy both objectives, whether he was an entrepreneur or an agent handling goods for an apparel manufacturer. If he is a member of the team producing goods in an integrated mill setup, he should be informed by the sales department as to the identity of the customer company and the objective that customer is striving to achieve. In other words, just what is the principal market of this manufacturer? It would be highly desirable, of course, if the dyestuff used could have satisfactory durabiltiy and colorfastness for the service of the article. More and more the textile industry is concentrating on continuous dyeing instead of batch processing. It is forecast that within the next year or two flat textiles will be printed at a speed up to 100 yards a minute. This alone is a challenge to the colorist.

GENERAL FINISHES AFFECTING CONSUMER SELECTION

Esthetic Finishes

Some of the esthetic, or sales-appeal, finishes in the following list are applicable to all fiber types that either are to be marketed as whites or are to be dyed or printed. These must be bleached because most textile fibers are not truly white. A typical yellowish color, which may range from yellow to ivory, tends to make white or pastel shades dull. Therefore, the rule is that the whiter the cloth the clearer the pastels and the better the dyeing operation will be.

Luster and fabric body are also enhanced by finishes:

1. The beauty of table linen is greatly enhanced by imparting additional luster and brightness through finishing.
2. The feel or handle of a cloth can be improved by increasing its weight or improving its draping quality. Silk fabrics can be weighted to make them heavy and firm.
3. Finishing operations are employed to stiffen some organdies; other fabrics, such as linen suitings, are given a finishing process to keep them smooth.

No fabric is given only one finishing process. The sales appeal of a fabric depends to a great degree on the way it has been processed after weaving. Bleaching and dyeing are properly included in any list of permanent finishes. Each textile fiber undergoes a series of finishing processes that are characteristic of the cloths made from it.

The nature and number of finishes for fabrics of different fiber origins vary because of their physical characteristics, such as color, texture, degree of combination with foreign substances, and the amount of sizing required to strengthen or to lubricate the fibers during the weaving operation. The lengths of fabric being finished can be artificially tinted for rapid identification by the weaver. The various fibers need different finishing processes and these sometimes are affected by the amount of dirt and other material collected during mechanical handling. As one would expect, natural fibers are less uniform and have been exposed to more contaminants, so these require a greater number and variety of processes in order to give them the desired esthetic appeals. For that reason, finishing operations for various fibers must be discussed in some detail.

SPECIAL PROCESSING FOR THE VARIOUS FIBERS

Cotton

Cotton fabrics are given the following finishing processes, usually in the order they are given here.

BRUSHING If a cotton cloth such as a percale or a gingham is to have a smooth surface, it must be brushed and sheared. The cloth is rubbed by means of revolving brushes that raise and fuzz the loose ends in the yarns so that they can be **sheared** off by knives.

GASSING The cloth is quickly passed through gas flames or over very hot copper plates to burn off any remaining fuzz. These two processes are known, respectively, as **gassing** or **singeing**. The cloth is prevented from burning by passing it through a water bath to quench any smoldering flames in the fibers. The singeing may be done on only one side, depending on the degree of fabric smoothness desired.

BLEACHING If the cotton yarns have not been **bleached**, the cloth as it comes from the loom will be dull and may be a grayish-brown or yellow color.

Cottons are boiled in large tanks called kiers to remove the natural gum or wax from the fibers. Cheap cloths, such as some muslins and those for cotton bagging, are sometimes sold unbleached. If the cotton fabric is to be bleached in the piece after weaving, it is commonly prepared for kier boiling and for bleaching by using carefully controlled baths with one or more chemicals including alkali, sulfites, and chlorine. This cycle can be repeated to make the fabric more receptive to bleaching with Javelle water. This same chemical, a hypochlorite solution, is commonly known in homes as chlorine bleach. Excessive bleaching and careless pretreating can seriously weaken the fabric.

MERCERIZATION Like bleaching, the **mercerizing** process can be performed either in the yarn stage or on the woven fabric.

This process is named after its discoverer, John Mercer. Briefly, the treatment of the cotton by a caustic soda solution causes it to swell and to lose its natural twist; both its luster and its tensile strength are increased. Later, H. Lowe, an English chemist, modified and controlled the process by keeping the cloth under tension in the caustic solution. A wide variety of fine cotton cloths are now mercerized to enhance their luster to rival that of silk.

The longer-staple cotton fibers are used in the yarns of fabrics that are to be mercerized. Because the visible effect of mercerization is a lustrous and smooth surface, it is important that the preliminary treatments insure as smooth a surface as possible before the cloth is mercerized. These processes are the careful combing of the fibers composing the yarn, singeing, and bleaching.

DYEING AND PRINTING   The coloring of cotton cloth is discussed in more detail on pp. 329–39. The coloring operations are integral parts of the finishing and can be done on both bleached and mercerized cloths. The latter have better absorptive power and take the dye more readily. If the cloth is to be **dyed** a deep color, it is not necessary to bleach it before immersing it in the dye bath. If one or more colors are to be printed onto a cloth, it is necessary to singe, bleach, and perhaps mercerize it.

SIZING   **Sizing**, or **dressing**, is an operation that increases the weight and improves the texture of a cloth. The stiffening of organdy, mosquito netting, and other sheer cloths, and the crispness of dimity and marquisette are typical results of sizing. The bleached, mercerized, or dyed cloth is passed between two rollers, one of which dips into the sizing mixture. Sizing may be of vegetable origin, such as a starch or flour paste; it may be inorganic, such as clay, magnesium chloride, or magnesium sulfate; it may be of animal origin, such as mucilage; or resin finishes may be applied. The stiffness imparted by the sizing is often modified and given a better handle by the use of oils, greases, waxes, or resins. The use of organic sizing agents makes cotton more susceptible to the attack of mildew, and an antiseptic solution, such as formaldehyde or zinc chloride, may be added to the sizing to prevent damage caused by mildew.

Excessive surface-covering sizing can be recognized by rubbing two layers of cloth together and noting whether small particles flake off. Scraping the fabric with a knife or one's fingernail or tearing it will also produced these fine flakes of sizing material. A dyed cloth that has been excessively sized may show **crocking**, or rubbing off, of the dye when it is rubbed against a white cloth.

NAPPING   Cotton fabrics can be given a fuzzy surface closely resembling that of wool. This raised surface, or **nap**, is imparted mechanically by rubbing the woven or knitted fabric with stiff brushes or bristles mounted on cylindrical rolls, much as blankets are napped. For ease in napping, the fabric should be a rather open weave of loosely twisted yarns made from short-staple fibers. Typical napped fabrics are outing flannels, cotton blankets, flannelette, and similar materials. The nap differs from the raised pile surface formed by weaving.

GLAZING   A stiff, lustrous surface is given cotton by means of **glazing**. The firm, lustrous surface is achieved by means of starches, glues, shellacs, and resins that are given a high polish by smooth, hot rollers called calenders. Chintzes for upholstery and draperies are given this glazed finish. They shed dirt readily because of the smooth surface. A great improvement has been made in recent years, and some of these glazed fabrics, such as **Everglaze**, the trademark product of Joseph Bancroft & Sons Co., can be washed successfully and retain the surface effect.

CREPEING   The most permanent crepe texture is given to fabrics in the weaving by using alternate filling yarns of right-hand and left-hand twist. It is possible, however, to impart a **crepe texture** by finishing processes. Two common methods follow:

1. The cloth is passed between hot rollers in the presence of steam. The rollers are indented to reproduce the pucker figures in the cloth. The method is inexpensive, but the crepe will wash and iron out.

2. Chemical **seersucker** or **plissé** crepes are much more permanent. A caustic soda paste is rolled onto the cloth in stripes or figures. When the fabric is washed, causing the parts to which the paste is applied to shrink, the rest of the cloth puckers or crepes. Sometimes the reverse treatment is used; the cloth is given a caustic-resistant paste finish in all spots and areas where crepeing is not desired. The whole cloth is then immersed in the caustic solution; it shrinks wherever the cloth is unprotected, thus puckering the other areas. Crinkled bedspreads are made in this manner to resemble the durable, slack-tension, woven genuine seersucker.

BEETLING   Heavy cottons can be given a linenlike finish by **beetling**. This finishing process is applied after the cloth has been bleached and printed. The cloth is slowly passed between rollers that subject the fabric to blows from tiny hammers. The cloth becomes compact and leathery because of the flattening of the yarns, but the finish may gradually disappear in use and washing. Genuine linen fabrics are usually beetled also.

EMBOSSING   **Embossing** is the process of imprinting or engraving a pattern onto cotton tablecloths and apparel fabrics to simulate the figures woven by the Jacquard loom. The designs are engraved on copper. rolls, and the combination of steam and high temperature imprints the design on the cloth. The finish is not permanent to laundering unless a resin treatment is used.

CALENDERING   The final finish given to the surface of cotton cloth is that of **calendering,** or polishing. The cloth is passed between hot, smooth rollers to iron out wrinkles and to impart a sheen to the cloth. The luster is increased by sizing the fabric before calendering or by passing it through the rollers several times. The principle of calendering is duplicated in the home when smooth cottons are ironed.

TENTERING   Tentering is a mechanical process to even or straighten the width of the cloth. All fabrics have to be **tentered** in order to straighten the selvage. The tentering frame resembles a horizontal runway, holds the selvages, and pulls sideways jerkily. The method of pulling is to advance each side alternately a few inches at a time by means of a chain drive and to stop it while the other side is advanced. This gives the cloth a series of slanting jerks over its entire length. A source of steam is located under the frame so that the cloth is easily shunk or stretched until the edges are straight. The cloth is dried in this condition.

PRESHRINKING   This is considered a functional finish.

IMITATIVE FINISHES   The techniques of cotton finishing have brought about a wider field of uses for cotton. It has become a more important style fiber because finishing methods have increased its luster, softness, and draping quality. Wash-and-wear finishes enable cotton to resist wrinkles to a degree comparable with synthetics. The low cost of cotton fabrics has also contributed to its increased popularity during recent years.

Cotton can be made to resemble linen, wool, and even silk. The use of nubby yarns produces a fabric closely resembling linen. Napping gives a wool-like texture to cotton cloths. Mercerizing gives a silky sheen to cotton fabrics.

Finishing Linen

BLEACHING   The natural color of the linen or flax fiber is tan or grayish tan. It is necessary, therefore, to bleach linen for fine white fabrics.

Chemical agents used in bleaching linen are listed in Table 2–6, p. 42. A brief summary of the methods of bleaching linen follows.

Grass Bleaching   Grass bleaching is still common in Ireland, and it is believed by many that the natural action of moisture, air, and sunlight produces the loveliest silvery color and strongest fiber.

Chemical Bleaching   The use of chemicals is becoming increasingly common in the bleaching of linen. The principal steps follow:

1. Boiling with a lime solution to remove wax and other impurities.
2. Rinsing and treating with dilute hydrochloric acid.
3. Rinsing and boiling in a caustic soda solution.
4. Bleaching with a chlorine-containing powder.

Chemically bleached linens are a dead white and lack the silvery luster of grass-bleached fibers. Overbleaching weakens the flax fiber and full-bleached linens are weaker than quarter-, half-, and three-quarter-bleached fabrics. It is advantageous to purchase linen towels and other durable linens that have been bleached only partially. As these fabrics are repeatedly laundered, they will become whiter; their initial strength is considerably greater than that of full-bleached cloth.

DYEING AND PRINTING Natural linens are printed without bleaching, but if a white background is desired, the linen must be bleached before printing. Solid-color linens are usually vat-dyed either in the yarn or the piece. Linen shows relatively poor dye absorption, and it is difficult to obtain a piece-dyed fabric whose yarns have a uniform depth of color throughout.

OTHER PROCESSES Beetling has been described in the section on cotton finishing. The uneven diameters of linen yarns and the usual irregularity of the weave cause openings in the fabric structure. Beetling to a firm, leathery texture makes the fabric weave compact and dense, desirable features in linens, especially in table damasks.

Linens are calendered to flatten the yarns and to impart a glossier finish. The firmness, glossy beauty, and characteristic drape of fine table linen are unmistakable.

Like all fabrics, linens can be tentered to straighten the selvages.

Dress linens and linen suitings can be given a crease-resistant finish similar to that of cotton cloth in order to make them neater and less likely to wrinkle. Linen does not respond as well as cotton to durable-press finishing.

The natural characteristics of linen make mercerizing, singeing, and sizing unnecessary. The fiber is long and nonelastic; hence, linens are never napped. These same properties make the spinning difficult enough so that linen is not given any crepe effects.

Finishing Rayon and Acetate

The rayon fabric produced by the weaver is almost ready for the consumer. The common practice is to dye the rayon yarn—as a matter of fact, rayon is rarely bleached in the piece. Peroxides and chlorine bleaches are used if the fabric is to be white or dyed a delicate shade. Rayon can be piece-dyed or printed much as is the practice for cottons. Some rayons are filled by means of resins in order to make them resistant to crushing or to give them an improved handle and greater weight. Rayons that have been subjected to an excessive and deceptive sizing will often lose much of this filler when washed.

Rayons are tentered. Those that are to have a smooth, lustrous surface are calendered. A distinction is made between spun rayons and continuous filament rayons. The spun rayons are often **napped,** are usually given a **wrinkle-resistant** finish, and can be finished with oils, waxes, or resins to give an improved tactile quality such as softness and handle. Rayon velvets are tentered and steamed.

EMBOSSING A rayon fabric can be given a figured surface resembling a woven design by **embossing**. The cloth is passed between steam-heated rollers that imprint the roller design on the cloth. This finish is not permanent, and the fabric cannot be sponged unless it has been given a water-resistant finish. A somewhat similar finish can be given to acetate or silk, called moiréing. A cloth with a fillingwise rib weave is passed in double thickness between rollers, one of which can be engraved in wavy lines. This moiré figure is a watered effect. Only in the case of cellulose acetate can the moiré finish or the embossed figures be washed. In the acetate the lustrous, watered lines have been made permanent by the combination of moderate heat and great pressure.

DIMENSIONAL STABILIZATION Rayons are generally stabilized by a chemical impregnation. The fibers are swelled by a caustic solution, after which the chemical or resin is more easily introduced into the fiber. This finishing procedure prevents rayon from stretching when wet or shrinking when dry.

Finishing Silk

BLEACHING Sometimes silk is woven with yarns from which the **sericin** or gum has not been removed. Such silks must be boiled in soap solution to degum them. Wild silks need not be bleached if the cloth is to be sold having "natural" color. These silks are bleached if they are to be dyed, and the cultivated silks are bleached if they are to be printed or if they are to be pure white. The boiling off of the gum often removes enough of the natural yellow color of the silk fiber. For more complete bleaching, hydrogen peroxide or sodium peroxide is used, or the fabric is exposed to the fumes of burning sulfur. Chlorine-type bleaches yellow silk.

PRINTING AND DYEING The dyeing characteristics of silk are given in Table 2–12, pp. 84–85. Silk fabrics can be printed, yarn-dyed, or dyed in the piece. Delicate silk fabrics, like georgettes, satins, and velvets, are hooked by their selvages onto hollow reels or rollers—allowing about an inch between successive folds of the fabric—and immersed in the dye bath. Crepes and other more durable cloths are passed through the dye bath on smooth metal rolls. After dyeing, the cloth is rinsed and sprayed with water and may be given a mild organic acid bath, such as in acetic acid, to increase the luster.

STRETCHING   Smooth-textured cloths can be stretched by passing them over rollers revolving at increasing speeds as the fabric passes from one to another. This tends to smooth the fabric and to increase its luster.

CALENDERING   In silk, as in the other fabrics previously discussed, calendering, or passing the fabric through heated, polished rollers, imparts a luster. No fabrics are more greatly improved by calendering than are satins. Satins can be given a very smooth and lustrous surface by using hydraulic presses in addition to the rollers.

OTHER FINISHES   All silks must be tentered, and they can be embossed or moiréd to give attractive and durable surface patterns. The weighting of silk has been discussed on p. 82. Controlled weighting is primarily for the purpose of replacing the sericin removed in degumming. but it can be overloaded (above 15 per cent), which will give a flimsy silk cloth the suggestion of strength and durability.

Finishing Wool

The finishing of wool goods depends on whether the fabric is a worsted or a woolen. Worsteds are practically finished when they leave the loom, and their beauty depends to a great degree on the clearness and compactness of the weave. The surface is firm and flat (except for unfinished worsteds).

The goods taken from the loom are spread out over a horizontal beam or rack and examined for defects in the yarns or the weave. Skilled needle workers repair most of these faults. This is called perching. **Mending, burling, specking**, and **crabbing** (holding the cloth under tension in alternate hot and cold baths to set the weave) are special wool finishes.

DYEING   Wool is usually bleached prior to weaving. The process takes place either in the fiber or the skein stage. It is often dyed in one or the other of these stages, or the woven fabric can be dyed. Only in the latter case is dyeing classed as a finishing process. Wool takes dye readily either in the fiber, yarn, or piece.

FELTING, OR FULLING   In order to make a woolen cloth more compact and **thicker**, the cloth is processed by a method variously known as **felting, milling**, or **fulling**. The woolen is immersed in a warm soap suds and is pounded and twisted to cause it to shrink a desired amount. Wool owes its characteristic felting behavior to the structure of the fiber.

NAPPING   Many woolen coatings and suitings are napped in the same way blankets are finished to give them their fuzzy surface. The fulled fabric is rinsed, dried, and tentered, after which it is passed over cylinders, the surfaces of which are covered with fine wire bristles. These bristles pull and raise individual wool fibers from the yarns to give a fuzzy surface. Natural plant burrs, especially the teasel, are often used to produce a softer nap— and with less physical damage to the yarns. Napping with teasel burrs is often referred to as **gigging**. The nap is sheared to a uniform length. Fragments of burrs can be removed by carbonizing (treating with sulfuric acid to char the cellulose).

OTHER FINISHES   Woolens are sheared, steamed, pressed, and sponged. They can be given a false appearance of weight by **flocking** or by **loading**. It is possible to force loose wool fibers from sheared cloth or reused fibers into the back of a cloth by steaming. This is considered a legitimate practice if it is not overdone and if it is not for the purpose of covering up defects. The loose balls of wool that sometimes form in the pockets of men's and boys' coats are an indication of flocking. The presence of these fibers can be shown by briskly brushing the back of the cloth with a stiff brush.

Wool is naturally hygroscopic and can absorb a large amount of water without feeling wet. Loading is practiced by unscrupulous manufacturers who treat the cloth with a hygroscopic, or water-absorbing salt, such as magnesium chloride. The woolen then can be made to absorb even more than its usual water content.

Finishing Worsteds

The finishing of worsteds is relatively simple and usually consists of the following steps:

1. **Inspection** is made to detect defects to be repaired.
2. **Dyeing** is done in the piece if the yarns have not already been dyed.
3. **Fulling** is performed only when worsted fabric needs to be softened.
4. **Napping** is rarely done to worsteds and is never done beyond a slight raising of the surface.
5. **Brushing**, sponging, and pressing complete the finishing.
6. **Shearing**, is sometimes done to remove raised fibers that have resulted from other processing.

Finishing Manufactured Fiber Fabrics

Woven fabrics from the synthetic fibers rarely require any finishing operation other than a mild washing if soiled or perhaps a tentering, if, for example, a print is off-grain—that is, out of perfect alignment. Many of these fabrics are given a heat-stabilization treatment. Generally, the synthetic fibers are sufficiently white and do not require bleaching, either for white goods or for those to be dyed in light shades.

In Table 7–1 a classification of textile finishing agents as reported in *Textile Chemist and Colorist* is shown. Brand names for new textile finishes currently on the market are given in alphabetical order. This summary lists the number of brand products in each textile finish category; that is, 230 of these brand names are classified as adhesives and 18 as antichlorine (chlorine bleach) protection.

More than 1600 dyeing assistants and general finishing agents are used in textile finishing. A great deal of emphasis is placed on fire resistance in textiles because fire protection is the only personal hazard control of im-

Table 7-1   Branded Products Classifications of Certain Textile Finishing Agents Listed for 1970, 1971, and 1972

	1970	1971	1972
Adhesives	230	246	392
Anticreasing agents	146	132	135
Antiseptics	69	173	56
Antislip finishes	170	158	162
Antistatic agents	369	373	488
Delustering agents	116	100	93
Detergents and assistants	998	929	1008
Enzymes and desizers	63	67	73
Finishing agents	1600+	1217	1046
Fire resistants	369	100	116
Insecticides and repellents	29	28	30
Mildew preventives	79	82	76
Odor control	41	45	48
Shrinkage controllers	154	152	134
Sizing agents	462	353	276
Water repellents	177	196	188
Wetting agents	697	616	614
Whiteners (fluorescent)	38	24	42

SOURCE: *Textile Chemist and Colorist* (Oct. 1972), p. 55.

portance in textile products and because of current legislation in this field. A listing of 369 finishing agents that have flammability control has been compiled for use in the industry.

It is to be noted that some of the proprietary process names listed for 1970 disappeared in 1971 for some categories. In other applications there are more finishes for 1971.

GROWTH OF TEXTILE FINISHING

Functional finishes are, in general, special-use treatments. In some cases, they are designed to make the individual fiber-family product behave in a completely unnatural way: for example, to render wool protection from moths and other insects, to make cotton fabrics resistant to wrinkling in wear, or to render flammable fabrics safe from fire. From the consumer's point of view, it is desirable that these finishes be as permanent as possible or, if they can be removed by washing or dry cleaning, that they be renewable. For this reason, many functional finishes are identified on labels as being permanent or renewable.

The great number of proprietary names for textile finishing compounds as listed in Table 7–2 suggest something of the dollar value of these finishes in the textile market. It has been estimated that the textile chemical industry in 1968 produced approximately 1520 billion pounds of finishing agents valued at $415 million; in 1973, this dollar volume is expected to be 50 per cent higher than in 1968. In a study made by C. H. Klein & Company, this market research organization reported that in the study of 59 individual textile resins and chemicals utilized in nine major product categories, the chemicals were used in the following proportion:

Chemicals	*Per Cent*
Coating and backing resins (principally for tufted carpets)	59
Sizing resins	15
Binding resins	7
Easy-care resins	7
Water and soil repellents	7
Hand modifiers and softeners	5
All others*	3

* C. H. Klein & Company.

Great growth can be anticipated in the "all-other" category because it includes some of the newest and most challenging demands being placed on textiles today—that is, in soil-release agents and flame retardants.

Table 7-2　Some Important Trademark Finishes

Purpose	Common Trade Names	C	R	A	W	S	N	Ac	P
Water-repellency (durable)	Zelan	x	x						
	Cravenette	x	x	x	x	x	x	x	x
	Permel	x		x					
	Norane	x	x	x		x	x	x	x
	Syl-mer	x		x	x	x	x	x	x
	Duridel	x	x						
Water-repellency, Renewable (nondurable)	Hydro-pruf	x	x	x					
	Aridex	x	x						
	Aqua-shed	x	x	x					
	Impregnole	x	x		x				
Flame-resistant	Ban-flame	x	x						
	Flame Foil	x	x						
	Fire Chief	x	x						
	Permaproof	x	x						
	Aerotex (renewable)	x	x						
Wrinkle-resistant and wash-and-wear	Bancare	x	x						
	Tebilized	x	x						
	Lanaset	x		x	x				
	Perma-fresh	x							
	Resloom	x	x						
	Wrinkl-Shed	x	x						
	Definized	x	x						
	Superset				x				
	Aqua-permanent				x				
	Zeset	x	x						
	Fresh-Tex	x	x						
	Bellmanized	x	x						
	Facility	x	x						
	Unidure	x	x						
	Sanco		x						
	Redmanized	x	x						
Glazed	Everglaze	x							
	Vita-glaze	x							
Insect-resistant	Eulan				x				
	Larvex				x				
	Mitin				x				
	Boconize				x				
	Mothsnub				x				
	Dieldrin				x				
	Woolgard								

Table 7-2 (continued)

Purpose	Common Trade Names	C	R	A	W	S	N	A_c	P
Shrinkage control	Sanforized	x							
	Sanforset		x						
	Harriset				x				
	Lanaset				x				
	Rigmel	x							
	Resloom				x				
	Redmanized	x	x						
	Apponized		x		x	x			
	Definized				x				
	Avcoset		x						
	Dylanized				x				
Mildew-resistant	Aridex	x	x						
	Drax	x	x						
Durable-press†	Koratron	x	x	x	x	x	x	x	
	Coneprest	x	x	x	x	x	x	x	
	Dan-Press	x	x	x	x	x	x	x	
	Never-Press	x			x	x	x	x	
	M-S	x	x						
	Burmi-crease	x			x	x	x	x	
Heat insulation	Milium	x	x	x	x	x	x	x	x
	Temp-Resisto	x	x	x	x	x	x	x	x
Soil- and	Scotchgard	x	x	x	x		x	x	x
stain-resistant	Syl-mer	x	x	x	x		x	x	x
Hygienic	Sanitized	x	x		x				
	Purasan	x	x		x				
	Doweide								
	Guardsman	x	x						
Starchless finish	Bellmanized	x	x						
	Salerized	x	x						
	Apponized	x	x						
	Vitalized	x	x						
	Trubenized	x	x						
	Aerotex	x	x						
	Heberlein	x	x						
	Wat-a-set	x	x						
	Defiance	x	x						
Softened finish	CMC	x	x	x					
	Sorbinol	x	x	x			x	x	x
Soil-release finish	Cirrasol PT		x	x					
	Come Clean		x	x					

Table 7-2 (continued)

Purpose	Common Trade Names	Fibers Using Process*							
		C	R	A	W	S	N	A_c	P
	Dual-action								
	Scotchgard	x	x						
	Fibrite	x	x	x					
	Visa	x	x						
	X-lt	x	x						
Antistatic	Astar				x		x	x	x
	Fybrite				x		x	x	x
	Permalose				x		x	x	x

SOURCE: *Textile Chemist and Colorist* (Sept. 1970 and 1971).
Note: Several finishes are effective in other functional requirements in addition to their principal role.
*C — Cotton
 R — Rayons
 A — Acetate
 W — Wool
 S — Silk
 N — Nylon
 A_c — Acrylic
 P — Polyesters
† Usually applied to *blends* of cellulose fibers and a thermoplastic. Not applied to the man-made fiber garments alone.

It must be remembered that permanence is a relative term in spite of its sound of finality. White silks and woolens may turn yellow because of mishandling, whereas bleached linens rarely darken. An incompletely or surface-mercerized cotton broadcloth may lose its luster in laundering long before a well-mercerized fabric will even begin to become dull. The dyed surface or printed pattern of a fabric may fade from sun exposure, or washing, or the effect of perspiration. The glaze of a chintz may be lost after a single washing because the sizing that gave body to the cloth was removed in the detergent suds. The napped surface of a woolen may be worn away by friction during wear.

The glazing of an otherwise washable cotton chintz is a nonpermanent finish if the glaze is lost during washing. The sun fading of the dye of a delicate fabric intended for indoor wear similarly shows a nonpermanent finish as far as the service condition is concerned. The moiré figure on a silk is not resistant to water spotting and washing, but one on an acetate fabric can be made permanent. Sizing, filling, flocking, embossing, and crepeing are common nonpermanent finishes.

Among the more important permanent functional processes are those of preshrinking and making fabrics water-repellent, fire-retardant, insect-resistant, mildew-resistant, and crease-resistant, as in wash-and-wear or durable-press garments. Errors may be made in applying even the best and most durable of functional finishes.

FABRIC PRESHRINKAGE

The **Sanforizing** process is an intricate mechanical method of reducing residual or service shrinkage to a minimum, including both the natural and relaxation shrinkage of cotton and linen fabrics. It can also be applied to special cloths containing yarns of cotton or linen fibers mixed with rayon filaments. The Sanforizing process was the first method capable of producing a fabric having a low-shrinkage guarantee: a 1 per cent residual shrinkge under the Federal Trade Commission ruling of 1938 for "Shrinkage of Woven Cotton Yard Goods and Articles Made Therefrom." This method produces a fabric that can be guaranteed to have a residual or remaining shrinkage not to exceed 1 per cent in either warp or filling when washed according to a standard method recommended by the U.S. Bureau of Standards (CS–59–44). Cotton and many other fibers have a natural shrinkage in washing. The mechanical pulling operations during making and finishing any cloth or manufacturing an article of clothing from any kind of fiber can introduce enough stress and stretching to cause the garment to have a length or width shrinkage in excess of the guaranteed maximum. This is generally termed **relaxation** shrinkage. Therefore, even garments made from Sanforized cloth must be tested for shrinkage if they are to be labeled as having been processed to reduce the natural shrinkage. A partial protection is afforded fabrics by **stabilization**, or yarn anchorage, by means of synthetic resins that prevent yarn shifting and slipping. Fabrics that have been preshrunk, or relaxed, simply by being dipped in water and then dried may still have a residual shrinkage of 5 to 15 per cent. Much of this is the normal shrinkage of the yarn and fiber.

Sanforization for Cotton

A brief description of the Sanforizing process follows. The fabric is washed by standard procedures under CS–59–44 (L–22 or ASTM standards) to determine the shrinkage of that piece of goods. The fabric then passes over smooth cylinders to have wrinkles removed before it enters the Sanforizing, or controlled-shrinkage, machine. It is then fed into a chamber in which it is dampened by steam or water to relax the yarns. The fabric goes from here through a tenter frame. As the cloth is carried along the tenter frame, it is **rippled**—or pulled first on one side and then on the other—while subjected to the relaxing steam. This sideways pull releases the tension on the warp yarns, which relax and crinkle as the filling is pulled. This results in a lengthwise, or warp, shrinkage to the predetermined value.

This pulling action on the filling yarns while they are wet and pliable causes them to straighten and to stretch slightly. This width dimension must now be brought to the predetermined measurement shown by the pretest of the fabric shrinkage. The fabric passes over additional cylindrical rolls to flatten the cloth and to regulate its rate of passage; it then goes to the belt-shrinking machine in which it adheres to the convex or outer surface of a heavy woolen blanket that passes over the surface of a revolving drum. The blanket and fabric are then turned over as they enter and pass into the drying drum in which the direction of curvature is reversed—the fabric is then on the inside surface of the drum. The surface of the heavy blanket contracts and the relaxed filling yarns experience a degree of compression or push from each side to further aid in their shrinkage. The fabric is then labeled Sanforized and the residual shrinkage, usually 2 per cent or less, is stated on the label.

Rigmel finish, a trademark of the Bradford Dyeing Association, can also produce preshrunk cotton fabric that will not have a residual shrinkage in excess of 1 per cent. This, too, is a compression method by which a tautly held fabric is steamed and worked into the predetermined normal wash-shrinkage limits.

The FTC regulation does not apply to any woven cotton fabric or garment unless there is a claim made for preshrinkage or any reference to a shrinkage limit or tolerance.

There is no economy for any customer to buy cotton garments for which fit is a desired factor unless these have been preshrunk by a dependable process. Some wash-and-wear articles of cotton may suddenly begin to shrink when the all-purpose resin has leached or dissolved out.

An added advantage given by a satisfactory preshrinkage process is that the strength of the fabric has been increased. This increase is due to the fabric having more yarns per square inch after shrinking. The fabric has an improved handle, luster, and softness as a result of the action of the rollers and the steaming. It is well worth the increase in price of 2 to 8 cents per yard for Sanforized cloth.

WATER-REPELLENT FINISHES

To consumers, the problem of water repellency in outer-wear apparel is simply whether or not the wearer becomes wet when it rains. The challenge is much more complicated than this when it comes to treating fabrics for the protection of the wearer and, at the same time, satisfying him with the texture and appearance of the garment. Two important criteria in consumer satisfaction are contradictory when it comes to the selection of fabric. **Water-shedding ability** is one important factor in protection against rain. A fabric of loose structure and a rough-textured, somewhat fuzzy surface *sheds* rain much better than a smooth-surfaced fabric. However, from the standpoint of water *penetration* of the material, the smooth-surfaced, closely woven construction is better. Typical of the natural shedding would be a rough-textured wool tweed; for the second property, **penetration-resistance**, a tightly woven Oxford, using fine yarns would be more satisfactory. When this fabric becomes wet, the fibers and yarns swell and the weave becomes even more compact. (This is the principle of construction of the large fire hoses on fire-fighting equipment. They are generally made of cotton with multilayers of fine yarns in tight weaves. When the water first enters the all-cotton hose, it is rapidly absorbed by the cotton fibers; as they swell, they form a watertight structure that perimts no leakage along the length of the hose.)

The protection expected of most rain-wear apparel is that it will resist the water penetration from the impact of the pounding action of raindrops on the back and shoulders of the wearer. It would be hoped that upon impact the large drops would be broken into very small droplets, which, in turn, would bounce off or fall from the fabric. On the other hand, many materials, such as those used for tents, tarpaulins, and such spread fabrics, are required to prevent the penetration of water from pools that collect on the surface. To complicate matters further, the various fibers applicable to water-resistant items require different finishing materials and techniques to increase their effectiveness.

A **waterproof** fabric is any cloth that has been coated with rubber or plastic or that has been filled with oil until it will permit neither water nor air to pass through it. Any less complete barrier to moisture must be classed as **water-repellent**. These methods use gums, resins, oils, waxes, metallic soaps, and other chemicals to produce a fabric that will not water-spot and that will shed water if the garment is worn in a light shower. For the most part, these finishes are **nonpermanent** or are classed as **renewable**—they are removed by washing or dry cleaning but can be reapplied by the cleaner. Children's snow suits, coats, and hats; men's coatings, suitings, and ski togs; and women's coats, hats, sportswear, and hosiery are all articles of wearing apparel that frequently are given a water-repellent finish. Common renewable process names are **Cravenette, Neva-Wet, Aridex**, and **Impregnole**. (See Table 7–3.)

Among the various useful types of water-repellent finishing materials are the following:

1. Oils and dispersions of wax
2. Metallic soaps
3. Wax dispersions with salts of aluminum
4. Wax dispersions containing zirconium salts
5. Pyridinium repellents
6. Resins and thermosetting repellents

Table 7-3   Water-repellent Treatments, Trademarked Permanent Finishes

Trademark Product*	Type*	Manufacturer
Cerol	Wax dispersion—Al salts	Sandoz
Cravenette	Stearamide type	Crown Metro
Impregnole	Wax dispersion—Al salts	Sun Chemical
Nalan	Organometallic complex (Cr · Al)	du Pont
Nepton D	Methylol stearate amide condensate	Crown Metro
Norane	Stearamide type—Zr salts	Sun Chemical
Paramul	Wax dispersion—Al salts, Zr salts	American Cyanamid
Permel	Fluorochemical	American Cyanamid
Persistol	Wax dispersion—Zr salts	BASF
Phobotex	Waxy solid–water dispersion	CBA
Quarpel	Pyridinium base and fluorochemical	U.S. Army QM
Quilon	Organostearate–chromium complex	du Pont
Quintolan	Organometallic complex	ICI
Scotchgard	Fluorochemical	3-M Company
Sylmer	Silicone	Dow Corning
Velan	Pyridinium type	du Pont
Zelan	Fluoropolymer	du Pont
Zepel	Polymer-wax type	du Pont

* Under each trademark, or proprietary name, there may be several formulations, each requiring a different dispersion solvent. There may also be renewable finishes under some of these trade names.

7. Organometallic complexes with chromium or aluminum

8. Silicones and fluorochemicals

The permanent finish generally involves impregnating the fabric with a thermoplastic material, sometimes by actually polymerizing the resin in the fiber. One of the chemical constituents is absorbed by the fiber, which is then subjected to the second monomer at a sufficiently high temperature to develop the resin. Under these conditions, the interstices of the cloth are not affected, and the fabric has the ability to stay comfortable, even in a warm rain. Anyone who has worn one of the impermeable fabrics or a plastic raincoat will recall that in warm weather the inside of the coat is almost as wet as the outside, as a result of the condensation of body moisture on the inner surface of the garment. In Table 7–3 some permanent finishes are listed. Many of these are both dry-cleanable and washable. However, in both the durable and the nondurable, or renewable, types one should pay particular attenion to the label. If the garment is marked "washable" or "wash only," it means that the water-repellent finish was impregnated into the goods from a solvent; therefore, a dry-cleaning solvent might dissolve some of it, making the fabric less water-repellent. On the other hand, washing would not remove any of the chemical. If the article is marked "dry-clean only," it indicates that the chemical treatment was applied in a water solution; therefore, the article cannot be washed without leaching out some of the material. No matter how such garments are cleaned, it is absolutely necessary that every trace of soap be removed, because the presence of soap causes the fabric to become wet instantly, and it will leak badly wherever any soap particles are left.

Zelan was the first really dependable permanent water-repellent finish. Other effective permanent finishes are **Neva-Wet** and **Unisec**.

Within recent years the silicones have come into a position of importance in water-repellent garments. One of the successful silicone processes is **Hydro-pruf**. Another is a **Norane** repellent further identified from its sister finish trademark in the durable class as **Norane Four Star SWR**.

FIRE-RETARDANT FINISHES

It has long been common practice to **fireproof**, or more accurately to make **fire-retardant**, the fabrics used in stage settings and costumes. All the fabrics used in decorating most of the new luxury steamships, hotels, and the more recent World's Fairs were made resistant to fire. One method used is to saturate the fabric with a chemical, usually an ammonium salt, that will slow down the rate of burning. The fabric will not support combustion, and will no longer burn when the match or torch is removed. The chemicals used should not affect the handle or draping quality of the cloth nor should there be toxic vapors produced.

Factors in Flameproofing

Probably, a majority of the public believes that the problem of flame-proofing textile materials is one of recent seriousness. One may attribute this to the more widespread usage today of manufactured fibers and of lighter and lighter textile fabrics formed from the cellulosics, cotton and rayon. According to recent statistics of the U.S. Department of Health, Education and Welfare, the annual number of deaths in the United States caused by fires of all types rose to over 12,000 in 1967 and 1968. Of an average of about 7000 deaths annually during the previous two decades, it is believed that about 2000 to 3000 of these were attributable to the ignition of clothing fabrics. These figures are lower than those reflecting the numbers of persons injured and requiring long periods of hospitalization and rehabilitation as a result of clothing that caught on fire. Some observers reported at a textile flammability conference in 1962 that the annual number of clothing fire victims might be as high as 250,000 annually.[1] In many fires, the cellulosic materials are the principal sources of fire. Cellulosics would, of course, include wood for buildings. This is not a new problem. F. J. Ward records that in 83 B.C. a solution of alum was used to protect the wooden storming towers at the siege of Piraeus.[2]

One of the most important factors in the burning of cellulosic materials is the availability of oxygen. It is for this reason, of course, that light and filmy or napped surface fabrics of cotton and rayon have been particularly vulnerable to rapid combustion—the by-products of which varied, depending on the rate of burning and its completeness. In an excess of air, carbon dioxide and water are given primarily. If the air supply is more limited, there is a complex mixture of volatile gases, tarry materials, char, and water. Untreated cellulosic fabrics in an excess of air burn quickly over the surface to leave a black char; then the char itself is gradually consumed by an edge afterglow until finally only ash remains. If such fabrics were chemically treated to prevent the afterglow, the wearers of the clothing, although they would be burned painfully, would be less seriously or deeply burned than if the fabric were completely consumed. There are many chemical preparations that can reduce the afterglow to a considerable degree. Phosphate ions have been found to be effective retardants, whereas the alkali metal ions enhance the afterglow. The melt dripping effect of some of the manufactured fibers is another serious problem because these dripping molten residues in contact with the skin tend to produce painful and deep burning. Manufacturers of flame-retardant finishes and converters called upon to protect fabrics face further challenges because the new Federal legislation still has not spelled out the objectives to be met in the different categories of textile products not only in apparel or clothing items, but also in household fabrics and many industrial products. Certain problems still need to be resolved:

1. What is the ultimate degree of flameproofing or fire retardancy required in the regular use of a textile material?
2. How do the requirements of other uses of this same material affect the kind of treatment given?
3. How effective must such a finish be?
4. How durable must a fabric's finish be to be worn, laundered, or dry-cleaned?
5. Are there health factors that must be considered, (such as sensitivity of the skin or damage to the lungs from the chemical vapors produced by charring)?
6. Is sensitivity of the skin increased by perspiration or by wearing the garment when it is wet?

[1] Sylvia Porter, "Your Money's Worth," *Pittsburgh Post-Gazette* (April 10, 1970).
[2] F. J. Ward, *Journal of the Society of Dyers and Colourists,* **71**, No. 10 (1955), p. 569.

7. If small amounts of a finish are taken internally, as when babies chew a treated blanket or clothing, will the finish have any ill effects on the child?

It is anticipated, of course, that standards will eventually define these various requirement criteria. However, subsequent to them such processing problems as the effects of the chemical or process on the color, hand, or luster of the treated cloth will be introduced. What of its compatibility with other finishes? As important as any criteria, how much will it cost? These various problems apply not only to the original finishing of the textile in the converter's plant but also to any kind of finish eventually accepted for retreatment of washed or dry-cleaned textile products.

NEW FEDERAL LAWS ON FLAMMABILITY

Additional Federal legislation was enacted in 1967 applying not only to apparel fabrics, but also to household textile products. The *Federal Register* has published proposed standards for flammability for the commodities listed in Table 7–4.

The Department of Commerce issued the *Flammability Standard* to cover children's sleep wear on July 27, 1971. The Department of Health, Education and Welfare supplied the Department of Commerce with 150 cases in which 1059 separate garments were ignited causing the deaths of 76 persons and injury to 504. Of 580 cases, 174 involved the spillage of flammable liquids on the garments. These were not considered to be the fault of the fabric; however, of the other 406 cases, 713 garments—in which children under the age of 5 were injured in greater numbers, 21.2 per cent of the cases—were tested by the National Bureau of Standards (NBS) by the proposed new test and failed to pass.

In brief, the standard proposes that five specimens of every item of sleep wear and the fabrics from which they are made be selected from the most flammable portion of the item, including trim and seams. Each specimen is tested in the vertical direction by subjecting it to a 3-second exposure to a standard methane gas flame. In order to pass, garments must meet certain char length and afterflame criteria, even after being laundered 50 times. All items of children's sleep wear must be labeled with precautionary instructions to protect the items from agents or treatment known to cause deterioration of the garments' flame resistance. Such labels must be permanent and otherwise in accordance with the rules and regulations established by the Federal Trade Commission.

Obviously, new and more realistic test methods have become necessary to stimulate actual use conditions more closely. These test methods continue to be studied because the number of end-use items to be covered increases. The compromise 45° angle test used in the first flammability law is no longer

Table 7-4 **Status of Federal Textile Flammability Legislation**

Items	Effective Date	Requirements
DOC–FF–1–70 Large carpets and rugs	April 1971	"Pill" test. A tablet of methenamine is placed on the brushed pile surface and is ignited. The flames must go out before spreading 3 inches. The test must again be passed after 10 washings. Carpet backings are to be tested in a similar manner because of foam flammability and toxicity of fumes. Fabrics failing cannot be sold.
DOC–FF–2–70 Small carpets and rugs, including bath mats	Dec. 1971	Items must be marked "Failed U.S. DOC Standard FF–2–70." These should not be used near a source of ignition.
DOC–FF–3–71 Children's sleep wear, including fabrics intended for children's sleep wear, sizes 0–6X	July 1972– July 1973 Revised July 28, 1973	"Vertical forced ignition" test. Samples exposed to flame before and after 50 washings must show char length less than 7 inches average (on 10-inch specimen). No aftermelt or drip longer than 10 seconds. Amendment modified sampling plan. Garments failing to meet test must be labeled "Flammable does not meet DOC Standard FF–3–71". Should not be worn near source of ignition. As of 7–28–73 revision, those not meeting the standard cannot be sold in market.
DOC–FF–4–72 Mattresses and mattress pads	Passed May 1972 Effective May 31, 1973	"Cigarette" test mattresses must resist ignition from 18 cigarettes placed on the mattress and between sheets. Year of grace expired as of May 31, 1973, and all mattresses failing to pass are banned from market.
FF–5–74 Flammability of children's sleep wear, sizes 7 through 14	May 1, 1975	Extension of DOC–FF–3–71. To become effective in 18 months.

applicable to all textile products and use conditions. It is significant that this 1967 law was passed before adequate standard test methods, definitions, and tolerances had been established; subsequently the fire exposure procedures in Table 7–4 were devised. These are described briefly here:

1. *45° angle or flash burning test for apparel (1967)*. In this test, samples are exposed at a 45° angle to a 1-second ignition source. Fabrics whose surfaces burn in fewer than 3½ seconds are considered dangerously hazardous. This test is applied primarily to articles of wearing apparel. It may soon be extended to blankets.

2. *Tablet test for carpets and rugs* (**large** and **small**). The surface flammability of carpets and rugs is tested by exposing eight 9-inch square specimens to an ignited tablet of methenamine that burns for 90 to 120 seconds. If the fire spreads more than 3 inches in any direction from the location of the tablet, the specimen fails. One failure out of the eight samples is permitted.

Small rugs and carpets that fail this test can still be sold, provided that they are *labeled* to warn the public of their potential flammability.

3. *Vertical forced ignition test for children's sleep wear* (pajamas, nightgowns, bathrobes). Five specimens are cut from garments in both the length and width directions, and then are oven-dried. In a vertical test cabinet, each sample is exposed to a gas flame for 3 seconds. This test is carried out on new fabrics and on fabrics after they have been laundered and dried 50 times. A simulated seam is sewn into samples in what is found to be the most flammable direction (length or width) and is tested by this method. If trim or decoration on the garment is greater than 2 inches in length, it too must be tested.

To pass, the average char length for the five specimens (before and after laundering) cannot exceed 7 inches; no *individual* specimen can have a char length of more than 10 inches. In addition, the average afterflame time (the time the specimen continues to melt and drip after the burner has been removed) must be 10 seconds or less because melt burn wounds can be very severe and deep.

Certain criteria can be set up for an ideal fire-resistant fabric:

1. When the fire source is removed, the flame extinguishes itself.
2. There is no change in the flammability hazards in use or following laundering or cleaning.
3. A fabric does not differ in appearance or performance properties from other fabrics accepted for similar end-uses.

This means that the esthetics of treated fabrics, feel and appearance, must be competitive with untreated fabrics, also treated fabrics must be free of toxic, allergenic, or irritating effects: skin irritation or irritating fumes if the fabric should smolder.

A treated fabric should also be competitive in price as compared with other fabrics for the same end-use.

Similarly, certain basic criteria should be set for the ideal fire-resistant treatment.

1. The treatment should be formulated from economical and efficient chemicals widely available from the chemical industry.
2. These chemicals should be applied in commercial equipment without requiring unusual or costly methods of application.
3. The treatment should give reproducible results in all laboratories and be applicable to a wide variety of textile fabrics.
4. It should not affect other processing steps such as finishing and dyeing.
5. It should be durable under all use and care conditions.

A brief survey of the burning characteristics of some of our more important fibers will emphasize the need for a treatment as close to the ideal as possible. However, it also will suggest that more than one finish probably will be required for specific fibers and that the durability of any finish may vary for different constructions and end-uses.

Cellulose Fibers

Cotton and rayon textiles are regarded as the most serious fire hazards. They ignite readily and are consumed totally. The organophosphorus compounds have been among the most successful in controlling afterglow effects. This is the lingering glow or flame left by some finishes that are effective only in preventing the actual flaming or burning away of the fibers. It is similar to the afterglow on a match that has had its flame blown out but that still possesses the dangerous power of igniting any flammable material in contact with it.

Wool

Loose wool has been known to burn, and large quantities of fine wool fibers in the air corresponding to the dust from grain or coal dust can burn and explode. In ordinary use conditions, however, wool is considered to be flame-retardant. If a fire should start from a live flame dropped on a wool carpet, such as from a lighted match or from a burning ember from a fire, it would burn a small ring in the surface of the carpet but would extinguish itself because of its low air-holding capacity.

Manufactured Fibers

No attempt can be made to draw conclusions as to the relative flammability of manufactured fibers considering the wide variety of the polymers in their chemical and physical properties and the effect of natural fibers mixed with them in blends. All thermoplastic fibers when exposed to a live flame tend to melt and to draw away from the flame. This does not necessarily mean that they are self-extinguishing, because if a single cotton or rayon thread is woven into such a yarn, this cellulose will serve as a wick causing the fire to pass rapidly and to consume the manufactured fiber. Thus, there is evidence that blends of cotton with polyester or with acrylics will actually burn at a more rapid rate than 100 per cent cotton or 100 per cent of the manufactured fiber. Such fabrics as blends or combination fabrics should probably be treated as a manufactured unit; that is, the fabric should be treated rather than the individual fibers before spinning or the yarns before weaving.

Fire-retardant Fabrics

Several chemical companies are currently working on durable fire-retardant finishes. Several finishes have been found to be commercially adaptable to cotton and to a somewhat lesser extent to rayon, but thus far no finishes are being used commercially to render thermoplastic manufactured fibers non-flammable. The 1967 revision of the Federal Flammable Fabrics Act of 1953 has been extended to include household textiles. Among the fibers not previously covered are the modacrylics, saran, and some of the nylons. The purpose of the original test was to eliminate from the market and from interstate commerce dangerously flammable materials for apparel. New standards and tests are to be required and of some 117 garments involved in burn accidents, all passed the CS–191 test (identical to the AATCC–33–1962) used in existing flammability legislation. The problem facing the textile industry is that, if a vertical test is adopted as a test method, much of our present textile product production will not meet the test. If children's apparel and the fabrics worn by older people are flammable, they can cause injury or death even if the present test methods are made more rigid—that is, even if the flammability time is changed from 3½ seconds to as much as 10 seconds, more than half of the 117 garments that had caused death would burn. In Britain, in 1964, special regulations on children's night-gowns went into effect and all fabrics used for such apparel are now required to be flame-retardant, according to British standards BS–2963 and B–3121. When the regulation was passed, a finish called Proban, based on THPC, was applied to cotton and rayon. It did not work, however, with thermoplastic fibers.

In 1969, the AATCC approved a modified vertical test for thermoplastic fibers that measures the advantages of fire-retardant fabrics, such as **Nomex** nylon with polyester and with polyesters and modacrylics. The heat of combustion of various fibers is given in Table 7–5.

Table 7-5

Fiber	Heat of Combustion, Btu/lb
Cotton or rayon	7,400
Acetate	7,700
Polyester	9,300
Nylon	12,950
Acrylic	13,000
Spandex	13,540

Without a fire-retardant treatment, all these fibers are flammable. Considerable research is still needed to measure some of the flame-propagating media, such as afterglow, melting and burning material, disintegration into flying particles or brands, flame intensity, and heat transfer.

The greatest market for such fabrics is in the household for bedding, curtains, draperies, and upholstery. However, the immediacy of need is greater from the standpoint of personal safety, especially for children and the elderly, even though the total potential market, as shown in Table 7–6, is smaller.

The Flammable Fabrics Act and its amendments calling for safer fabric-flammability standards indicate greater public and congressional awareness. The textile industry has long been concerned with this matter, but the original interest was primarily in apparel. In other words, great importance was devoted to the accidents experienced by individuals whose apparel became ignited. When the acrylic fiber first began to affect the carpet fiber market, there was some unfair adverse publicity calling attention to the burning

Table 7-6   Potential Markets of Fire-resistant Fabrics, Based on 1968 Use

Markets	Millions of Square Yards
Automotive fabrics	285
Children's nightwear	235
Children's play clothes	245
Bedding and bedclothes	2371
Curtains, draperies, and upholstery fabrics	1497

Table 7-7   Statistics on Fabric Flammability Accidents

Yearly deaths from flammable fabrics, 4,000
Total burns each year, medical attention or activity restricted, 2,000,000
Bed cases, 300,000
Burn cases involving fabric ignition, 175,000
Burn cases involving clothing ignition, 150,000
Death from clothing ignition, 20,000
Estimated economic losses per year $400,000,000

---

characteristics of the fiber in comparison with such fabrics as wool and nylon. At that time carpet flammability was considered to be such an insignificant danger that there were few, if any, state laws or local ordinances dealing with the problem. The Marietta Nursing Home fire in 1970, however, indicated a factor hitherto largely neglected. That factor was the effect of fumes from fires as health hazards, because most of the victims in that fire died of smoke inhalation. The greater number of the 142 deaths at the Boston Cocoanut Grove fire in 1942 had been classified as the result of inhalation of toxic fumes from plastic decorations. Some of the polymers used in the 1940s as coating materials are among today's textile products.

The new law also takes under consideration the burn damage resulting from the melting of thermoplastic fibers. Some molten material may drop onto the flesh of the wearer before the fabric actually bursts into flame, causing serious burns that may require eventual skin grafting. Just as cellulosic fibers are more susceptible to burning in lightweight filmy fabrics or in those with a napped or pile surface, the burning and melting intensity of thermoplastic fibers are increased by similar structures. It has been noted that blended fabrics sometimes exhibit a greater burning intensity than those made of either fiber alone. A case in point is cellulose acetate with nylon, or acrylic with nylon or with a cellulosic fiber. In the case of these blended yarn fabrics, there is a minute grid effect in which either the more flammable or the lower-melting fiber is suspended in a minute layer of the more flame-resistant ingredient. These complications will require more extensive research than just the protection required by individual fibers or fiber families. More information will be required in order to determine the degree of flame- or fire-resistance of fiber families in constructions for various end-use items. Not only must their initial protection requirements be considered, but also those demanded by the conventional methods of cleansing and care.

Limitations of Fire-resistant Finishes

The Committee of the National Bureau of Standards has worked closely with the Federal Trade Commission for the purpose of developing a series of test methods to evaluate fire-resistant finishes for the great number of end-use items to which it is now applied. FFA 67 (Flammable Fabrics Act of 1967) applies to flat-lying textile products such as carpets, rugs, and mats; vertically hanging fabrics, such as curtains, draperies, and other decorative textile products; and to wearing apparel whose exposure to flame may be at any angle. Thus, various tests and interpretations leading to standards of performance will necessarily be varied. The finishes to be selected also must be considered in relation to conventional methods of cleaning the product. Because the majority of these textile products are cleaned in the presence of water, one of the requirements must certainly be resistance to water solution or leaching out. The next limitation is the durability of the material. If durability is removed by water, then there should be a renewable type of finish, such as the standard borax-boric acid mixture, which is in itself water-soluble and causes some stiffening of the fiber texture.

The next group of products are the semidurable finishes. Unfortunately, some of them are adversely affected by certain water conditions; because of the widespread variety in water treatments against pollution through chemical refuse, removal of excess hardness, and excessive detergents, they will lose their effectiveness after a few washings. These nondurables and some of the chemicals being proposed for durable finishes are costly. The pyramiding of costs incurred in the finishing operation might well price certain well-known fabric constructions out of traditional apparel outlets. The consumer simply could not afford the extra retail price of the dress, shirt, coat, sweater, or whatever the article might be.

ANTIBACTERIAL FINISHES

Sanitizing is a relatively old hygienic process that makes fabrics sterile and **bacteria-static**; that is, it inhibits the growth of bacteria on the fabric. The cloth is saturated with an odorless chemical that does not affect the texture of the fabric in any way. This treatment is readily removed by washing or by the action of plain water, but it is said to be relatively permanent in dry cleaning. It is applied to hotel linens, mattress covers, women's wearing apparel, shoe linings, luggage fabrics, and underwear.

Cyana-finish, perfected by the American Cyanamid Company, is applied to textiles to reduce the possibility of odor-forming bacteria growing on the fabric. Much of the early research was carried out in Army field hospitals for the purpose of preventing the development of odor from fluid matter exuding from wounds and from perspiration. The chemical formula has been reported as having five major attributes:

1. It is effective against bacteria associated with perspiration.
2. The finish is durable and is removed by washing or dry cleaning only with extreme difficulty.

3. It is inexpensive not only in cost but in application.

4. The finish does not affect the appearance or hand of the fabric.

5. It is not irritating to the skin.

Laboratory washing tests (50 in number) have not removed this finish from cottons and rayons. The producers claim it is durable for the life of the fabric. The finish is not required for manufactured fibers.

WARMTH RETENTION

Wide use has been made of finely dispersed aluminum powder in a resin base as a reflective surface to help maintain body comfort in both cold and hot ambient conditions. This resin base is deposited on a lining fabric, often rayon or acetate, with the metal face toward the body to reflect the body's own heat rays and keep the wearer warmer. In practice, these methods, such as **Milium**, **Tempresisto**, and others, are only moderately successful. One problem is that some finishers use a cheap, open lining fabric and depend on the impermeable resin layer to serve as a windbreaker also and thus retain warmth. At times the resin is dissolved or is partly removed by dry cleaning, and the bright metallic surface darkens and defeats the objective of the product. The metallic surface can cause local chilling by conducting heat from the body at points of direct contact.

SPOT- AND STAIN-RESISTANT FINISHES

Synthetic fibers are sensitive to staining by oils and greases. The claim made for them that they are spot- and stain-resistant applies only to water-borne materials. It is important, therefore, that special finishes be developed to protect carpets and rugs, as well as upholstery fabrics of nylon, acrylics, polyesters and other synthetics, against oily spots. **Scotchgard** and **Zepel** are examples of a finish that is applicable to synthetics and to wool for resistance to water- and oil-borne stains.

MILDEW-RESISTANT FINISHES

The natural fibers, particularly cellulose, will, if left to the effects of nature, eventually decompose or become consumed by organisms. This deterioration resulting from bacteria and mildew is more rapid in hot, moist climates than in the temperate areas of the world. In order to preserve useful articles made of these materials from the deteriorating atmosphere, it is necessary to protect them against organic bodies. This is generally done by means of toxic compounds that destroy mildew or bacteria but that are not harmful to humans. Metal salts, metal soaps, and various sizing materials can be used. Generally, these protected cellulosic fabrics become stiff and harsh in texture and discolored, particularly if copper soaps are used. However, most of these fabrics are protected for military or industrial use rather than for the average consumer; thus, the changes in physical appearance are not objectionable.

INSECT-REPELLENT FINISHES

Wool is the only common fiber subject to damage from the larvae of clothes moths or of carpet beetles. These larvae may eat through other fibers, but generally it is to get at a source of wool or other protein fiber such as hair, fur, or feathers, or to escape from a confined space. It ought to be mentioned here that chemicals such as silicofluorides are used. A number of these methods and chemicals can now be used to make wool resistant to insects for the life of the garment. **Mitin, Dieldrin**, and **Boconize** are permanent mothproofing methods for wool. One of the principal safeguards for the home is to see that wool articles when stored for a season are cleaned before being packed away and that no soiled garments are left in contact with them or in the same container—moth eggs might have been laid on the soiled garments.

STARCHLESS FINISHES

Because the traditional use of starch and other filling agents may be accompanied by a dusting of the stiffening material when rubbed or a loss of this material upon washing, a number of chemical finishing methods have been developed for the purpose of giving a crisp, starchy appearance without loss or change in texture during repeated washings. This is usually done on cottons either by an acid or resin treatment. Often it is tied in with wash-and-wear if a stiffened fabric is desired. It is used mostly on sheer cottons, such as lawns, veils, and organdies, and to a considerable extent on cotton and rayon marquisette curtain materials. A permanent finish helps hold the individual fibers close together in the yarn. Some of these finishes are listed in Table 7–2. Resin-finished fabrics may develop either a bad fishlike odor or that of formaldehyde if the resin is not completely cured in the fibers. These odors may disappear if the garment is well aired, but if they do not, the consumer is justified in expecting the garment to be returnable to the store and producer.

STATIC-RESISTANT FINISHES

The static electrical results encountered in wearing some fibers or fabrics, especially indoors in a very dry ambient atmosphere, are familiar to most consumers. Among evidences of static are the sparks produced by contact between one person who has become charged by moving around and one who has been standing—long-recognized also to many people as the popular childhood game of sparking. It is also evident in the clinging, creeping, and bunching up of garments and in the attraction of dust and lint to hosiery, to the cuffs of slacks, and to some untreated curtain and drapery materials. There are other objectionable qualities: slacks and trousers cling to the legs and to the waistline of shirts. Sleeping garments also tend to cling as the result of static; and garments of dissimilar natures dried together in a household dryer cling and tangle (for example, a nylon slip with an acetate dress).

On a number of occasions this writer has had a demonstration of static electricity. The first time it occurred, it was quite startling. In donning a pair of polyester slacks while standing on a wool carpet, the static produced appeared to be of exactly the right wavelength to turn on a remote-control television set.

The following factors are related to, or affect, the static in apparel:

FIBER TYPE   At an indoor condition of 15 per cent relative humidity, a condition common in many homes in colder regions of the United States, certain of our fibers are rated in the following order with the worst static-producing fiber mentioned first: polyester, acrylic, nylon, acetate, wool, and cotton.

ENVIRONMENTAL CONDITIONS   The 15 per cent relative humidity creates a condition producing the optimum objection; however, the kind of rubbing surface, the pressure, and the time of rubbing all contribute to the total charge of static accumulated.

PERSONAL CHARACTERISTICS OF THE WEARER   This static is affected by the rubbing of the fabric against the skin of the wearer.

Some persons seem to be more static prone than others, and it may be that even under the dry ambient conditions, the skin surface of some wearers is slightly more moist. This might help reduce the static charge, while the charge to those with drier skin would be expected to be greater. The accumulation of static is gradual, and whether or not a textile material is satisfactory or an antistatic finish is effective will depend to a considerable extent upon the time the static actually persists in the garment. Thus, fibers that are recorded as most resistant to static discharge their electric capacity quickly, compared to those that are objectionable. Fibers differ slightly in their ability to conduct electricity; the better conductors cause the static to flow out through the yarns to a grounded surface more quickly. It is clear, therefore, that those fibers that store static are those having the greatest amount of electrical insulating capacity—that is, they are resistant to the flow of electricity. During the summer months, or in damp ambient conditions, there is little difference to be noted between any of these fibers in clinging or in actual spark production. Relative humidities as low as 40 per cent are virtually static-free with any of these fibers.

A sail test devised by R. H. Pike was described by Wilkinson in an article entitled, "Static Electricity, Domestic and Commercial Implications in Textile Materials." [3] Test subjects wearing garments of various fibers rubbed against a sail of polyester 4 or 5 feet wide, mounted vertically on an insulated rack. The time in minutes for the static charge to disappear under different relative humidities of from 10 to 65 per cent was recorded. For maximum static build-up, rubber-soled shoes were worn to prevent conduction to the floor.

Among the companies attacking the antistatic feature with good success are Celanese with their **Fybrite** and ICI with **Permalose.** These finishes cause a fabric to resist the impingement of dirt and its entrapment in fiber ends brought erect by the static charge. At the same time, they reduce the tendency of such garments to cling to the body or to a protein fiber garment, such as a silk dress or a wool skirt or suit.

WASH-AND-WEAR FINISHES

Wash-and-wear, although it has been replaced by durable-press for some uses, is one of the most important textile programs in many years. Actually, the more accurate terminology is **minimum care. Wash-and-wear,** taken literally, implies that absolutely no iron touch-up is required to restore the smoothness of the garment and to make it completely presentable. A wash-and-wear fabric is one that resists the wrinkles and mussiness imposed during wearing; it retains creases, pleats, and other ironed-in formations; and, after washing, it shows a minimum evidence of wash-wrinkling to the extent that it can almost be worn immediately after drying without pressing. Generally, however, most double-thickness areas benefit from a touch-up from the iron. It is not necessary to iron the entire garment, and this saves considerable time and energy. The public tends to forget the equally significant fact that these garments stay fresh-looking for many more hours' wear than do the average articles of wearing apparel.

[3] *Modern Textiles* (Dec. 1970), pp. 35–40.

A garment gains this minimum-care characteristic in one of three ways: (1) it may be a quality or property of the fiber itself, as in the case of most thermoplastic synthetic fibers; (2) it may be a property added to the fabric by means of blending a thermoplastic fiber with cotton; or (3) it may be gained by chemically treating an all-cotton or rayon fabric.

Wash-and-wear articles—whether all synthetic, or blended, or treated cotton—should be washed under moderate conditions. Normal wash temperatures and detergents can be used, but bleaches, especially the chlorine type, should be avoided. A chlorine bleach will discolor some of the manufactured synthetic fibers and will combine with most of the resin types used in the chemically treated cottons to the eventual deterioration of the cotton. Furthermore, wrinkles induced by washing are often more serious than those resulting from wear because, being applied to the fabric under a relatively high temperature, there is some danger of their being sealed into the fabric, especially with the synthetics. A light wash load, possibly half the normal washing capacity, and not more than half a dryer load can safely be tolerated by these fabrics without heat-sealing wrinkles into them.

We cannot have the easy-care properties associated with wash-and-wear without some sacrifice. One such sacrifice is that the resins tend to make the fibers brittle, with the result that a cotton fabric treated with wash-and-wear resin will lose about one third of its wear resistance. It is, therefore, poor economy to buy a wash-and-wear item if one is going to use it as one would an untreated garment. That is, wash-and-wear should not be treated as ordinary fabrics. The more they are placed with heavy loads in the washer and in the dryer, the more wrinkles will be induced and the more ironing will be necessary.

The resin used to provide this crease retention and wrinkle resistance has other advantages also. It helps stabilize the fabric—that is, it keeps the fabric from shrinking and from stretching. Inded, this is sometimes the only stabilization process given to cotton fabrics. The resin also helps hold the dyestuff in the fabric, and, of course, it adds a certain degree of body or weight to the material. Thus, if this finish is not permanent and is gradually removed by repeated washings, there may come a time when the fabric, almost overnight, will appear to be faded, shrunken, and wrinkled. Odors may develop if the garment is not properly cleaned; this is a justifiable consumer complaint.

Wash-and-wear Trademark Processes

Among the more prominent producers of wash-and-wear fabrics certain trademark names stand out in the memory of the average customer. These are the names that most frequently appear in advertisements in the newspapers and magazines and on labels on goods in the better stores. Many of these names are featured in the catalogues of mail-order companies.

1. **Bellmanized**: The Bellman Brook Bleachery name for a durable, crisp, starchless finish particularly useful for dress and curtain fabrics.

2. **Everglaze**: This trademark designates fabrics finished and tested according to the process standards of the Joseph Bancroft & Sons Co. It is applicable to patterned and embossed surface effects; it gives fabrics durable wrinkle resistance and shrinkage control. The use of this trademark as an identification of yarns, fabrics, and garments is set forth on "Everglaze" trademark tags.

3. **Facility**: The Reeves Brothers, Inc., hold this trademark for a wrinkle- and shrinkage-resistant finish; it is useful also for perspiration and acid resistance.

4. **Fresh-Tex**: This wash-and-wear trademark is from the Cranston Print Works Company. It is also said to control shrinkage and damage from perspiration and mildew.

5. **Permel-Plus**: This washable, water-repellent finish is an American Cyanamid Company trademark. It is claimed also to add to the strength of the goods.

6. **Redmanized**: This trademark belongs to the F. R. Redman Company to control relaxation shrinkage for woolen and cotton-knit goods. It is identified within the processor's quality-control plan and applies more to shrinkage control than to wash-and-wear, although it has some attributes in that field as well.

7. **Resloom**: Monsanto Chemical Company offers this resin finish for cotton, wool, and rayon for wrinkle resistance and shrinkage control.

8. **Sanco 400**: This trade name of the Sanco Piece Dye Works, Inc., is used primarily for wash-and-wear rayons.

9. **Unidure**: This trademark is held by United Piece Dye Works for a permanent wash-and-wear finish.

10. **Wrinkl-Shed**: This process is the trademark of Dan River Mills for permanent crease resistance, shrinkage control, and mildew resistance in fabrics.

11. **Zeset**: This trademark of E. I. du Pont de Nemours & Co., is for crease resistance and shrinkage resistance for fabrics made of cellulosic fibers.

A problem in washable durable-press and wash-and-wear items, especially resin-finished cotton and blends of cotton with polyester resins, is the requirement of optical brighteners to mask the yellowing or grayish dulling caused by the redeposition of dirt during washing. Another problem is the removal of soil from the neckbands of collars, the insides of cuffs, and various other locations where dirt and oil have accumulated. Research in the detergent industry has contributed numerous types of enzyme-active products aimed at both preventing and removing this type of soil. Unfortunately, these products generally require a degree of presoaking in the active material prior to the actual washing operation. Several of these products have been advertised widely.

There is some evidence of skin irritation from too frequent contact with these enzyme-containing detergents and of bronchial distress in breathing their dust.[4]

Household detergents have been found to be a serious pollutant material in our water sources because of their phosphate and enzyme content. It is now necessary that the ingredients be **biodegradable**—that is, they must break down or decompose upon exposure to water, air, and sun.

Durable-press

Durable-press is one of the peaks of progress achieved by textile research and development. It is, in fact, more perfect and more durable than wash-and-wear, although the predecessor is still an important commercial product. Durable-press means also durable fit. At present the garments that have been durable-press finished are blended with one of the thermoplastic fibers. Some manufacturers supplying gray goods for this new, more sophisticated and demanding market are using 85 per cent cotton and 15 per cent of du Pont's 420 nylon. Others are still utilizing 65 per cent polyester, 35 per cent cotton, or 50 per cent blends of the two fibers.

This new finish demands great care in dyeing. Generally, the cotton and the other fiber are dyed separately to as close to the same shade as possible. The complication in dyeing is that the dyes must be exposed to high temperatures during the curing operation. Furthermore, full absorption of the dyes cannot be achieved because the fibers must be left free to absorb sufficient amounts of the curing resin. Color changes in durable-press garments can also result when the garment has been pressed at a relatively high temperature, along the creases of trouser legs, jacket sleeves, or in permanent pleats in a dress. Other areas of the garment not subject to as great a temperature in pressing may show shade differentials after the garment has been worn for a time. Also, the conditions of curing and the pressing that follows seem to make some dyestuffs more subject to light fading. The term *fixing* as used in the durable-press process simply means the fixing or insolubilizing of about 6 per cent of resin (synthetic polymer) in the fabric. The resin used

[4] Ralph Nader, *Pittsburgh Press* (June 14, 1970).

should be nonchlorine retentive and should not pick up soil from the wash load.

There are several different processes, but the two most prominent categories are (1) **delayed cure**, where the sensitizing chemicals are applied in the finishing operation but are not completely fixed and (2) **precured**, where the fabrics are finished and cured—the final permanent-press character is given by the fabric manufacturer's pressing equipment at a higher temperature. **Koratron**, the first commercially used process, licensed by Koracorp Industries, Inc., is an example of the delayed-curing method. The resin is applied during the finishing of the fabric, which is then cut into garments, sewn together, and placed in an oven at a high temperature. Here the resin is cured and is fixed in the creases or pleats permanently. At the same time, other wrinkles and puckers are sealed out. There is a certain vulnerability to pressing of this kind: Many manufacturers are inexperienced, and lack confidence, in the art of curing resins and other finishes in fabrics and may not completely fix the resin in place. The result is that the garment will not hold its crease and may even lose shape after some wear.

The precure method, in which many textile companies are interested, is being experimented with by such large textile producers as Cone Mills, Deering-Milliken, and others. The precure finished garment is then pressed at a temperature of 450°F and under pressure far beyond any temperature or pressure it will meet during the life of the garment.

Another method is represented by Burlington's **Burmi-Crease** and Wamsutta's **Never-Press**. This method does not require chemical treatment; the fabric is impregnated with a heat-settable resin so that when the fabric is pressed at a high temperature, permanent creases are set in.

Quite good durable-press results have been achieved through the high-temperature pressing of fabrics blended with two thermoplastic fibers, such as 50:50 polyester and acrylic, as opposed to results through finishing.

Sanitary No-iron Linens

There has been some question in the minds of homemakers as to whether a satisfactory level of sanitation is possible with the mild washing procedures recommended for the no-iron or durable-press bed sheets. The American Hotel and Motel Association through its research committee recently conducted a series of chemical tests on the bacterial count on 50 per cent cotton/50 per cent polyester sheets. After removing the sheets from the beds and washing them according to the association's procedure for washing lightly soiled linens,[5] research workers found that washing even without sanitizers

[5] The American Hotel and Motel Association revised edition of the *No-iron Laundry Manual* by L. A. Bradley, published by the Cornell Hotel and Restaurant Administration Quarterly, Ithaca, N.Y.

reduced the bacterial content considerably. The no-iron sheets appear to contain fewer bacteria than the conventional cotton sheets, both before and after laundering; and furthermore, chlorine bleach proved to be a satisfactory sanitizing agent.

SOIL-RELEASE FINISHES

The path of any new technological development is alternately light and shadow; that is to say, there are high expectations and some successes, followed by failures and disappointments as unexpected problems present themselves. The wave motion exists in the laboratory, in the promotion, and finally, in the acceptance by the ultimate user of the process or its product. In no field does this become as troublesome to all concerned as in the textile industry. It is a very competitive industry; each new finish, new texture, new color, and new design is immediately in competition with the existing products on the market and with improvements coming out of the laboratories of competing companies. Invariably, new products and finishes —such as the most recent, soil release—are introduced with great enthusiasm by sales and promotion departments. However, sometimes a product has not yet been adequately proved in the laboratory or in a semi-commercial-scale study. The new finish may be applied to textile products for which it is not suited. The apparel manufacturers seize upon such products and add their voices of enthusiasm to those of the manufacturing company. Then, in turn, the products tend to be overly praised by the retailers to the consuming public, so that the consumer may expect far more than even a praiseworthy product may be able to give. Users may find that during a period of use and cleaning the finish will lose its effectiveness. This disappointment may lead to their avoiding the product.

Our modern textile industry has provided us with a progression of serviceable and easily cared-for merchandise; we have seen the advance from all-day freshness to easy care, wash-and-wear, durable-press, soil release fabrics. Far more was expected of soil-release in improving the acceptability of durable-press, whose finish is oleophilic (the durable-press textile readily absorbs oils and greases).

The soil-release finish really involves three phenomena.

1. A truly effective release finish must first have the ability to repel stains; that is—to prevent the entry of stains, spots, and soil into the textile; therefore, it must be hydrophobic.

2. The second property is that of soil release. This means that a finish must permit the entry of soap and water to some extent so that during laundering the soil in the fabric will become attached to, or combine with, the detergent agent through chemical action. In other words, this is a moderately hydrophilic condition.

When the soil has been released to the wash water, either through solution or by a chemical combination with the detergent, the chemical finish must resist a redeposition. This is a protective measure reminiscent of the home washing of cottons in which the soap or detergent did not attract dirt sufficiently well to prevent the resoiling of the wash load, resulting in what is referred to as "tattletale grey."

3. A soil-release finish applied to a durable-press fabric must also resist spots and stains, mostly oily in character, coming from the body of the wearer as well as from all the different kinds of soiling materials encountered during wear. These various stains may be either water-borne or carried by oil. The problem is complex, and it is improbable that any single chemical will be found that will prevent both the entry of soil into a fabric and effect its ready release during laundering. The problem of redeposition is additional and depends, in part, on the nature of the chemical used to effect soil release from the garment and the retention of the soil by the specific detergent system used.

Soil release is in commercial operation, and its great appeal to the consumer is attributed to one or perhaps two of these primary objectives, with the idea being that there may be a greater or lesser degree of combination of results—that is, when a fabric is prevented from yellowing, the intensity of the oily stains may also be reduced. Also, if a finish is capable of resisting oil and grease staining, it will perhaps respond more favorably to the action of the newer detergents when it comes to completely removing the stains that may have occurred.

The complexities of the many roles the soil-release finish must play are not fully appreciated by the homemaker. However, about 40 different materials or methods have appeared on the market since 1969 in order to combat the gradual color damage to durable-press articles and certain other manufactured fiber products after repeated use and washing. Polyester fibers, in particular, are the most readily stained of these fibers and thus require a soil-release finish most frequently. Possibly, part of the specific criticism results from the fact that the polyesters have played such an important part in white fabrics, either alone or blended with cotton or rayon. Among the early methods were ICI's **Cirrasoft**; Burlington-Klopman's **Come Clean**; Celanese's **Fybrite**; 3-M's **Dual Action Scotchgard**; Milliken's **Visa**; and MacCampbell-Grantville's **X-it**. The earliest of these, **Visa**, was aimed at improving the oil and stain resistance of polyester fibers, particularly those used in durable-press garments. The products are applicable also to resin-treated cottons in similar durable-press cottons with the resin finish. These fibers are hydrophobic and, therefore, resist the penetration of water-base detergents and optical brighteners in formulas. It is also well known that these fabrics, in common with those made completely of manufactured fibers, attract oil—that is, they are oleophilic. In both, a gradual loss of brightness resulting from the accumulation of dirt and the graying of oil stains results in a dulling of many of the whites and light shades in durable-press apparel. (There is a very simple method for understanding these technical terms clearly, even if at first they seem confusing. The terms *hydro* and *oleo,* of course, refer specifically to water and to oil or grease. The suffix *philic* can be translated "to be filled"; *phobic* means having a phobia against. Thus, a fiber described as hydrophobic would be one that resists or has a phobia against water; an oleophilic fiber would be one that accepts or absorbs oil.)

Mere surface soil resistance, however, is not the same as soil-release. Soil-release finishes depend on two diametrically opposite conceptions. In one case, a film is deposited over all the fibers so that neither oil nor water can penetrate them. At the same time, the soil-release finish has a chemical effect on the fiber so that its surface becomes hydrophilic and attracts water together with the detergent and brightener in solution. The claims for the durability of these finishes vary considerably, but it appears that 20 washings constitute a reasonable claim for maintenance of the effectiveness of the finish. Claims of as many as 50 washings have been made in some cases.

There is much research under way incorporating fluorocarbons and the acrylics into the fibers as finish polymers for soil-release results. The fluorocarbons have the very elaborate chemical compositions. The acrylic acid emulsions are hydrophilic copolymers, and a third group, now causing a stir of interest, is the soluble acrylates, which includes a new product called FC 281 made by 3-M Company. Generally speaking, the fluoro chemicals have good soil-releasing properties but do not resist redeposition as well as do the acrylics, which have quite effective results against both soil redeposition and the accumulation of static. It is claimed that the FC 281 product is unique because, when the fabric is being worn and exposed to air, it has hydrophobic properties and resists water in addition to stains. But during washing, it becomes hydrophilic, thus permitting the easier removal of stains and spots. It also is oil-resistant—that is, oleophobic—and is quite resistant to redeposition and reabsorption. At the present time, the claims made for this product outstrip those of its competitors. The specific soil-release finish to be applied to any garment should be based on the conditions of use and exposure to the soil-producing materials.

Summary of Resin Finish Side Effects

Store salespeople and their customers should realize the combination of problems attending new finishes. For example, durable-press apparel is vulnerable to soiling around the inside of the cuffs of men's shirts and women's blouses, and on the inside of the collar band. Similarly, the stains from oil and some hair grooming preparations appear on the cushions of upholstered furniture. One term for this type of soilage is *soil deposition*—a similar over-all appearance is found in some cases when a bright, white durable-press shirt is washed in a mixed load with dirty articles. This is a continuing phase of what the soap companies, many years ago, characterized as tattletale grey. Soil may be deposited on and be made to cling to some of these fabrics as the result of static electricity. The effect of static as another source of soiling is most pronounced during the winter months when home interiors are warm and the humidity is extremely low. Many types of dirt, including household dust in the air, respond to a static attraction and will impinge on unprotected fabrics. For this type of control, the cellulosic finishes having the hydrophilic effect on the outside of the fibers appear to give good protection. Homemakers should regard the soil-release finishes as helpful, especially when they are promoted for articles that have the advantages expected of durable-press.

COLOR APPLICATIONS

Color has probably been a method of adornment for mankind since prehistoric times. Pigments extracted from roots and herbs, colored muds, and other sources have been daubed on the skin of many primitive peoples; the practice existed in our own country, for color played an important part in the lives of the Indian tribes in North America for ceremonial occasions and as part of their dress for war. Many of the peoples of Africa had distinctive ways of coloring their bodies, faces, and hair according to tribal customs. The effect, extent, and method of coloring among the people of other continents differ only in kind but not in purpose, when compared with our own practice of coloring the lips and cheeks, or applying an artificial sun tan to our bodies. Color is an important economic factor in today's textile industry. In this time of an infinite variety of shades and kinds of dyestuffs, it is difficult to imagine that only a very few years ago the available synthetic dyestuffs were limited; and 100 years ago, we were dependent entirely upon nature to provide the coloring materials for our fabrics.

Color as a Form of Energy

It is recorded that Plato conceived of vision as being the result of particles emitted from the eye that bounced back from the object. In 1666, an Italian mathematician named Grimaldi compared the wave action of light with that of water. Within the past 100 years physicists and mathematicians of several nations have made independent discoveries of the wavelengths of various kinds of radiation.

Now an electromagnetic spectrum extends from very short gamma rays of wavelength (distance from crest to crest) of between 1×10^{-5} and 10^{-10} centimeters. Gamma rays are a product of radioactive materials and are similar to X rays. Visible light is an extremely narrow band in this entire spectrum. The shortest of these are 37×10^{-5} or 370 millimicrons; the longest are in the red range 76×10^{-5} centimeters or 760 millimicrons. The solar spectrum has as its upper limit in wavelength 53×10^{-4} centimeters or 5300 millimicrons. Longer rays in order are infrared; microwaves, radar, TV, and FM radiation; short-wave radio, another narrow band; and then AM radio.

The rays in the visible light range can excite a reflectance or certain wavelengths, each of them associated with a specific color that is reflected back to the eye of the observer. These reflectances are given color names. It is generally said that without light one is not aware of the presence of color and one "sees" black. Conversely, the complete reflectance is white. The brighter the light with which one views a colored surface, the brighter the colors seem to be. But there are other colors excited by other wavelengths that fluoresce, or glow, in the dark. Certain of these are termed *black-light* produced colors. The electromagnetic rays vary in wavelength—that is, the actual measurement from crest to crest—from as short as 0.01 millimicrons or 10^{-8} centimeters to as much as 10,000 meters. The range of visible light is only between 370 millimicrons for the shortest to 760, the longest visible rays (see Table 7–8). Thus, in the visible range, violet has the shortest wavelength of the colors and red, the longest. The color we see in a fabric is the wavelength reflected when white light rays strike the surface. White light is made up of all the colors in the spectrum, which are separated, rainbow-like, by passing light through a prism. On a surface, the color seen is the reflected color that is the complement of the one absorbed—that is, the wavelength absorbed by the article.

In a fabric, the color, or **hue**, is one of the first qualities noticed. However, the hue may vary in **value**—that is, it may be lighter or darker, depending on the amount of light striking it. This explains why a fabric may appear to be one color in daylight and an entirely different hue under artificial light; the light varies in both intensity and wavelength. This is one of the problems in color matching in the selection of a dress or suit in a store in which the light is not very intense. Sometimes one finds that an ensemble that is harmonious, or of equal value in daylight, is not harmonious under artificial or fluorescent light.

When a beam of blue light falls on a white cloth, the spectrum is broken into three portions. Part of the light goes through the fabric—this is the transmission of light. A certain percentage is absorbed in the fabric—this light-absorption energy turns into heat, raising the temperature of the cloth or causing a chemical transformation of the fibers. The remainder of the blue light is reflected back—this is the blue color because the light projected was of that shade. The fabric itself has a bluish hue. The use of optical brightners

Table 7-8 Radiation Range of Waves

	Millimicrons*
Gamma rays (shortest)	0.01 — 0.1
X rays (longest)	0.1
Ultraviolet	0.1–60
Visible light (shadow)	370–760
Maximum chemical effect (solar)	400
Violet	400
Blue	460
Green	520
Yellow	560
Orange	600
Red	670
Red (largest visible rays)	760
Infrared	760–5,300
Radio waves	5,300
Micro radar	5,300–100,000
TV–FM radio	100,000–1,000,000
Short wave radio	1–12 meters
AM radio	12–10,000 meters

* 1 millimicron $= 0.001$ micron
  1 micron $= 0.0000001$ meters
  1 micron $= 0.00001$ centimeters

in textile finishes achieves somewhat this same result. Infrared rays are invisible to the eye and are concentrated as heat energy in the fabric.

Light and Comfort

It is recorded that Benjamin Franklin, one of our earliest scientific experimenters, was interested in the relative comfort of certain colored fabrics in regard to light absorption and absorption of other energy waves, including heat. One of his experiments consisted of putting fabrics of different colors on banks of snow and exposing them to winter sunlight. He observed that black cloth sank more quickly and more deeply as the snow melted under it. Intermediate colored fabrics sank more slowly, and the white cloth remained on top of the snow. Recent studies at the Philadelphia College of Textiles and Science have given more information and indicate that the infrared absorption characteristics of dyestuffs used in fabrics are an important factor in their relative warmth or coolness. It is the infrared spectra with wavelengths between 2900 and 3600 millimicrons that also contribute to the fading of dyestuffs. It was found that some of the infrared absorption is chemical—certain black dyes, for example, will absorb infrared more rapidly than the other. Similar techniques provided actual figures for heat fabrics on cakes of ice and exposing them to infrared light from a lamp showed that the ice under the infrared absorptive dyestuff melted more rapidly than the other. Similar techniques provided actual figures for heat absorption that paralleled experiments or the experience that white is the "coolest" color and black, the "warmest," in summer weather. In Table 7–9 some ratings obtained by the Philadelphia school are shown, based on the arbitrary figure of 100 per cent heat absorption by white.

Table 7-9   Per Cent of Heat
Absorbed by Various Colors

Color or Fabric	Absorption, Per Cent
White	100
Pale yellow	102
Dark yellow	140
Light grey	152
Dark green	161
Red	168
Light brown	198
Black	208

Dyeing Textiles

It is generally assumed by the person making a purchase that the color of the dress or suit being purchased is truly permanent. This is referred to as the degree of colorfastness. This property is only relative. The degree of colorfastness or serviceability of the dye depends on many different factors: the type of dyestuff; the method of application; the service to which the fabric is put in use; the kind of washing or cleaning; the amount of soil that will be allowed to accumulate on and in the textile product itself; and then, of course, its exposure to prolonged sunlight or to certain chemicals in the air. Dyestuffs are chemical compounds applied to textiles by chemical processes to produce color.

Dyestuffs

Fabrics are colored by impregnating the fibers or by covering the surface of the yarns or fabrics with a coloring substance known as a **dyestuff**.

Throughout the history of textiles until 1856, when William Henry

Perkin discovered the first artificial dyestuff, fabrics were colored by dyes obtained from the products of nature. Many of these natural materials are now synthesized in chemical plants and laboratories; others have been abandoned because synthetic dyestuffs of superior quality have been perfected to produce better and more permanent colors. Some idea of the variety of sources for the older coloring materials can be had from the following discussion of common natural dyestuffs. These materials only suggest the enormous amount of experimental work that early dyers of cloth must have done to collect, prepare and experiment with these coloring materials.

The principal colors used by the textile workers of ancient China and India were **indigo**, a blue dye obtained from a plant, and **kermes**, a red color obtained from the dried bodies of a scale insect.

An ancient Egyptian papyrus, **Papyrus Graccus Hornkensis**, preserved in the museum in Upsala, Sweden, gives seventy recipes dealing with the cleaning, mordanting, and dyeing of wool. (A **mordant** is a chemical pretreatment sometimes needed to improve the dyeability of a fabric.) In it are mentioned the following dyestuffs known to the ancient Egyptians: alkanova (red), safflower (yellow and red), kermes (red), madder (red), and woad (blue). The methods of applying the color were basically the same as those used in dyeing today.[6]

The dye **Purple of Tyre** is identified with the ruling families of the Roman Empire. This dyestuff was probably obtained from a sea snail. The dyers of Oriental rugs, as late as a century ago, kept secret the methods of dyeing certain colors. Families were skilled in making certain sunfast and waterfast dyes, the secret of which was handed down from father to son.

The peoples living around the Mediterranean Sea became skilled in the art of dyeing with the colors known to them. Secrets of formulation and methods of dyeing were jealously guarded. The discovery of America brought to European dyers many new dyestuffs, principally dyewoods. The most important of these, and the only one still used commercially, is **logwood.** The dye is extracted from the brown-red wood of the Campeche, a large tree native to the West Indies and Central America. The Spaniards found a valuable scarlet red dye in Mexico. This was **cochineal**, a dyestuff extracted from the insect of the same name, which replaced kermes red. Most of these "New World" dyestuffs were used by the Inca and Aztec Indians in South and Central America for dyeing wool and cotton.

The First Synthetic Color

The art and science of dyeing were completely changed by William H. Perkin, a 17-year-old English boy who worked as a chemist's assistant. In

---

[6] W. von Bergen and H. R. Mauersberger, *American Wool Handbook* (Metuchen, N.J.: Textile Book Service, 1939), p. 573.

1856, while working in his own laboratory with a coal-tar derivative, aniline, Perkin discovered that the substance colored white silk. Continuing his research efforts, he developed a dyestuff he called mauve, a word derived from the French name for the mallow flower.

The immediate result of Perkin's discovery was an extensive study of other derivatives of coal tar and their allied compounds, and the manufacture of a vast variety of dyestuffs from these materials. Prior to and during World War I, Germany was pre-eminent in the dye-production industry. Many German patents became available to the American chemical industry when they were seized by the Alien Property Custodian and, after the war, were sold to the public. This step and the growth of industrial chemistry in the United States since 1920 combined to raise this country to the top of the tremendously profitable dyestuffs industry. Although new and improved coloring materials are constantly being discovered and developed, much of the attention of the great manufacturers of dyestuffs during recent years has been devoted to the standardization of dyeing procedures and to the fastness properties of the color produced in the cloth. New challenges to the ingenuity of the dyers and the producers of chemical colorants came about with the synthetic fiber industry, especially after the middle 1940s. Each new fiber type has required new dyes and new methods of application.

Approximately 4000 dyes have been produced. According to their method of application, dyestuffs are classified in the following nine groups:

1. Acid dyes
2. Mordant and chrome colors
3. Vat dyes
4. Basic dyes
5. Direct colors
6. Sulfur dyes
7. Naphthol or azoic dyes
8. Developed dyes
9. Disperse dyes

The acid dyes have as their chief chemical constituent an acid group, and basic dyes have salts of color bases or alkaline groups. Both the acid and basic dyestuffs can be applied directly to animal fibers. In order to color cellulose fibers with these dyestuffs, it is necessary to give the fibers a preliminary treatment with a mordant, a chemical that has an affinity both for the dye and the fiber. Thus, for a basic dyestuff an acid mordant is used, and vice versa. Despite the fact that dyestuffs are chemical compounds, just as are the textile fibers themselves, the exact mechanisms of dyeing the various fibers are not known. There is some evidence, especially in wool dyeing, that the process is chemical in nature. On the other hand, the physical theory of absorption has strong adherents, especially for the cellulose fibers. Synthetic fibers demonstrate still other properties.

ACID DYES   Acid dyes are commonly used for wool, especially for brightly colored sweaters, women's clothing, upholstery yarns, bathing suits, and other fabrics. The dyeing is usually done in a solution of a neutral sodium salt and an acid to set the dye.

MORDANT AND CHROME COLORS   These colors are used most frequently for wool, principally for men's clothing. The colors are more fast but less brilliant than those from the acid dyestuffs. In addition to the salt and acid bath, a metal salt is required to fix the dye in the wool to produce the desired shade. This metal salt, or mordant, is frequently a chrome salt,—hence the name **chrome color** for that particular group. The theory of this method of dyeing is that the acid combines with the wool, making it more absorptive to the dyestuff. The metal salt is then added and converts the acid-wool color compound into an insoluble metal **color lake** that is firmly and chemically united with the fiber. (See Table 7–10.)

Table 7-10   Dye Classes for Certain Fibers

Fiber	Dye Classes
Cotton and rayon	Direct; naphthol or azoic; vats; sulfur; anthraquinone; etc.
Wool	Acid dyes
Acetate	Disperse dyes
Nylon	Disperse dyes; acid; cationic
Polyester	Disperse; cationic
Acrylic	Cationic; acid; disperse
Olefin	Disperse; acid; metalizable

VAT DYES   Many fabrics are labeled *vat-dyed*, and to most customers this connotes the highest quality in serviceability.

This class of dyestuffs can be used for wool, cotton, rayon, linen, and silk. Vat colors can produce the greatest colorfastness to sunlight, washing, and other service conditions. They are especially useful for shirtings, uniforms, draperies, and other fabrics that must be both durable and colorfast. The most famous vat dye is indigo, which is widely used for men's work clothes and for blue denims. Other vats are anthraquinoids and sulfur dyes.

Vat dyes are insoluble in water. The strongly alkaline bath required for this process must be diluted in dyeing silk to prevent chemical damage to the fiber. The principal difficulty in vat dyeing—and a very important one—is that of matching colors. The dyer has no idea what the shade is going to be until the color is actually developed when the cloth is dried. This is much different from exposing a fabric to a dye bath until the desired shade is developed.

BASIC DYES   Basic dyes are used to color cotton, silk, or wool. They are seldom used on wool, however, because of the superior fastness of acid dyes. This class of dyestuffs was the first to be discovered; even now they are often referred to as aniline colors because the first few were derived from that compound by Perkin and his followers. Silk and wool are dyed directly with these dyestuffs, but it is necessary to fix the colors in cotton by means of a mordant. It is customary to dye cotton with some other type of coloring material and then to **top**, or brighten, the color by means of an application of a basic dyestuff. A brilliant color is given silk fabrics with these colors. Basic dyes have rather poor colorfastness to washing, sunlight, and perspiration. *Naphthol* dyes, a modification of basic dyestuffs, are used almost exclusively in coloring and printing cotton piece goods.

DIRECT COLORS   Although these dyestuffs are used for silk and wool, they are generally regarded as cotton dyes. No mordant is required for coloring cotton by means of these dyes, but the colors are generally dull and require brightening. They can be used for wool yarns and shoddy. They give excellent fastness, especially with wool and silk.

SULFUR DYES   Sulfur dyes are used on vegetable fibers and can be used for wool and silk with fair colorfastness when a small amount of glue is used in the dye bath. Although these colors as a class have good fastness to light and washing, certain ones, such as the yellows, are fugitive. Sulfur black had good lightfastness, but prolonged sun exposure weakens the fabric because of the gradual oxidation of the sulfur compound into sulfuric acid. For this reason, the black stripes in awnings are usually the first places where breaks occur during use and exposure.

COLORING MAN-MADE FIBER PRODUCTS   Regenerated cellulose rayon can be dyed with all the classes of colors applicable to cotton. The vat dyestuffs and the direct dyes are commonly used for rayon. Cellulose acetate, being chemically different from other textile fibers, requires an entirely different group of dyestuffs. These special dyes, sometimes termed *acetate dyes,* are derived from basic dyes, developed dyes, water-soluble dyes, or a type classed as dispersed dyes. The cross-dyeing of acetate-rayon mixed fabrics offers interesting effects. Arnel, cellulose triacetate, may be dyed with these same dyestuffs. Many of these are used in **solution** or **spin dyeing** for acetates.

PIGMENT DYES   Pigments are very finely ground colors, insoluble in the dye bath and fiber but carried in by the liquid medium in emulsion form and fixed by a resin or other binder. They are applicable to almost any fiber and are especially useful for spun or staple yarn fabrics. These colors are generally padded on the goods passing rapidly through the color box and then through a series of squeeze rolls, they also are mixed in the spinning solution to produce spun-dyed yarns.

DISPERSE DYES   This group of dyes was identified for a long time by the name **acetate** dyes because of their development for the coloring of acetate fabrics and fibers. They are principally derived from anthraquinone; the colored substance is ground to an extremely fine colloid or suspension of particles from 1 to 100 millimicrons in size and suspended in the dye bath. In this very fine suspension, they are absorbed by the fibers. They develop bright shades and are widely used, not only for acetates but for nylon, acrylic, modacrylic, and polyester fibers. They are also used in printing. The fastness of the color to light and to washing varies somewhat with the color itself and with the fiber on which it has been used. This group of dyes causes problems with the gas fading of acetate and other fibers unless the coloring is carried out in the fiber-producing liquid.

Methods of Dyeing

The actual application of color to textile fibers is performed by highly technical operations. A review of some of the more common dyeing methods follows:

1. *Dyeing the raw fibers.*   By this method the fibers are dyed before they are carded or combed. It is often utilized in coloring wool fibers, and fabrics dyed by this method are referred to as **dyed in the wool**. This method gives a uniform and very fast color. The interesting mixtures found in fine suitings for men and women are formed by mixing colored fibers from different dye baths.

2. *Dyeing the sliver.*   Some fibers are dyed in the slub or sliver, the smooth rope of roughly parallel fibers formed by the carding or combing machines. The sliver may be dyed all one color, or it may be differently colored or printed at intervals. When the latter sliver is drawn and spun, interesting mixtures are produced. The method is used for wool mixtures, and good dyefastness is obtained because the absence of twist permits a rapid and uniform dye absorption by all the fibers.

3. *Dyeing the yarn.*   All kinds of textile yarn can be dyed. The fabrics woven from yarn-dyed fibers are usually colored more deeply and richly than those dyed in the piece after weaving. The dye penetration is deeper in yarn-dyed cloths, and when a yarn is unraveled, it does not show a varying depth color toward the core of the yarn as is often found in piece-dyed cloth. Plaid fabrics are good examples of yarn-dyed cloths. In hosiery, the

term **ingrain** is synonymous with **yarn-dyed** and the term **dipped** corresponds to **piece-dyed**.

4. *Dyeing the fabric.* When the woven fabric is dyed, it is termed piece-dyed. The quality of the dyeing varies more widely when done by this method than by any other. The reason is that it is more difficult to obtain deep and uniform dye penetration after the fabric has been woven. This method is economical for the manufacturer of hosiery and of woven goods because he can store up stocks of knitted or woven goods in the gray and then have them dyed to order. This is especially advantageous because of the rapid changes in the color fashion for women's hosiery. Many women are wearing nylon hose of the same hue as their dresses or suits.

5. *Cross-dyeing.* Cross-dyeing is based on the fact that the different textile fibers do not have the same affinity or speed of dye penetration. When a cloth is composed of a mixture of animal and vegetable fibers, or natural fibers and synthetics, it is possible to produce interesting effects by proper selection of the dyestuff or the conditions in the dye bath. The dye may color one fiber and leave the other undyed or colored to a lesser degree. The fabrics known as **unions** often contain mixtures of wool and cotton. Almost any combination of fibers can be mixed in the yarns to form a blend, or the warp yarns may be one fiber and the filling another to form a combination fabric. Proper selection of the dyestuff, usually the acid type, will color the wool and leave the cotton white. By other methods of dyeing, both fibers may be dyed to the same color or to contrasting colors.

Fabric and Color Design

Design, accompanied by color, constitutes the principal esthetic appeal to catch the eye of the store customer and to give lasting pleasure to the owner of the textile product, whether it be a wall hanging, a carpet, draperies, or wearing apparel. In textile products, design is the pattern of the fabric and its decoration; usually, it is considered to be a pattern or figure repeated many times and at regular intervals on the surface of the fabric.

There are two basic types of design recognized in the textile business. One is the formation of patterns in the fabric by the manipulation of the yarns in weaving or knitting.

In the other, the design is applied to the surface of the fabric after the fabric has been formed. This is done by printing operations. We refer to the first type, which is part of the sinews of the fabric, as **structural** design. The surface type is known as **applied**. As in most general rules, there are exceptions and one such in textile design is warp printing. Here, we have a fabric designed while it is in the process of being formed. The color or pattern is printed on the warp yarns, and the pattern only appears in a shadowy form after the weaving operation has been completed.

Printing

Printing is simply the controlled application of color to selected areas or figures on the cloth. It is obvious that dyestuff in liquid form is too fluid and uncontrollable for such precise figure coloring; thus, most printing employs the dyestuff in the form of a paste that will color the fabric area to which it is exposed but will not flow beyond the prescribed borders. The following procedures are among the most important printing methods.

BLOCK PRINTING   Block printing may well have been one of the very first attempts by man to produce figures on fabric, and it is still one of the most popular handcraft methods of **producing design** on fabric and on paper. Its origin as an art medium for textiles is lost in antiquity. The cutting away of the surface of a block of hard wood to leave raised areas or lines to be reproduced as a print on the fabric or paper is still done. Colored paste or stiffened ink is smeared on the face of the block, which is then applied firmly to the surface of the cloth or paper on which the colored design is to be reproduced. Other blocks with different patterns of surfaces and lines related to the picture desired can be used to apply other colors within the picture area. One to three colors are generally the limit for block prints.

STENCILING   Differing slightly from the block method of printing is the art of *stenciling*. In this method the areas to be colored by any one stencil are cut out, and the paste or ink is brushed or smeared on. A complicated and elaborate figure can be developed by the use of many stencils, one for each color to be applied. The Chinese were the earliest to develop this into a fine art. It is still one of the most prized art forms in the Indian textile industry.

RESIST DYEING   Other ancient methods of dyeing employed one or another of the techniques associated with resist printing, or dyeing, in which protected areas of a fabric are kept from being exposed to a liquid dye bath. Either certain portions of the cloth are covered with wax, or little puffs or balls are tied with waxed threads and plunged into the dyestuff. The unprotected part of the textile receives color; the waxed portion remains white; and white rings appear on the surface of the cloth where the wax threads and little **tie-dyed** puffs had lain. In tie dyeing, the color borders blend into the tied-off areas by seepage of the dye.

One form of the wax-resist method, known as **batik**. is still used by native craftsmen in Java and to some extent in other countries of the Indies. The design is covered with wax, after which the fabric is dipped in dye to provide the background with color. The wax is then removed with boiling water or by means of a suitable solvent, and the design portion appears white. In the case of a multiple-color batik (some have been known to contain as many as 16 different colors), the wax is carefully removed bit by bit to expose the portions of the fabric that are to be colored by the next dye bath.

MADDER PRINTING   **Madder printing**, associated with the beautiful British tie silks, is the modern application of the mordant printing technique. Today's method was known as early as the fifth century B.C.; the writings of Pliny, the Greek historian, describe the printed garments worn by inhabitants of the Caucasus mountains. The Egyptians used a similar process a short time later. So-called Indian chintzes were forerunners of this type of printing technique, which involves covering a cloth with mordants, or binders, rather than with a color. By using different mordants, which react differently in the same dye bath, varying colors are produced. This could be combined with the wax-resist process or with tie-dye for more intricate results. The British tie silks originally used madder as a dyestuff, but it has since been replaced by synthetic dyes. Basically, the fabric is still printed first with the mordant and then with different colors from the single dye bath.

SCREEN PRINTING   **Screen printing** is still done by hand for many exclusive fabrics. It can also be done automatically. This essentially slow and tedious method has the virtue of a true handcrafted appearance. Because it requires far less equipment than any roller method, screen printing lends itself to experimental and creative designs; indeed, recognized artists and creators of textile patterns provide interior decorators and manufacturers of high-priced furniture with their personalized products.

The screen used today is generally of nylon or sometimes of silk or a fine metal. This fine fabric screen is then covered with a film. A frame is laid on the fabric; the color is sprayed, painted, or squeegeed on. A separate screen is required for each color to be applied to the pattern. Texstyle Creators of New York are using a special grade of silk screening stretched over wooden frames for their silk-screening operation. The silk is given two coats of a gelatin compound containing ammonium bichromate. The designs are painted on translucent acetate sheets, one design sheet for each color in the print. The sheets are placed on a glass-topped frame, and each screen to be developed is laid over it in succession. Under the frame is a bank of fluorescent lights, when turned on, these lights insolubilize the gelatin bichromate mixture. After sufficient exposure, the screen is taken up and washed in water. Areas protected from the light dissolve out. The screen is ready to use after it is dried; the printing color passes through the open areas developed by the light and colors the fabric stretched below the silk screen.

Automatic screen printing is possible with electronic control over both the pattern selection and the dye to be used. Today 2 men can do the work formerly done by at least 15. Generally, the machine has 8 frames, each of which may apply a different color, using different screens. As the machine runs all the frames operate simultaneously, the cloth simply moving forward one frame width between each application of color. It is, therefore, equivalent to printing 8 colors at one time. When the fabric leaves the last frame on the printing table, it goes into a drying box in which the paste colors are dried in place.

ROLLER PRINTING   Roller printing is the process by which most cloth is printed today. Essentially, it is the same process by which a newspaper is printed. The original design is etched into copper rollers, which are then covered with dye; as the fabric and roller come in contact, the design is transferred to the fabric. Many intermediate steps requiring great accuracy are involved. Each color requires an etched roller.

1. *Making the repeat.*   The original artist's drawing is made into a repeat, so that it can be reproduced over and over again as the rollers and fabric come in contact.

2. *Photographing the design.*   Every design element representing a single color is photographed onto a sensitized copper plate; each color requires a different copper plate.

3. *Painting the plate.*   The artist paints in a pattern from the traced outline of the original drawing, transferring it to the roller using a pantograph. The engraver traces the lines of the design as they appear on the flat plate, but they are automatically transferred to the curved and protected surface of the roller. The roller is etched by acid to imprint the cut pattern in the metal.

4. *Photo engraving.*   Rollers are also be engraved by a photochemical process that reproduces the detail and shading of the photograph. This type of roller printing is popular for decorative fabrics and in wallpaper.

5. *Hand engraving.*   A skilled artist duplicates a design or pattern, and it is reproduced on copper plates, each etched to imprint one color to the fabric. An engraver then goes over each copper plate with a fine needle or awl to remove any loose fragments of copper that might mar the clarity or perfection of the design.

Operation of the Roller: Each roller is securely locked in place and passes through its own color tank, or bath, from which it picks up the dyestuff. Before the fabric comes in contact with the roller, a doctor knife, or squeegee, scrapes away the excess dye from the smooth face of the roller, so that a clear, even print is made. The cloth passes through all the rolls and emerges with the completed print clearly transferred. Machines can print up to 16 colors at one time at the rate of 150 yards a minute. The colors are then set by heat for permanence against bleeding or fading when washed or exposed to sunlight. Direct roller-dye prints require only drying. Developed dyes require several aftertreatments, including curing or aging.

In any printing operation, the value of the final product lies in the accuracy and perfection of the work and the avoidance of the shady edges, white breaks, or overprinting where the placement of a roller was faulty.

SPECIAL TYPES OF PRINTING

1. *Discharge printing.* In this process, the fabric is dyed throughout with the chosen background color. It is then printed with a bleach that removes the color to form the white pattern. Generally, these fabrics are found to be white patterned on a uniform background color. However, by means of roller printing with varying strengths of bleach, it is possible to get two or more intermediate shades between the ground color and the white. Careful washing is required to remove all of the reacting chemicals. In general, when these fabrics begin to fail in use, after many washings or exposure to the sun, it is the bleached portion that first breaks. Its reduced strength is the result of exposures to the chemical solutions.

2. *Air brushing.* A mechanized air brush, guided by hand, is used to blow the dye into the cloth in this method. A blended, shadowy pattern is produced that is used principally on smooth-surfaced silks.

3. *Duplex printing.* This is simply a double printing on both sides of the cloth so that the pattern outline coincides on each face of the fabric to simulate a woven pattern. The cloth is first printed on one side and then on the other. It is a necessary operation if the cloth is to be reversible.

4. *Textured printing.* This term was coined to represent printing onto a fabric base such textured materials as metallic dusts, sequins, or the soft, fuzzy effect created by minute particles of fiber or flock. In this operation, the fabric is screen-printed or, more commonly, roller-printed with an adhesive of slow-drying quality forming the patterned areas. The desired coloring and texturing material is then dusted on the surface. It adheres to the adhesive patterns, after which the printed fabric is dried over rollers and the particles are set tightly onto the surface of the cloth. Some plain-weave fabrics for women's dresses are printed in this manner. Also, very inexpensive dotted swiss fabrics for curtains may be patterned by a similar glued method. Although the result is very attractive in appearance, these fabrics have distinct limitations and usually give poor serviceability because much of the design may be rubbed off in normal wearing. The designs can often be picked off, especially in the case of larger grains of metallic fiber or sequins; the latter are more permanent if stitched on. There is often some question as to the water solubility of the adhesive resin used and whether the fabric can be dry-cleaned without the resin going into solution and all the pattern disappearing.

5. *Flock printing.* Sometimes longer fibers are printed on in this same manner in such a way that they stand erect, giving a pronounced fuzz to the surface, either as an over-all covering or in patterns. This is done by an **electrostatic printing method**. Again, the fabric is covered with an adhesive and passed through a chamber in which an electromagnet beneath the fabric

attracts the loose fibers that have been allowed to float in the air above the fabric by means of a current of air. These fibers have an opposite charge to that attractive force, are attracted to it, and impinge themselves endwise in the goods.

6. *Textile printing from transfer papers.* Complex multicolor prints can be put on woven, knitted, and nonwoven textile products using a color-coated paper made by the Paper Corporation of the United States. This method is in direct competition with roller printing and can operate on widths as great as 63 inches and at a speed of 8½ yards per minute. These papers, termed sublistatic, are said to transfer the dispersed dyes from the paper to the fabric by sublimation as the two materials pass around a heated cylinder whose temperature is 370°F. The sublimation is almost immediate for the duration of the contact with the large cylinder surface is only 15 to 20 seconds. The fabric emerges dry and warm. The rejects, or seconds, are said to constitute less than a quarter of 1 per cent of production, whereas in roller-screen printing, the seconds may be as high as 10 to 15 per cent. Other important advantages are the total elimination of overlaps and the ability of the developed colors to stand up under dry cleaning and machine washing. This printing method is likened to the rotogravure.

DEPOSITED DESIGN FINISHING

Flocking Fabrics

Design-flocked fabrics are those having an all-over covering of patterned dots or figures of a fibrous nature adhering to the face of the fabric. The flocked fabrics of the 1940s simulated the small dots or patterns woven in by some of the specialty weaving procedures, such as the clip spot and lappet. These fabrics were introduced as novelties but proved to be unsatisfactory in use because the adhesive failed to withstand repeated launderings. Also, the small dots in the early swiss-dot fabrics were too easily picked off or rubbed off in use. Today, adhesives are selected on the basis of the end-use to which the fabric is to be put and the way in which the article is to be cleaned. Some of them are machine-washable; others must be washed by hand; and still others are for fabrics that must be dry-cleaned and for articles one would prefer to dry-clean rather than wash. The use of these adhesives permits the application of a flocked surface not only to textiles, but also to paper, plastic, jute, foam, and even metal foil. A new process employing a combination of the electrostatic process and a beater bar system permits rapid production, thus putting these materials on a competitive basis with other structures. It is also possible to apply such surfaces to three-dimensional articles: gift boxes, toys, hats, and other objects. Among the flocked fibers in use today are cotton, rayon, and nylon, in wide varieties of colors and fiber diameters.

A completely flocked surface is now less expensive to produce for cushioning fabrics and surfaces than the conventional napped or pile materials. Sound cushioning is necessary in airplane and automobile interiors, in speaker grilles, and in the seat springs in aircraft, automobiles, and furniture. This surface is used also to provide shock- and scar protection from bookends, vases, lamp bases, and similar articles that scar the surfaces of wooden tables and chests. Interesting and colorful surface effects are utilized in soft coverings for children's toys, in the illustrations in children's books, in visual displays, greeting cards, and packaging, as well as in patterns on textiles. The modern plant producing flocked fabrics, such as Floc Industries, Inc., integrates the procedures from the raw, dyed flock to the finished product: from fiber cutting and dyeing to adhesive development and the surfacing of materials. No-iron nylon is a product used widely for covering paper for designers and decorators who want something new in wallpaper. Sheets flocked with nylon are screen-printed in wide varieties of patterns and colors, and they are also patterned with metallic inks.

Some unique techniques have been developed in the United States, in Europe, and in Japan. Carpeting with a one-flock pattern on top of a flocked base and the simultaneous application of flocked fibers of two different fiber lengths for a three-dimensional appearance are now available.

A new item is flock applied to a nylon or rayon yarn to produce a yarn resembling that used in chenille or in plush velvet. These yarns have unusual durability against abrasion. Flocking and tufting appear to have taken over by far the greatest volume of carpeting and rug manufacturing.

EIGHT

Selecting Fabrics for Apparel and Household Uses

On many occasions throughout the chapters in this book, reference has been made to consumer guides of several types.

1. Legislative action pointed toward consumer protection.
2. Voluntary standards, such as those of Federal government purchasing agencies.
3. Commercial standards developed by the U.S. Bureau of Standards through cooperation with industry.
4. Voluntary standards developed through the American National Standards Institute[1] (ANSI) by all interested parties, which included consumer representation.
5. Informative labeling developed by trade associations, standards promulgators, and individual retail establishments.

[1] Formerly the American Standards Association (ASA).

341

It cannot be overemphasized, however, that none of these tools can be utilized to full advantage unless the consumer has some *basic knowledge* of textiles and clothing as well as of his own needs and habits.

TEXTILE LEGISLATION

On September 26, 1914, the FTC was created by an act of Congress. This act defined the powers and duties of the commission and its jurisdiction over commerce between states and between the United States and foreign nations. Briefly, its main function is to investigate and to prevent unfair methods of competition. Thus, the power and authority of the commission can be invoked the most quickly when the question of unfair competition arises between two companies or associations whose business is competitive.

The five appointed commissioners generally specialize in specific fields of business. From time to time, the commission has issued fair trade practice regulations to correct some malpractice on the part of industry. This interpretation has led to calling on the FTC for regulations to clarify and to control practices leading to lowering the quality or value of textiles. The commission also draws up the specific rules and regulations prescribed by Congress in its several labeling laws.

Trade Practice Conference Rules

Typical of these trade practice regulations revoked April 5, 1960, when they were incorporated in the fiber identification law, are the following: silk industry, November 4, 1928; linen industry, February 4, 1941; rayon and acetate textile industry, 1952. Two rules which dealt with textile products: hosiery industry, promulgated May 15, 1941, amended April 7, 1942, revised August 30, 1960; and shrinkage of woven cotton yard goods, 1936, were also revoked.

Care Labeling

The FTC's trade regulation rule covering care labeling of textile wearing apparel became effective July 3, 1972. This meant that, with few exceptions, garments of every type produced after that date had to be permanently labeled with appropriate care instructions. These labels represent the single most important source of information for consumer use. This ruling followed many years of voluntary efforts on the part of the textile industry and retail business associations to provide consumer information. For several years before the FTC regulation governing the labeling of textile products, both industry and government studied the advisability of the use of care symbols before deciding that care *terms* were more feasible for consumer use. To assure the successful use of the care labeling regulation, the consumer must be responsible for reading the instructions provided and following those instructions carefully.

The rule states that each finished article of wearing apparel requiring care must have a tag or label permanently affixed to it by the person or organization that is responsible for its manufacture. Piece goods, other than remnants, must be accompanied by a label or tag that (1) clearly discloses instructions for care and maintenance to be provided by the person or organization that directed or controlled the manufacture of the piece goods, and (2) that eventually, by normal household methods, can be attached permanently to the finished article by the ultimate consumer.

There are a few exceptions permitted after written petition has been made to the FTC. These include articles where either the utility or appearance would be substantially impaired by the attachment of a permanent label. However, such articles must be *accompanied* by care instructions. Articles retailing for $3 or less and that are completely washable under all normal circumstances are also exempt.

Federal Labeling Laws Affecting Textiles

1. **The Wool Products Labeling Act** of 1939 became effective July 15, 1941, and has been amended several times, the latest being November 20, 1965. One purpose of the act is to protect producers, manufacturers, distributors, and consumers from the unrevealed presence of substitutes and mixtures in spun, woven, knitted, felted, or otherwise manufactured wool products.

A principal objective of this law is to define the three types of fiber derived from sheep. The first, **wool**, is the new virgin, or unused fiber from the fleece of sheep or lambs or the hair of angora or cashmere goats and includes also specialty fibers with the normal physical and chemical properties of wool. The second, **reprocessed wool** is a fiber that had been made into cloth or yarn but had never been used by the ultimate consumer and had been reduced back to the fiber state. The third, **reused wool**, results when wool or reprocessed wool, having been spun, woven, knitted, or in other ways gone into wool products and used by the consumer, is subsequently reduced to a fiber again. Any other textile fiber present must be identified also and the percentage of composition given. A 5 per cent tolerance is allowed for decorative yarns and fibers. The Wool Products Labeling Act specifically exempted from the law rugs, carpets, upholstery fabrics, and a few other specialty uses.

2. **The Fur Products Labeling Act** was passed August 8, 1951, and

became effective August 9, 1952; it was amended March 15, 1961. The purpose of the act is to protect consumers and others against the misbranding, false advertising, and false invoicing of fur products and furs.

This is essentially a truth-in-advertising bill, designed to correct the prevalent mispractice of the time of giving all kinds of fictitious and misleading names to fibers and furs. The principal offenders were those processing rabbit (lapin) pelts that bore all kinds of romantic names, suggesting that the original animal had been anything from seal to mink. Not only must furs be correctly identified as to animal type, but the label must also disclose the country of origin and whether or not the furs have been dyed or in any other way had their color altered.

3. **The Textile Fiber Products Identification Act** was approved in 1958 and became effective March 3, 1960. The FTC rules amended and effective July 26, 1960, have been amended several times since to provide for new generic definitions.

This act protects producers and consumers against the misbranding and false advertising of fiber content in textile fiber products. This law requires that the label disclose the name or registered number of the person or firm marketing the product in commerce. If the textile product is imported, the name of the country where the goods were processed or manufactured must appear on the label. The fiber name and the generic or family name of all fibers present in amounts greater than 5 per cent must be listed in the order of their predominance, giving the content of each as per cent by weight. The regulations also provide a system of 19 generic groups. Few additional generic names have been approved by the Federal Trade Commission under this regulation. In order to obtain FTC approval, a new polymer must differ substantially in chemical origin, chemical composition, and demonstratable use from existing fibers to justify its variations. These names have appeared in each chapter with the fibers corresponding to their generic name group (nylon, acrylic, and glass, for example). Thus, such terminology as 65 per cent Dacron polyester, 35 per cent wool; or 80 per cent silk, 20 per cent mink fiber, or 50 per cent wool, 30 per cent mink hair, 20 per cent nylon are all acceptable labels. This law does not include fabrics or end-use products exempted from the Wool Products Labeling Act, except for carpets and rugs. Therefore, upholstery fabrics on furniture and a few other specialty uses are still exempted from identification labeling. Upholstery fabrics sold as piece goods are included in the act.

4. **The Flammable Fabrics Act** was passed in 1953; it became effective July 1, 1954, and was amended December 14, 1967. The original purpose of the act was to prohibit interstate commerce of articles of wearing apparel and of fabrics so highly flammable as to be dangerous.

This act is an example of textile law having a distinct health or safety point of view, much as in the case of regulations under food, drug, and cosmetic laws. It has been discussed under fabric flammability, particularly under the cellulosic fibers, cotton and rayon, the two fibers most affected. Briefly, it defines the scope of prevention. It requires the Federal Trade Commission to devise a method of test and ground rules under which certain fabric constructions of dangerous flammability potential can be excluded from interstate commerce until they are permanently treated with a satisfactory flammability-control chemical or compound. The Consumer Products Safety Commission is now responsible for carrying out the provisions of the act.

The Flammable Fabrics Act was amended on December 14, 1967, and signed into law by President Johnson. The amendment widened the scope of the previous law and introduced new features. As amended, this law covers all articles of clothing and all interior furnishings, including rugs and carpets. The scope involving clothing is extended to define clothing as "any costume or article of clothing worn or intended to be worn by individuals." The new, all-inclusive scope also covers household furnishings, "any type of furnishing made in the whole or in part of fabric or related material and intended for use or which may reasonably be expected to be used in homes, offices, or other places of assembly or combination." It should also be noted that other trade products related to the construction of textile fabrics, such as plastics, synthetic film, foams, rubber, and paper are included. These inclusions introduce the additional hazard of toxic fumes from the burning or smoldering of some chemical compounds, even though they may not actually burst into flame. The amended act provides that "whenever the Secretary of Commerce finds . . . that a new or amended flammability standard or other regulation, including labeling, for a fabric, related material, or product may be needed to protect the public against unreasonable risk or the occurrence of fire leading to death or personal injury, or significant property damage, he shall institute proceedings for the determination of an appropriate flammability standard. . . ." It is under this provision that flammability standards for children's sleepwear and carpets have been established.

Current Legislative Requirements and Test Methods for Flame Retardance

The first flammability standards to be issued dealt with carpeting and rugs (DOC FF 1–70 and FF 2–70). Standards for children's sleepwear, sizes 0–6X (DOC FF 3–71) and sizes 7–14 (FF 5–74), have been issued. A standard for mattresses (DOC FF 4–72) has also been issued; standards for blankets and upholstered furniture are under discussion.

Flame-test specifications are complicated at all levels of commerce, not only because of the slow development of Federal specifications and test methods, but also because several states and a number of municipalities have set their own specifications, which are subject to control by local fire marshals. Five different types of tests are currently being conducted under the guidance of the American Association of Textile Chemists and Colorists and the American Society for Testing Materials: (1) AATCC-33-1962, 45° angle test; (2) methenamine pill test for carpets; (3) AATCC-34-1969, vertical; (4) Federal specification-191B, 5906, horizontal; and (5) ASTM E84-61, tunnel test. The original Flammable Fabrics Act of 1953 used a 45° angle test.[2]

There is a need for uniform specifications based on each of the prevailing test procedures. In that way the test procedure most suitable for the end-use item will give dependable and useful information for consumer safety, regardless of such textile fabric variables as

1. The nature of the fiber.

2. Fabric construction.

3. Durability of special finishes—such as water repellency, washability, dry-cleanability, and texture control—dimensional stability, and fire resistance.

4. The effect of the retardant finish on the hand, drapeability, strength, or color of the fabric.

5. Reasonable cost.

Flammability has from the beginning been a source of great interest and concern to the manufacturers of nonwoven textile materials and the users of these textiles in a wide variety of end-use products. The public has been concerned with the flammability of these nonwoven materials because of their close resemblance in many cases to paper, which the public recognizes as being a flammable material. In some cases, these nonwovens are even more flammable than paper, as when certain binders are used to impart strength. It is not necessary to use a durable type of flame-retardant finish on these products because, for the most part, they are classed as disposables. Therefore, the consumer does not expect to wash them once they become soiled. On the other hand, certain textile attributes must be retained, such as the hand, texture, color, and good fastness of dyes and any special finish, such as water repellency. Historically, nonwoven products have been tested by a vertical method. The disposal of nonwovens may in some cases pose a challenge to antipollution ordinances. They must be burnable with a minimum amount of smoke or ash and should produce no toxic vapors or by-products during combustion.

[2] Robert Weinstein, *Textile Chemist and Colorist* (Feb. 1971), pp. 49–51.

FLAMMABILITY—FURTHER RESEARCH

In a recent article, Kenneth A. Howry[3] reminded the textile industry and the consumer that the textile fabric flammability situation is becoming more complicated because of the continued lack of data as to what is required to produce safe and marketable textile products. Even with all the research work that has been conducted since the Flammable Fabrics Act was revised, there is still no satisfactory test available. It has been pointed out already that, considering the conditions of exposure and the wide variations in the structure of the textile materials entering into such kinds of merchandise as dress fabrics, children's wear, mattresses, carpets, and plastic materials, numerous different tests will be required. The Department of Health, Education and Welfare is cooperating with the National Bureau of Standards in this problem of testing and then interpreting the data. For example, in a fire in an Ohio nursing home, the carpet that had been blamed for the seriousness of the fire passed the existing test of the Social Security Administration; however, the latex backing not covered by the test was responsible for the suffocating fumes. Thus, a different test must be developed. This demand for protection against fabric flammability has been made by the Social Security Administration; it affects 4,850 nursing homes that receive Federal funds. Carpets failing to meet the test must be removed. The Federal Trade Commission has requested the Commerce Department to provide stricter standards not only for carpets, but also for small bath mats and throw rugs; despite the fact that at the time of the first fire control act, which applied only to wearing apparel, carpets and rugs were deemed to be safe against the rapid propagation of fire. The carpet test method and standard are now in use.

A Commerce Department study showed that 99 of 135 hotel fires started in beds. This study also showed that in the Virginia-Washington area 26 per cent of house fires started in bedding. In other localities, the percentage was lower, especially in Maryland County, in which the National Bureau of Standards is located, where only 2.9 per cent of fires were started in bedding. Now comes the requirement that bedding be defined. Is bedding only sheets and sheeting or does it include mattresses, bedspreads, and ticking? Canada is currently conducting tests and studies on this subject. One serious problem is that if the standard is soon to be applied to dresses and fabrics sold retail over the counter, it may be several years before there is a sufficient supply of protective chemicals to make significant progress in protection. Fire is still the most serious hazard for the cellulosics, but tests should consider the molten droppings from overheated manufactured fibers and

[3] Kenneth A. Howry, "Flammability—Confusion Compounded," *Modern Textiles,* **51,** No. 4 (April 1970), pp. 36–37.

from plastics. These burns are deeper, more painful, and more serious than a surface burn of even a more extensive area. Medical experience has shown also that melt burns are slower to heal and often require plastic surgery.

Research and development in the textile industry will probably continue along the patterns of the last 20 years insofar as such efforts are supplied by the chemical industry, which makes the new fibers, finishes, dyestuffs, and other chemical additives for textile producers. On the other hand, it appears that more scientific knowledge at the Ph.D. level in physics and mathematics will become available to the textile industry if there is any significant further cutback in space studies and other programs under Federal control. This might mean a considerable increase in the speed of fiber and fabric production not only in faster weaving looms, but also in knitting equipment and in nonwovens. Computerization and other automatic controls will also have a great effect on developments in the building industry during the late 1970s. It has been interesting to note the rapid growth of textile research in what is now described as the Research Triangle in North Carolina—in the Greensboro, Chapel Hill, and Durham areas.

The Federal government's purchasing standards do not apply directly to the consumer but are of some guidance value to large institutional and commercial purchasers.

The commercial standards deal primarily with garment sizes and the results of their use contribute to the economic benefit of the ultimate consumer in that homemakers are assured that garment sizes for boys and girls and adults are accurate for the products of all the dependable garment makers using them. These are identified by the designation CS, commercial standard; for example, CS-135-46, which covers men's shirts. The importance of such size specifications is that a manufacturer will not then cheat on the sizing by perhaps reducing the tail length or by lessening the girth around the chest. In women's wear the principal effort has been in standardizing pattern sizes throughout the pattern-making industry. Ready-to-wear garments and outer apparel have not been as uniformly sized for women.

AIDS TO THE CONSUMER IN SELECTING TEXTILES

Standards

Large mail-order chains and some of the more prominent department stores in the United States exercise laboratory control over many of their textile and other merchandise purchases. These standards were developed in the early 1930s and stiffened progressively through the years as the laboratories gained more experience in the evaluation of products. These laboratories have continued to labor under one great difficulty, the number of items available for testing from any one manufacturing resource. In other words, the laboratories have had to rely on the degree of quality control in the producer's plant and to hope that the sample being evaluated was representative of the manufacturer's line—that is, that it was neither better than nor lower in quality than the average. This is where experience and past data become valuable in the case of staple items that a store may purchase year after year. It is not of as great aid in the appraisal of a new product or of a new finish for which there is an insufficient backlog of test information available.

Manufacturers of fibers and yarns have also set up their standards for fabrics and in some cases for apparel made from their fibers. Some of the textile companies provide this kind of standard guidance information to consumers. The significance of this information lies in the fact that the manufacturer of a fiber who wants to protect the quality of his product will not approve the sale of fabrics using his fiber trademark unless those fabrics meet standards set up by him. If, for example, a producer manufactures, finishes, or colors a fabric containing a blend of cotton and a proprietary name polyester and the fabric does not meet the testing standards of the manufacturer of the polyester, then that proprietary name cannot be used in any promotion or sale. The fabric can be sold as a blend of cotton with polyester, the origin of which will not be disclosed. This is, incidentally, a rather strong argument for consumers who buy proprietary name blends. At least it is a kind of implied warranty that is not present in the unidentified fiber material. One might say that merchandise identified by the fiber name is one produced by and, in a sense, guaranteed by the primary producer, in addition to the fabric weaver and the store from which the apparel was purchased.

Today all these laboratories make use of the L-22 standard of the American National Standards Institute, Inc. (ANSI). This is the L-22-1968 standard and applies to 27 articles of women's and girls' apparel items, 21 end-uses for men's and boys' apparel fabrics, and 15 standards for home furnishings. The original standard, L-22-1952, applied only to articles made of acetate and rayon and was sponsored in what was then the American Standards Association by the National Retail Merchants Association (at that time the National Retail Dry Goods Association) and was very largely based on the test methods and standards of the Crown Tested Program of the American Viscose Corporation. These L-22 standards were necessary because of wide fluctuations in the properties and performance of rayon and acetate garments following World War II.

For each of the apparel items, the L-22 standard has specified acceptable minimum performance figures for most anticipated service conditions, such as strength, wet and dry; dimensional change; colorfastness to washing, dry cleaning, or chlorine bleach; and to other properties any individual item might be expected to encounter. Degrees of color washfastness and colorfastness to light are based on the anticipated exposure in use. These minimum values were established by actual consumer experience. The laboratories of commercial testing establishments, women's magazines, consumer advisory organizations, the American Institute of Laundering, the National Association of Drycleaners, and store laboratories submitted quantities of data showing the floors of minimum quality above which consumer complaints were rarely encountered but below which there were numerous complaints. There was some compromise in setting performance levels in the case of certain fabrics that had been used for specific end-use items for many years without much criticism by the users but that might fall slightly below the minimum standard in one or another test.

The L-22 program is not recommended for partial compliance; however, where this is claimed, the label must show in the same size type any deviation: for example, USAS L-22, 10.3-W except shrinkage.

In Table 8–1 the L-22-1968 USA standard performance requirements for women's and girls' woven blouse and dress fabrics are shown; the code letter product identification is L-22-10.3-1968. Table 8–2 (L-22-10.3-1968) covers women's and girls' knitted apparel. It will be noted that the testing procedures dealing with the physical performance of the fabric are those of the ASTM, D-13. The ASTM is essentially an engineering technical society dealing with test methods of engineering characteristics for all kinds of products. The tests dealing with chemical performances are those of the American Association of Textile Chemists and Colorists. In rare cases in which neither society has yet developed a laboratory testing procedure of satisfactory reproducibility, the origin of the test method is given. These so-called private methods of testing are done at, for example, Textile Distributors Institute (TDI), Fabric Laminators Association (FLA), and the Apparel Manufacturers Association.

There has been much disappointment among consumers in the fact that the L-22 standards have not been greatly publicized and that their use appears to be confined mostly to laboratories rather than sales floors. An inherent problem is having permanent labeling or identification of products meet the standard requirements of the L-22 standard as far as washfastness characteristics are concerned as well as those of the L-23 standard developed for the institutional buyers—the hotels, motels, ship lines, universities, hospitals, and other large-volume consumers. It has been proposed that a permanent sewn-in label be in the garment or other textile identifying the item by its code number in the standard in the manner shown in the identifications in Table 8–1. The color of the lettering on the label would identify the appropriate washing conditions in the following manner.

USAS L–22–B, washable at 160°F, with bleach—purple
USAS L–22–W, washable at 160°F, no bleach—green
USAS L–22–C, washable at 120°F, no bleach—blue
USAS L–22–H, washable at 105°F, no bleach—yellow
USAS L–22–D, dry-cleanable—red

Special care directions can be added to these basic performance requirements that can be detachable. It is conceivable that such supplementary information might be "wash only, do not dry-clean," or vice versa or, "do not bleach," or "iron on the wrong side."

Similar information has been given in graphic form in so-called Sure Care labeling. The **Sure Care** label is shown in Figure 8–1. It should be noted that the washing, ironing, and bleaching requirements here are similar to those in the L-22 program. For a time these Sure Care labels were used extensively in boys' and children's wear, but in the late 1960s, they became less prominent. It must be remembered that in the case of the Sure Care labels the evaluation is only on the washability characteristics, whereas in the L-22 program it is implicit that all the other tests have been made and that the textile product has been found to be satisfactory. (See Table 8–3.)

POSSIBLE LIMITATIONS OF THE L-22 STANDARD

The original L-22 standard on rayon and acetates contemplated that their usefulness probably would extend to some 20 per cent of the products of the two fibers. These would constitute a quality level and would conceivably command a higher retail price because of the guarantee and the fact that fabrics so identified could be traced back through each stage of production to find out where any failure or weakness first developed—that is, whether the responsibility rested with the finisher, the weaver, the spinner, or perhaps with the fiber itself. Obviously, any testing program would demand a considerable amount of time, and for this reason it was thought that high-fashion merchandise would never be included. It still does not seem possible that any textile fabric requiring rapid marketing, such as high-style merchandise, can be subjected to standards. The traditional pattern of apparel use of such fabrics indicates that durability is not an important factor. These fabrics are primarily of high esthetic value and are rarely subject to regular wear. It is probable that standards would apply only after a few seasons, when a new finish or a unique color proved itself well enough to be extended into lower-priced merchandise.

The ASTM and the AATCC cooperate through a joint committee under the auspices of the ANSI and other technical committees; each recognizes the standard test methods of the other. It is not within their domain to set up standards of quality; they are concerned with test methods. Interpretation and standards resulting from the tests are the responsibility of the ANSI and other organizations promoting standards programs.

The National Bureau of Standards has a limited staff engaged in textile research and testing, but it acts as a liaison for the various technical societies. It is influential in the evaluation of textiles, especially in those phases having to do with Federal legislation or with the trade practice rules of the Federal

Table 8-1   **USA Standard Performance Requirements for Women's and Girls' Woven Blouse or Dress Fabrics**

| Property | Minimum Requirements | | | | | Test Method |
	L-22.10.3-B Washable 160° F	L-22.10.3-W Washable 160° F No Bleach	L-22.10.3-C Washable 120° F No Bleach	L-22.10.3-H Washable 105° F No Bleach	L-22.10.3-D Dry-cleanable	See Part VII*
Breaking strength						
Dry (see note 1)	20 lb	20 lb	20 lb	20 lb	20 lb	USAS L-14.184 Grab Test (ASTM D 1682)
Wet	12 lb	12 lb	12 lb	12 lb	12 lb	USAS L-14.102 (ASTM D 434)
Resistance to yarn slippage	15 lb	15 lb	15 lb	15 lb	15 lb	USAS L-14.207
Tongue tear strength (see note 2)	1 lb	1 lb	1 lb	1 lb	1 lb	USAS L-14.103 (ASTM D 2261)
Yarn shifting						(ASTM D 1336)
Maximum opening						
Satins	0.10-in.	0.10-in.	0.10-in.	0.10-in.	0.10-in.	1-lb load
Others	0.05-in.	0.05-in.	0.05-in.	0.05-in.	0.05-in.	1-lb load
Maximum dimensional change—each direction (see note 3)	2.5 per cent	2.5 per cent	2.5 per cent	2.5 per cent	2 per cent	USAS L-14.138 (AATCC 96) (ASTM D 1905) Table II Test No. III Test No. II Test No. I AATCC 108
Odor	Class 3	Class 3	Class 3	Class 3	Class 3	TDI No. 3
Colorfastness to						
Atmospheric fading after						
Washing (see note 4)	Class 4	Class 4	Class 4	Class 4		USAS L-14.54 (1 cycle) (AATCC 23)
Dry cleaning (see note 4)					Class 4	
Laundering	Test IVA	Test IIIA	Test IIA	Test IA		USAS L-14.81 (AATCC 61)
Alteration in shade	Class 4	Class 4	Class 4	Class 4	Class 4	International Gray Scale
Staining	Class 3	Class 3	Class 3	Class 4	Class 4	
Dry cleaning (see note 5)	Class 4	Class 4	Class 4	Class 4	Class 4	AATCC 85

Crocking						
Dry	Class 4	Class 4	Class 4	Class 4	Class 4	USAS L-14.72 (AATCC 8)
Wet	Class 3	Class 3	Class 3	Class 3	Class 3	
Wet-washed crock cloth (see note 6)	Class 4	Class 4	Class 4	Class 4	Class 4	Color Transference Chart
Perspiration						
Alteration in shade	Class 4	Class 4	Class 4	Class 4	Class 4	USAS L-14.56 (AATCC 15)
Staining	Class 4	Class 4	Class 3	Class 3	Class 3	International Gray Scale
Light	L-4-20 hr	L-4-20 hr	L-4-20 hr	L-4-20 hr	L-4-20 hr	USAS L-14.53 (AATCC 16A)

Pressing

Whenever the pressing temperature specified in any testing procedure is too high for heat-sensitive fibers, pressing should be done at temperatures as high as possible without glazing or fusing.

Retention of Hand, Character, and Appearance

A fabric shall not change substantially in hand, character, or appearance as a result of three launderings by the applicable shrinkage procedure or dry cleaning by USAS L-14.121 (AATCC 86), except laminated (bonded) fabrics which shall be tested by FLA Test No. 1. In addition, the fabric shall not lose more than 3 per cent of its weight as a result of this treatment.

Durability of Laminates

A fabric shall exhibit no delamination, cracking, or peeling as a result of three launderings by Fabric Laminators Association Test No. 2 or three dry cleanings by Fabric Laminators Association Test No. 1, according to whichever standard is used.

Special Performance Characteristics

When a claim is made for a special performance characteristic not covered by this standard, see Part IV of these standards.

FABRICATION AND COMPONENTS PROPERTIES

Components

All textile components and components other than textiles incorporated into the textile article shall conform to applicable performance requirements of this standard in order not to cause alteration in appearance of fabrics meeting these requirements after appropriate refreshing tests. If the provisions of this standard do not cover refreshing requirements suitable for removable components, other L-22 end-use standards may be specified.

Seam Strength (Garment or Textile Items)

Each original seam shall possess a breaking strength of at least 17 pounds (ASTM D 1683).

Raveling Test (Seams in Garments or Textile Items)

Fabrics containing filament yarns shall be tested for seam strength after three launderings using the applicable shrinkage procedure, or after dry cleaning by USAS L-14.121 (AATCC 86), except laminated (bonded) fabrics which shall be tested by FLA Test No. 1. Seam failure due to excessive free-edge raveling indicates the need for another type of seam.

PERMANENT LABELS AND DETACHABLE TAGS

Permanent labels and detachable tags indicating compliance with the specific L-22 standard shall be in accordance with requirements as set forth in Part V of these standards.

SOURCE: USAS L-22.10.3-1968. (Revision of L-22.10.3-1960.)

Notes:
1. Fabrics known to exhibit a wet strength in excess of the dry strength requirement need not be subjected to a wet test.
2. Use of USAS L-14.203 (ASTM D 1424—Elmendorf) Test Method is permitted if preferred with existing requirements as given in this standard. However, in case of controversy, USAS L-14.207 (ASTM D 2261) shall prevail.
3. Use AATCC Test Method 99 when applicable. Use FLA Tests No. 1 and No. 2 for laminated (bonded) fabrics.
4. Use corresponding test methods as provided in the columns under laundering and dry cleaning.
5. Under this standard, a washable fabric shall also be colorfast to dry cleaning, unless specifically labeled: *Do not dry-clean.* Dry-cleanable goods are dry-cleanable only.
6. For wet-washed crock cloth use CS 59-44, Part VIII, Colorfastness to Crocking, Para 31a.

* The references to the test numbers in this column give only the permanent part of the designation of the USA Standard, AATCC, ASTM, and other test methods. The particular edition for year of issue of each method used in testing the material for conformance to the requirements here specified shall be as stated in the current edition of Part VII of these L-22 standards.

Table 8-2   USA Standard Performance Requirements for Women's and Girls' Knitted Blouse or Dress Fabrics

Property	Identification: L-22.10.5-B Washable 160° F	L-22.10.5-W Washable 160° F No Bleach	L-22.10.5-C Washable 120° F No Bleach	L-22.10.5-H Washable 105° F No Bleach	L-22.10.5-D Dry-cleanable	Test Method See Part VII*
Bursting strength						USAS L-14.67 (ASTM D 231)
Man-made cellulosic fibers						
Dry	32 lb	32 lb	32 lb	32 lb	32 lb	
Wet	25 lb	25 lb	25 lb	25 lb	25 lb	
Other fibers						
Dry (see note 1)	50 lb	50 lb	50 lb	50 lb	50 lb	
Wet	30 lb	30 lb	30 lb	30 lb	30 lb	
Maximum dimensional change— each direction (see note 2)						Washable, USAS L-14.138 (AATCC 96) (ASTM D 1905) Table I
Warp knit (heat-set)	3.5 per cent	3.5 per cent	3.5 per cent	3.5 per cent	3.5 per cent	E1
Other two-bar knits	5 per cent	5 per cent	5 per cent	5 per cent	5 per cent	C1
Other knits	5 per cent	5 per cent	5 per cent	5 per cent	5 per cent	E2
						Dry-cleanable, AATCC 108
Odor	Class 3	Class 3	Class 3	Class 3	Class 3	TDI No. 3
Colorfastness to						
Atmospheric fading after						
Washing (see note 3)	Class 4	Class 4	Class 4	Class 4		USAS L-14.54 (1 cycle) (AATCC 23)
Dry cleaning (see note 3)					Class 4	
Laundering	Test IVA	Test IIIA	Test IIA	Test IA		USAS L-14.81 (AATCC 61)
Alteration in shade	Class 4	Class 4	Class 4	Class 4		
Staining	Class 3	Class 3	Class 3	Class 4		International Gray Scale AATCC 85
Dry cleaning (see note 4)	Class 4	Class 4	Class 4	Class 4	Class 4	

						Test Method [*]
Crocking						
Dry	Class 4	Class 4	Class 4	Class 4	Class 4	USAS L-14.72
Wet	Class 3	Class 3	Class 3	Class 3	Class 3	(AATCC 8)
Wet-washed crock cloth (see note 5)	Class 4	Class 4	Class 4	Class 4	Class 4	Color Transference Chart
Perspiration						
Alteration in shade	Class 4	Class 4	Class 4	Class 4	Class 4	USAS L-14.56 (AATCC 15)
Staining	Class 4	Class 3	Class 3	Class 3	Class 3	International Gray Scale
Light	L-4-20 hr	L-4-20 hr	L-4-20 hr	L-4-20 hr	L-4-20 hr	USAS L-14.53 (AATCC 16A)

Pressing

Whenever the pressing temperature specified in any testing procedure is too high for heat-sensitive fibers, pressing should be done at temperatures as high as possible without glazing or fusing.

Retention of Hand, Character, and Appearance

A fabric shall not change substantially in hand, character, or appearance as a result of three launderings by the applicable shrinkage procedure or dry cleaning by USAS L-14.121 (AATCC 86), except laminated (bonded) fabrics which shall be tested by FLA Test No. 1. In addition, the fabric shall not lose more than 3 per cent of its weight as a result of this treatment.

Durability of Laminates

A fabric shall exhibit no delamination, cracking, or peeling as a result of three launderings by Fabric Laminators Association Test No. 2 or three dry cleanings by Fabric Laminators Association Test No. 1, according to whichever standard is used.

Special Performance Characteristics

When a claim is made for a special performance characteristic not covered by this standard, see Part IV of these standards.

FABRICATION AND COMPONENTS PROPERTIES

Components

All textile components and components other than textiles incorporated into the textile article shall conform to applicable performance requirements of this standard in order not to cause alteration in appearance of fabrics meeting these requirements after appropriate refreshing tests. If the provisions of this standard do not cover refreshing requirements suitable for removable components, other L-22 end-use standards may be specified.

Seam Strength (Garment or Textile Items)

Each original seam shall possess a bursting strength of at least 27 pounds for man-made cellulosic fibers and 43 pounds for other fibers (U.S. Testing Company Method).

PERMANENT LABELS AND DETACHABLE TAGS

Permanent labels and detachable tags indicating compliance with the specific L-22 standard shall be in accordance with requirements as set forth in Part V of these standards.

SOURCE: USAS L-22.10.5-1968. (Revision and consolidation of L-22.10.5-1960; L-22.10.6-1960; L-22.10.7-1960; and L-22.10.8-1960).
Notes: 1 Fabrics known to exhibit a wet strength which is in excess of the dry strength requirement need not be subjected to a wet test.
2 Use AATCC Test Method 99 when applicable. Use FLA Test No. 1 and No. 2 for laminated (bonded) fabrics.
3 Use corresponding test methods as provided in the columns under laundering and dry cleaning.
4 Under this standard, a washable fabric shall also be colorfast to dry cleaning, unless specifically labelled: *Do not dry-clean*. Dry- cleanable goods are dry-cleanable only.
5 For wet-washed crock cloth use CS 59-44, Part VIII, Colorfastness to Crocking, Para 31a.
* The references to the test methods in this column give only the permanent part of the designation of the USA Standard, AATCC, ASTM, and other test methods. The particular edition for year of issue of each method used in testing the material for conformance to the requirements here specified shall be as stated in the current edition of Part VII of these L-22 standards.

Follow these symbols to WASH or DRY-CLEAN and IRON your clothes or home furnishings with satisfactory results. Look for the labels with these simple guides to happier washdays.

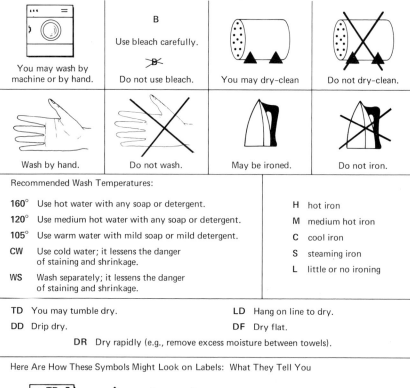

You may wash by machine or by hand.	**B** Use bleach carefully. Do not use bleach.	You may dry-clean	Do not dry-clean.
Wash by hand.	Do not wash.	May be ironed.	Do not iron.

Recommended Wash Temperatures:

160° Use hot water with any soap or detergent.

120° Use medium hot water with any soap or detergent.

105° Use warm water with mild soap or mild detergent.

CW Use cold water; it lessens the danger of staining and shrinkage.

WS Wash separately; it lessens the danger of staining and shrinkage.

H hot iron

M medium hot iron

C cool iron

S steaming iron

L little or no ironing

TD You may tumble dry.　　　　　**LD** Hang on line to dry.

DD Drip dry.　　　　　　　　　　**DF** Dry flat.

　　　　DR Dry rapidly (e.g., remove excess moisture between towels).

Here Are How These Symbols Might Look on Labels: What They Tell You

Wash by machine or by hand in hot water with any soap or detergent. Use bleach carefully. Tumble dry. Do not dry-clean. Iron with hot iron.

Wash by hand in warm water with any soap or detergent. Do not bleach. Dry-clean. Little or no ironing.

Wash by hand in lukewarm water with mild soap or detergent. Do not bleach. Dry rapidly. Dry-clean. Do not iron.

Courtesy of National Retail Merchants Association

Figure 8-1. Sure Care chart. (Courtesy of National Retail Merchants Association)

Trade Commission. The FTC, like the NBS, is a part of the Department of Commerce. Its traditional responsibility has been to administer laws and regulations dealing with fair trade practice. As already mentioned, the FTC can initiate action on its own—that is, without a complainant requesting permissive action in what he considers to be an unfair trade practice within the industry.

Table 8-3   Consumer Care Guide for Apparel

	When Label Reads:	It Means:
Machine-washable	Washable Machine-washable Home launder only	Wash, bleach, dry, press by any customary method including commercial laundering Same as above, but do not use commercial laundering
	No bleach	Do not use bleach
	No starch	Do not use starch
	Cold wash Cold setting Cold rinse	Use cold water from tap or cold washing machine setting
	Lukewarm wash Warm wash Warm setting Warm rinse	Use warm water (hand-comfortable), 90–110°F
	Medium wash Medium setting	Use warm water (medium washing machine setting), 110–130°F
	Hot wash Hot setting	Use hot water (hot washing machine setting), 130°F or hotter
	No spin	Remove wash load before final machine spin cycle
	Delicate cycle Gentle cycle	Use appropriate machine setting; otherwise wash by hand
	Durable- press cycle Permanent- press cycle	Use appropriate machine setting; otherwise use medium wash, cold rinse and short spin cycle
	Wash separately	Wash alone or with like colors
Nonmachine Washing	Hand-washable Wash by hand	Launder only by hand in warm water. May be bleached. May be dry-cleaned
	Hand wash only	Same as above, but *do not* dry-clean
	Hand wash separately	Hand wash alone or with like colors
	No bleach	Do not use bleach

Table 8-3 (continued)

	When Label Reads:	It Means:
Home Drying	Tumble dry	Dry in tumble dryer at specified setting—
	Machine dry	high, medium, low, or no heat
	Tumble dry	Same as above, but in absence of cool-down
	Remove promptly	cycle remove at once when tumbling stops
	Drip dry	Hang wet and allow to dry with hand shap-
	Hang dry	ing only
	Line dry	
	No squeeze	Hang dry, drip dry, or dry flat only
	No wring	
	No twist	
	Dry flat	Lay garment on flat surface
	Block to dry	Maintain original size and shape while drying
Ironing or Pressing	Cool iron	Set iron at lowest setting
	Warm iron	Set iron at medium setting
	Hot iron	Set iron at hot setting
	No iron	Do not iron or press with heat
	No press	
	Steam iron	Iron or press with steam
	Steam press	
	Iron damp	Dampen garment before ironing
Miscellaneous	Dry-clean	Garment should be dry-cleaned only
	Dry-clean only	
	Professionally clean only	*Do not* use self-service dry cleaning
	Commercially clean only	
	No dry-clean	Use recommended care instructions. No dry-cleaning materials to be used

SOURCE: Produced by the Consumer Affairs Committee, American Apparel Manufacturers Association, Inc., 1969.

Consumership

An excellent summary of information on man-made fibers is the annual *Man-Made Fiber Fact Book* distributed by the Man-Made Fiber Producers Association, Inc., 1150 Seventeenth Street, N.W., Washington, D.C. 20036; it can be obtained by writing to the Educational Director of the Association at that address.

Table 8–4 represents the type of information available through the various member corporations manufacturing these fibers. This table indicates the several media by which product information is disseminated: booklets, leaflets, film strips, and other educational material for classroom

Table 8-4   Educational Material Sources Among Members of Man-Made Fiber Producers Association, Inc.*

	Charts and Folders	Booklets	Kits	Film Strips Motion Pictures	Technical Bulletins
Allied Chemical Corporation	x	x			x
American Cyanamid Company	x	x			x
American Enka Company		x	x		x
Beaunit Corporation	x	x			x
Celanese Corporation	x	x		x	x
Courtaulds North America, Inc.	x	x			
Dow Badische Company	x	x			x
E. I. du Pont de Nemours & Co., Inc.	x	x		x	x
Eastman Kodak Company Tennessee Eastman Company Division	x	x	x		x
FMC Corporation, American Viscose Division	x	x	x	x	x
Hercules, Incorporated	x	x			
Hoechst Fibers, Incorporated		x		x	x
J. R. C. Fibers Company, American Cyanamid Company		x	x		x
Monsanto Company, Textile Division	x	x			x
Phillips Fibers Corporation		x			
Union Carbide Corporation	x	x	x		

SOURCE: As listed in the *1970 Man-Made Fiber Fact Book*, Man-Made Fiber Producers Association, Inc., Washington, D.C.
* These companies are members of the Man-Made Fiber Producers Association, Inc.

work and issues dealing with general consumership. It is suggested that, for technical bulletins and reports, an order be sent on the college or university letterhead. As a general rule this material is not applicable to students' use, nor would it be particularly important to the merchandise-selection problems facing the consumer.

PRODUCERS' AIDS TO FABRIC SELECTION CARE

Progressive producers of textiles have provided much helpful information for the consumer, but it is keyed more directly to the teacher and student in textile and clothing courses.

Labeling programs of fiber producers, garment manufacturers, retailers, and state laboratories are referred to on pp. 347–48. It is more appropriately discussed there than under textiles because it is to the apparel as an entire unit that both labels and standards should apply.

Apparel Performance Standards

The men's apparel industry established a research organization in 1964 called the Apparel Research Foundation. It has undertaken a number of projects to improve the functional qualities of apparel and to bring about greater efficiency in garment production. To do so requires a program of standards based on the testing programs of the various members to fill the void created by the lack of industry-acceptable standards by which the utility and cleanability of a garment could be established. Research for this Apparel Performance Level Standards (APLS) is being extended from the conventional methods of garment construction by sewing to include the use of adhesives in forming the seams through several procedures somewhat similar to the formation of laminated fabrics—that is, the use of films, monofilaments, thermoplastic yarns, and liquid adhesives. Ultrasonic welding—the use of sound waves as an energy source—is also one of the projects under study.

This association, too, has concerned itself with consumer guidance in the care and maintenance of apparel. The descriptive phrases in Table 8–3 express what the L-22 colors and Sure Care graphics portrayed. It is interesting to observe that all three methods endeavor to be concise and clear. Because some outer wear can be washed successfully without color damage, shrinkage, or loss of finish at a moderate temperature, 130°F is the highest washing temperature suggested.

Consumer Consciousness

Between 1963 and 1970, the United States Congress enacted a series of major laws whose basic philosophy involved consumer consciousness. One might define the basic objective of these laws as the preservation of the consumer (that is, maintaining his freedom from overpowering debt due to poor purchasing habits and from deception on the part of the producers and sellers of certain goods). Few of these laws pertain specifically to textiles, but they lend weight to certain textile problems still facing the Congress. Two earlier acts of Congress, the Textile Fiber Identification Act of 1960 (p. 344) and the Wool Labeling Act of 1953, amended in 1965, (p. 343), more or less set the pattern. After long study, the FTC issued the Permanent Care Labeling Trade Regulation, which became effective July 3, 1972. Care labels are now permanently sewn or printed on garments. Eventually these labels may go beyond the simple directions for care that appear on the Sure Care labels, Canadian Care Direction Labels, the British Textile Care Labeling Code, the International Care Labeling Code, and the Color Code of the L-22 standards on textile fabrics. In 1972, the FTC stated that it would be an unfair method of competition and an unfair or deceptive act or practice to sell any textile product "which does not have a label or a tag permanently affixed or attached thereto which accurately and clearly discloses proper instructions for the laundering and cleaning of such products." In 1971, the FTC had begun considering the possibility that the language of such a rule implied a guarantee. Because no product—textile or otherwise—will last forever, a great deal of consternation has appeared, of course, throughout the textile industry. However, worries concerning the care of manufactured fiber fabrics could be reduced if consumers knew more about the identity of fibers and realized that many essentials of care are so similar as not to require special attention.

TECHNICAL ASPECTS OF SELECTION

In Chapter 1, which dealt with basic concepts in the study of textiles and clothing, a number of instances were pointed out in which the concern of the professional investigator was with the finished apparel more than with its individual ingredients or the finish and color applied. It is the textile item in the ready-for-sale condition that interests many of the home economics graduates employed by the textile industry, retail store, and technical laboratories. They serve also as textile and clothing experts, judging textile products for consumer advisory laboratories and commercial testing laboratories. They work as technologists in the laboratories of the servicing associations, both laundering and dry cleaning, and many of them similarly are employed by manufacturers of home appliances. This, of course, is to be expected because their appraisals are for the benefit of the home manager, the ultimate consumer of textile apparel.

We now know a good deal about the various aspects of the manufacture of these garments: fibers, yarns, and fabrics; the kinds of finishes applied; color; and wear and durability. These factors have been taken for granted by the homemaker. Among the profusion of possible selections complicating the problem of selection, are the following: (1) How can she be sure that the dress she has selected is really the best value? (2) Will the dress give as good service and long-time satisfaction as another at which she may have looked? (3) Will her husband be happier with an all-cotton sports shirt, a cotton-polyester blend, or with an all-synthetic for summer wear? (4) To what extent will her energies be saved with a durable-press shirt, instead of one that will require ironing each time it is washed?

Similar perplexing questions face the customer regarding many household fabrics, including such things as bed sheets. Does she have the equipment, the time, and the energy to wash and iron these sheets at home? Is she satisfied with the high prices of the sometimes poor work done by many of the commercial laundries? If durable-press sheets are purchased and sent to the commercial laundry, will they be treated with regular cotton sheeting with a chance of distortion damage from careless pressing or the use of excessive bleach if the finish is chlorine-sensitive? Each kind of textile product has its own selection criteria that enter into the evaluation made by the homemaker at the time a purchase is to be made. By **evaluation** is meant that in addition to specifying the fibers and fabrics and the effects of the use of the application of color and finish, technology must endeavor to weigh the various results of these applications in terms of their influence on the end-use performance of the apparel. Such a product evaluation will also include the workmanship, component parts of the product, and the kind of maintenance care it may require in use. Judgment and experience are necessary in addition to the technical competence and accuracy of a technologist, and the significance of all these parts to consumers' satisfaction must be established. In many staple products bought repeatedly, such as infants' wear, children's and boys' wear, uniforms, housedresses, and similar apparel, judgment and experience are just as necessary to the laboratory technician as to the ultimate consumer. The advantage held by the laboratory person is that numerical test data can generally be coordinated fairly well with the subjective data supplied by the observation of merchandise returned by consumers in the form of complaints. The significance of consumer complaints is amplified in the discussion of the L-22 standards.

As a result of its research studies on complaints and its compilation as to responsibility for damaged textile products (Tables 8–5 and 8–6) the NID issued Table 8–6, which deals with a wide variety of textile products. One might term this an actuarial approach toward compensation for the premature destruction of one's purchases.

PSYCHOLOGICAL SELECTION CRITERIA

To What Do We React in Buying?

The general consensus is that the average store customer, the homemaker, like other members of her family, tends to make her textile product selections more on the basis of esthetic or appearance factors than on durability or potential performance in service. Many of these esthetic qualities defy actual testing in terms of figures and precise ratings. They are essentially **subjective** reactions and, to a considerable degree, depend on the taste and selective ability of the individual. We must use words to describe the drape or hang of a skirt, or the graceful folds in curtain and drapery material. We must use words to describe relative dullness or luster. Fabric textures are more a matter of sensory response than of precise measurements. Similarly, we say that one fabric feels cool and comfortable to the skin; another does not.

The advertisements of new textile products and finishes that appear in fashion magazines, in the daily paper, or on a store's display signs emphasize fashion rightness, beauty, texture, and price with rare attention being called to the durability of the fabric or of its color or finish. Minimum-care fabrics (now referred to as durable-press) have begun to call the attention of the customer to the serviceability and the care conditions to which these new materials, principally the synthetic fibers, respond so well in service. These are **objective** reactions with differences measurable by laboratory testing procedures and to which numbers or rating values can be assigned. With these new fibers and with the chemical changes that have been imposed on the natural fibers, principally cotton and wool, and on other cellulosic fibers, such as linen and rayon, some of the potential use-experience, or consumer influence, is beginning to be felt at the point of sale.

Despite these changes, which are still small in comparison with the total textile volume sold in our large department stores, it is safe to conclude that when an individual makes a purchase it is with esthetics principally in mind. These can be described as *customer influences*. After the article has been used for some months, the same individual becomes more critical and begins to compare performance with what she expected or hoped for. These are the *consumer elements*; they guide the individual in future action. Does she repurchase the product? Does she silently condemn it? Does she return it for credit or replacement? The housewife is a realist and probably bases her returns more on the failure of the article to meet her expectations than

Table 8-5 Implied Serviceability Designations and Life Expectancy Rates

Men's and Boys' Wear

Item	Renovation Method	Rate (years)
1. Bathing suits	Hand wash	2
2. Coats and jackets		
Cloth, dress	Dry-clean	4
Cloth, sport	(See no. 20)	
Pile (imitation fur)	Dry-clean. Cold tumble only; no steam	
Fur	Fur clean	10
Leather and suede	(See no. 7)	
Plastic	(See no. 10)	
3. Formal wear	Dry-clean	5
4. Gloves		
Fabric	Medium wash; dry-clean	1
Leather	Leather clean only	2
5. Hats		
Felt and straw	Clean by hat renovation specialists only; water-resistant	
Fur	Fur clean (See nos. 2 or 11)	5
6. Jackets		
7. Leather jackets and coats Suede and grain leather products require special care in cleaning. Colors normally subject to fading and some loss in		

Item	Renovation Method	Rate (years)
13. Shoes Can be cleaned and polished, resoled, heeled. Thread in uppers holds sections securely for normal service life without undue breakage		
Men's		3
Boy's		1
14. Shirts		
Dress and plain sports		
White and partly colored	Hot wash	2
Colored	Hot wash; no bleach	
Sports (fancy)		
Cotton and blends	Medium wash, dry-clean	3
Wool or silk	Dry-clean; hand wash	2
15. Shorts	(See no. 17)	
16. Ski jackets	(See no. 11)	
17. Slacks and shorts (including matching sets)		
Wool or wool blends	Dry-clean	4
Cotton	Medium wash; dry-clean	2

cleaning. Suedes and most grain leathers restorable by application of color and finishing products

Item	Care	Rating
8. Neckties	Dry-clean	1
9. Sleepwear		
White goods	Hot wash	
Colored goods	Medium wash	2
10. Plastic apparel— (See no. 11)		
Imitation leather and suede	Hand wash; no pressing	3
11. Rainwear		
Film and plastic-coated fabrics	Hand wash; no pressing	2
Fabric		
Unlined	Medium wash; dry-clean	3
Lined and quilted	Dry-clean	
Rubber	Wipe down with damp cloth; no pressing	3
12. Robes		
Silk or wool	Dry-clean	3
Other:		
Unlined	Medium wash; dry-clean	2
Lined	Dry-clean	

Item	Care	Rating
Synthetics	Dry-clean	2
18. Sneakers	Medium wash; bleach; air or tumble dry	0
19. Socks		1
Wool	Hand wash	
Other	Medium wash	
20. Sport coats		
Wool and wool blends	Dry-clean	4
Cotton and synthetics	Dry-clean	2
21. Suits		
Summer weight:		
Wool or wool blends	Dry-clean	3
Cotton and synthetics	Dry-clean	2
Winter weight	Dry-clean	4
Wash suits	Medium wash; dry-clean	2
22. Sweaters		
Wool and synthetics	Hand wash; dry flat only; dry-clean; wet clean	3
23. Underwear		
White	Hot wash	2
Colored	Medium wash	
24. Uniforms		
Unlined and work types	Medium wash; dry-clean	1
Lined and dressy	Dry-clean	

Table 8-5 (continued)

Item	Renovation Method	Rate (years)
25. Vests		
Fancy and regular	Dry-clean	2
26. Windbreakers	(See no. 11)	
27. Work clothing		2
Customarily shows noticeable signs of wear to greater or lesser degree depending on amount of use. Color may be expected to appear rubbed off in areas. Fabric has strength to withstand strains of use and laundering at 160°F. With heavy-duty soap.		
Women's and Girls' Wear		
28. Aprons		
Regular	Medium wash; bleach white only	1
Fancy	Hand wash; dry-clean	4
29. Blouses		
Dress and sports		

Item	Renovation Method	Rate (years)
35. Jackets	(See nos. 2 or 11)	
36. Negligees		
Cotton and nylon types	Medium wash	2
37. Sleepwear		2
White goods	Hot wash	
Colored goods	Medium wash	
38. Rainwear	(See no. 11)	
39. Robes	(See no. 34)	
40. Scarves		2
Wool	Dry-clean	
Other	Mild wash; dry-clean	
Fur	Fur clean	5
41. Shoes		
Dress and walking	(See no. 13)	2
Work		1
Evening, formal		5
42. Shorts	(See no. 44)	2
43. Skirts		
Winter and fall	Dry-clean; wet clean	
Resort and summer	Medium wash; dry-clean	2
44. Slacks and shorts		
Lounging and tailored	Dry-clean	2

Item	Care instructions	No.
White cotton	Hot wash; dry-clean	3
White synthetics and all colored	Medium wash; dry-clean	2
30. Coats and jackets	(See no. 2)	
31. Dresses		
House and sports	Medium wash; dry-clean	1
Afternoon	Dry-clean	3
Street	Dry-clean	2
Evening or cocktail: High fashion	Dry-clean; special handling of delicate and decorated styles	3
Basic	Dry-clean	5
32. Gloves		
Fabric	Medium wash, separate; dry-clean	1
Leather	Leather clean	2
33. Hats		
Felt	Clean by special hat-renovation methods	1
Straw	Same unless trim details precludes cleaning	2
Fur	Fur clean	5
34. Housecoats and robes		
Lightweight cottons and synthetics	Mild wash; dry-clean	1
Quilted and heavy	Dry-clean	3
Active sport	Hand wash; dry-clean	2
Dress	Dry-clean	3
45. Sneakers	(See no. 18)	
46. Socks	(See no. 19)	
47. Sport coats	(See no. 2)	
48. Suits		
Basic	Dry-clean	4
High fashion	Dry-clean. Special handling on delicate and decorated styles	3
49. Sweaters	(See no. 22)	
50. Swim wear	Hand wash	2
51. Underwear		
Slips	Mild wash; bleach white cottons	2
Foundation garments	Medium wash	1
Panties	Medium wash; bleach white cottons	1
52. Uniforms		
Unlined and work types	Medium wash; dry-clean	1
Lined and dressy	Dry-clean	
53. Wedding gowns	Dry-clean	
54. Windbreakers	(See no. 11*)	
55. Work clothing	(See no. 27)	

Table 8-5 (continued)

Item	Renovation Method	Rate (years)
Children's Wear		
56. Coats	Dry-clean	2
57. Coat sets	Dry-clean	2
58. Dresses	Medium wash; dry-clean	2
59. Hats, bonnets	Dry-clean	1
60. Playclothes	Medium wash	1
61. Snow suits		2
Wool and wool blends	Dry-clean	
Cotton and synthetics	Medium wash; dry-clean	
62. Suits	Dry-clean	2
63. Undergarments		1
White goods	Hot wash	
Colored	Medium wash	
Household Furnishings		
64. Bedspreads		
Cotton, synthetics	Medium wash; dry-clean	3
65. Blankets		
Heavy wool and synthetic fabrics	Mild wash; dry-clean	10
Lightweight	Mild wash; dry-clean	5
Electric	Mild wash	5
66. Curtains		
Sheer	Medium wash; dry-clean	3
Glass fiber	Hand wash; wet clean	

Item	Renovation Method	Rate (years)
67. Draperies		
Lined	Dry-clean	5
Unlined	Medium wash; dry-clean	4
Sheer	Medium wash; dry-clean	3
Glass fiber	Hand wash; wet clean	4
Linings (attached)	Same as drapery	4
Linings (separate)	Medium wash; dry-clean	4
68. Sheets and pillow cases		
White and colored	Hot wash	2
69. Slip covers	Medium wash; dry-clean	3
70. Table linen		
Fancy	Mild wash	5
Service		
(white)	Hot wash	2
(partly colored)	Hot wash	
(colored)	Medium wash	
71. Towels		
All types	Hot wash	2
72. Upholstery fabrics		
Hand-cleanable with dry-cleaning solvent or foam cleaners. Color- and finish-resistant to water		5

SOURCE: National Institute of Drycleaning, from "National Fair Claims Guide for Consumer Textile Products," 1965.
* Indefinite life expectancy. (See Section 6, para. I.)

on the extent to which it falls short of perfection in service. Perfection might mean almost indefinite serviceability, with no attrition or damage to fabrics, texture, color, or finish during normal wear. Expectations differ, too; the weight, texture, or delicacy of the article may change from what the customer previously may have purchased. Thus, the realistic customer or housewife, recognizing that today's nylon hosiery is much finer in filament and, therefore, much more transparent than those with which she first became familiar, would not expect the same degree of wear she had with pre-World War II full-fashioned nylon stockings. She should not expect the same serviceability from a sheer blouse that she obtained from a heavier, firmer poplin. And, certainly, today's 8-ounce summer suiting will not wear as long as the former 11- or 13-ounce wool suiting for men's summer tropicals.

Attributes of Fabrics

A fabric or the end-use products made from it contains a combination of properties or attributes that influence not only customer selection but also consumer experience in use. Some of these properties pertain to the individual fiber or fibers making up the yarn structure. Others are imparted through the art and science of fabric finishing and dyeing. However, the combination of properties—both esthetic and functional—that was originally possessed by the textile should be reasonably permanent, so that the wearer or user can continue to enjoy the product. Two notable exceptions that are supposed to lose color are India madras prints—which are widely advertised as "readily fadeable" or "guaranteed fadeable"—and blue denims —which, reflecting perverseness in human nature, must be stiff and deeptone-dyed initially but become increasingly pleasing to the wearer as they soften in texture and in tone through frequent wearing and washing.

No single textile product would ever have all of the fabric properties appearing in Table 8–7. Some of those appearing together are direct antitheses; others are comparatively insignificant when one considers what is wanted or expected in terms of serviceability in use.

Fashion

Today's costume may be tomorrow's custom. Changes in fashion have been described for several hundred years. We see such descriptions when we examine the photographic evidence of recent history and the drawings and paintings from those periods that preceded the development of the camera. We tend to view these apparel items of the past as costumes in much the same way as we view the traditional garments worn in other countries and in older civilizations or eras of history. This tendency persists not only in courses on past fashions given in colleges and universities but in museum

Table 8-6 Calculation of Claims Adjustment Values

Life Expectancy Rating of Article (from Table 8-5)					Age of Article in Years	Adjustment Values		
Age of Article in Months						Percentage of Replacement Cost		
1	2	3	4	5		Excellent	Average	Poor
0–4	0–4	0–4	0–4	0–4	Less than 1 year	100	100	100
4–7	4–7	4–10	4–13	4–16	2–4 years	75	75	60
* 7–9	* 7–13	10–19	13–25	16–31	4–6 years	70	60	45
* 9–11	13–19	19–28	25–37	31–46	6–8 years	50	40	30
* 11–13	19–25	28–37	37–49	46–61	8–11 years	30	20	15
13 mos. and older	25 mos. and older	37 mos. and older	49 mos. and older	61 mos. and older	11 years and older	20	15	10

SOURCE: Developed by the Textile Trade Relations Department.
* Use only with "Average" column in figuring Adjustment Value.
Note: Ages are given to, but not including, the first day of the month or year shown.

Step by Step Use of Tables 8-5 and 8-6

1. Determine the cost of replacing the article. This is called Replacement Cost.
2. Determine the Actual Age of the article in months (in years for "10-year" items).
3. Determine the condition of the article as Excellent, Average, or Poor.
4. Select the Life Expectancy rating of the article from Table 8–5.
5. Refer to the column in Table 8–6 at the top of which is shown the Life Expectancy rating selected in Step 4. Read down in this column to the box showing the Actual Age and across to the Adjustment Value.
6. In Table 8–6 select the box under "Adjustment Values" that applies, according to the condition of the article.
7. Multiply the per cent figure given in Table 8–6 by the Replacement Cost figure determined in Step 1. This will be the Adjustment Value.

> *Example 1*—High fashion cocktail dress. Replacement Cost—$200. Life Expectancy—3 years (Table 8–5.) Actual age—30 months (Table 8–6). Condition—Excellent. Adjustment Value—30 per cent or $60. (Table 8–6.)
>
> *Example 2*—Man's leather coat. Replacement Cost—$80. Life Expectancy—5 years. Actual Age—5 months. Condition—Excellent. Adjustment Value—75 per cent or $60.
>
> *Example 3*—Man's wool, slacks. Replacement Cost—$18. Life Expectancy—3 years. Actual Age—60 months. Condition—Poor. Adjustment Value—10 per cent or $1.80.
>
> *Example 4*—Custom-made, lined draperies. Replacement Cost—$250. Life Expectancy—5 years. Actual Age—48 months. Condition—Average. Adjustment Value—20 per cent or $50.

371

Table 8-7

Group I. Esthetic or Sensory Factors, Customer-oriented

Fashion or style rightness
Texture: smooth or rough
Texture: soft or firm
Comfort: coolness or warmth
Sheerness or opacity (compactness)
Drapeability: grace of fold or rigidity
Dimensional stability (resistance to shrinking, stretching, or
  distortion in use)

Group II. Service Properties, Consumer-oriented

Permanence of esthetic properties
Breaking strength
Tear strength
Bursting strength
Weight
Wear or abrasion resistance
Yarn slippage resistance
Seam strength
Crease retention
Wrinkle resistance
Odor resistance
Sun damage resistance
Colorfastness to washing
Colorfastness to sunlight
Colorfastness to cleaning
Colorfastness to crocking
Colorfastness to bleach
Resistance to chlorine retention
Resistance to insects
Resistance to mildew
Resistance to perspiration
Resistance to bacteria
Flammability resistance
Water repellency
Water absorbency

---

displays as well, even to the display of Inaugural Ball gowns worn by our
Nation's first ladies at the Smithsonian Institution in Washington, D.C.

For the most part, these historic costumes have been examples of the
high fashion of each age. We know what the men and women wore, but we

have much less information about the children and generally we do not know why certain designs were selected. There is also little evidence that utility has ever played a major role in fashion changes or developments. The basic aim of fashion change, it has been claimed, is to attract the opposite sex. However, we also must admit that often abrupt change and not gradual development features a new matrix fashion. One must suspect that such revolutionary shifts as changing hems and waistlines, disclosure areas, and other new features have often been brought about through economic pressure. In other words, a radical change is needed in order to give a financial transfusion to a lagging apparel business, despite the fact that at times these changes are not welcomed at first by the women who wear them or by the men who presumably are to find them attractive.

Both men and women now appear on the streets in rather incongruous grab. Certainly, a young man wearing cowboy boots on a city street looks both uncomfortable and foolish, with their narrow pointed toes and their high heels sloping forward so that contact with the ground is almost under the instep. Nor does the 10- to 12-inch-high boot top contribute any useful features on a city street. These boots were designed for strictly utilitarian purposes associated with their daily use by the cowboys of the horse age that predates today's jeep and motor-bike age. The pointed toe and thin sole were designed to fit into the stirrup readily and to slip out easily if the rider were to fall from the saddle. The forward slant and length of the heel were designed for similar purposes—to prevent the stirrup from being caught in the instep of the boot and to prevent the heel from sliding all the way through. The high top of the boot gave additional protection to the leg of the wearer from the brush and branches through which the riders had to go to round up wandering cattle; it also kept the bottom of the rider's jeans from flapping and perhaps from being caught by brush and branches. They were never intended to be comfortable walking boots, as evidenced by the somewhat mincing gait of the cowboy who always walked as if he had sore feet.

In modern society it is rare for street clothing to have much to do with protection. Hazardous tasks, professions, and sports require practical garments. On rare occasions, a utilitarian item may become a fad of brief duration or it may be a fashion item and last for several years. The snood worn by women engaged in war industries during World War II in factories, in repair work, in various trade unions, and in restaurants or lunchrooms later appeared in high fashion as a highly decorated net for long hair.

Fashion and the concept of a new automobile every year are the two most noticeable evidences of "conspicuous consumption," Thorstein Veblen's descriptive qualifications for status in our own society.[4] Until the

---

[4] Thorstein Veblen, *Theory of the Leisure Class* (New York: New American Library, 1954), pp. 60–75.

invention of the sewing machine, women of wealth depended on the skill of many seamstresses to provide them with the voluminous items of clothing associated with the wardrobe of the day. Even when the sewing machine greatly widened the market for fashion within the reach of a larger buying public, the cost of garment construction continued to add considerably to the cost of merchandise.

It is reasonable to foresee future fashion tending to be designed for a specific purpose with comfort, utility, and cost the three predominant factors in selection. It is expected that the next century will probably be marked by an ever-decreasing work week in terms of hours, resulting in more leisure time for all income groups. The so-called everyday wear of working men and women, unless a particularly hazardous job requires special protection, will probably become more comfortable and simple in line and texture and more closely resemble leisure wear. The accelerated demand for the manufactured fibers forecast, Table 2–2, may amount to 75 per cent of our textile consumption by the year 2000. Undoubtedly, it will expand at a more rapid rate as our population multiplies. Costs of natural fibers also will increase and their availability will decrease as we and other nations will require more land for food production and for dwelling areas. Much of the best arable land even now is being used for housing developments, for recreational areas adjacent to our cities, and for highways and air terminals. Truck gardens, dairy farms, and orchards are being turned into suburbs and even into small cities. Newer and faster methods of clothing construction, such as bonded seams, increased simplification in structural form, and greater dependency on multilayered fabrics will lead to simpler design and probably better fit.

Psychological Response to Color

Some color experts have advanced their opinions on the psychological effect of certain colors in our homes. These color observations have nothing to do with shades that might currently be in vogue. It is said, for example, that bright, warm colors tend to cause a measurable increase in heart action, respiration rate, and muscular tension, and to slightly raise blood pressure and brain activity. On the contrary, dim lights and cool colors, particularly blues, have a restful effect; similarly, experts venture the opinion that these same psychological factors should be considered in the effect one wishes to create with one's wearing apparel. If one wishes to attract attention, as so many individuals do, red is advisable. If one wishes to create a feeling of calm and quiet through dress, then blue is advised. Psychologists also advise against the use of green in apparel if one wishes to attract attention. It is said that green suggests the quiet of nature, grass and trees. Regardless of the effect one wishes to create, contrast is said to result in greater attraction than any one over-all ensemble hue. The mixture of white with any of the atmosphere-creating colors seems to enhance the value of the latter as far as attracting attention is concerned; black with red, yellow, or green, is described as a magnified attention-getter.

Individual Response to Color

Faber Birren, a noted researcher in the field of personality responses to color, states that conservative persons have a natural predilection for soft, subdued hues, preferably in the cool range, whereas persons of more dynamic temperament feel most comfortable in clothing and surroundings of brighter colors. To expose either to the opposite environment, either in clothing or surroundings, results, according to Birren, in embarrassment and increased shyness on the part of the retiring personality, and an apparent artificiality in the case of the more emotional one.[5]

One of the conclusions reached on studies of this sort is that when a manufacturer of apparel is seeking colors for his new line, he should consider the seasonal weather. Light exposures and temperature conditions should govern his selection of dyestuffs; that is, the dyestuff with the more appropriate infrared absorption characteristics should be chosen for cold weather, and that with the least amount of infrared absorption should be chosen for summer wear. Similarly, fabrics for different purposes or conditions should be chosen with the comfort of the wearer in mind.

This is a very important application of research. It involves not only the selection of the merchandise, but the color and design of displays, packages, and selling areas. Color affects not only one's outward appearance but one's emotional or inner being as well.

APPAREL CONSUMERSHIP

The term **consumership** connotes a degree of mastery of the problems and risks involved in the efficient selection of and utilization of apparel and other textile products. It involves sound judgment and efficiency. It requires the ability to make the proper selection based on values—some of which defy actual measurement but that clearly identify for one's peers the taste of the individual and his ability to keep certain values in mind in making a selection. Just as certain values in mental capacity or personal habits or abilities determine whether one is a statesman or whether one is qualified in seamanship, consumership has its own set of values. One big difference is that all

[5] Faber Birren, *Light, Color, and Environment* (New York: Van Nostrand Reinhold, 1969), pp. 29–31.

of us are consumers, whereas by comparison few are charged with responsibilities for a career in foreign relations or in operating a vessel at sea or other professional competence.

Were we master of consumership, we would approach the problem of buying apparel—for example, a raincoat—on a truly professional basis and would have in mind certain sets of values. These would, of course, include esthetics, price, size, fiber identification, type of finish applied, and other factors of significance. Some of these various factors are purely esthetic, as we have learned from studying textile finishes. Others are functional and have to do with the performance of the article. For most of us the influence of customer-oriented appeals are the only ones seriously considered in making the original purchase. These are the esthetics—the factors that appeal to our sense of touch, of sight, and of fashion taste. The features provided by functional finishes such as water repellency, fire resistance, shrinkage control, and others entering into the end-use experience are the consumer influences. Most of us do not consider these factors seriously when we make the original purchase, but they do become significant if we are disappointed in the performance of the article. For example, the raincoat may not live up to our expectation as far as rain protection is concerned or it may have shrunk the first time it was cleaned. These failures, and perhaps a loss of some of the esthetic features during successive washings and wearings, cause us to return goods (refer to the fabric properties listed in Table 8–1).

Influences Affecting Customer Selection

The Agricultural Marketing Service of the Market Research Division of the U.S. Department of Agriculture has carried out several research studies on consumer preferences and consumer attitudes toward various fibers for certain apparel items. Most of these are old studies and were conducted before the development of the manufactured fibers. Nevertheless, the general conclusion that it is esthetics that appeal primarily to the customer can be drawn from them. One such study was reported by F. L. Nolan and Daniel B. Levine.[6] This study involved interviewing consumers about an abbreviated list of factors:

1. Ability to hold shape
2. Amount of shrinkage
3. Appearance of the weave

---

[6] F. L. Nolan and Daniel B. Levine, "Consumer's Concepts of Fabrics," Market Research Division, U.S. Department of Agriculture, Washington, D.C., 1959.

4. Colorfastness
5. Degree of sheerness
6. Degree of warmth or coolness
7. Degree to which it will show or pick up soil
8. Degree to which it will wrinkle
9. Durability
10. Ease of pressing or ironing
11. Feel on the skin

It is doubtful if our preferences have shifted much even with our greater technical awareness today.

Knowledge, as well as appreciation, of textile performance is not easily achieved. Names and details of performance challenge even the experienced home economist and store buyer, to say nothing of the salesperson. These goods have been bought for the purpose of pleasing the majority of the buying public who are regular customers of the store. They will not please every customer; they will not satisfy the consumer unless she makes her selections carefully with her own particular needs in view. Whether buying for herself or buying for her family, she can be regarded as the purchasing agent for that unit of our society; and if she is a good purchasing agent, she should buy with the interest of her family in mind, not only in **cost** and in terms of what she expects by way of **performance** but with the idea of **value**.

Definition of Value

A mathematical equation can be set up for the individual consumer if she has the ability and experience to study thoroughly in advance her own habits in use and cleaning; the state of her wardrobe; and her expectations in terms of garment performance. The retail cost of the several garments in which she may be interested as possible additions to her wardrobe or to those of her family members should not be overlooked.

Value can be defined as the degree to which her present needs and wants and particular care requirements are satisfied per dollar retail cost of the various dresses or other articles under consideration. Expressed as an equation, then,

$$(V) \text{ value} = N \text{ (needs)} + W \text{ (wants)} + C \text{ (care)}$$

all divided by D (dollars).

Generally, a **need** is an important requirement the article must meet, or an important role the article must fill in the textile use pattern of the individual person or family. A **want** is something secondary; it is desirable but not imperative. **Care** involves method of cleansing, potential frequency of cleansing, ease of ironing, color permanence, and any special storage or care conditions required by the material or article.

As an example of this calculation, let us assume that a college freshman in home economics is considering the purchase of a light blue dress, primarily for afternoon parties or for trips to town, but suitable also to wear to class on occasion. It should be a dress that will be comfortable in comparatively warm weather such as in late spring and early fall. The style must be suitable for this college freshman, but she might also need to take into account the possibility that it will be used by her younger sister who, at present, is somewhat heavier than she is, although both can wear the same size. The selection has come down to two dresses: an all-cotton poplin, rather loosely fitting dress at $19.95, and a more sheer, polyester and cotton blend, sheath type at $29.95. From the needs, or primarily requirements, this girl selects appearance, style, size, drapeability, general utility, durability, crease retention, and sheerness as her bases of selection. Among the wants, or secondary factors, to be considered are the coordination of each dress in terms of her wardrobe, the trimming, the workmanship observed, potential resistance to soiling, retention of dimensions, colorfastness to light, the presence of a standards label, comfort, and the hand-me-down potential of each dress. In terms of care, the washability of the fabric, the possibility of removing trimming, and the ease of ironing are the three important factors. She draws up Table 8–8.

Taking the totals of needs, wants, and care for each dress and dividing by the appropriate dollar values, the equation for the all-cotton dress is

$$V = (70 + 78 + 24)/20 \text{ or } 8.6$$

The second dress has as its equation

$$V = (77 + 80 + 30)/30 \text{ or } 6.2$$

(Note that the dollar values have been rounded out to the nearest whole dollar for ease of calculation.) These differences are well within the error of estimation on the part of the shopper. The lower-priced dress is the higher value in terms of the money this young lady has to spend.

Treating the three analytical categories separately, the shopper may be better able to evaluate her own buying patterns and habits than if all three are added together. It may be that an individual will find that the wants, or the special care requirements, are of much less importance than the needs, and she can assign her own private weighing or significance to these other two analytical summations.

Perhaps a more experienced shopper than this college freshman would have put considerable trust in the name of the manufacturer if she had had experience with garments made by the firm. She might also have had experience with the polyester-cotton blend. The college freshman may well

Table 8-8   Concept of Value*

Value = (Needs + Wants + Care)/Dollars

	Cotton	Blend
Needs		
Color	10	10
Style	8	10
Appearance	10	10
Drape	10	10
Utility	10	7
Durable-press	7	10
Crease retention	7	10
Sheerness	8	10
	—	—
	70	77
Wants		
Coordination	10	8
Workmanship	8	10
Soil resistance	7	10
Standards label	10	8
Comfort	8	10
Hand-me-down	8	6
Shrinkage resistance	7	10
Colorfastness to light	10	8
Trimming	10	10
	—	—
	78	80
Care		
Washability (labels)	8	10
Ease of ironing	8	10
Trim removal	8	10
	—	—
	24	30
Total	172	187

* Rank (10–0).

have misjudged the quality of the trimming on the two garments; perhaps that on the more expensive dress was not as good. It is possible, too, that in her generosity she gave too great a penalty to the $29.95 dress for its more limited hand-me-down features.

Relationship of Quality to Price

Arlee Galen and Rachel Dardis[7] at Cornell University conducted an evaluation of 10 white, short-sleeved shirts that represented the production of 4 manufacturers and 6 distributors. These shirts varied in retail price from $3 to $8.50, the majority being approximately $5 in price. Their data indicate that, quality, in terms of fabric durability and performance, bore little relationship to price. However, when garment construction was taken into account, then there was a much more definite relationship between price and consumer satisfaction. It was an intensive test involving as many as 80 washings and wearings.

It would appear that other departments of home economics might well conduct similar tests on other items of apparel, because one of the protective shelters into which consumers have often fled is the belief that the higher the price the more durable and better the quality. Admittedly, such studies would be more complex today, with the variety of fiber compositions, types of finish, and varying functional demands—all of which would have an influence on the price of the finished apparel.

When similar studies were made on various types of apparel by the Kaufmann Department Store Fellowship at Mellon Institute, the same situation existed, even though at the time the most common fiber in the items studied was cotton. Resources were explored from which such articles as men's shirts, children's wear, undergarments, and similar staples for Own Brand promotion could be purchased at several different price levels. In a rather rough estimate, arrived at over many such tests involving both laboratory techniques and wear tests with frequent observations, the maximum performance in terms of durability generally was found at a price about two thirds of the way between the most inexpensive article in the department and the most expensive. The general observation was that fabrics of lower count and less durability were found in the lower-price bracket; in the higher-price bracket, finer and more delicate yarns and fabric constructions again brought about a decrease in strength and durability. But construction refinements and detail were more marked in the higher-priced merchandise, so that, from the standpoint of esthetics, they did give superior value.

Outer-wear Comfort Protection

When we listen to a weather report, we are given not only the temperature recording for the day, but also the wind velocity and sometimes a rather

---

[7] Arlee Galen and Rachel Dardis, "Predicting Product Performance by Price," *Textile Chemist and Colorist*, **2**, 10 (May 20, 1970), pp. 159–63.

mysterious factor identified as the wind-chill temperature. Research scientists from the United States Weather Bureau and other laboratories interested in weather extremes have developed a technique by which the rate of chilling a heated material or person protected by various textile materials is affected by a combination of the room temperature and the amount of air blown against the object. For example, if one is out-of-doors in an air temperature of 10°F, the wind-chill temperature is −9° at a wind speed of 10 miles per hour. If the wind speed increases to 20 miles per hour, the chill effect would be equivalent to 24° below zero. (See Table 8–9.) It is this wind chill that guided our armed forces to revolutionize its cold-weather garb during World War II by using the layer principle. Prior to that, man's effort had been to pile on more and heavier protective clothing in order to keep warm. In the layer principle the outer garment fabric generally is a closely woven lightweight material that prevents the entry of chilling wind; the undergarment has sufficient insulating material to retain the body heat. The Eskimo developed this same principle in his clothing. The seal skin and other hair or fur-bearing pelts are worn with the hair side toward the body to hold warm air. The vapor-impermeable leather surface is on the outside.

The term "**clo**" is used as a unit of insulation and is defined by F. H. Newburgh as follows:

The clo is a unit of insulation and is the amount of insulation necessary to maintain comfort and a mean skin temperature of 92°F in a room at 70°F

Table 8-9   Wind-chill Index*

Wind Speed (mph)	Actual Thermometer Reading (°F)						
	30	20	10	0	−10	−20	−30
	Equivalent Temperature						
Calm	30	20	10	0	−10	−20	−30
5	27	16	7	−6	−15	−26	−35
10	16	2	−9	−22	−31	−45	−58
15	11	−6	−18	−33	−45	−60	−70
20	3	−9	−24	−40	−52	−68	−81
25	0	−15	−29	−45	−58	−75	−89
30	−2	−18	−33	−49	−63	−78	−94
35	−4	−20	−35	−52	−67	−83	−98
40	−4	−22	−36	−54	−69	−87	−101

* To find the wind-chill temperature locate the actual temperature in the top row and the wind speed in the left-hand column. The equivalent (wind chill) temperature is found where these two intersect. For example, with a temperature of 10° and wind speed of 10 mph, the wind-chill temperature is −9°.

with air movement not over 10 feet per minute, humidity not over 50 per cent, with a metabolism of 50 calories per square meter per hour.[8]

Thus, it is obviously both a physiological and engineering term. In a very simplified concept of comfort, it may be said that several factors must be taken into account.

1. The protective clothing layer close to the body of the wearer must have ample fiber surface to trap air; that is to say, it must hold the body-heated air. Wool has an advantage here in that it does not pack down and close the voids holding air.
2. An outer shell or windbreaker prevents the inflow of cold air and the escape of body-heated air.
3. Body moisture must be allowed to escape from the skin surface to avoid frost accumulation.
4. Protecting of the face and extremities from cold prevents the leakage of metabolic heat. The Eskimo does this with the furry rim from his headpiece about his face.

H. S. Belding reports that 4.3 clos will protect a sleeping man indefinitely at 50°F. If there is no wind, 81 per cent of this must be provided by the bedding. If there is a 12-mile per hour wind, 95 per cent must be provided by the bedding.[9]

HOUSEHOLD TEXTILES

Traditionally, furnishing fabrics have fallen into three broad classifications: **domestics**, or utility fabrics, including towels and other textiles used in the bath; table "linens," bedding, sheets, blankets, and spreads; **home furnishings**, principally floor- and furniture-covering fabrics; and **decorative** textiles, such as curtains and draperies. These distinctions are not universal and in many stores separate departments are set up for each category. However, the same fabric may be found in more than one broad classification. For example, the same fabric may be used in draperies and to slip cover overstuffed furniture; some tufted carpet and rug constructions are used not only on the floor but also as a decorative and sound absorbing wall covering.

Upon entering a store with which they are not familiar, many older consumers will ask for the location of the several categories of domestic textile products as "linens," meaning towels, table linens, bed linens, or blankets.

[8] F. H. Newburgh, *The Physiology of Heat Regulation and the Science of Clothing* (Philadelphia: W. B. Saunders Company, 1949).
[9] H. S. Belding, ibid.

The latter are generally adjacent to departments selling bedspreads, pillows, and other bed supplies.

Towels and Toweling

The well-appointed bathroom or powder room will have an adequate supply of guest towels, sometimes referred to as face towels. These are generally made of cotton, of blends of cotton, or with rayon or polyester. However, they may be made of linen, or linen and cotton mixtures, linen being preferred because of its lower lint-carrying ability. Some of the finer-textured towels have added luster, which is achieved by blending fibers with rayon. These towels may be woven in a diamond pattern, which is often referred to as the honeycomb or huckaback weave. Characteristic of this fabric is the fact that the yarns are given a low twist; this results in a relatively soft but very absorbent fabric. Much of the quality depends on the way in which the towels have been hemmed. This can be done at home, or they can be purchased already hemmed. Huck towels are available in a variety of sizes such as 17 × 32, 18 × 32, 18 × 34, and 18 × 36 inches. The fabric can also be purchased as yardage in 18-inch widths.

TERRY TOWELS AND WASHCLOTHS   The terry cloth is a characteristic weave of the turkish bath towel. There are numerous well-known brand names in the terry cloth field, but the brand name alone without specifications or manufacturing details does not tell one the full story of what the quality of a towel is—even though the primary purpose of each is rapid moisture absorbency. There is a rigid standard for terry towels in the L-22 standard. It is not unusual for a manufacturer to produce twenty or more different terry towels, when one considers such variables as basic fabric construction, height and density of the loops, and changes in the dimensions of the towels. The purpose of the loops, of course, is to provide as much loosely twisted yarn volume as possible within the area of the towel. The looser and softer the terry loops, the more rapid will be the moisture absorbency; at the same time, the greater the number of piles or loops per square inch, the higher the total water-capacity rating of the towel will be. Therefore, more expensive towels usually have a longer pile, or longer terry loops. These are, however, somewhat more fragile than the shorter loops, because they can be caught and pulled loose more easily. Short loops tend to make the fabric seem scratchy, and they reduce its capacity to hold water. The poorer grades of terry are made with a single thread in each loop, in contrast to the better grades, which have a double-thread construction in which each loop has been made with two parallel threads. These threads are virtually without twist, for greater absorbency. The selvage on towels should be firm, and the filling yarns should bind the warps to the finished edge of the selvage. The selvage wear of terry towels can be improved by increasing abrasion resistance; some manufacturers reinforce their products with polyester yarn in the selvage. Decorative polyester and Mylar metallic yarns are used in some terry towels as well as in huck towels. (The polyester fibers and polymers are preferred because they are color-fast to the vat dyes used in the dyeing of the towels.) Other decorative effects are patterned or colored borders or stripes; solid colors, printed or woven in an all-over pattern and with matching washcloths and guest towels coordinate the bathroom ensemble. The finest quality towels are made on the Jacquard loom and are decorated by weaving complicated figures.

The sizes of towels vary greatly. The usual face towel sizes are 16 × 28 and 18 × 36 inches; medium bath sizes are 20 × 40 and 22 × 44 inches; and oversized bath towels are 24 × 48 and 32 × 64 inches. Beach towels, bath sheets, and terry for beach robes and for bathrobes are much larger in size. A fairly high amount of shrinkage in terry towels is to be expected, reaching as much as 14 to 15 per cent in some cases. If the towel is large enough, the shrinkage will not interfere with serviceability. However, uneven edges and a greater shrinkage in decorative stripes are very unsightly, causing ripples down the sides or across the ends of towels. Terry towels should never be ironed as they are much fluffier, more absorbent, and more attractive when they have been tumble-dried, despite the fact that this drying method does contribute to shrinkage. One must remember that the bold dark colors are less fast in washing than lighter shades; there may be a gradual loss of color depth over a period of time, especially if these towels are washed at a high temperature. Dark-colored towels should be rotated in use so that the color loss in washing is equalized. Colored towels should never be exposed to chlorine bleach or drying outdoors in the sun.

DISH TOWELING Among the several requisites for a satisfactory towel for drying dishes, and glassware especially, is a high count in proper balance so that the fabric will absorb as much moisture as possible and its strength will be the same in both directions. Thus, linen is generally preferred, but cotton is also acceptable. Some of the most common linen and cotton fabrics used for dishes are **crash**, a plain-weave fabric; **damask**, a Jacquard-loomed fabric; terry cloth; **glass cloth**, cotton with a hard twisted yarn comparatively free from linting; **cottonade**, somewhat resembling woolens in weave; and **Osnaburg**, a strong plain-weave fabric of very coarse yarns. Nonwovens are strongly competitive in this field; they have good wet and dry strength and enjoy the further advantage of eliminating linting. An interesting combination of asbestos with cotton in the proportion of 80 per cent cotton to 20 per cent asbestos has been marketed under the name **Carosel** and is manufactured by the United States Rubber Company.

Viscose rayon alone or blended with cotton or linen has become increasingly important in the dishtowel field because of its resistance to linting. In addition to softness and evenness, rayon contributes high luster and has good moisture absorbency. Towels of 100 per cent rayon have proved to be very satisfactory. One objection is the tendency of the fibers to shrink lengthwise as they swell with water. Because these fibers are notably hydrophilic, the towels may shrink as much as 10 per cent in length when wet. Much of this, however, is restored when the towels are ironed, especially with a lengthwise tension. The L-22 standard on towels made of rayon requires that the maximum permanent lengthwise shrinkage not exceed 8 to 10 per cent.

Shower Curtains

Shower curtains generally represent the center of color and pattern interest in the bathroom—although the modern trend is more and more to correlate them with the coloring of the walls, whether these be of tile or of another washable surface. Some shower curtains are simply sheets of plastic or rubber; others have the sheeting placed over a textile fabric base. Still others are of a woven fabric that has been given a satisfactory permanent water-repellent finish. Some of the fabrics used either alone or in combination with a water-impermeable layer are ducks, taffetas, and satins. The standard curtain size is 70 × 70 inches and may be sold alone or together with a small-sized window curtain of matching material. This imposes the extra demand on the material of sunfastness for window exposure.

Table Linens

In fine table damasks, linen is still the preferred fiber for dining room use because of its increased luster and appearance through many years of service. These qualities have been described previously in some detail in Jacquard weave. Other fibers are found in more casual use, such as in bridge table covers, the standard size being 34 × 36 inches. Other table settings may be of linen, crash, lace, or embroidery; sets of runners or placemats may be used, runners being 18 × 36 or 18 × 72 inches, and placemats generally 12 × 18 or 14 × 20 inches. Small matching napkins are usually available. Informal entertaining and the cost of laundering, even of a durable-press fabric, have brought about the wide use of nonwoven covers. Paper or paperlike fabric napkins have almost completely replaced fabric napkins.

Bed Sheets

Woven sheets have long been an example of practically a 100 per cent one-fiber product, and cotton accounted for almost all of the bed sheets used in homes in America. Linen sheets are smooth and comfortable but are very high-priced and are distinctly a luxury item found in few homes. From time to time, attempts have been made to promote rayon or nylon sheets, but the reaction of the public has been unfavorable: they are too warm; the bed covers slip off of them; and, over a period of time, the nylons tend to discolor in laundering, becoming grey or yellow looking. Nonwoven sheets are widely used, especially by institutions, such as hospitals.

The new competition to 100 per cent cotton sheets is in polyester-cotton blends for durable-press. In a recent fall and winter Sears catalog, the following sheet types were shown:

50:50 polyester/cotton	128 muslin	white, solid colors, prints
50:50 polyester/cotton	180 percale	white, solid colors, prints
100 per cent cotton	128 muslin	white
100 per cent cotton	180 percale	white, solid colors, prints

In a recent fall and winter Penney's catalog, the following sheet types were shown:

50:50 polyester/cotton	130 muslin	white, solid colors, prints
50:50 polyester/cotton	180 percale	white, solid colors, prints
100 per cent cotton	133 muslin	white
100 per cent cotton	186 percale	white

This indication will be confirmed by the inspection of the bed sheet department in any large department store; it shows a strong trend toward the durable-press sheets. Some people have predicted that one day it may become as hard to find an all-cotton white sheet as it is to find 100 per cent cotton shirts.

It was reported that the noncellulosic fiber consumption for sheets and sheeting rose from 0.5 million pounds in 1964 to 86.4 million pounds in 1970. In this same year, the cotton consumption for sheets and sheeting was 464.3 and 444.2 million pounds, respectively.[10]

Bed sheets and sheeting were the first of the consumer products for which a voluntary standard was adopted by distributors and consumers (see Table 8–10). This standard defines four types of sheeting in terms of the number of yarns per square inch. Sheets are of plain weave and have been previously referred to in the discussion of this weave where the advantage of a fabric balance was emphasized. Thus, when the type is expressed in number of yarns per square inch, such as type 128 (lightweight muslin),

[10] *Textile Organon,* **44,** No. 11 (Nov. 1971).

type 140 (heavy muslin), type 180 (utility percale), or type 200 (fine percale), the figure represents the total of warp and filling threads per square inch. The closer the actual count is to an equal number in both directions, such as 64 × 64 for type 128, 90 × 90 in the percale, or type 180, for example, the more even will be the strength of the sheet in both directions unless there is a distinct disparity in the size of yarns. Usually such differences are avoided for the reason that the sheet must be uniform in appearance if it is to appeal to the consumer.

Table 8-10   Count Standards for Sheets and Sheeting

	Type 128, Carded Yarns	Type 140, Carded Yarns	Type 180, Combed or Carded Yarns	Type 200, Combed Yarns
Combined thread count, warp and filling	128	140	180	200
Warp breaking strength, pounds	55	70	60	60
Filling breaking strength pounds	55	70	60	60
Maximum adding sizing, per cent	6	4	2	1
Weight, ounces per square yard	4	4.6	3.6	3.6

As a general rule, the warp and filling counts will not differ in the sheet by more than 10 per cent; thus, a 60 × 60 count would be too low arithmetically for a type 128 and would not be accepted; the difference in count would be too much. On the other hand, the 61 × 67 would barely pass. Another safeguard in this standard is that the breaking strength in terms of pounds per inch (minimum breaking strength by grab test) for the type 128 muslin is 55 pounds in the weaker direction; for type 140, it is 70 pounds. As for the combed or carded type 180 percale, a strength of 60 pounds is required, and in the combed type 200, 60 pounds is required for the weaker direction.

Another set of sheet standards is that of dimensions for the various sizes of beds most commonly used in the United States. These dimensions are in terms of torn length of sheet and make allowance for a 1-inch turnover at the foot and a 3- or 4-inch turnover for hemming at the top of the sheet. Thus, the actual sheet length will be 5 inches shorter than the torn length. It should also be mentioned that some manufacturers use the same hem size

Table 8-11   Sheet Sizes (in inches)

Bed	Mattress Size	Flat Sheets	Fitted Bottom Sheets
Crib	27 × 52	42 or 45 × 77	Crib
Youth	33 × 66	54 × 90, 99	Youth
		63 × 99, 108	
Studio or day bed	33 × 74–76	63 × 104, 108	Day bed
		72 × 104, 108, 113	
Twin	39 × 75–76	72 × 104, 108, 113	Twin
Extra-long twin	39 × 80	72 × 115, 117, 120	Extra-long twin
Single	36 × 75–76	72 × 104, 108, 113	Single
Three quarter	48 × 74–76	72 × 108, 113	¾ or sofa bed
Sofa bed	48 × 76	72 × 108, 113	¾ or sofa bed
Double or full	54 × 76	81 × 104, 108, 113	Double
		90 × 104, 108, 113	
Extra-long double or full	54 × 80	81 × 115, 117, 120	Extra-long double or full
		90 × 115, 117, 120	
Queen	60 × 80	90 × 115, 120	Queen
California king	72–75 × 84	108 × 113, 115	California king
		108 × 120	
Hollywood (2 twins forming 1 bed)	78 × 76	108 × 115, 120	Hollywood
King	78 × 80	108 × 126	King
Foam Rubber			
Twin	39 × 76	See twin above	Twin for foam rubber
Double	54 × 76	See double above	Double for foam rubber

SOURCE: From Wamsutta Mills, 1972.

at both ends, sometimes a 2- or sometimes a 3-inch turnover. Sheet sizes are listed in Table 8–11.

The size of the sheet to be selected should be adequate to provide a firm placement of the sheet with enough material at the sides, top, and bottom to be turned under the mattress. A skimpy sheet requires too much pulling and tugging, with the danger of tearing after the sheet has been laundered repeatedly and lost a significant amount of its original strength. The principal wear area of a sheet is at the shoulder level.

An average double mattress is 75 × 54 × 4 inches thick, but double mattresses are standardized at 11 inches in thickness, and the average sheet is 108 inches in length, torn length for adequate fitting lengthwise. This would require 75 inches plus 26 inches of turnover for the bottom sheet for both ends for mattress thickness and turnunder, plus a shrinkage allowance of 2 inches (usually preshrunk to 2 per cent), plus hems of 5 inches, sufficient fabric to give a minimal turnunder at each end. Extra-sized beds, such as queen or king sizes, require extrasized sheets in order to provide the same fit surpluses. Generally, the top sheet is tucked under approximately 7 inches at the lower end and the upper or head end folds over the blanket in order to protect it from edge wear during the night. The total top-sheet foldover is usually about 18 inches.

Fitted sheets, or **contour** sheets, which are made of manufactured fibers, either alone or in blends, or of cotton sheeting with a resin treatment, rarely require ironing. Further, this kind of sheet eases the task of bedmaking because the sheet is formed to fit over the mattress and to accommodate the shape of the mattress smoothly. These nonshrinking sheets are available also in durable-press.

These same fabrics are available for pillow cases (see Table 8–12). The standard hem size for pillow cases is 3 inches and, as in heavier sheets, the stitches are 14 to the inch.

Table 8-12   Pillow-case Sizes (in inches)

Size of Pillow	Size of Pillow Case
20 × 26	42 × 36 or 42 × 38½
20 × 28	42 × 38½
22 × 28 (standard size)	45 × 36 or 45 × 38½
22 × 30	45 × 40½

Blankets

It is recognized that a well-insulated house is cool in summer and warm in winter. The insulating capacity of the materials stuffed into the walls and laid under the roof depends greatly on the amount of air enmeshed in the spaces between the fibers or within the hollow cells. This trapped air acts as a barrier to the rapid passage of heat through the insulating material. It prevents the sun's heat from warming the house in summer and delays the escape of the furnace heat into the outside air in winter. In a similar manner, the warmth of a blanket depends on the air retained in its finely napped construction; a blanket does not add warmth, it retains it. Tests have proved that an equally heavy felted blanket is not as warm as a napped blanket. A well-napped cotton blanket, when new, retains heat well, but the fibers are not as springy as wool; after repeated launderings, the air spaces are gradually reduced by the flattening of the fabric and the warmth-retention decreases. Blankets of crimped nylon, acrylics, and other synthetic fibers retain their napped structure longer than do cellulosic fibers, but not as long as wool.

Blankets are purchased less frequently than most other staple articles, but their selection is of great importance. Firm, dense blankets are quite expensive; all-wool blankets range in price from $7.50 to $28.00, the synthetics are slightly lower. When a customer buys a blanket, she is interested in warmth, weight, durability, attractiveness, and price. Selection will depend on the order of importance of these factors as far as specific needs are concerned. If the greatest amount of warmth combined with comfort is the primary concern, a lightweight all-wool blanket or one of synthetic fiber will be selected. If a moderate price is of special importance, an all-cotton blanket or a cotton-wool mixture may be chosen. Whatever the choice, knowledge of the characteristics of the fibers and of the desirable qualities of blankets will aid the potential customer. (For blanket sizes see Table 8–13.)

Lower-priced blankets are produced by some of the newer and faster construction methods, including Malipol, the multilayer pile machine, and tufting. These do not have the warmth retention of the conventional blanket.

Wool blankets are woven of yarns in which the individual fibers are loosely gathered together with very little twist, so the random fibers will hold more air. The yarn count in the warp and filling must be well balanced—that is, of approximately the same number of yarns to the inch. The warp yarns must be strong in order to withstand the friction and tension of weaving. The filling yarns are made loose and then are rendered still fuzzier by pulling or napping with teazle burrs or fine wire brushes. The well-napped blanket offers a construction characterized by a great deal of air-holding capacity.

With these construction facts in mind, the several factors influencing the customer's choice will be elaborated on here.

WARMTH   A fabric with an open weave permits cold air to pass through it quickly. If the fabric is so constructed that a considerable amount of air is enmeshed between the fibers, the cold air from the outside will pass through so slowly that it will be warmed before it reaches the body. Thus, the blanket with the greater air-holding capacity is the warmer one.

COMFORT   Warmth and comfort are not synonymous. A heavy, felted blanket may have sufficient warmth, but it will not feel comfortable to the person under it. The lighter the blanket, the more comfortable it is. A lightweight all-wool blanket, properly napped, is warmer than a heavy blanket. The use of electric blankets is increasing over that of heavy blankets because

Table 8-13   Bed and Blanket Sizes (in inches)

Bed	Width of Bed	Width of Blanket	Total Allowance	Allowance at Each Side
Double	54	66	12	6
Double	54	70	16	8
Double	54	72	18	9
Double	54	80	26	13
Twin	39	54	15	7.5
Twin	39	60	21	10.5
Twin	39	66	27	13.5
Single	36	54	18	9
Single	36	60	24	12
Single	36	66	30	15
Narrow single or day bed	33	54	21	10.5
Narrow single or day bed	33	60	27	13.5
Day bed or cot	30	54	24	12
Day bed or cot	30	60	30	15

Length of Bed	Length of Mattress	Length of Blanket	Total Allowance
78	76	76	0
78	76	80	4
78	76	84	8
78	76	90	14
72	70	76	6
72	70	80	10
72	70	84	14

they are lightweight and are effective without placing a heavy, restricting weight on the sleeper. A well-napped cotton blanket is warmer than a felted wool blanket of the same weight because it has greater air capacity. The extent to which the blanket can be napped depends on the looseness of the twist of the filling yarns, the strength of the core around which the loose fibers are loosely twisted, and the amount of napping which can be done without weakening the filling yarns beyond serviceable limit.

Another factor influencing comfort is the moisture-absorbing capacity of the fiber itself. Wool can hold as much as 30 per cent of its own weight of moisture without its feeling wet and cold. Cotton can hold much less water and will feel damp in wet weather. The synthetics hold practically no moisture and would give little protection as out-of-door bed covers and would feel clammy in humid weather.

DURABILITY   Whatever the yarn composition may be, there are certain factors that govern the durability and serviceability of a blanket.

1. *Length of fibers.*   Short fibers pull out easily. The napping process may have worked the fibers loose and actually weakened the filling yarn. Long fibers are more securely caught in the yarns and will not slip or pull out readily. Cotton fibers pull out more easily than wool. Always pinch some of the nap between the thumb and forefinger when lifting a blanket; the nap should not pull out even when the weight of the blanket is suspended.

2. *Tensile strength of fibers.*   Weak or brittle fibers will break off during use and during washing. It is important that strong fibers be used in blankets. The strength of individual fibers varies over a wide range.

3. *Yarn tensile strength.*   The warp yarns must be strong enough to withstand the tension in the loom and be compact enough to withstand the friction during weaving. Warp yarns are often multi-ply; that is, two or more yarns are twisted together to form the warp yarn. The filling yarns are made looser so that the nap can be brushed up easily.

4. *Construction.*   A balanced fabric having an even distribution of warp and filling yarns is desirable for long wear. A loosely woven blanket that has been excessively napped in order to make it look firm and compact is much too weak for good service and washability. There will not be enough yarns to give adequate strength, and the chances are that the filling will have been weakened still further during the raising of the profuse nap. The minimum strength for the warp and filling, respectively, should be 30 and 20 pounds. A good idea of the closeness of the weave can be judged by looking through the blanket with a bright light on the other side.

SIZE   The matter of the proper size of the blanket affects both its comfort and its durability. Too small a blanket does not adequately protect the sleeper in cold weather. In addition to that, it is subjected to excessive pulling in order to be tucked in at the foot and sides or to cover the shoulders of the sleeper.

There are eight standard sizes recommended for blankets: 60 × 80; 60 × 84; 60 × 90; 66 × 80; 70 × 80; 72 × 84; 72 × 90; and 80 × 90.

FIBER IDENTITY—LABELING   The labeling of wool or wool-blended blankets falls under the Wool Products Labeling Act. Accordingly, the Federal Trade Commission has ruled that if a blanket contains less than 5 per cent wool, the finished blankets cannot carry the word *wool*. Blankets bearing the word *wool* must be labeled as follows:

1. Fiber content must be listed, with wool described accurately as reprocessed or reused.
2. A blanket of above 98 per cent wool can be labeled "All Wool."
3. The label "Virgin Wool" means that only new wool (not previously used in a fabric) is contained in the blanket.

The Wool Product Law (1941) forced the labelers of wool fabrics into giving the content of reprocessed and reused wool. The labeling of other blankets is covered by TFPI.

APPEARANCE   A fine grade of virgin wool is lustrous and clear in appearance, and the colors are uniform and clear. A delicate pastel shade is usually more pleasing than a bright, glaring color. The finishing of the ends is a factor influencing the blanket's appearance. A binding of taffeta, nylon, or rayon satin remains bright even after repeated washings, but it must be washed with care. Acetates may gradually change color due to contact with the wool. Mercerized cotton sateen is strong and durable but tends to become dull. A blanket-stitched edge is practical and inexpensive.

Table 8–14 shows the USA standard for the performance of woven blankets.

CARE OF BLANKETS   No matter how well made an article is or how carefully it was selected, it cannot be considered to be serviceable unless it can be cleaned without loss of strength or impairment of its appearance. Blankets are no exception, but they must be cleaned and cared for according to definite methods because of the nature of the fibers and construction of the cloth.

Blankets can be dry-cleaned or washed. In washing blankets, it is necessary to avoid heat, excessive manipulation while wet, and too great pressure. Abundant lukewarm suds of neutral soap should be used. The blanket should be washed quickly with as little manipulation as possible; it should never be twisted, rubbed, or wrung. The suds should be squeezed out without twisting, and the blanket thoroughly rinsed twice in lukewarm water. Excess water should be squeezed out. Wet blankets must be carefully hung to dry in the shade; it is advisable to lay the blanket across two parallel lines; it should be shaken gently while it is drying. The household dryer can be used for blankets if a single blanket is cycled at a time; the blanket should be removed from the dryer before it is absolutely dry. This method avoids wrinkles from the tumbling of the blanket. The binding should be stretched flat after the blanket is dry and then ironed at the appropriate temperature for the binding fiber. The nap can be fluffed up by gently brushing with a soft brush.

Blankets must be cleaned before being stored. Moths are attracted to dirty woolens. Pack blankets rather loosely in a mothproofed drawer or box. A handful of paradichlorobenzene thrown on top of stored woolens affords good protection against moth damage if the container is kept closed.

THE ROLE OF SYNTHETICS IN BLANKETS   As we have seen, wool has been a natural fiber for blankets in almost every sense of the term, and yet there are certain disadvantages to the fiber that cannot be minimized. First, the problem of insect damage requires special storage conditions; these necessitate some extra care provisions on the part of a consumer. In certain climates wool mildews, again requiring special care. Probably, the principal disadvantage is in the tendency of wool blankets to shrink. This is a continuing problem in spite of the shrinkproof treatments that can be given to wool and wool fabrics. These treatments are almost inevitably accompanied by a slight harshening of the fiber, and the blanket will not have the same degree of softness and luxury one associates with a really fine blanket fabric. Lower-priced wool blankets may not have the fibers fully bleached and thus do not produce the clean, rich-looking pastel shades now so popular in blankets made of the synthetic fibers.

All blanket manufacturers produce several grades of blanketing materials, and even those depending primarily on wool for their quality blankets do make cheaper lines with rayon blended with nylon or an acrylic fiber. These give excellent thermal properties, bright colors, dimensional stability in washing, and lightness in weight. Blankets can be made of almost any of the more common synthetic fiber fabrics: nylons, polyesters, acryilcs, modacrylics, and others. Because they are staple fibers and can be processed like wool, they require no great amount of change in manufacturing. Furthermore, the fibers are uniform, much more so than in the case of natural products, as we have already seen. The pricing of the synthetic fibers is subject to less variation and manipulation than that of the natural fibers, and it can be depended on for a year or more in advance, thus enabling the manufacturer to calculate his costs closely. When one combines the inherent advantages possessed by the synthetics, there is little wonder that these fibers, especially the acrylics, have met the competition of quality wool blankets head-on. They have gone into the field of highest quality, rather than working up through lower grades into the top price ranges. The brightness of color, especially of the pastels, possessed by these acrylics cannot be matched by wool. In addition to that, the fibers retain their loftiness in the nap; thus, their thermal properties are maintained to a high degree. There is no tendency to shrink or full. (Fulling in this sense means that fibers mat and stick together.) Insects cannot damage them, nor are they subject to mildew attack. Their tensile strength is fully equal to that of wool. Being somewhat bulkier than wool, the actual fiber weight of a blanket of the same nap height and apparent density is lower in the case of the synthetic. Static electricity is still a problem, however; also, these synthetic fiber blankets are not as good protection as wool when used out-of-doors or at camps or lodges when the room or ambient conditions are low in temperature and high in humidity. In these circumstances, wool will out-perform the synthetics, if one is to translate the fiber properties into the physical performance of the fabric. No test figures have been seen, however, to substantiate this theory. The thermoplasticity of these fibers should affect only those who are foolish enough to smoke in bed and run the risk of burning holes in the blanket. There is deep concern about the flammability of rayon blankets and one of the consumer advisory organizations, Consumers Union, issued a warning on this in February 1971.

ELECTRIC BLANKETS   The electric blanket, first considered to be a luxury item for the affluent customer of advanced age, has become a widely sold type of blanket, especially in competition with all-wool blankets of good quality. The price differential is not great. The electric blanket possesses one great advantage over wool in conventional blanket structure—it is light in weight without sacrificing warmth to the sleeper. These blanket structures are open in weave, have a very short nap, and afford controllable comfort. Some blankets have double controls so that in a double bed the degree of heat can be controlled on each side. Man-made fibers are widely used in this type of blanket—nylon, acetate, acrylics, and modacrylics have all been utilized. There are also some of rayon. In using these blankets, it is good practice to use another sheet on the bed on the top of the blanket to help protect against abrasion (the nap will wear away under rubbing). According to the Duquesne Light Company of Pittsburgh, these blankets consume about 120 watts of electricity—20 per cent more than a 100-watt electric light.

The temperature control element should be removed before washing the blanket in relatively cool water. No damage will be done to a sound heating wire system by washing. Dry-cleaning, however, will affect the plastic- or rubber-coated wires.

COMFORTERS   Quilted bed covers stuffed with soft filling materials, such as cotton linters, wool down, feathers, or manufactured fiber staple, are often referred to as **comforters**. These are soft, very lightweight covering materials that keep the bed occupant warm in cold weather. They are generally less restrictive than blankets but give comparable protection. They should be buoyant and resilient, otherwise the filling materials tend to mat and lump-up over a period of time. For this reason, long-staple cotton filling is used instead of linters and is actually superior to inferior short fibers of reused wool. Another source of cheap wool is the waste from slivers. Feather down is the softest and lightest filling material and is the most expensive. The breast feathers from the eider, a sea duck, have traditionally been the choice

Table 8-14   USA Standard Performance Requirements for Woven Household Blanket Fabrics

Property		Minimum Requirements			Test Method See Part VII*
	Identification:	L-22.30.4-C Washable 120 F No Bleach	L-22.30.4-H Washable 105 F No Bleach	L-22.30.4-D Dry-cleanable	
Breaking strength					
6.5 oz/sq yd and under dry and wet (see note 1)		25 lb	25 lb	25 lb	USAS L-14.184 Grab Test (ASTM D 1682)
Over 6.5 oz/sq yd					
Dry (See note 1)		15 lb	15 lb	15 lb	
Wet		20 lb	20 lb	20 lb	USAS L-14.138 (AATCC 96) (ASTM D 1905) Table II
Maximum dimensional change—each direction (see note 2)		5 per cent	5 per cent	2 per cent	Test No. II Test No. I
Odor		Class 3	Class 3	Class 3	AATCC 108
Colorfastness to					
Atmospheric fading after					
Washing (see note 3)		Class 4	Class 4		TDI No. 3
Dry cleaning (see note 3)				Class 4	USAS L-14.54 (1 cycle) (AATCC 23)
Laundering		Test IIA	Test IA		
Alteration in shade		Class 4	Class 4		USAS L-14.81 (AATCC 61)
Staining		Class 3 (see note 4)	Class 4		International Gray Scale

				Test method*
Dry-cleaning (see note 5)	Class 4	Class 4	Class 4	AATCC 85
Crocking				
Dry	Class 4	Class 4	Class 4	USAS L-14.72 (AATCC 8)
Wet	Class 3	Class 3	Class 3	
Wet-washed crock cloth (see note 6)	Class 4	Class 4	Class 4	Color Transference Chart
Light	L-4-20 hr	L-4-20 hr	L-4-20 hr	USAS L-14.53 (AATCC 16A)
Loss of thickness (maximum) (see note 7)	10 per cent	10 per cent	10 per cent	BFTB Test No. 3

Pressing: Whenever the pressing temperature specified in any testing procedure is too high for heat-sensitive fibers, pressing should be done at temperatures as high as possible without glazing or fusing.

Retention of Hand, Character, and Appearance: A fabric shall not change substantially in hand, character, or appearance as a result of three launderings by the applicable shrinkage procedure or dry cleaning by USAS L-14.121 (AATCC 86), except laminated (bonded) fabrics which shall be tested by FLA Test No. 1. In addition, the fabric shall not lose more than 5 per cent of its weight as a result of this treatment.

Durability of Laminates: A fabric shall exhibit no delamination, cracking, or peeling as a result of three launderings by Fabric Laminators Association Test No. 2 or three drycleanings by Fabric Laminators Association Test No. 1, according to whichever standard is used.

Special Performance Characteristics: When a claim is made for a special performance characteristic not covered by this standard, see Part IV of these standards.

COMPONENTS PROPERTIES

Components: All textile components other than textiles incorporated into the textile article shall conform to applicable performance requirements of this standard in order not to cause alteration in appearance of fabrics meeting these requirements after appropriate refreshing tests. If the provisions of this standard do not cover refreshing requirements suitable for removable components, other L-22 end-use standards may be specified.

PERMANENT LABELS AND DETACHABLE TAGS

Permanent labels and detachable tags indicating compliance with the specific L-22 standard shall be in accordance with requirements as set forth in Part V of these standards.

SOURCE: USAS L-22.30.4-1968 (Revision of L-22.30.4-1960).

Notes: 1 Fabrics known to exhibit a wet strength which is in excess of the dry strength requirement need not be subjected to a wet test.
2 Use AATCC Test Method 99 when applicable, except laminated (bonded) fabrics which shall be tested by FLA Test No. 1.
3 Use corresponding test methods as provided in the columns under laundering and dry-cleaning.
4 For evaluating, use gray scale.
5 Under this standard, a washable fabric shall also be colorfast to dry cleaning, unless specifically labeled: *Do not dry-clean.* Dry-cleanable goods are dry-cleanable only.
6 For wet-washed crock cloth use CS 59-44, Part VIII, Colorfastness to Crocking, Para 31a.
7 Measurements shall be made on original specimen and after one laundering or dry cleaning (whichever is applicable) according to shrinkage test, followed by light brushing.

* The references to the test numbers in this column give only the permanent part of the designation of the USA Standard, AATCC, ASTM, and other test methods. The particular edition for year of issue of each method used in testing the material for conformance to the requirements here specified shall be as stated in the current edition of Part VII of these L-22 standards.

material for light weight, resiliency, and warmth, not only in comforters but also in sleeping bags. This material, when available, sells for $15 per pound.

The coverings of these comforters are usually gay and bright and should be closely woven in order to avoid any loss of fiber filler. The usual weave is a short-float twill or satin, because this seems to cling to the other bed covers more firmly than a long-float satin. Also, a fine cotton or silk-cotton mixture will slip less than will a fabric of rayon, acetate, or manufactured fibers. Some comforters are made with one color on one side and another on the reverse; others have a patterned fabric on one side and a plain color on the other in order to provide variations in decoration. The standard sizes are double-bed size, 72×78 or 72×84 inches; extra-sized, 80×90 inches; and twin-bed size, 60×78 or 60×84 inches. In large king-size beds, the size may be 72×108 inches.

BEDSPREADS A bedspread helps set the decor of the bedroom, both in material, texture, and color. The fabrics used should not wrinkle or crush easily. They should be easily washed and should be large enough for the bed. The lengths generally should be a minimum of 100 to as great as 108 inches. The bedspread industry has traditionally been one of the most important in the tufted fabric field (p. 244).

Rugs and Carpets

The terms *rugs* and *carpets* are not interchangeable. From a technical point of view, a rug is a soft-surfaced floor covering, usually patterned, of a size to cover the greater part of the floor area in a room. Carpets are made of the same fibers as rugs but generally have a plain surface and are cut to cover the floor of the room from wall to wall. Their patterns, if any, are simple and small and are formed by dyeing or by special weaving techniques that give a variable pile height to geometrical figures. Carpets that are woven in wide widths to fit the entire cross section of a room are called broadloom. Narrower strips, which are suitable for covering most stairs or for piecing in a room of irregular shape, are generally less expensive per square yard.

Rugs and carpets have a pile surface that can be characterized as cut pile: the fiber ends stand vertically or they are of tufted or twisted construction with vertical loops of pile yarns as the wearing surface. Such a construction gives a floor covering that is heat-retentive and absorbs noise; it is less tiring to walk on than are hard-surface coverings, such as wood, vinyl resin, tile linoleum, and even tightly twisted braided fabric rugs, mats, and pads.

Rugs and carpets are major textile purchases for most homemakers. The carpet mills in the United States now use approximately thirty times as much manufactured fiber in the pile as the amount of natural fibers. Figure 8–2

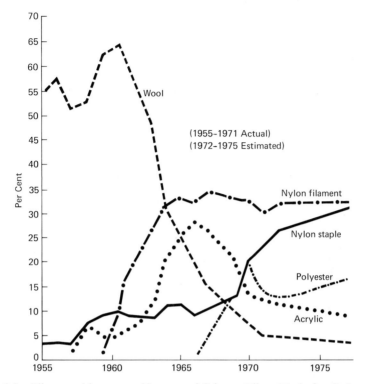

Figure 8-2.   Fibers used in carpets. (Courtesy of Celanese Fibers Marketing Co.)

shows the consumption pattern of the various fibers in percentages from 1955 to estimates for 1975.

Figure 8–2 is of interest because it shows the plummeting of wool as a carpet face fiber from 65 per cent in 1960 to about 5 per cent 10 years later. The growth fibers now appear to be polyesters and the nylon staple fiber yarns. The figure deserves special study on several counts.

1. In what way do the fiber properties account for the shift?
2. To what extent does fiber cost enter into this shifting?
3. What impetus was given to synthetic fibers by the development of newer and faster methods of tufted fabric production?
4. What influence did indoor-outdoor carpeting for athletic fields have on consumer habits?
5. How do consumers regard these cheaper, less durable floor coverings for use on patios, automobile floors, in mobile homes, summer cottages, and in similar modern applications?

In 1969 the volume of business done by the carpet industry was $2 billion. The industry anticipates that the consumption of carpeting in the

United States by 1977 will reach approximately 1 billion square yards, based on the present increasing residential market, especially of developments in low-cost housing, and also anticipating increased demands for automobiles, mobile homes, and second homes outside the city.

The traditional rug construction names are of little significance today. With the growth of the tufting and stitch-thru methods of rug formation, traditional weaving methods are used in the textile industry to produce fabrics other than rugs (Figure 8–3). Stuffer yarns of linen or cotton, the

Figure 8-3. Polypropylene fabric to be used as carpet backing nears completion on one of the new Sulzer looms at the Wilson, North Carolina, plant of Burlington Industries. (Photograph courtesy of Burlington Industries, Inc.)

use of different warps to reinforce the base, and tying down the loops and the pile loops themselves have been replaced by other methods. The old names associated with jute backing have been replaced by such fabrics as olefin, which is widely used in backing today.

Three nylon fibers used for rugs are shown in Figure 8–4. Regardless of the actual method by which the rug is formed, there are a few guides for the careful homemaker to follow in making a selection. The backing, if visible, should be closely woven and compact to hold the tufts in place firmly. Many of today's rugs have an adhesive backing that serves two purposes: It protects the base yarns and the bottoms of the loops from premature wear, and it makes the rugs firmer and less subject to sliding. Such a backing also helps prevent the passage of abrasive dust and dirt through the rug to the floor where, during normal attrition in wear, the base might be cut by these

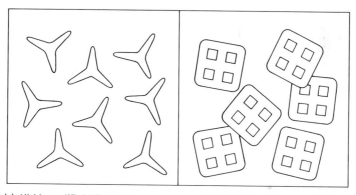

(a) Highly modified trilobal nylon yarn This fiber is designed to reduce crushing and packing and give a luxurious softness.

(b) Soil-hiding nylon yarn Hollow conduits in fibers scatter light and conceal dirt.

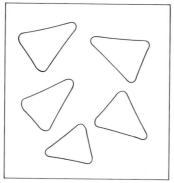

(c) Lustrous encalure yarn The sides are flat and mirrorlike to reflect light rather than scatter it. If a bright polymer is spun, the rug is very lustrous.

Figure 8-4. Three unusual nylon fibers for carpets and rugs.

irregular fragments. When a corner of the rug is turned over, it should be quite stiff and resistant to bending. One that is too soft in its bending resistance is likely to be too loosely woven for great durability. This test is not quite as applicable to modern tufted carpetings because the bases for these could not be expected to be as rigid as the woven backings were.

A significant change in backing in recent years has been a twisted paper, kraft paper, slit and then twisted into a yarn called **Kraftcord**. It tends to make carpet backing stiffer than that using the natural fibers; also, the resistance to shrinkage is greater. Note the stuffer and filling yarns in the backing construction in the various sketches of carpet construction. These are the yarns referred to as being of hemp, paper, and similar materials. Recently, a very high-strength, water-resistant, and dimensionally stable backing yarn of kraft paper yarn twisted around a glass fiber core has made its appearance.

Another change in the backing of rugs has been the increased use of laminated foamed backings. Thus far, this backing has been used more on scatter rugs and small throw rugs in order to reduce their tendency to slip on waxed floors. It also gives a washable backing, so that the rugs themselves can be washed and dried in conventional equipment.

Tufted Fabrics

One of the fastest growing branches of the textile industry is processing pile fabrics for bedspreads, blankets, and carpets by new high-speed tufting machinery. It is done by punching extra yarns into a ground or base fabric that may be anything from a thin cotton scrim to jute, heavy nylon duck, and even to polyurethane foam reinforced with embedded nylon scrim and other fibers. The choice of ground material and the pile fibers can be of any kind —rayon, nylon, polyester, cotton, wool, or acrylics—depending on the end-use. The man-made fibers have been found by the U.S. Department of Commerce to account for 85 per cent of the 1965 production of tufted fabrics. In 1964, this industry used the following quantities of fibers.[11]

Fiber	Quantities (millions of pounds)
Nylon	170
Rayon	114
Acrylics	70
Wool and blends	50
Cotton	50

[11] "Trends in Tufting," *Modern Textiles Magazine,* **47** (May 1966), pp. 18–32.

This is a revolutionary change from the cottage and handcraft tufting of spreads and carpets. The machine control of the industry began in the 1930s. The new machines insert the tufts or pile by means of a series of needles, all of which descend at once, passing through the horizontal base fabric; as the needles retreat, a hook holds the loop in place beneath the fabric. The pile can be left as a top-surface loop or it can be cut. Loop and pile height can be varied for textural effects. A blanket can be completely tufted in 2 minutes and a 9 × 12 carpet in 4 minutes, compared with a Jacquard loom, which would take longer than an hour. This speed enables the producer to sell these products more cheaply than those made by conventional methods and has brought about the widespread use of the soft floor coverings in corridors and on floors in hospitals and schools. Some consumers are suspicious of the tufted blankets, but they appear to live up to every service demand.

The principal choice facing today's consumer is which pile fiber is most appropriate for the end-use intended—which type of pile will be most satisfactory in a hall or on stairs, in a living room, dining room, a bedroom, around the pool, or elsewhere in and about the home. As a general guide, the following factors are suggested.

1. *Wool.* Wool is soft and warm; it has good durability and excellent springiness (it resists the flattening of the pile under heavy wear); it is colorfast in pastels, but is not as clear and bright as the synthetics. It is subject to insect damage; it is moderately fire-resistant, washable, and dry-cleanable, and it is water-absorbent.

2. *Cotton.* Cotton is no longer significant as a pile fiber because of its poor resiliency and durability compared with other fibers.

3. *Rayon.* Rayon is still used in some blends and occasionally in all-rayon fabrics. The rayon filaments must be given a permanent crimp or crease in order to provide sufficient resiliency to avoid traffic lanes. It is weak when wet; it is a fire hazard; it is washable and dry-cleanable; and it is dyed easily. It is very inexpensive.

4. *Nylon.* Nylon is the most wear-resistant of carpet fibers. The use of heavier deniers and irregular cross sections, with or without permanent crimp, and a greater dependence on staple nylon yarns have cured the tendency of nylon to flatten out under load; nylon pastels are clean and clear. It is dyed easily; it is washable and resistant to water-borne stains; but it is subject to permanent staining by oil and grease unless given a protective finish. Fine filament nylons are likely to pill in low twist yarns.

5. *Acrylics.* Acrylics approach the wear and durability of nylon. They are somewhat more flammable than other fibers; somewhat less static prone than many other synthetic fibers; and are subject to oil and grease stains. They can be blended with other fibers or with different deniers and cross sections of the same acrylic to produce unusual effects.

6. *Modacrylics.* Modacrylics are frequently blended with acrylics to increase flame resistance in tufted carpeting for both indoor and outdoor use.

7. *Polyesters.*   The polyesters are the fastest growing of the manufactured fibers in carpets because of their excellent durability, ease of dyeing, and color-fastness, indoors and out. They are subject to oil and grease staining but are resistant to sun fading.

8. *Olefins.*   Olefins are stiffer than other fibers. They are used for athletic fields and for indoor-outdoor carpeting. They are colorfast to sun and to moisture, but are subject to oil and grease stains. They are inexpensive, but are not as springy as other fibers in recovery from load. They are fire resistant, however.

9. *Saran.*   Saran is stiff and wiry, but it is wear-resistant and has satisfactory sun resistance. It is subject to oil and grease stains, but it will not burn.

Worldwide figures for the production of tufted, needle-punched, and woven carpets in 1969 and 1971 (estimated for 1973 and 1976) are given in Table 8–15.

Pillows

Pillow casings are generally made of ticking in the twill or satin weaves. A standard weight is approximately 6 ounces per square yard. Cotton is by far the most widely used ticking material; rayon is sometimes used as a ticking, as is cotton blended with a manufactured fiber. The weave has traditionally been close in order to prevent the escape of filling material, especially when natural products such as down, duck feathers, finely cut chicken and turkey feathers, or kapok are used. The wide use of soft staple manufactured fibers, especially polyester and the acrylics, has resulted in great variations in ticking material and permits a lighter material to be chosen. Most of the natural stuffing materials were allergenic to some users. Foam rubber and plastic have also been utilized in order to reduce any dusting and allergenic effects.

Upholstery Fabrics

Generally, the fiber types best suited for carpets and rugs are well suited for use in upholstery fabrics. However, they are subject to the same weaknesses. The primary purpose of each is to afford surfaces with wear resistance, attractiveness, color appeal, and easy cleanability (and, when feasible, spot and stain resistance). The degree of wear will vary with the conditions of use. Thus, it is only natural that those manufactured fibers that have proved successful for the rug manufacturer will be the greatest interest to the manufacturer or weaver of fabrics for upholstery materials. Special nylons, such as **Enkaloft,** made by the American Enka Corporation; **du Pont 501**; Allied Chemical Corporation's **Caprolan**; Chemstrand's **Cumuloft**; and **Nyloft**

Table 8-15 *Production of Soft Floor Coverings, Worldwide*

(in millions of square meters)

Market	1969	Per Cent	1971	Per Cent	1973	Per Cent	1976	Per Cent
EEC (Common Market)								
tufted carpets	79	35	129	47	165	51	222	57
needle-punched	66	33	88	33	109	34	131	33
woven	58	32	50	20	46	15	43	10
total	203		267		320		396	
EETA (other 7 European countries)								
tufted	71	53	90	56	109	58	131	61
needle-punched	6	5	14	9	20	12	25	12
woven	57	42	57	35	58	30	57	27
total	134		161		187		213	
COMECON (Eastern Europe block)								
tufted	9	14	15	20	24	23	63	40
needle-punched	5	9	9	12	15	15	30	11
woven	49	77	57	68	64	62	70	49
total	63		82		103		163	
USA								
tufted	470	87	521	88	623	88	767	90
needle-punched	39	7	43	7	54	8	69	8
woven	30	6	23	5	22	4	20	2
total	539		587		699		856	
Remaining countries (all others)								
tufted	80	55	105	51	150	58	230	60
needle-punched	15	11	25	19	45	18	80	21
woven	50	34	55	30	62	24	70	19
total	145		185		257		380	
Worldwide								
tufted	709	64	861	67	1071	69	1413	70
needle-punched	131	14	179	14	243	15	335	16
woven	244	22	242	19	252	16	260	14
total	1084		1282		1666		2008	

SOURCE: Based on *Modern Textiles Magazine*, **54**, No. 1 (Jan. 1973), p. 44.

made by Firestone Tire and Rubber Company, are among the special nylons being used for rug and decorative fabrics. A nylon from Guilford Mills, Greensboro, North Carolina, known as **Trilon,** consists of continuous filament. An interesting suedelike fabric of nylon is Chemstrand's **Islon.** This is bonded to a foam backing and illustrates one of the many uses for these urethane foams. Not only has the foam appeared as a backing material in upholstery fabrics to help keep them firm and to give additional warmth, but it has replaced some of the traditional springing and foam rubber in upholstered chairs and sofas.

Of interest to decorators is du Pont's **Pattina**, an expanded vinyl sheeting that resembles leather. This has been used to some extent in shoes. Recently, it has been made into garments, luggage, and leatherlike coverings for furniture. It is a polymer of the olefin group and has a knitted cloth backing. The fabric has tremendous resistance to abrasion, scuffing, and marking. It has even been used successfully for seven years on an experimental basis as a covering for furniture in a high school.

The term **expanded vinyl** does not refer to a stretch fabric, although moderate stretch is one of the characteristics of this material in connection with leatherlike fabrics for wearing apparel, shoes, and upholstery materials. The expanded vinyl-coated fabrics are those to which a cellular structure has been given by a heat-treating or baking process. The result is that the customary polymer coating achieves a softness and texture resembling that of natural leather. A thin, honeycombed interior is brought about by a rising or vertical expansion mechanism that might be compared with the rising of yeast in a dense dough in the baking process which results in a soft, cellular loaf of bread.

Another application of the olefin polymer is in the form of a novelty yarn of polyethylene around a core of a nonshrinkable yarn that is then woven into a fabric with this coated yarn as the pile. A novelty effect is created upon dyeing, because the polyethylene winding tends to shrink during the process. The core yarn is thus spread and crimped, creating a textured effect of great permanence. Mention has also been made of the comparative prevalence now of metallic yarns which are used as decorative or splash features in the figures woven into many of our materials for upholstered furniture. Generally, colored aluminum with a Mylar coating is the fiber chosen for this purpose.

TYPES OF UPHOLSTERY MATERIAL   The fabrics used to cover furniture, to serve as slipcovers, or to be used in the cloth seats of chairs are termed **upholstery fabrics**. There are four general classifications:

1. Friezes are springy pile fabrics with looped pile.
2. Velvets have cut loops that result in a pile that is thick, dense, and patternless.
3. Damasks and brocades are generally intricately woven Jacquard designs, but small patterns can be woven by the dobby attachment on the regular loom.
4. Ribbed fabrics include armures, reps, tapestries, and whip cords.

Although any fiber can be used for these fabrics, wool and cotton are the most common from the combined standpoints of wear, ease of cleaning, and sunfastness. Rayons, acetates, and manufactured fibers, such as nylon, the polyesters, acrylics, and olefins, have been used alone or in blended fabrics. However, the man-made fibers are generally more slippery and nylon, in particular, requires special reinforcement in the sewing of soft pillows and cushions lest the yarns in the fabric slip or shift during stress in use. For maximum durability and permanence of appearance, especially when staining in use is a hazard, such as in homes with small children, a tightly twisted yarn in a small inconspicuous pattern should be used. Silk can be used but it is a luxury fiber and will not stand as much abrasion as the other fibers; furthermore, it is adversely affected by sunlight. The factor of sunlight has become increasingly important in recent years because stylists have begun to relate the same fabric used in upholstering one or more pieces in the room to draperies. The amount of sun exposure is so different in these two applications that, unless the fabric has been dyed in fast colors, the drapery may show fading or yellowing long before any sign of color change is seen in the upholstered piece.

A worn upholstered chair can be covered with a slipcover if one does not wish to go to the expense of having it reupholstered. Slipcover fabrics often include cotton chintzes or cretonnes; but they can be blends with linen, nylon, polyester, or other fibers. Decorative effects are also achieved by the use of metallic threads in the patterns.

Handcrafted fabrics are treasured in chair seats, occasional cushions, and on the tops of benches. These are in needlepoint, crewel work embroidery, or needling a pattern usually using wool yarn through a heavy burlap or linen backing cloth.

Slipcovers and piece goods for furniture recovering are subject to Federal legislation on fiber identification.

DEVELOPMENT OF SKILLS FOR SELECTING
AND USING TEXTILES

Advancing textile technology in the field of new fibers and of new finishes designed to contribute new conveniences and new ways of life to the consuming public has resulted in ever greater critical opinion by the public. The historic causes of complaints, such as sun fading, rapid wear, shrinkage, and the like have now changed as consumers begin more and more to judge performance in terms of the degree to which special functional advantages are realized. That is, if a garment is sold as wash-and-wear or durable-press, the consumer does not expect to have to iron the article. If more than a touch-up is required, then there is a legitimate cause of complaint. Standards of performance, therefore, become more and more important. The significance of such standards as those in L-22 and the ANSI[12] (formerly the ASA), as well as the data received from standard test methods designed by the AATCC and the ASTM, will aid in selection and use. In a recent wear trial symposium,[13] it was noted that some people will never be satisfied. They are psychologically motivated to note some fault with almost any apparel item and possibly other materials as well.

Having directed a questionnaire survey among homemakers and home economists, the results shown in Table 8–16 were obtained on three often-mentioned, possible failings of manufactured fibers: pilling, static, and stain and oil retention.

Table 8-16

Problem	Homemakers			Home Economists		
	Major	*Minor*	*None*	*Major*	*Minor*	*None*
Pilling	30.7	30.7	38.6	42.4	24.3	33.3
Static	14.0	36.0	50.0	22.5	31.5	46.0
Stain-soil	24.6	10.5	64.9	30.6	21.6	47.8

SOURCE: *Modern Textiles Magazine*, **51**, No. 3 (1970), p. 89.

In this study it was found that the home economists, being better trained in chemical appraisal and therefore more demanding in their expectations, were the more critical. If a fault were found, they also were more inclined to give it a major degree of seriousness. It seems a real achievement for the textile industry that the failure to observe any flaws occurred almost as frequently in the opinions of the home economists as in those of the home-makers. The study covered other types of failure and in one, as expected, the home economists were much more critical than the homemakers. That was in wrinkling characteristics; 25 per cent of the home economists said that it is a serious or major fault, but only 9 per cent of the homemakers agreed.

The several studies reported by Powderly substantiate the findings of this writer—which appear in a report made to the Textile Research Institute titled, "Ten Thousand and One Consumer Complaints"—that consumer experience is the best method of obtaining conclusions in advance regarding anticipated types of garment failure. Laboratory procedures carried out in advance of sale provide an indication of whether there is any widespread potential hazard of consumer dissatisfaction. After all, it must be remem-

[12] American National Standards Institute, Inc., 1430 Broadway, New York, N.Y. 10018.
[13] Daniel D. Powderly, "The Changing Standards of the Consumer," *Modern Textiles Magazine,* **51**, No. 3 (March 1970), pp. 88–92.

Table 8-17   Fiber Fabric Problems

	Pilling	Stain/Soil	Snagging	Shrinkage
Times mentioned	185	122	102	86
Per cent of problems	15.9	10.5	8.8	7.4
Fiber/fabric				
Nylon	14.1	1.6	32.3	2.3
Cotton	2.7	21.3	1.0	31.4
Prints	9.2	3.3	28.4	23.2
Wool	19.5	7.4	6.9	8.1
Acrylics	22.7	.8	2.9	21.3
Polyesters	7.0	6.6	2.0	1.2
Perm Press	0.5	12.3	—	—

bered that the degree of performance in Textile Standard L-22 as well as in the textile standard for the Institution Customers L-24 were based on consumer experience. The degree of performance requirement for shrinkage, stretching, colorfastness, and other results designed to avoid dissatisfaction were based on the levels of performance acceptable to consumers. Now, with new factors introduced, such as durable-press and spot resistance, it is necessary that many of the evaluation procedures be brought up to date and new standards be required for the functional criteria imposed by technology.

Rough approximations of the service-use ratings of textile fibers are given in Table 8–18. These ratings are to some extent based on the relative absence of consumer complaints concerning a fiber for a specific end-use item, on the chemical nature of the polymer, and on the fiber properties. It must be realized that these fibers are used in so many different items of apparel and in household fabrics that in some constructions they are rated 1, or excellent; in another 3, only fair; or even 4, rated poor. At any rate, these are guides to be read by the consumer in examining labels and in determining the way in which an article is cared for in its use. It is generally safe to say also that as the presence of the weaker fiber in a blend becomes larger, the fabric or garment must be cared for more as if it were made entirely of the weaker or least serviceable component.

Damaged Merchandise

A significant source of economic waste in our system of apparel distribution is in imperfect or seriously damaged merchandise being shipped by a manufacturer to a retail establishment. Careless workmanship and incompetent inspection, possibly induced by the element of speed in getting the order out of the manufacturer's shop and into the hands of his customers, often

Table 8-18 Service-use Ratings of Textiles (average ratings)*

| Service-use Factors | Natural Fibers | | | Glass Fiber | Cellulose-base Man-made Fibers | | | |
| | Cotton | Wool | Silk | | Regenerated | | Thermoplastic | |
					Rayon	Fortisan	Acetate	Arnel
Durability								
Wear or abrasion	2	2	2	3	3	2	3	3
Breaking strength, dry	2	4	2	1	3	1	4	3
Breaking strength, wet	1	4	3	1	4	2	4	3
Tearing resistance, dry	1	4	2	1	3	1	4	3
Tearing resistance, wet	1	4	3	1	4	2	4	3
Sun resistance (fabric, not color)	3	3	4	1	4	2	3	3
Insect resistance (moth and carpet beetle)	1	4	4	1	1	1	1	1
Mildew resistance	4	2	2	1	4	3	2	2
Acid resistance	4	3	3	3	4	3	3	3
Alkali resistance	2	4	4	2	4	2	4	4
Bleach resistance	2	2	4	1	4	2	2	2
Burning resistance	4	2	2	1	4	2	3	2
Iron damage resistance	1	3	3	1	2	3	4	3
Appearance and comfort								
Draping quality	4	1	1	1	4	1	1	2
Crease retention	4	2†	2†	1	4	2†	3	2
Wrinkle resistance (and recovery)	4	1†	2†	1	4	3	3	1
Softness of hand	3	1	1	2	2	2	2	3
Ease of dyeing	1	2	2	4‡	1	1	2	1
Bulk and warmth	4	2	2	1	4	2	3	3
Warmth retention after prolonged use	4	2	2	2	4		3	3
Comfort in all weather	2	1	1	4	3		3	3

Service-use Factors	Nylons	Acrylics	Modacrylics	Polyesters	Saran	Olefins
Durability						
Wear or abrasion	1	2	2	1–2	2	2
Breaking strength, dry	1	2	2	2	3	1
Breaking strength, wet	1	2	2	2	3	2
Tear resistance, dry	1	2	2	2	3	2
Tear resistance, wet	4	1	2	2	3	2
Sun resistance (fabric, not color)	1	1	1	1	1	4
Insect resistance (moth and carpet beetle)	1	2	1	1	1	1
Mildew resistance	4	2	1	2	1	1
Acid resistance	1	3	1	2	1	1
Alkali resistance	3	3	3	3	2	3
Bleach resistance	2	2	1	1–2	1	4
Burning resistance	3	4	4	4	3	4
Iron damage resistance	3	2	2	2	2	1
Appearance and comfort						
Draping quality	1–2	1	2	1	2	2
Crease retention	1–2	2	2	1	3	4
Wrinkle resistance (and recovery)	3	2	2	2	4	3
Softness to hand	2	2	3	3	2	4
Ease of dyeing	2	1	2	3	3	3
Warmth retention after prolonged use	2	1	1	3	3	3
Comfort in all weather	4	3	1	3	3	2

* 1—Excellent
2—Good
3—Fair
4—Poor
† Dry rating—4 when wet.
‡ Colored by other methods.

411

result in a considerable number of garments being damaged to the extent that they are unwearable. On the receiving end, the element of speed persists and the garments may be given a cursory examination and inspection and then are rushed to the sales floor. Flaws such as incompleted hems, incompletely sewn seams, inadequate seam allowance under the arms and at other points of strain, or soil and spots on the garment are found daily in the stock coming into a store. At a seminar with apparel manufacturers in 1968, William Bursten, then vice-president and manager of the merchandising division of the National Retail Merchants Association, reported that one retailer found 121 imperfect dresses in one day and two days later found 172 defective garments that had been accepted and stocked in his store. In addition to the listed flaws, he found some had different fabrics in the same style and same number—he received four different shades of navy in one style. In three months time 1600 dresses were returned by this retailer, 12½ per cent of the total number he had received from that source. Not all retailers are as particular as this one. If, then, the customer in her haste neglects to look carefully over the entire garment for such flaws, she is likely to get it home and only discover the damage after she has worn the garment. Then it becomes a consumer complaint and the chances of the garment being returned to the manufacturer are minimal. The finished garment, when it leaves the manufacturer, is simply a hole in a computer card or some other simple statistic. Unless a great number of defective items are sent back to the store and returned to the manufacturer, the defective garment will remain a statistic. If statistical figures are too small to warrant correction, no correction will be made for future production. There are headlines when a manufacturer of an automobile accepts a few thousand cars for replacement of a defective part. Economically the cars are more important than a similar number of dresses, blouses, or suits; however, the drain on the individual consumer's pocketbook is only relative. It is shrugged off by far too many individuals.

Even large department stores with laboratory facilities sometimes find a sudden increase in consumer complaints. As a case in point, this writer recalls an experience that occurred about 15 years ago. Alerted by several consumer complaints about dress with dolman sleeves having gone into holes under the arms, a member of the Kaufmann Department Store at Mellon Institute went to the store in which they were being sold and examined a shipment of one gross of dresses all retailing at about $30. One hundred and seventeen dresses were damaged under the arms as a result of too much trimming of material in the underarm area. In some cases the sewing thread was cut; in other cases, there were openings up to as much as an inch and a half where there was no stitching at all. The garments in the entire shipment were returned to the manufacturer. One wonders what became of those dresses! Were they restitched and sent to some other less particular retailer, and were his customers brave enough to return them if they failed to serve their purpose? Other common flaws in manufacturing are failure to match the pattern, poor button adhesion, fabric flaws, crooked zippers, and uneven hems. These are facts that should be ascertained by the customer when inspecting a garment. They are just as important to the appearance of the dress as the fit.

Consumer Responsibility

The real responsibility of the individual purchaser to improve the efficiency and economics of textile purchasing is unrecognized by many homemakers. When entering the store as a customer, one tends to forget or to neglect past experience and knowledge and to overlook the significance of even the meager amount of material available on labels or hang tags. Customers may be so excited and exhilarated by the quality of beautiful merchandise around them and so affected by the esthetic qualities of color, design, and texture that they may become overconfident in their selections and buy articles totally unsuited to their real needs and wants. Thus, the value concept is overlooked. On the other hand, this volume of merchandise may cause defensive buying; frustrated in selection, consumers may become fearful of making a bad buy. Often they fall back on price as the criterion, believing that the higher price will give greater durability and satisfaction. Again, the value is overlooked.

These conditions both lead to what one might term *impulse buying*. Several important factors having to do with efficiency in buying for one's personal means are commonly overlooked. One such factor is the coordination of the article being considered with one's wardrobe. Will the color, design, or texture require further expenditure for a more appropriate handbag, shoes, scarf, or other accessory items? Another factor is the suitability of several competitive dresses or skirts or other articles of apparel for the individual's usual activities, whether they be social, business, or athletic. The weight, texture, and pattern may limit the usefulness of a garment for the wearer's own requirements. Color suitability is another factor sometimes overlooked. The hue may be pleasing under the store lighting or in its position with contrasting garments on the display racks, but at home it might not be the most flattering color for the wearer. Perhaps most homemakers are sufficiently color-conscious to avoid this problem; however, various depths of hue can make a pleasing and becoming color less attractive. Sometimes, especially during periods of economic pinch, recognition should be given to the question of whether one garment might be better than another for its hand-me-down potentiality. This, of course, is more rare, but in many families there exists a pattern in which the garment purchased originally for one member of the family is so admired by someone else that the original owner will pass it on to the other person with the necessary alterations.

Another responsibility of the consumer at the customer or selection level is to read with care all labels and all pertinent information available. The customer should also have as much basic information as possible with regard to the fibers present in the garment to be prepared to care for them in the most efficient manner.

Just as the homemaker has certain responsibilities as a customer, the consumer's responsibilities as a user and caretaker of apparel and other textile items are important. Reference has been made in several places in this book concerning the functional finishes, their requirements, and the extent to which the consumer can help garments retain these properties. Also, the question of maintenance of color, texture, and dimension enters into the intelligent use and care of apparel. Textile products are not permanent; users will have different criteria as to what constitutes satisfactory and unsatisfactory durability or colorfastness. A poor buy may have been made; on the other hand, the damage may be primarily caused by consumer misuse, or possibly because of an error made in the cleaning and laundering of a product by a commercial cleaning establishment. Almost any of these failures may appear later as consumer complaints. The significance of legitimate consumer complaints has been mentioned in the commercial standards L-22.

Too few organizations collect consumer complaints for statistical analysis relating to cause, so that constructive steps can be taken to correct the condition and so that the source of damage, whether in fiber, yarn, fabric, apparel construction, wear, or servicing, can be isolated. It is only through this kind of attention at each level in the development of a textile that the source of an error can be found and corrected. The consumer who believes that a complaint is fully justified should return apparel to the store. The buyer then should return it, with complete data as to what happened to it, to the garment manufacturer, who in turn can reach his fabric resource. The history of the material should be traced back as far as necessary to isolate the cause of the damage. If a store simply satisfies the individual consumer and then discards the article for destruction or to be turned over to some charitable organization, if it is still wearable, he has satisfied the one customer but has not lived up to his responsibility to the other clients of the store, or, in fact, to the manufacturer of the garment. This factor has been mentioned as one of the reasons for the manufacturer's shifting from one fabric construction, finish, or color to another.

Prior to the advent of manufactured fibers, it is significant that the consumer was in error in approximately 65 per cent of more than 15,000 consumer complaints analyzed in the laboratory of the Kaufmann Department Store of Pittsburgh, Pennsylvania.[14] Table 8–19 indicates that, in the

---

[14] Jules Labarthe, "Ten Thousand and One Consumer Complaints," *Journal of the Textile Research Institute.*

experience of the laboratory of the NID, in 1969, the customer was responsible for 26 per cent of the damage cases. These cases were forwarded to the National headquarters, where 25 different causes of damage were identified as attributable to the customer. The total number of cases was 7940.[15] Old stains of caramelized sugar and oxidized oil were the most prevalent. Presumably these and mineral acid stains had been ironed into garments.

Table 8–20 indicates a variety of damage causes attributable to either the merchant or the manufacturer. These numbered 10,543 and accounted for 47.6 per cent of the cases reaching the NID laboratory. It should be noted that color loss of pigment prints constituted a major case of damage, 6.35 per cent of the total problems, with shrinkage in other than bonded fabrics accounting for 6.3 per cent of the total. The research laboratory of NID tabulates in Table 8–21 the number of cases in each of 25 damage causes attributable to the dry cleaner. Alkaline color change was identified as being 2.9 per cent of the total. Table 8–22 gives data on the processing errors that result in dry-cleaning damage of garments.

These tables allow producers, distributors, and consumers to locate the most common causes of failure. It is difficult to realize the full significance of the damage causes attributable to the manufacturer. Possibly many of the problem articles that have reached store and service industry laboratories have been isolated cases; there is no indication as to how frequently a single fabric, or pattern, or apparel item appeared in the various plants of the National Institute of Drycleaning. If one considers the volume of production today, it is reasonable to assume that each of these cases represented a vast number of actual or potential failures that were never reported by consumers or cleaners through laziness, frustration resulting from previous contacts with a complaint, or because of a feeling of guilt. Perhaps many of these failures were so slight in certain garments that they were overlooked. It would be interesting to know how many similar items are hanging in closets in homes in the United States. It is this hidden number of economic tragedies that add so much importance to each individual legitimate complaint. This is the responsibility of the consumer.

Background Information for the L–22 Voluntary Standards

With consumerism becoming so great a political and economic issue, it might be well to study some of the historical background of such voluntary standards as the L-22 voluntary standard of 1952 and its revision in 1960. The problems faced in the development of this standard still hold true in any standard program whether voluntary or mandatory; there are certain prac-

---

[15] National Institute of Drycleaning, *Technical Bulletin P-459* (March 1970).

Table 8-19   *Types of Damage Observed in Garments and Responsibility Assignments*

Damage Classification	Customer	Manu- facturer or Merchant	Dry Cleaner	Unknown	Total	Per Cent
Dimensional change	316	2685	516	74	3591	11.9
Fabric damaged	2903	2857	1443	264	7467	24.8
Finish damaged	76	994	617	5	1692	5.6
Color or design damaged	1327	5783	2339	52	9501	31.5
Stains	3318	1271	2810	40	7439	24.7
Other materials in garment		455			455	1.5
Failure to follow label instructions*			5		5	0.0
Total	7,940	14,045	7,730	435	30,150	100.0
Percentage	26.33	46.6	25.6	1.5	100.0	

SOURCE: Courtesy of NID.

* It is difficult to measure the actual amount of care aid provided by labels because they become lost or are never referred to by the consumer. There is also the unresolved question of whether the labels are adquate. Perhaps it is overly optimistic to believe that permanently attached labels, required by the care labeling act, will be used as effective care guides by most consumers. Their use will result in the proper care of textile products and help the garment producer to select his fabrics for his end-use products with more attention to the conditions of use and care of that item.

ticalities and concessions that neither the consumer nor the producer can overlook. The L-22 standard was a bold effort to present the concept of rightness in service for a part of the textile products offered to the consumer.

At the risk of some duplication between this background information and other discussions on the subject of L-22, the standards development is as follows: Prior to World War II, the rayon and acetate industry found itself in ill repute with consumers because of the variable quality in performance in use and a considerable amount of uncertainty with regard to differences between rayons and acetates. The issues became so serious that the National Retail Drygoods Association (now the National Retail Merchants Association) sponsored a voluntary standard (L-22) for rayon and acetate textile products through the American Standards Association. This association has now been reorganized under the name of the American National Standards Institute, Inc. Several of the producers of rayon and acetate fabrics had developed standards of quality for their own brands. Noteworthy among these were the American Viscose Corporation, which had developed its Crown Test Program. This program enlisted all of the then-known textile test methods developed by the ASTM, AATCC, and the Federal government, along with some private test methods from the corporation's own laboratory, and from other textile laboratories. These were

Table 8-20   Causes of Damage in Cases Where Responsibility Was Assigned to Merchant or Manufacturer

Cause	Number of Cases	Per Cent
Shrinkage—other than bonded fabrics	1433	6.47
Color loss—pigment prints	1405	6.35
Blistering or separation of bonded fabrics	678	3.06
Fluorescent dye discoloration	503	2.27
Color loss—sun fading	480	2.17
Solvent-soluble dyes or pigments	427	1.93
Stiffening of plastic	375	1.69
Water-soluble dye	307	1.39
Shrinkage—bonded fabrics	272	1.23
Stretching	248	1.12
Loss of finish	248	1.12
Fabric construction defects	225	1.02
Alkali-sensitive dyes	224	1.01
Foam laminate deterioration	203	0.92
Fume fading	200	0.90
Foam laminate yellowing	190	0.86
Rubber-lined jackets	179	0.81
Sun-tendered drapes	148	0.67
Soil-prone finish	145	0.66
Silk splits	142	0.64
Low strength	140	0.63
Damaged velvets	130	0.59
Salt-sensitive dye	120	0.54
Pilling	114	0.52
Color change by acid	112	0.51
All others	1895	8.56
Total	10543	47.64

SOURCE: Courtesy of NID.

nationally used but there was no official list of national standards. Because reference was made in advertising to the effect that the Crown Test Program was based on the national standards, the FTC issued a cease-and-desist order. All the Crown Test material was invaluable to the L-22 committee and actually formed the basis on which the test methods were selected and used. Under the aegis of the ASA, these methods have achieved national recognition and are the official methods also of the government commercial standards for textile products.

Table 8-21   Causes of Damage in Cases Where Responsibility Was Assigned to Dry Cleaner

Cause	Number of Cases	Per Cent
Mechanical damage	715	3.23
Alkaline color change	638	2.88
Color loss from prespotting	454	2.05
Stains from dry-cleaning bath	431	1.95
Soil redeposition	401	1.81
Carbon stains	309	1.40
Delustering	291	1.32
Heat damage	283	1.28
Prespotter stains ·	269	1.22
Color loss from spotting	243	1.10
Nonvolatile material	211	0.95
Acid color change	204	0.92
Shrinkage (wool felting)	154	0.70
Color fading—glass fabrics	148	0.67
Color loss from wet cleaning	85	0.38
Chafing	78	0.35
Stains from wet cleaning	71	0.32
Acrylic fiber yellowed	70	0.32
Metallic stains	59	0.27
Nap or pile distorted	49	0.22
Dye bleeding	44	0.20
Stretching	39	0.18
Chemical damage to fabric	37	0.17
Color fading—wet cleaning	33	0.15
Loss of pleats	27	0.12
All others	268	1.21
Total	5611	25.35

SOURCE: Courtesy of NID.

In order to develop a standard for testing, equating, and promoting a product, the ASA required that every element of business and consumer interest must be invited to serve on the committee. On this L-22 were representatives of fiber producers, fabric producers, converters, retailers, government departments, commercial testing laboratories, consumers, government and service industries, such as the dry cleaners and launderers. In the rayon-acetate standard there was no participation on the part of apparel manufacturers, especially the producers of men's and boys' wear, although they had been invited. They were active subsequently in the revision of the

Table 8-22   Kinds of Processing Errors Causing Dry Cleaners to Damage Garments

Process Error	Number of Cases	Per Cent
Spotting or prespotting errors	1461	26.0
Poor solvent maintenance	1102	19.6
Physical mishandling	754	13.4
Incorrect dry cleaning or finishing procedure	725	12.9
Excessive heat	472	8.4
Carbon in washer	309	5.5
Incorrect wet cleaning	189	3.4
Excessive water	163	2.9
All others	436	7.8
Total	5611	100.0

SOURCE: Courtesy of NID.

L-22 program of 1960 when the inclusion of all fibers more directly affected their business.

Textile products were divided into three main groupings—men's and boys' wear, women's and children's wear, and household fabrics—with subcommittees dealing with specific topics such as upholstery materials, curtains, domestics, blouses, dresses, suits, coats, underwear, hosiery, and so on.

All the test methods used in Crown Test programs and others used by laboratories were evaluated and compared. The development of any test method, as has been stated elsewhere in this book, requires that it be reproducible not only within the laboratory in which it was developed, but also by other laboratories—and that the results be consistent. Another rule is that if the laboratory test does not duplicate the pattern of wear or deterioration suffered by the article of apparel in use, the degree of damage and the ranking of performance between two or more articles be of the same order of magnitude in the laboratory test as in consumer experience. On this basis, the series of test methods was approved as national by recognized American standards, or as tentative standards, depending on further research and investigation.

The establishment of levels of performance was the responsibility of the organization issuing the standards—that is, of the ASA. The technical societies supplying the test methods set the measurements of quality evaluation as test results but did not set the base or floor level at which the product would be rated as satisfactory or unsatisfactory. It was, therefore, necessary to have a source of information dealing with consumer experience so that a floor or satisfactory minimum could be set for such factors as light-fastness, washability, strength, shrinkage, and other physical and chemical factors affecting consumer use. This information came principally from the records of store laboratories, commercial testing laboratories, and the service industries, as well as from the experience of home economists active in universities and in agricultural extension work. Only then was it possible to say that a fabric for a certain end-use should withstand a certain number of hours of sunlight, a certain washing program or condition, or functional performance with regard to fire-resistance, water repellency, or other use factors.

These committees met frequently during the war years and up until the rayon standard was issued in 1952. There was some lost motion, or as one of the representatives said one day, "It seems to me all we did today was spin the wheels." This kind of delay was caused by having to orient new committee members on occasions when an alternative would attend the meeting in place of the regular member or when an organization—such as a women's club, labor union, university or commercial testing laboratory, or any other —might appoint a new person to the committee to replace the experienced member. All these new members had to be reoriented for they were bound to ask the obvious questions that had been threshed out months or perhaps a year or two before.

Certain practical problems had to be faced. Some of these required compromises between two or more of the interested representative groups.

1. When a converter finishes and dyes a fabric, he does not always know the end-use to which that fabric may be put. The same textile material might appear in children's wear, women's dresses, men's shirts, beach wear, pajamas, or lightweight draperies. The fabric could be a standard weave for each of these widely varying end-uses. Should it therefore be dyed for the outer-wear applications with sunfast colors, or for pajamas, which would be exposed to very little sunlight? Should it be preshrunk? Need it be water-repellent? How could the fabric producer guarantee to the manufacturer of the goods that the fabric would stand up under that manufacturer's requirements and then perform satisfactorily in service? How could a consumer complaint be traced back through the various steps of his textile products development to identify the source of weakness? Obviously, standards were essential.

2. It was found that some fabrics and constructions that did not quite meet the standard for strength or elongation or some other physical property as judged by the laboratory methods were well established in the industry and for years had been staple constructions used for such divergent products as men's shirts, boy's pajamas, or women's housedresses without many consumer complaints. Satisfactory experience was more important than minor deviations from the laboratory-testing floor level. Again, experience was important, as when these floors or minima were selected on the basis of a

laboratory test value below which consumer complaints were often encountered but above which few, if any, complaints had been registered.

3. In a standards program, consumers must face the reality that a somewhat limited pallette of colors will be possible. All dyestuffs will not provide the required colorfastness for all of the end-use items. A dress manufacturer with a large variety of colors in his line may find as many as a third of these will not meet the standard required, for example, in sunfastness, wash fastness, resistance to bleach, or other kinds of exposure. The same thing is true in men's shirts and in upholstery materials or in draperies. On one occasion, one of the converter industry members brought a large box in which he had in windows every color his firm was dyeing acetates or rayons that year in one of the most widely used fabric constructions. Within this box was a light and with a control button he blocked out all of the shades that would not meet the L-22 standard for pajamas, then for housedresses, then for beach wear or sportswear. Nearly 40 per cent of the colors failed to meet the L-22 standard for rayons and acetates. This is one of the practical problems faced by consumers.

4. The use of label on L-22 has been discussed on pp. 349–50. Such a label would be a guarantee applicable to perhaps only 15 or 20 per cent of the rayon and acetate products being used by the American public. It was not then intended that L-22 would be applicable to all textile fibers and it is obvious that new constructions, new finishes, and new colors cannot quickly be tested and subjected to the L-22 or any other testing program. This difficulty has been mentioned elsewhere in the book. L-22 merchandise was intended to be of prestige nature and of guaranteed performance.

When the L-22 program was issued in 1952, some of the hardest working members on the committee were suddenly classified by their employers as liaison or observer members and not as voting members of the committee adopting and approving the standard to be submitted to the Certification Committee of the ASA. Many of the fabric and fiber producers found themselves in this quandary because their parent organizations became apprehensive as to what this standard might mean to their entire market line and particularly, this writer believes, feared it might become a mandatory standard. They did not cast a negative vote; therefore, when the final record was taken, there were no negative votes against the standard and it could, therefore, be approved by the Certification Committee. Under the ASA procedure one negative vote could remove a standard and it would then go back to the committee for reconsideration and for enough changes to make it acceptable to all.

The revised L-22, or all-fabric, standard of 1968 has on its flyleaf the following statement:

A USA standard implies a consensus of those essentially concerned with its scope and provisions. A USA standard is intended as a guide to aid the manufacturer, the consumer, and the general public. The existence of a USA standard does not in any respect preclude anyone whether he has approved the standard or not from manufacturing, marketing, purchasing, or using products, processes, or procedures not conforming to the standard. USA standards are subject to periodic review and users are cautioned to obtain the latest editions. Producers of goods made in conformity with the USA standard are encouraged to state on their own responsibility in advertising, commercial material, or on tags or labels that the goods are produced in conformity with particular USA standards.

It has been pointed out that these new standards, the 1968 revision, are being used widely in laboratories engaged in textile testing—in stores, commercial testing laboratories, dry-cleaning laboratories, laundry laboratories, and those of textile manufacturing companies. Some of the apparel manufacturers are using these standards, but they are not being promoted to the public. The standards are in a rather peculiar position. Each company, association, or group contributing to the development of the standards has shown great interest in them, and most have expressed willingness to proceed when the request is made by its customers. Thus, it appears that the ultimate users—consumers and the home economics interests—will have to extend the final pressure for the use of these standards. Our experience when working for Kaufman Stores at Mellon Institute was that most store buyers never heard of the standards, but all a buyer had to do was place on his order blank the requirement that the goods under the order conform to the L-22 standard. This would mean that the manufacturer would put the same demand on his orders to his textile resource and so on, all the way back to the converter whose responsibility it is to make a textile product saleable and useful.

It must be kept in mind that a program of certification and rechecking is expensive and time-consuming. Probably it is for this reason, too, that the textile industry, although depending on the standard in much of its quality-control operations and in many of the serviceability claims, still hesitates to produce a prestige-guaranteed line of goods (even at a higher price) in competition with run-of-the-mill production. A corrective step in this direction is provided in the care-directive labeling programs of the textile product manufactured in the United States, Canada, and Great Britain.

AIR POLLUTION AND TEXTILES

The average homemaker recognizes that abrasive wear, frequency and severity of washing, the conditions of ironing, and the amount of sun exposure all contribute to damaging the color of apparel and of household fabrics and reduce the service life span. Unless there is some unusually severe and easily noted accident from a concentration of exposure to a pollutant material, we overlook the constant attrition textiles suffer from our polluted environment of both air and water. It has been estimated by Dr. Victor S. Salvin, professor of home economics at the University of North Carolina, at Greensboro, that air pollution costs the average family in the United States between $400 and $600 yearly and that the annual cost is close to $11 billion.

Some consumers and numerous retail stores selling textile products recognized one phase of this problem as early as the 1930s. At that time the most dramatic victim of our pollution was acetate fabric containing a blue component dye. This color damage resulted even in the small quantities used in blends of dyes to produce a chocolate brown or grey. At that time, this was described as gas fading, but it also accounted for the fading of certain acetate fabrics in contact with wool. In this case, the color change was caused by the slightly acid nature of the wool fiber. Thus, acetate bands on men's felt hats changed color; for example, browns changed to a reddish hue. If acetate was used in lining men's suits, the color might change as a result of the destruction of the blue component dye. If a robe of blue acetate was hung in a closet for a considerable period of time touching wool or touching against certain kinds of plastic envelopes, it might change color on the outer folds. This kind of damage has now been virtually eliminated by the solution- or dope-dyeing of acetates (p. 90); this technique, of course, has been applied to other manufactured fibers as well. (See Chapter Seven on dyeing and coloring fabrics.)

In general, we tend to overlook the effects of our atmosphere. Acid vapors from a large heating plant may be windswept against the legs of passersby, or the exhaust fumes from an automobile muffler may weaken nylon hosiery or apparel fibers even though a color change is not noted. Ozone has been found to affect the colors of some fibers. This ozone can come from the lightning in an electric storm charging the oxygen. Ozone forms peroxides with some of the by-products of gasoline combustion engines and from nitrogen oxides in the air. Certain of the conventional finishing operations, such as the heating in durable-press, may activate some of the complex chemical formulations that have gone into textile finishing, with the result that the dyestuff may become discolored. A percentage of consumer complaints about the abnormally rapid wearing out of a garment may also be accounted for by some kind of chemical exposure of which the consumer is completely unaware.

MECHANICAL ATTRITION

Clay and sand tracked into a home on the bottom of children's shoes, especially sneakers—the soles of which entrap more dirt than do the smooth-soled shoes of adults—may necessitate more rug cleaning. Another wear factor is that rubber soles are more abrasive than those of smooth leather, thus contributing to a more rapid wearing out of carpets and rugs. To a certain extent dust and dirt are further evidences of our pollution. These exposures in the average household do not in any way approach the terrific mud damage resulting from flooding in areas from which trees and vegetation have been stripped. More and more must we rely also on chemical formulations to make our water supply potable, to reduce its hardness, and rid it of the by-products of certain detergents. Some cleaners and laundries, probably lacking the research and advisory facilities of their national or state associations, will rely on stronger and more rigorous methods of cleaning textiles, especially those arriving in badly soiled condition. This can hardly be conducive to greater durability.

Among the organizations producing standards for consumer textile items are the American Institute of Laundering, National Fabricare Institute, Joliet, Illinois; The Association of Home Appliance Manufacturers (AHAM) 20 North Wacker Drive, Chicago, Illinois 60606; Fabric Laminators Association (FLA), 110 West 40th Street, New York, New York 10018; National Institute of Drycleaning, Inc. (NID), 309 Burlington Avenue, Silver Spring, Maryland 20810; Soap and Detergent Association (SDA), 485 Madison Avenue, New York, New York 10022; and American National Standards Institute, Inc. (ANSI), 1430 Broadway, New York, New York 10018.

The consumer should learn to respond to legislation or rules dealing with such functional properties as fire resistance. Water repellency, dye permanence, shrinkage control, and perhaps even durability may reach performance levels that can be guaranteed in some, if not all, price lines. The average homemaker can look forward to textile products of increased quality in addition to housing conditions and food supplies considerably above the subsistence levels of the past. With the increased leisure forecast by shorter work weeks, and perhaps the liberation from work of the young wives who would really prefer more time with their families, it is possible that garb will be chosen more from the standpoint of convenience and comfort than utilitarian factors on one side and extremes in self-expression on the other. There have been indications that by the middle of the 1970s no more than 25 per cent of all workers will be engaged in manufacturing, mining, farming, or even in the construction of the vast number of new homes and new transportation facilities so greatly needed.

Sales and services will be the principal fields for many of the workers formerly included in the blue-shirt category. This move in itself will lead to great conservatism in dress, for industry will not tolerate unconventional appearance in its representatives, nor will business. It is among the man-made fibers that the greatest amount of special functional service requirements may be found, and it is estimated that by the end of the 1970s the per capita consumption of man-made fibers will be more than 42 pounds as compared to 10 pounds in 1960. Such a market would consume somewhere around 10 billion pounds of man-made fibers, the declining cost of which will probably continue, in view of the increasing demand for efficiency in production. On the other hand, the prices of fibers may be affected by the needs of producers to spend much larger amounts of money on research and development in the control of air, water, and land pollution. It is probable that the more enlightened consumers, enlightened not only in economics but also in the problems of environmental and social issues, will respond to the brand names of those textile companies doing the best job in the field of race relations, in the social and economic status of employees, and showing the greater amount of social consciousness in the field of pollution of our natural resources. The brand names backed by the reputation of the primary producers of fibers will probably become the prestige items, rather than garments and other clothing identified only as to fiber type. On the other hand, some experts feel that the volume products in man-made fibers will be those identified only by family name because this will allow greater market competition among fiber resources. The apparel line then would not be so closely identified with one fiber producer whose private name is well known. As discussed in Chapter Six, this group of fabrics will become much more important during the next decade due to speed of production, lower costs, and what appears to be a liking for softer textures. It is expected that the knits will grow at a rate of 10 to 15 per cent per year, as compared with a growth of about 2 per cent per year for woven fabrics.

Research and development in the textile industry will probably continue along the patterns of the past 20 years insofar as chemistry is concerned, with much of the research effort being supplied by the chemical industry making the materials for the textile industry—not only in the form of new fibers, but also in finishes, dyestuffs, and other textile modifications.

THE FUTURE OF TEXTILES

Anyone interested in forecasting the future of textiles from the standpoint of fiber production, yarn spinning, fabric weaving, garment utilization, and technical changes in finishing and coloring would do well to examine the centennial issue of *Textile World*, the name of which was, "The Pace of Change—Textiles, 1868 to 2068," published in April 1968. Pressley anticipates great changes in textile fabric formation as the result of increased use of the more sophisticated technical discoveries of recent years, many of which have not been applied to textile production in any way. Among these devices for control of fabric formation equipment would be the increased use of electronics, computerization of patterns, film memory, digitized computerization, fluidics (air jets transporting the filling yarn rapidly and gently), ultrasonics (for more efficient dyeing and cleaning as well as selective shrinkages of yarns to produce novelty fabrics), laser beans (for cutting, control, and accuracy), and radar (to detect any deviation in the path of the shuttle).

Looking forward 100 years, he and others have estimated that whereas

Table 8-23   *Selected Textile Product End-use Volumes in 1971*

		Fiber Consumption (in million pounds)							
	Total	Rayon Acetate		Noncellulosic Man-made Fibers		Cotton		Wool	
End-use	Pounds	Pounds	Per Cent	Pounds	Per Cent	Pounds	Per Cent	Pounds	Per Cent
Apparel									
Women's and girls'									
Dresses	66.5	222	34.6	350	52.6	85	12.7	8	1.0
Slacks	189.8	34.8	18.3	110	58.0	42	23.6	3	1.6
Blouses and shirts	163.2	36	22.1	61.8	37.9	65	39.0	0.4	1.0
Knit underwear	146.2	33.7	23.0	86.5	59.0	26	18.4	—	—
Women's and children's nightwear	112	10	9.0	33	29.5	68	60.7	1	1.0
Men's and boys'									
Shirts	465.6	26.8	5.7	195.3	42.1	241	51.7	2.5	0.4
Utility clothing	440.2	0.7	—	59.5	13.5	380	86.5	—	—
Slacks	300.1	22.8	7.6	175.3	58.4	95	31.6	7	2.3
Knit underwear	169.9	2.7	0.1	16.5	9.1	150	88.2	0.7	—
Hosiery	107.8	—	—	72	66.7	33.5	31.0	2.3	2.1

Apparel linings	289.7	106.5	36.7	79.9	27.0	100	34.4	3.3	1.5
Household fabric products									
Carpets and rugs (face yarns)	1320	63.7	4.1	1163.8	88.0	14.8	1.5	77.7	5.9
Drapery and upholstery	598.9	202.5	33.8	134.8	22.5	260.5	43.5	1.1	0.3
Bedding	545	25.6	4.8	121.4	22.2	398	73.0	—	—
Towels	290.4	14	4.7	—	—	276.4	95.1	—	—
Bedspread and quilts	154.9	19.8	12.7	8.3	5.3	126.8	81.8	—	—
Tire cord	588.5	127.8	21.7	460.4	78.0	0.3	—	—	—

SOURCE: Textile Organon, **43**, No. 11 (Nov. 1972), pp. 162–67.

today weaving accounts for 65 percent of textiles; 100 years from now, it will be only 17 per cent, with knitting rising from 28 to 55 per cent, and all others from 7 to 28 per cent.[16]

Computer simulation of the textile industry has been used by Walter S. Fedor to predict the industry's production and growth during the 1970s. Some of the projections are startling:

1. Investment in facilities will nearly double by 1980.
2. Sales of textile mill products will increase 70 per cent.
3. Profits will increase 97 per cent.
4. Production of textile mill products will increase 50 per cent.
5. By 1980, the textile industry will purchase nearly $8 billion in chemicals and chemical products compared to about $4 billion in 1969.[17]

The computer was fed information dealing with internal and external factors that would affect the volume of textiles produced and also give some information as to the types. The internal factors dealt with such areas as the investment of money for plant expansion, for replacement of parts, and for salaries and wages, and, in general, productivity changes through investment on the part of the company. The external factors dealt with changes in consumer ages, habits, and movements and other economic possibilities influencing the demand for textiles. Three broad major markets were recognized for textiles: apparel was estimated as accounting for 40 per cent; home furnishings, 48 per cent; and industrial textiles, mainly for automobile use, the balance of 12 per cent. One overpowering factor in these estimates was that the war babies of World War II will be the big textile-volume buying group of 35- to 44-year-olds whose purchase patterns have accounted for the consumption of 29 per cent of clothing and accessories, 28 per cent of home furnishings and equipment, and 27 per cent of all automobiles. Furthermore, this group will, during the 1970s, have the highest median income in history, nearly $9500. By 1980, it is estimated that the level will be near $16,500, and 40 per cent of all family heads in the United States will have incomes between $10,000 and $15,000 by 1980. Simultaneously, our population will have grown to an estimated 235 million by 1980.

It is forecast that 75 per cent of all fibers produced will be man-made and that knit goods will be contenders for the leadership. According to the Federal Reserve Board Indexes of Production, the textile mill products index grew 57 per cent during the 1960s. See Table 8-23 for 1971 textile end-use

---

[16] Richard B. Pressley, "Fabric Formation, The Next 100 Years," *Textile World* (April 1968), pp. 128–131.
[17] Walter S. Fedor, "Textiles in the '70's," *Chemical & Engineering News,* **48** (April 20, 1970), pp 64–73.

volumes. During the next decade, the increase will be about 45 per cent, with the textile product index reaching 239 (1957 to 1959 = 100).

It is forecast that in the decade of the 1970s a tremendous expansion for capital spending and for research and development will be seen. New products will constitute a large proportion of these gains, and shifts in fiber consumption will be reflected in the further expansion of blends of natural and man-made fibers. The computer forecasts that research and development will increase from $32 million in 1960 and $52 million in 1970, to as much as $100 million by 1980. Capital spending for expansion for 1970 and 1980 is estimated by the Department of Commerce to be $810 million and $1600 billion, respectively. The expansion in research and development reflects an increased interest on the part of large textile producers, whereas prior to this time much of the research money was spent by the chemical companies providing fibers and finishes to the textile industries.

It is forecast that these large financial investments by 1980 will meet the anticipated textile consumption shown in Table 8-24.

Table 8-24

Textile Fiber Consumption Will Increase 50 Per Cent by 1980

		Per Capita Consumption	
	Total Consumption	*All Fibers*	*Man-made Fibers*
	Billions of Pounds	*Pounds*	
1960	6.49	36.2	9.9
1965	8.49	45.0	18.3
1970	10.50	50.9	31.0
1975	12.50	56.0	40.0
1980	15.60	64.0	48.0

Home Furnishings Will Become Major Outlet for Fibers

	Apparel	*Home Furnishings*	*Industrial*	*Miscellaneous*
		Billions of Pounds		
1960	2.86	1.30	0.84	1.49
1965	3.56	1.87	1.44	1.62
1970	4.10	3.05	2.00	1.37
1975	4.63	4.00	2.37	1.50
1980	5.30	5.62	3.12	1.56

SOURCE: Walter S. Fedor, "Textiles in the '70's," *Chemical & Engineering News*, **48** (April 20, 1970), p. 66.

An interesting sidelight on the impact of a style change on our textile industry is illustrated by men's shirts. According to a study made by the Men's Fashion Association of America, in 1967 an estimated 80 per cent of all the men's dress shirts sold in the United States were white, and approximately 50 to 60 per cent of these shirts had button-down collars. Today the white button-down is much less popular, with 80 per cent of men's shirts found in stripes, checks, prints, woven patterns, and a variety of solid colors. Apparently, this revolution was a timely one for the men's shirt industry in the United States, because the statement was made that the oriental countries—Japan, Taiwan, China, and Korea—could produce unlimited quantities of white shirts and more cheaply than the American manufacturers. As of 1971, 40 per cent of the white shirts sold in this country were oriental imports.

The rapid changes in fashion between colors and pattern types are the saviors of the American shirt industry, for white shirts retail at prices under $5.00, with many selling for a little as $2.95. In 1969, 9.8 million dozen shirts were imported from the Far East; in 1970, 7.8 million dozen—and the dollar volume was reduced from 10.8 million in 1969 to 9.8 million in 1970. It costs $0.50 more to make a colored shirt than a plain white one, so that the American shirt manufactureres are making more money—a few years ago most men's shirts sold at about $6.50. Today most are around $8.50. In 1966, U.S. manufacturers sold 10.4 million dozen shirts; in 1970, 12.3 million dozen. The dollar value at wholesale was 347.6 million in 1967 and in 1969, was $411 million. Whether this color change or color phenomenon was inspired by the youthful or the older customers is still a matter of controversy. Each has been credited. One observer stated that the recession of 1969–1971 may have helped the men's accessories business; because suits are expensive, fashionable new shirts and ties can help a man achieve a "dressed up," individualistic look even with an everyday suit. Profits may get a further shove upward as the result of knits in shirts. The equipment for these is imported from Germany and is in short supply. Therefore, knits are very expensive retailing at about $13.00.

The Adaptation of Textiles Through the 1970s

Much of the census data obtained in 1970 has been analyzed and compared with that from earlier decades. The 1960s were challenging and sometimes violent with social, political, and environmental problems affecting our economy. The issues have not been resolved, but there are signs of progress with public pressure on government at all levels from local to Federal. Any program attempting to solve these problems must consider the status quo of the 1960s as well as the fact that there will be more persons affected during the 1970s.

Much of the social concern for poverty, race relations, pollution, and isolationism has been activated by high school and college-age individuals and groups. Many clothing extremes also have been exhibited among these young people.

Textiles may come under the influence of more governmental interest and control in the future as the issues of quality, standards, informative labeling, safety, and serviceability become radical issues. It is to these phases of textiles that most of the leading minds in the textile industry are directing their attention. These are the problems that industry is trying to iron out; they become even more significant when one considers that our economy will continue to expand with increasing prices. The per capita and per family income rose greatly during the 1960s. It is estimated that the annual family income will be $12,000 by 1980. The buying power of that income will, of course, be affected by any increase in the cost of living.

Variations in dress among today's youth show little if any relation between an individual's economic standing and his attire. Contemporary dress has been marked by a revolutionary repudiation of the tailored and conservative garb of professional and business leaders in the so-called establishment. If the remaining years in the 1970s are to be years of stock-taking and of progress in solving social and economic inequalities, perhaps this rapidly expanding youth market will swing back to a more conservative pattern. The textile industry, which anticipates that approximately 70 per cent of all textile products will be made of manufactured fibers by 1980, is in the unique position of being able to produce clothing and other textile products that will satisfy individual requirements more satisfactorily than at any time in the past.

Bibliography

Students of textiles and clothing will be required to do a certain amount of collateral reading. Therefore, a number of standard textbooks and references, as well as sources of abstracts of significant articles, are included here. These books, encyclopedias, and technical and fashion journals can be found in college and university libraries.

A few suggestions may benefit the student before he or she embarks upon those outside reading assignments. At the basic level—that of students just beginning the study of textiles and clothing—assignments will probably be in specific textbooks, wherein certain topics are discussed at greater length than in this volume, or to encyclopedias, such as *Encyclopedia Britannica, Encyclopedia Americana, Encyclopedia of Textiles,* or *Man-made Textile Encyclopedia,* for an elaboration on specific topics or facts already well established in the literature. Such reading assignments will probably deal with the description of a loom, information on batik prints, the history of silk, information regarding materials from which rayon fiber is made, how a new fashion develops, or the psychology of dress.

For information on textiles, the next group of reference materials would include, for example, Matthew's *Textile Fibers,* edited by H. R. Mauersberger; *Technology of Synthetic Fibers* by Sherman and Sherman; *Man-made Fibers* by Moncrieff; and other advanced books on textile technology. Other sources of information can be found in the technical information booklets and bulletins issued by some of the principal fiber-producing companies, such as du Pont, Chemstrand, American Viscose, and Celanese. Generally, these resource materials will tell the student how a fiber is produced and how it is dyed or finished.

The more advanced student, especially one interested in textile research, must know the answers to "why" certain work was carried out, as well as the results achieved. Specific projects, term papers, and similar requirements set up

432

by the instructor in an advanced course will require that the student study certain important primary sources of material—that is, *original articles* from technical journals.

It is intended that the student do his own searching on specific topics, which can be aided greatly by first reading the annual indexes of journals. The index generally appears in the January issue and lists all articles that appeared in a journal during the previous year. One should always begin with the latest index and work back. Another source, but covering worldwide textile publications, is the *Review of Textile Progress*, Textile Institute, Manchester, England.

As a rule, the journals pertain to specific fields:

1. *American Fabrics*: fashions, trends in marketing
2. *American Dyestuff Reporter*: dyeing and finishing, new products
3. *Textile Chemist and Colorist*: finishing, consumer interests, new techniques
4. *Modern Textiles Magazine*: data on new fibers and constructions
5. *Textile World*: manufacturing methods
6. *Textile Organon*: imports and exports
7. *Textile Research Journal*: physics and chemistry of fibers and fabrics

BOOKS

Baity, E. C. *Man Is a Weaver*. New York: Viking Press, 1942.

Clarke, Lincoln. *Consumer Behavior*. New York: University Press, 1955.

Crawford, M. D. C. *The Heritage of Cotton*. New York: G. P. Putnam & Sons, 1942.

Editors of American Fabrics Magazine. *Encyclopedia of Textiles*. New York: Doric Publishing Company, 1960.

Edwards, Alice. *Product Standards and Labeling for Consumers*. New York: Ronald Press, 1940.

Hamby, D. S. The American Cotton Handbook, Vol. I. New York: Wiley-Interscience, 1966.

Harris, M. *Handbook of Textile Fibers*. Harris Research Laboratories, Inc., 1954.

Hathorne, B. L. *Woven, Stretch and Textured Fabrics*. New York: Wiley-Interscience, 1964.

Hollen, N. R., and J. Saddler. *Textiles*, 4th ed. New York: Macmillan Publishing Co., Inc., 1973.

Joseph, M. L. *Introductory Textile Science*. New York: Holt, Rinehart and Winston, Inc., 1966.

Kaswell, E. R. *Wellington-Sears Handbook of Industrial Textiles*. Wellington Sears Co., 1963.

Labarthe, J. *Textiles, Origins to Usage*. New York: Macmillan Publishing Co., Inc., 1964.

Leggett, W. F. *The Story of Linen.* New York: Chemical Publishing Company, 1945.

Linton, G. E. *Applied Basic Textiles.* New York: Meredith Corp.: 1966.

―――――. *Natural and Man-made Textile Fibers.* New York: Meredith Corp., 1966.

Lyle, D. S. *Focus on Fabrics.* Silver Spring, Md.: National Institute of Drycleaning, 1964.

Mark, H. F., S. M. Atlas, and D. Cernia., eds. *Man-made Fibers, Science and Technology.* Vols. I–III. New York: Wiley-Interscience, 1967 (Vol. I); 1968 (Vols. II and III).

Marsh, J. J. *An Introduction to Textile Finishing.* London: Chapman and Hill, 1966.

Mauersberger, H. R. *The American Handbook of Synthetic Textiles.* New York: Wiley-Interscience, 1952.

―――――. ed *Matthews Textile Fibers.* New York: John Wiley & Sons, Inc., 1954.

Moncrieff, R. W. *The Man-made Fibers* 5th ed. New York: John Wiley & Sons, Inc., 1970.

Peters, R. H. *Textile Chemistry*, Vol. I. New York: American Elsevier Publishing Co., Inc., 1963.

Potter, M. V., and B. P. Corbman. *Fiber to Fabric.* New York: Gregg Division of McGraw-Hill Book Company, 1967.

Press, J. J., ed. *Man-made Textile Encyclopedia.* Metuchen, N.J.: Textile Book Service, 1959.

Sherman, J. B., and F. L. Sherman. *The New Fibers.* New York: Van Nostrand Reinhold Company, 1946.

Stout, Evelyn E. *Introduction to Textiles*, 3rd ed. New York: John Wiley & Sons, Inc., 1970.

Von Bergen, W., ed. *Wool Handbook*, Vol. 1. New York: Wiley-Interscience, 1963.

―――――, and H. R. Mauersberger. *American Wool Handbook.* Metuchen, N.J.: Textile Book Service, 1948.

Ward, K. *Chemistry and Chemical Technology of Cotton.* New York: Wiley-Interscience, 1955.

Weibel, A. C. *Two Thousand Years of Textiles.* New York: Pantheon Books for the Detroit Institute of Art, 1952.

JOURNALS

Anon. "Flocking Techniques Defy Traditional Textile Methods." *Modern Textiles Magazine,* **49** (June 1968), 22–23.

―――――. "Indoor-Outdoor Carpeting Invades New Areas." *Modern Textiles Magazine,* **49** (Jan. 1968), 51.

————. "Man-made Fibers Dominate Carpet Industry." *Modern Textiles Magazine*, **49** (May 1968), 24.

————. "New Process Electroplates Fabrics." *America's Textile Reporter*, **82** (June 20, 1968), 37.

————. "New Disposable Fabric Enters U.S. Market." *America's Textile Reporter*, **81** (Oct. 19, 1967), 63.

Ball, Fred W. "Feed Yarns Spurn Texas Ring." *Modern Textiles Magazine*, **50** (Aug. 1969), 23–34.

Blanks, Cranston C. "Textured Polyester Woven Fabrics." Papers of AATT. *Modern Textiles Magazine*, **52** (Sept. 1971), 74–78.

Brockway, G. H., B. Meadows, and L. Smith. "Cotton Waste." *Textile Research Journal*, **20** (Oct. 1950), 10.

Bromthall, E. V., and J. Lomartine. "Polyester Fibers: Problems and Solutions." *Textile Chemist and Colorist*, **2** (July 1, 1970), 218–24.

Brysson, R. J., B. J. Trask, and A. S. Cooper, Jr. "The Durability of Cotton Textiles: The Effects of Exposure in Contaminated Atmospheres." *American Dyestuff Reporter*, **57** (July 1, 1968) 15–20.

Burnett, R. "The Carpet Market." *Modern Textiles Magazine*, **49** (May 1968), 26–27.

————. "Needle Punch." *Modern Textiles Magazine*, **49** (June 1968), 33.

Canter, G. T., G. D. Jones, and J. W. Weaver. "Rupture of Cellulosic Fibers in Durable-Press Blends." *American Dyestuff Reporter*, **57** (Jan. 15, 1968), 43–47.

Chow, C. M. "Direct Spun Yarns." *Modern Textiles Magazine*, **49** (July 1968), 63–65.

Committee on Dyeing and Finishing of AATT. "The Status of Soil Release Finishes in the Marketplace." *Modern Textiles Magazine*, **49** (April 1968), 65.

Condit, B. C., and G. B. Johnson. "Film Fibrillation Spurts." *Modern Textiles Magazine*, **50** (Aug. 1969), 23, 48–55.

David, H. J., and R. S. McCullough. "Analysis of Wearer: Trials of Wool-Nylon Socks." *Textile Research Journal*, **38** (July 1968), 679–83.

Davis, Charles, Jr. "Rainwear Finishing." *American Dyestuff Reporter*, **56** (July 17, 1967), 124–27.

Depper, Harry J. "Men's Tailored Knit Clothes—The Pitfalls and Potential Market." *America's Textile Reporter*, **82** (June 20, 1968), 10–11.

Douty, Helen J. "Influence of Clothing on Perception of Persons." *Journal of Home Economics*, **55** (March 1963), 197–201.

Editorial. "Durable-Press." *America's Textile Reporter*, **82** (June 13, 1968), 36–38.

————. "Ingenuity Spreads Texturizing—Rapidly." *Modern Textiles Magazine*, **50** (Aug. 1969), 21, 24.

Editors. "Allied's Source." *Modern Textiles Magazine*, **49** (July 1968) 48–50.

————. "Testing and Consumer Legislation." *American Dyestuff Reporter*, **57** (March 11, 1968), 17–21.

Fortess, Fred. "Consumer Legislation as Related to the Textile Industry." *AATT Technical Review* (1970), 38–44.

_____. "Consumerism and the Textile Industry." *Textile Chemist and Colorist*, **3** (May 1971), 47–50.

Fratto, Kenneth. "Textured Yarns, A Progress Report." *Modern Textiles Magazine*, **48** (Aug. 1967), 53–58.

Fynn, P. J. "Knitted Fabrics and the Retailer." *AATT Technical Review* (1970), 7–9.

_____. "Voluntary Guide for Permanent Care Labeling." *Modern Textiles Magazine*, **48** (Nov. 1967), 26–27.

Gusman, A. D. "Textile Replacements and Their Fibers." *Modern Textiles Magazine*, **49** (Feb. 1968), 56–61.

Harvey, Gordan B. "Updating Nonwovens." *Modern Textiles Magazine*, **49** (April 1968), 60–63.

Heffner, L. L. "The State of the Art of Flame Retardant Fabrics." *American Dyestuff Reporter*, **57** (Feb. 26, 1968), 29–32.

Hessler, L. E. "The Relationship Between Cotton Fiber Development and Fiber Properties." *Textile Research Journal*, **31** (1961), 38–51.

Howlett, F. "Fibers and Plastics." *Journal of the Textile Institute*, **40** (1948), 241.

Howry, Kenneth A. "We Don't Know Much About Fabric Flammability." *Modern Textiles Magazine*, **50** (Aug. 1969), 56–60.

Jelly, Raymond. "Textured Yarns, Unlimited Market." *Modern Textiles Magazine*, **49** (July 1968), 19–25.

_____. "It's Only the Beginning for Textured Yarns." *Modern Textiles Magazine*, **48** (Aug. 1967), 46–49.

Johnson, Albert E. "Are the Most Frequent Consumer Complaints Predictable with Available Test Methods?" *American Dyestuff Reporter*, **57** (June 17, 1968), 69–71.

Johnson, Joyce. "Color and Print Explosion." *Modern Textiles Magazine*, **48** (Oct. 10, 1967), 30–31.

Lewis, H. M. "A Comparison of the Stain Release Characteristics of Fabrics Made of Polyester, Cotton, and Polyester/Cotton." *American Dyestuff Reporter*, **57** (Feb. 26, 1968), 19–26.

Lobl, Victor. "Ornamentation of Apparel Fabrics. Part 1. Deflected Thread Effects." *Modern Textiles Magazine*, **49** (April 1968), 26–30.

_____. "Ornamentation of Apparel Fabrics. Part IV. Mock Leno Stripes." *Modern Textiles Magazine*, **49** (Sept. 1968), 71–73.

Lohrke, James L. "Tow Processing More Flexible." *Modern Textiles Magazine* **50** (Aug. 1969), 23, 46–48.

Lynn, J. Edward. "New Developments in Durable-Press Performance Today and Tomorrow." *AATT Technical Review* (1971), 24–27.

MacFarlan, M. V. "How Rayon Became the Fiber Sensation of the Decade." *Modern Textiles Magazine*, **48** (Nov. 1967), 28–29.

McNeirney, Frank. "Drycleaning Durable-Press Shirts." *American Dyestuff Reporter*, **57** (Aug. 12, 1968), 19.

————. "Nonwovens, How Big an Impact?" *American Dyestuff Reporter*, **57** (July 15, 1968), 21.

"Making Good Cotton Better." *Pacific Gas and Electric Progress*, **38**, No. 3 (March 1961), 1.

Mehta, P. U. "International Wool Secretarial—Mothers Are Willing to Spend to Protect Baby." *Modern Textiles Magazine*, **50** (July 1969), 20–21.

"New Flame Retardants—NCC Conference." *American Dyestuff Reporter*, **56** (Nov. 20, 1967), 40.

O'Connell, R. A., C. E. Pardo, and W. Fong. "Preliminary Observations on Durable-Press Wool-Blend Fabrics." *American Dyestuff Reporter*, **57** (April 8, 1968), 17–19.

Perkins, R. B. "Fibers Past and Present." *Bulletin Southern Research Institute, Special Issue, Birmingham, Alabama* (1971).

Perry, E. M. "Soil Release—A New Chemical Concept in Polyester Finishing." *American Dyestuff Reporter*, **57** (May 20, 1968), 42–45.

Pingree, Raymond A. "Effective Soil Release Treatment." *Modern Textiles Magazine*, **49** (June 1968), 62–64.

Riggert, D. K. "Progress in the Manufacture of Polyester and Polyamide Fiber." *Modern Textiles Magazine*, **48** (Sept. 1967), 27–29.

Schappel, J. W. "Flammability from the Fiber Producers' Point of View." *American Dyestuff Reporter*, **49** (July 1960), 54–60.

Segall, William M. "Flammability Testing and Legislation." *American Dyestuff Reporter*, **57** (March 11, 1968), 37–40.

Shimauchi, S., and H. Mizushima. "Soil Redeposition of Polyester Fiber and Its Test Methods." *American Dyestuff Reporter*, **57** (June 17, 1968), 35–42.

Sloan, William G., A. S. Cooper Jr., M. J. Hoffman, and W. A. Reeves. "Effect of Changes in Fabric Structure on Properties of Cotton Stretch Fabrics." *American Dyestuff Reporter*, **56** (July 31, 1967), 11–14.

Smith, H. "Textile Fibers, An Engineering Approach to Their Properties and Utilization." *Proceedings AFTM*, **44** (1944), 543–92.

Staff. "New Durable-Press Post-Cure System for Cotton and Cellulosic Blends." *Modern Textiles Magazine*, **48** (Oct. 1967), 32–34.

Stearns, E. I. "How the AATCC Technology Committees Accomplish Their Purpose." *American Dyestuff Reporter*, **57** (Aug. 12, 1968), 36–40.

Strong, Peter M. "Cotton Manufacture, Cotton Growing, and the National Economy." *American Textile Reporter*, **76**, Nos. 2, 3, 4, and 5 (Jan. 11, 18, 25; Feb. 1, 1962).

Taylor, Marvin E. "Color Physics and Color Measurement." *American Dyestuff Reporter*, **56** (Dec. 18, 1967), 31–39.

Tables

Table 1 Yarn Numbering and Count Systems

Indirect or Length per Unit of Weight	*Number per Pound*
Asbestos and glass fiber (American cut)	100-yard hanks
Cotton count	840-yard hanks
Spun silk	840-yard hanks
Spun rayon staple	840-yard hanks
Linen count (wet spun)	300-yard hanks (or leas)
Worsted count (and special wools)	560-yard hanks
Woolen count (American cut)	300-yard hanks
Typp* (a proposed universal system)	1000-yard-hanks
Tex (a proposed metric system)	1000-meter hanks per kilo
Direct or Weight per Unit Length	*Weight*
Denier, silk and all filaments	Grams of 9000 meters of yarn
Grex (a proposed universal unit)	Grams of 10,000 meters of yarn
Tex	Grams of 1000 meters of yarn

Conversion from One Count to Another (count to denier)

Assume we have a 1's cotton yarn. By definition, 840 yards weigh 1 pound. From the conversion table, 1 pound = 0.453.6 grams; 1 meter is 39.37 inch.

$$840 \text{ meters weigh } 453.6 \times \frac{39.37}{36} \text{ grams.}$$

The ratio for determining the denier of 1's cotton is therefore:

$$\frac{9000}{840} = \frac{x}{453.6 \times 39.37/36} \quad \text{or} \quad x = \frac{9000 \times 453.6 \times 39.37/36}{840}$$

$$\therefore \ x = 5315 \text{ grams,}$$

so that 1's cotton yarn is 5315 denier in size.

Thus, for any cotton count such as 40's, the constant conversion factor for 1's would be used; this would be divided by the cotton count to give the denier. For example, 40's cotton would be

$$\frac{5315}{40} = 133 \text{ denier.}$$

---

*Typp. Acronym of thousands of yards per pound.

Table 2   Conversion Factors of Importance to Textile Study

	Multiply by
Meters to yards	1.0936
Meters to feet	3.28084
Meters to inches	39.370
Square meters to square yards	1.196
Square meters to square feet	10.764
Square inches to square centimeters	6.4516
Cubic inches to cubic centimeters	16.387
Cubic inches to liters	0.0164
Cubic feet to liters	28.339
Gallons (U.S.) to liters	3.875
Liters of water to pounds	2.2046
Pounds to kilograms	0.45359
Ounces to grams	28.349
Grains to grams	0.0648
Grams per square meter to ounces per square yard	0.0295
Pounds per square inch to grams per square centimeter	70.31

For the reverse conversion, divide by the constant.

Direct or Weight per Length (denier to count)

If we know the denier and wish to calculate the equivalent cotton count, the same constant is used and the denier is divided into 5315. For example, a 150-denier yarn would be equivalent to $5315/150 = 35.4$'s cotton yarn. This would properly be rounded out to the nearest whole number, 35's.

One might wish to compare the fineness of cashmere, calculated by the worsted count, with that of a synthetic reported by the denier system. A new conversion factor is required because the worsted system uses the 560-yard hank units to weigh 1 pound. Following the same procedure, the conversion factor or constant is found to be 7972.

Thus, a 60's cashmere count = 7972/60 or 133 denier (approximately), and a 200-denier yarn would = 7972/200 or 40's worsted count (almost).

Table 3   Conversion Factors: Count Values to Tex Numbers

Divide	By
Denier no.	9
Spindle no.	0.02903
4960.5	Asbestos cut[a]
590.54	Cotton count (English)[b]
4960.5	Glass cut[c]
1653.5	Linen cut[d]
1000.0	Metric no.[e]
310.03	Woolen run (American)[f]
885.8	Worsted count (English)[g]
	OR
Multiply	*By*
Denier no.	0.1111
Spindle no.	34.45

[a] Na_A, equals 100-yard hanks per pound.
[b] Ne_C, equals 840-yard hanks per pound.
[c] N_G, equals 100-yard hanks per pound.
[d] Ne_L, equals 300-yard hanks per pound.
[e] Nm, equals kilometers per kilogram.
[f] Nar, equals 1600-yard hanks per pound.
[g] Ne, equals 500-yard hanks per pound.

For example, then, if we had a 60's count cotton yarn, a yarn so fine that 60 of the 840-yard hanks weighed 1 pound, the Tex number would be 590.54 divided by 60, which in rounded Tex number would be about 9.8.

Approved Fiber Nomenclature
with Definitions

American Society for Testing Materials, Committee D-13

References

ASA:	American Standard Association (now American National Standards Institute)
ASTM:	American Society for Testing Materials
CVS:	Combination of definitions of various states
TFPIA:	Textile Fiber Products Identification Act
Unv:	Universal
USP:	United States Pharmacopoeia
WID:	Webster's International Dictionary

Cotton Fiber of seed of cultivated varieties of Gossypium hirsitum or of other species of Gossypium. (USP)

Wool Fiber from fleece of sheep or lamb or hair of Angora or cashmere goat (and may include so-called specialty fibers from hair of camel, alpaca, llama, and vicuña) which has never been reclaimed from any woven or felted wool product. It shall be free from kemp and vegetable matter. (TFPIA)

Virgin wool Wool which has never been used, reclaimed, reworked, reprocessed, or reused from any spun, woven, knitted, felted, or manufactured or used product, nor from fiber reworked or reclaimed from yarn or clips regardless of whether such yarn or clips are new, used, or were made of new or reprocessed or reused material.

441

Feathers Peculiar light, horny epidermal outgrowths which make up external covering or plumage of birds. (WID)

Goose feathers Feathers of any kind of goose, which are whole in physical structure, with natural form and curvature of the feather. (Unv.)

Duck feathers Feathers of any kind of duck, which are whole in physical structure, with natural form and curvature originally found in the feather. (Unv.)

Turkey feathers Feathers of any kind of turkey, which are whole in physical structure. (Unv.)

Chicken feathers Feathers of any kind of chicken, which are whole in physical structure. (Unv.)

Damaged feathers Feathers, other than crushed, chopped, or stripped, which are broken or which have been damaged by insects. (ASA)

Down Undercoating of water fowl consisting of light fluffy filaments growing from one quill point but without any quill shaft. (ASA)

Chopped feathers Feathers which have been chopped or cut into pieces. (ASA)

Crushed feathers Feathers which have been processed by a curling or crushing machine which has changed original form of feather without removing quill. (ASA)

Hair Coarse filamentous epidermal outgrowth of such mammals as horses, cattle, hogs, and goats. (Unv.)

Curled Hair Hair which has been put through curling process.

Manufactured Fibers

Acetate fiber Manufactured fiber in which fiber-forming substance is cellulose acetate. Where not less than 92 per cent of hydroxyl groups are acetylated, term *triacetate* may be used as generic description of the fiber. (TFPIA)

Acrylic fiber Manufactured fiber in which fiber-forming substance is any long-chain synthetic polymer composed of at least 85 per cent by weight of acrylonitrile units ($-CH_2-CH-$). (TFPIA)
$$\underset{\displaystyle CN}{|}$$

Azlon Manufactured fiber in which fiber-forming substance is composed of any regenerated naturally occurring proteins. (TFPIA)

Glass fiber Manufactured fiber in which fiber-forming substance is glass. (TFPIA)

Metallic fiber Manufactured fiber composed of metal, plastic-coated metal, metal-coated plastic, or core completely covered by metal. (TFPIA)

Modacrylic fiber Manufactured fiber in which fiber-forming substance is any long-chain synthetic polymer composed of less than 85 per cent but at least 35 per cent by weight of acrylonitrile units ($-CH_2-CH-$). (TFPIA)
$$\underset{\displaystyle CN}{|}$$

Nylon, nylon fiber Manufactured fiber in which fiber-forming substance is any long-chain synthetic polyamide having recurring amide groups ($-C-NH-$)

(TFPIA)   O

Nytril, nytril fiber   Manufactured fiber containing at least 85 per cent of long-chain polymer of vinylidine dinitrile ($-CH_2-C(CN)_2-$), where vinylidine dinitrile content is no less than every other unit in polymer chain. (TFPIA)

Olefin fiber   Manufactured fiber in which fiber-forming substance is any long-chain synthetic polymer composed of at least 85 per cent by weight of ethylene, propylene, or other olefin units. (TFPIA)

Polyester fiber   Manufactured fiber in which fiber-forming substance is any long-chain synthetic polymer composed of at least 85 per cent by weight of an ester of dihydric alcohol and terephthalic acid (p-$HOOC-C_6H_4-COOH$). (TFPIA)

Rayon   Manufactured fiber composed of regenerated cellulose, as well as manu-factured fibers composed of regenerated cellulose in which substituents have replaced not more than 15 per cent of the hydrogens of the hydroxyl groups. (TFPIA)

Saran   Manufactured fiber in which fiber-forming substance is any long-chain synthetic polymer composed of at least 80 per cent by weight of vinylidene chloride units ($-CH_2-CHCl-$). (TFPIA)

Spandex   Manufactured fiber in which fiber-forming substance is a long-chain synthetic polymer comprised of at least 85 per cent of a segmented polyurethane. (TFPIA)

Vinal fiber   Manufactured fiber in which fiber-forming substance is any long-chain synthetic polymer composed of at least 50 per cent by weight of vinyl alcohol units ($-CH_2-CHOH-$), and in which the total of vinyl alcohol units and any one or more of the various acetal units is at least 85 per cent by weight of the fiber. (TFPIA)

Vinyon, vinyon fiber   Manufactured fiber in which fiber-forming substance is any long-chain synthetic polymer composed of at least 85 per cent by weight of vinyl chloride units ($-CH_2-CHCl-$). (TFPIA)

Miscellaneous

All-pure, 100 per cent   Terms used to disclose the product to consist entirely of material thus described and permitting of no tolerance whatsoever. (EF)

Cattail plant fibers   Fibers obtained from tall marsh plant (Typha latifolia). Also any other species of Typha. (WID)

Coconut husk fiber   Fibers obtained from husk or outer shell of coconut.

Coir fiber   See "Coconut husk fiber."

Comber   Tangled fibers removed during combing process of textile fibers. (CVS)

Creped cellulose fiber   Material formed in layers of compressed and creped cellulose fiber (Penn.)

Flax fiber, flax tow   Coarse, broken, and refuse parts of flax separated from fine fibrous parts in preparing flax for spinning. *Note*: Fiber is more correctly de-scribed as *flax tow*.

Fly   Fibers which come off the machines during carding, drawing, or similar textile operations. (CVS)

Fur fiber   The fine soft underfur, with or without the usual guard hair, removed from the tanned or untanned pelt of mammals of the class of fur bearers. (CVS)

Jute fiber   Fiber obtained from various species of Corchorus plants, growing principally in India and East Indian Islands. (ASA tent)

Jute tow   Broken and refuse parts of jute separated from fine fibrous parts in preparing fibers for spinning. (ASA tent)

Kapok   Mass of fibers investing seed of kapok tree (Ceiba pentranda). (ASA and Unv.)

Milkweed   Fibrous growth attached to seed within pods of Milkweed (genus Asclepias) plant. (Unv.)

Moss   Processed fibers from an epiphytic plant forming pendant tufts upon branches and trunks of live oaks and other trees. (Cal.)

Noils   Short fibers removed during combing process of textile fiber or fibers other than jute, flax, and sisal from which it is produced. (CVS)

Palm fiber   Fibrous material obtained from leaf of the palm, palmetto, or palmyra tree. (Unv.)

Redwood bark fibers   Fibers obtained from bark of California redwood tree (Sequoia Sempervirens.) (Penn.)

Rubber   Manufactured fiber in which fiber-forming substance is comprised of natural or synthetic rubber. (TFPIA)

Silk   Fine, strong lustrous fiber produced by certain caterpillars (silkworms). (WID)

Sisal fiber, tow   Residual fibers left after extraction of spinnable sisal fiber from leaf. It shall not contain over 3 per cent pulp. (Unv.)

Steel felt   Steel wire which has been carded in layers or sheets when passed through some form of garneting machine.

Straw   The stalk or stem of grain, such as wheat, rye, oats, rice, and the like, after threshing. Shall be free from chaff, beards, bristles, husks, glumes, dirt, or other extraneous matter. (ASTM and Unv.)

Tow   (As applied to bast fibers.) Short fibers removed by hackling. (ASTM)

A

Absorbency, determination of, 12–13
Acetate. *See also* Arnel; Cellulose
    acetate
    defined, 91–93, 106
    dyeing of, 108, 109, 332
    fibers
        classification of, 113*t*
        properties of, 110*t*
    finishing of, 291–92
    garments, burning characteristics of,
        107
    primary, 113
    production of, 96, 107–109, 111–112
    quality of, standards for, 416
    spinning of, 112
Acetic anhydride, 107
Acetylation, of cellulose, 111
Acrilan acrylic
    Acrilan-Spectran, 147
    characteristics of, 146–47
    production of, 146
    use of, 147–48
Acrylic(s), 140
    fibers
        Acrilan acrylic, 146–48
        comparisons of, 143*t*
        Creslan, 148–49
        growth of, 149*t*
        Orlon, 141–46
        use of, 394
        Zefran, 148
    problems in, 409*t*

Acrylic(s) (*cont.*)
    trade names of, 140*t*
    use of, 402
        in tufted fabrics, 403
Acrylonitrile, 149, 150
Adjustment values. *See* Claims adjust-
    ment values
Aeress modacrylics, 153–54
Agilon, 255
    characteristics of, 207
Air pollution, textiles and, 422–23
Airco vinal, 178
Alien Property Custodian, 330
Alkalies, action of, on wool, 63
All-fabric standard. *See* L22 standard
Ambari, 48
American Association of Textile
        Chemists and Colorists
        (AATCC), 105*n*, 311, 346,
        350, 355, 416
American Enka Corporation, 106
American Hotel and Motel Associa-
        tion, 321, 321*n*
American Institute of Laundering, 424
American National Standards Institute
        (ANSI), 341, 408, 416
    L-22 standard and, 349–57
American Society for Testing Materials
        (ASTM), 91, 102, 191, 266,
        346, 350, 355, 416
American Standards Association (now
        ANSI), 349, 416–19, 421
American Viscose Corporation, 416
Anidex fibers, 175

Antibacterial finishes, 313–14
Apparel
    consumer guide for, 357–58*t*
    consumership in, 375–76
    fabrics for, selecting of, 372*t*
    knit versus woven, 262*t*
    of nonwoven fabric, 274–75*t*
    performance standard of, 360
Apparel Manufacturers Association,
        350
Apparel Performance Level Standards
        (APLS), 360
Apparel Research Foundation, 360
Arabeva method, 279
Arachne method, 279
Aridex, 302
Arnel, 107
    manufacture of, 113–14
    properties of, 112
Association of Home Appliance Manu-
        facturers, 424
Avisco vinyon, 177
Avril filaments, 213
Azlons
    production of, 114–15
    properties of, 115–16

                    B

Bacteria-static fabrics, 313
Balance, of fabric structure, 221–22
Ban-lon, 208
Barre, 258–59
Bast fibers, 48
Batik, 335–36
Battings, 266
Bed sheets
    count standard for, 386–87
    fabrics for, 385–86
    sizes of, 388–89
Bedspreads, 398, 402
Beetling
    of cotton cloth, 289
    of linen, 291
Belding, H. S., 382
Bicomponent fibers, 179, 209

Biconstituent fibers, 179, 180
Biodegradable ingredients, 320
Birren, Faber, 375
Blankets, 245, 402
    appearance of, 393
    care of, 293
    comforters, 397–98
    construction of, 389–90
    durability of, factors in, 392
    electric, 390, 391
    purchase of, factors in, 390–94
    synthetics in, 394, 397
    tufted, 402–404
    woven, USA standards for, 395–96*t*
Bleaching, 229, 286
    of cotton cloth, 287
    of linen, 290–91
    of silk, 292
    of wool, 63
Blending feeder, 192
Boconize method, 315
Bonding, *See also* Laminated fabrics
    foam bonding, 281
    of nonwoven fabrics, 267–72
        machine-stitch, 268
British Textile Care Labeling Code,
        361
Brushing
    air-brushing, 338
    of cotton cloth, 287
    of worsteds, 294
Bulk yarns, 205
Burling, 293
Burmi-Crease, 321
Bursten, William, 410

                    C

Calendering, 271
    of cotton cloth, 289
    of linen, 291
    of silk, 293
Camel hair, 72
Canadian Care Direction Labels, 361
Cantrece nylon, 137–38, 179, 255

Cantrece nylon (*cont.*)
  fiber joining in, 209
  hosiery, knitting of, 212
Capillarity
  defined, 13
  of wool, 62
Caprolan, 134, 404
Carding operation, 199
  for cotton yarns, 193
Care, 368. *See also* Sure Care
  of apparel, 414
    consumer guide for, 357–58*t*
    instruction for, labeling of FTC
      and, 342–43
  related to value, 378, 379*t*
Carnegie-Mellon University, 1
Carosel, 384
Carothers, Wallace H., 126
Carpets, 245, 402, 404. *See also* Rugs
  broadlooms, 244, 398
  characteristics of, 398
  fibers used in, 398–99
  flammability of, 312
  worldwide production of, 405*t*
Cashmere
  characteristics of, 72
  production of, 71–72
Celabond, 281
Celanese, 317
Celaperm, 109
Cellulose, cellulosics, 15
  acetylation of, 111
  alpha, 97
  chemical, 98
  fibers, 46. *See also* Acetate; Rayon
    classification of, 90–92
    decomposition of, 314–15
    flammability of, 309
    production of, 96
  materials, flammability of, 305, 347
  molecule, in cotton fibers, 19
  purification of, 109, 111
  of raw material, 96–98
Cellulose acetate 106
  chemical formula of, 107–108
  properties of, 107
Cellulose triacetate fiber. *See* Arnel
Certifab, 281

Chadalon, 207
Chemicals, used in bleaching, 290–91
Chemstitch, 281
Chemstrand Corporation, 133
China grass. *See* Ramie
Chrome colors, 331
Chromspun, 109
Circular knit, 246
  in hosiery, 255, 257
  jersey, 249–50
  purl, 250
  rib, 250
Cirrasoft, 323
Claims adjustment values, calculation
  of, 369*t*
Clipped-spot design, 239
Clo, defined, 381, 382
Cohesion of fiber, conditions for, 11
Color, 325
  black-light, 326
  chrome, 331
  direct, 332
  effect of radioactive rays on, 326,
    327*t*
  effect on heat absorption, 328*t*
  as a form of energy, 325–27
  hue, 326
  in natural fibers, 13
  psychological response to, 374–75
Colorfastness, degree of, 328
Color lake, 331
Colorado River hemp, 48
Colorspun, 109
Combing, of cotton cloth, 193
Come Clean, 323
Comfort
  of blankets, 390
  of outer-wear, protection of, 380–81
Comforters, 397–98
Conjugated fibers, 179
"Conspicuous consumption," 373
Consumer, 1
  acceptance of new fibers by,
    research on, 185, 187
  evaluation by, 377–80
  guides for, 341
  participation by, 4–5
  planning by, basic steps in, 2

Consumer (*cont.*)
  purchase by
    aids to, 348–55
    influences on, 368, 371, 372*t*, 376–77
    responsibility in, 413–15
  research, 189–90
Consumer care guide for apparel, 357–58*t*
Consumer consciousness, laws related to, 361
Consumer elements, 368
Consumership, 1
  basic hypothesis in, 6–7
  factors in, 375–76
  personal need in, 5
  responsibility in, 3–5, 6
Conversion factors, for textile study, 439–40*t*
Converter, role of, 284–85
Cornell University, 380
Coronizing process, 120
Cotton, 11, 383–84, 400
  classification of, 30–33
  fabrics, versatility of, 24
  fibers, 392
    characteristics of, 19–22
      chemical, 22–23*t*
      physical, 22*t*
    glucose molecule, 19
  finishing process for, 24, 287–90
  growing of, 27–29
  Pima, 29, 31
  price support of, 33
  problems in, 409*t*
  production of, in United States, 26–27
  Sanforizing process for, 300–01
  Sea Island, 29, 31
  sources of, 24–26
  spinning of, 196–97
  Supina, 29
  Upland, 29
  use of, 402, 404
    decline in, 34–39
    in tufted fabrics, 403
  weave, 224
  yarn

Cotton, yarn (*cont.*)
    classification of, 194–95
    formation of, 192–94
    textured, stretchable, 213
Cotton linters, 24, 96, 98, 107, 109
Cottonade, 384
Count system
  for fabrics, 219–221
  for yarns, 438–39*t*
Crabbing, 293
Crash fabric, 384
Cravenette, 302
Crease-resistant finishes, 291
Crepeing, methods of, 289
Creslan acrylic
  characteristics of, 149
  marketing of, 149, 150
  types of, 149
  use of, 149
Crimp, 11
  defined, 10
Crocking, 288
Cross dyeing, 334
Crown Test Program, 349, 416–17, 419
Cumuloft, 404
Cuprammonium process, 99–100
Curtains, shower. *See* Shower curtains
Customer influences, 368
Cuticle, 19
Cyana-finish, attributes of, 313–14
Cybernetics, 246

D

Dacron, 152, 163
Dacron polyester
  deviations from, 161
  polymerization of, 156–57
  properties of, 157, 159
    affecting use, 159–61
  type 655, 159
Damaged merchandise, causes of, 410, 413, 415
  by dry cleaner, 418–19*t*

Damaged merchandise (*cont.*)
  by merchant and manufacturer, 416*t*
Damasks, 235, 384
Dardis, Rachel, 380
Darvan, 179
Decorative textiles, 382
Delayed cure, 321
Denier, calculation of, 439–40
Density
  determination of, 11
  low-bulk, 141
Design
  structural, 239–40, 334
  types of, 334
Deterioration, of fibers, 125, 314–15
Dieldrin method, 315
Dimensional stabilization, of rayon, 292
Distribution, problems of, 187
Dobby loom, 235
Dobby weave, 237
Domestics, 382
  bed sheets, 385–89
  blankets, 389–97
  pillows, 404
  shower curtains, 385
  table linens, 385
Double knit jersey, 249–50
Doup weave. *See* Leno weave
Drawing, of cotton yarn, 193, 194
Drawing frame, 193, 194
Dressing. *See* Sizing
Dry cleaner, damage by, 418–19*t*
du Pont (E. I. du Pont de Nemours and Co.), 127, 130, 141, 144, 154, 219, 404
Durable-press fabrics, 317, 324, 368
  composition of, 320
  dyeing of, 320
  fixing of, 320–21
  no-iron linen, 321
  process for, 321
Dyeing, 1, 13. *See also* Color
  colorfastness in, 328
  of cotton cloth, 284
  dope, 148
  of linen, 291

Dyeing (*cont.*)
  materials for. *See* Dyestuff
  methods of, 330, 333
  of nylon, 134–36
  piece dyeing, 334
  resist dyeing, 335
  of silk, 292–93
  of wool, 293
  of worsteds, 294
Dyestuff
  classification of, 330
    acetate dyes, 332–33
    acid dyes, 331
    basic dyes, 332
    direct colors, 332
    disperse dyes, 332–33
    mordant and chrome colors, 331
    pigment dyes, 332–33
    sulfur dyes, 332
    vat dyes, 331
  history of, 329–30
Dynel, 154
  characteristics of, 151
  consumer use of, 152–53
  production of, 151
  property of, 152

E

Eastman Chemical Products, 162
Eisenhower, Dwight D., 14
Elastic limit, 11
Elasticity, 21
  variations in, 11
  of wool fiber, 61–62
Elastomeric fibers
  anidex, 175
  categories of, 171–72
  disadvantages of, 172
  lastex, 171
  lycra, 172–73
  spandex, 172–73
  use of, 170
Electrical conductivity, 14
Electrification, 258
Embossing
  of acetate and rayon, 292

Embossing (*cont.*)
  of cotton cloth, 289
  of silk, 293
Engraving, 337
Enkaloft, 404
Esthetic(s), 376
  finishes, sales-appeal and, 286
Esterification, 127, 130
Everglaze, 289, 319
Experimentation, 5

F

Fabric(s)
  body of, 286
  count of, 219–21
  fire-retardant, 310–12
  problems with, 409*t*
  properties of, influence on con-
    sumer, 369, 372*t*
  selecting of, 369, 372*t*
  structure, balance of, 221–22
Fabric Laminators Association
    (FLA), 281, 350, 424
Fair trade practice regulations, 342
Fashion, change in, 371–74, 430–31
  knits and, 259–60
Federal Flammable Fabrics Act, re-
    vision of, 310
Federal Reserve Board, indexes of
    production, 426
Federal Trade Commission (FTC),
    15, 57, 75, 91, 96, 105, 114,
    124, 126, 150, 154, 181, 254,
    300, 306, 312, 347, 357, 361,
    417
  Flammable Fabrics Act and, 344
  function of, 342
  labeling and
    of blankets, 392–93
    of care instructions, 342–43
  Textile Fiber Products Identifica-
    tion Act and, 344–45
Federal Wool Products Labeling Act,
    57–58

Felt, 266
Felting
  of wool, 293–94
  of worsteds, 294
Fiber(s)
  consumption of, 34*t*, 36–38*t*
  contents of, 94
  defined, 7
  dye classes for, 331*t*
  economic requirements for, 15
  joining, 211–13
  length, importance of, 9
  man-made. *See* Man-made fibers
  new, 18, 185, 187
  production of, 182–83*t*
  properties of
    chemical, changing of, 18
    essential qualities of, 9–14
    physical, 18
  raw, dyeing of, 333
  uncategorized, 184*t*
  variance in, 7
Fiber-fill, 161
Fiber identification law, industries con-
    cerned with, 342
Fibril(s), 19, 21
  defined, 9
Filament, defined, 9
Filling-knit, 246
Filling pile method of weaving, 240–41
Filling yarns, 217–18
Fineness, of fiber, determination of,
    9–10
Finish(es). *See also* Color
  antibacterial, 313–14
  esthetic. *See* Esthetic finishes
  functional. *See* Textile finishing
  imitative, 290
  insect-repellant, 315
  mildew-resistant, 314–15
  permanence of, 299
  soil-release, 322–24
  spot-and-stain-resistant, 314
  starchless, 315
  static-resistant, 316–17
  warmth-retention, 314
  wash and wear, 317–22
Finisher, 285

Finishing. *See also* Printing
 agents, branded products of, 295*t*
 process of
  for cotton, 287–90
  deposited design, 339–40
  for fire-retardation, 304
  for linen, 290–91
  for manufactured fiber fabrics, 295–96
  for rayon and acetate, 291–92
  for silk, 292–93
  for water-repellency, 301–304
  for wool, 293–94
  for worsteds, 294
 textile. *See* Textile finishing
Fire, from clothing
 prevention of, 305
 statistics on, 304–305
Fire-retardant finishes, 296, 403
 criteria for, 308–309
 of dynel, 152
 flame-proofing, factors in, 304–306
 legislation on, 311–12
 limitations of, 311–13
 method of, 304
 potential market for, 311*t*
 standards for, problems in, 305–306
Fixing, of durable-press finishes, 320–21
Flame-proofing. *See* Fire-retardant finishes
Flammability
 of fabrics
  accidents from, 312*t*
  Federal laws on, 306–309
  test methods for, 306, 308, 310, 312
 of fibers, 14
 research on, 347–48
 test for, 346–47
Flammability Standard, 306
Flammable Fabrics Act, 14, 311
 amendment of, 345
 flame-test specifications by, 345–47
 purpose of, 344
 requirements of, 313
Flat knit, 246

Flat knit (*cont.*)
 jersey, 248–49
 purl, 250
 rib, 250
Flat machine, 247
Flax. *See also* Linen
 fibers, properties of, 39–40
 papers, 44
 production of, 43–44
Flock(ing)
 printing, 338–39
 process of, 339–40
 of wool, 294
Fluflon, 208
Formelle yarn, 257
Fortrel polyester
 characteristics of, 161–62
 use of, 162
Franklin, Benjamin, 327
Fulling. *See* Felting
Functional finishes, 376
Fur, 75
 fibers, identification of, 75
Fur Products Labeling Act, 75
 purpose of, 344
Fybrite, 323

G

Galen, Arlee, 380
Gassing, of cotton cloth, 287
Gauge, of knitted article, 253–54
Gigging, 294
Glass
 cloth, 384
 fabric, uses of, 116–18
 fibers, 15, 116
  listing of, 118*t*
  manufacture of, 118–21
  physical properties of, 87
Glazing
 of cotton cloth, 289
 nonpermanence of, 299
Glospun, 173
Glucose, 19
Gossypium, 19

Grass bleaching, 290
Gray goods, 284, 320
Grimaldi, 325

Hydrophobic properties
of manufactured fibers, 125
of nylon, 134–35
Hydroscopic moisture, of wool, 62
Hydro-pruf, 304

H

Hackling, 44
Hair fiber(s)
camel hair, 72
cashmere, 71–72
minor, 72*t*
mohair, 70–71
Handcrafted fabrics, 407
Harness, 217
Heat
absorption, colors and, 328*t*
effect of, on wool, 63
setting, 258
Heddle, 217
Helanca NT, 207
Helanca yarn, characteristics of, 206–207
Hemp fiber(s), 46
Colorado River, 48
kudzu, 48
Herculon, 169
Herringbone twill, 231–32
Home economics, defined, 7
Home economist, responsibilities of, 5
Home furnishings, 382
of nonwoven fabrics, 275
rugs and carpets, 398–402
upholstery fabrics, 404–407
Honeycomb, 383
Hosiery, nylon
annual production of, 256*t*
Formelle, 257
knitting of, 254–57
Hospitals, use of nonwoven fabrics in, 273–74
Household textiles, classification of, 382–83
Howry, Kenneth A., 347
Huckaback weave, 383
Hydrocellulose, 21
Hydrolysis, of cellulose, 111–12

I

Identification of fabrics, method for, 234
for right face, 234–35
Impregnole, 302*t*
Impulse buying, 413
Industry, use of nonwoven fabrics, 275
Inflammability, 14
Inorganic fibers, 116
glass, 116–21
Insect-repellent finishes, chemicals for, 315
Insulation. *See* Clo
International Care Labeling Code, 361
Islon, 405

J

Jacquard loom, 235–37, 239, 245, 403
Jacquard weave, 384–85
Jersey knit
circular, 249–50
flat, 248–49
Johnson, Frank Y., 269
Johnson, Lyndon B., 345
Jute fiber(s)
handling of, 45
properties of, 45–46
uses of, 46

K

Kaufman Department Store, 380, 410, 414, 422
Kemp, 55

Kenaf, 48
Keratin, feature of, 50–51
Klein, C. H., 296
Knit(s)
  apparel
    fashion change and, 259–60
    versus woven, 262*t*
  fabrics
    characteristics of, 246
    disadvantages of, 258–59
    fibers in, 252–53, 259*t*
    fineness of, 253–54
    pile, 257–58
      deep pile, 265–66
    production of
      forecast of, 260–65
      in United States, 263*t*
    USA standard performance
      requirements for, 353–54*t*
    warp knits, 252
Knitting
  methods of, 246–47
  progress in, 246
  types of, 247–52
  of underwear, 254
Kodel polyester, 162
Koratron, 321
Kraftcord, 402
Kudzu hemp, 48

L

L-22 standard, 351, 360, 409, 417
  color code of, 361
  historical background of, 415–23
  limitations of, 355–57
  performance requirements of, 349–
    50
    for knitted fabrics, 353–54*t*
    for woven fabrics, 351–52*t*
  problems in, 420–21
  revised, 421–22
Labarthe, Jules, 414*n*
Labeling, 254, 341
  of care instruction, FTC regulation
    on, 342–43

Labeling (*cont.*)
  Sure Care, 351
  of washing conditions, 350
Laminated fabrics
  bonding techniques for, 280
    foam bonding, 281
  problems with, 282–83
Lanolin, 65
Lap, 193
Lappet design, 239
Lastex yarns, 171
Lastrile, 172
Layer principle, 22
Layered constructions
  chemstitch, 281
  laminated fabrics, 280–81
  stitching, 278
  stitch-thru fabrics, 278–79
Leaf vegetable fibers, 49
Lee, William (Rev.), 246
Legislation related to textiles, 342–47
Leno weave, 238–39
Levine, Daniel B., 376
Life expectancy rates, of textiles, 364–
    68*t*, 370
Light
  effect of
    on color appearance, 326–27
    on wool, 62
  infrared, effect on comfort, 327–28
Linen, 383, 384, 400. *See also* Flax
  characteristics of, physical, 41–42*t*
  count of, 44
  elasticity of, 2
  finishing of, 286
  history of, 43
  no-iron, sanitation level of, 321–22
  properties of, 40, 41, 43
  tow, 44
  use of, in table damask, 385
Linen tester, 220
Llama, wools from, 72, 74
Loading, of wool, 294
Lowe, H., 287
Lumen, 11
  fineness and, 9–10
Lus-trus, 176
Luster, 286

Luster (*cont.*)
  desirability of, 13–14
Lycra, 173–74

M

Mali unit, 279
Malifleece method, 279
Malimo method, 279
Maliwatt method, 279
Man-made fiber(s), 245. *See also*
      Manufactured fibers
  acetate, 91, 92–93, 106–14
  arnel, 113–14
  categories of, 15
  characteristics of, 87
  coloring of, 332
  consumption of, 35, 39
  economic requirements for, 15
  inorganic, 116–21
  metallic, 121–23
  organic, 114–16
  production of, 182–83*t*, 185*t*
  rayon, 91–106
  sources of educational material on,
      359*t*
  spinning of, 88–90
  U.S. export of, 186
Man-Made Fiber Producers Associa-
      tion, 358–59*t*
Man-made textile(s), U.S. imports of,
      186*t*
Manufactured fiber(s), 15, 374
  acrylic, 140–50
  elastomeric, 171–75
  flammability of, 310
  future of, 431
  modacrylic, 150–54
  nylon, 126–40
  olefin, 164–70
  properties of, 124–26
  Saran, 175–77
  status of, 180–84
  tetrafluorethylene, 178–80
  vinal, 178

Manufactured fiber(s) (*cont.*)
  vinyon, 177–78
Manufacturer, cause of damage by,
      417*t*
Market research procedures, 188, 190
Mauersberger, Herbert R., 52*n*
Mechanical attrition, factors in, 423–
      25
Mellon Institute, 380, 410, 422
Mending, 293
Mercer, John, 287
Mercerization process, 20, 229
  for cotton cloth, 287
Metallic fibers, 15
  listing of, 122*t*
  steel staple, 123
  use of, 121–22
Milanese knit, 252
Mildew, effect of, on wool, 62
Mildew-resistant finishes, 314–15
Milium, 314
Milling. *See* Felting
Mineral fibers, 15
Minimum-care fabrics. *See* Durable-
      press
Mitin, 315
Modacrylic(s), 310, 311
  fiber(s)
    Aeress, 153–54
    defined, 150
    Dynel, 151–53
    growth of, 149*t*
    trade names of, 150*t*
    Verel, 154
  use of, in tufted fabrics, 403
Mohair
  production of, 70–71
  properties of, 71
Moisture
  absorbency. *See* Hydrophobic
      properties
  content, determination of, 12–13
  regain, 13
Monk's cloth, 228
Monomers, 124
Mordant colors, 331
Mothproofing, 315
Mylar metallic yarns, 384

N

Napping, 292, 392
 of cotton cloth, 288
 of wool, 294
 of worsteds, 294
National Bureau of Standards, 312,
  347, 351, 357
 proposals on fire retardation, 306
National Fabricare Institute, 424
National Institute of Drycleaning
  (NID), 361, 368, 415
National Retail Merchants Association, 349, 410, 416
Natural fiber(s)
 bast, 48–49
 cost of, 374
 cotton, 19–37
 flax, 39–44
 hemp, 46
 jute, 45–46
 protein, 49–50
 ramie, 47
 silk, 75–86
 wool, 50–75
Need(s), 377
 related to value, 379t
Needle count, 254
Neva-Wet, 302, 304
Never-Press, 321
Newburgh, F. H., 381
Nirane Four Star SWR, 304
Noils, 66, 72, 193
Nolan, F. L., 376
Nomex aramis, 125, 138, 311
Nonwoven fabric(s)
 bonding of, 267–68, 270–72
 defined, 265–67
 fiber use in, 275t
 flammability of, 346
 future of, 276–77
 industries concerned with, 268–70
 producers of, 267
 properties of, 272–73
 uses of, 273–76
Norane, 304
Novelty weave(s), 204
 dobby, 237–38

Novelty weave(s) (*cont.*)
 jacquard, 235–37
 leno, 238–39
Numbering system, for yarns, 438–39t
 indirect system, 205
Nyloft, 404–405
Nylon, 310–11
 Cantrece, 137–38
 dyeing of, 134–36
 early disappointments with, 137
 fiber
  trade names for, 128–29t
  use in rugs, 401
 filament, production of, 131
 hosiery, 254–57
 manufacture of, polymerization,
   127, 130–31
 problems with, 409t
 properties of, 131–34
 Qiana, 139–40
 research on, 126–27
 sparkling, 255
 use of, 127, 402
  in carpets, 399, 401
  in textured yarns, 206, 208
  in tufted fabrics, 403
  washing of, 135–36
Nylon tricot, 137
Nytril fibers, 179

O

Olefin fibers
 Herculon, 169
 listing of, 167–68t
 manufacture of, 166, 168–70
 properties of, 165–66, 170
 Trilok, 169–70
 use of, in tufted fabrics, 404
Organic fiber(s)
 azlons, 114–16
 production of, 115
Orlon, 147, 149, 152, 154
 characteristics of, 141, 144
 history of, 141
 manufacture of, 144–45

Orlon (*cont.*)
  Sayelle, 144, 179
  use of, 145
Oxford cloth, 226, 228

P

Paper(s), 266
  yarns, 216
Patterns, applied, 239–40
Pattina, 406
Perching, 293
Performance, standards of, 419. *See also* Serviceability
  of apparel, 360
  testing of, 312
Perkin, William Henry, 328–29
Perlon, 134
Permanent Care Labeling Trade Regulation, 361
Permanent press, problems with, 409*t*
Philadelphia College of Textiles and Science, 327
Pick glass, 220
Picker lap, 193
Picks, 217
Pike, R. H., 317
Pile, 240
  fabrics
    characteristics of, 244
    deep, 265–66
    knitted, 257–58
  fibers, use of, in tufted fabrics, 402–404
  weaves, 240
    handling of, 244–45
    weaving methods for. *See* Weaving of, pile
Pilling, problems in, 409*t*
Pillow(s), fibers for, 404
Pillow-case(s), sizes of, 389*t*
Plain weave(s)
  advantages and disadvantages of, 228*t*
  construction of, 224
  fabrics of, 225*t*

Plain weave(s) (*cont.*)
  variations in, 225–28
Plasticity, conditions for, 11, 12
Plato, 325
Ply, of yarn, 201–202
Polycaprolactam, 134
Polyester(s), 311, 383–84
  fibers
    characteristics of, 163–64
    Dacron, 156–61
    defined, 154
    Fortrel, 161–62
    Kodel, 162
    listing of, 155–56*t*
    properties of, 158*t*
    Trevira, 163
    Vycron, 162
    WD2, 162–63
  problems with, 409*t*
  use of
    in carpets, 399
    in tufted fabrics, 404
Polyethylene, 166
  yarns, 170
Polymer(s), 11, 19, 124
  new, search for, 184–85
  use of, in tufted yarns, 206*t*
Polymerization, 124
  addition polymerization, 144
  condensation polymerization, 130–31
  of Dacron, 156–57
  of Dynel, 151
  by esterification, 127, 130
  in Saran, 177
Polynosic, 105, 106
Polypropylene, 156
  fibers, consumption of, 172*t*
  yarns, 171
Porosity, 11
  defined, 13
  of wool, 62
Powderly, Daniel D., 408
Precure, 321
Preshrinking, 290
  of fabric, 300–301
    Rigmel finish, 301
Pressing, 229, 294

Price, of apparel, relationship to quality, 380
Printing
  air brushing, 338
  block printing, 335
  of cotton cloth, 288
  discharge printing, 338
  duplex printing, 338
  electrostatic method, 338–39
  of linen, 291
  madder printing, 336
  problems with, 409t
  resist dyeing, 335–36
  roller printing, 337
  screen printing, 336–37
  of silk, 292–93
  stenciling, 335
  textured printing, 338
  from transfer papers, 339
Proban, 310
Professions related to textiles, 7, 8
Protein fibers, characteristics of, 49–50
Purl knit
  circular, 250
  rib, 250

Q

Qiana nylon, 139–40, 212
  properties of, 139t
Quality, of apparel, relationship to price, 380
Quivat, 75

R

Radioactive rays, effect on color appearance, 326, 327t
Ramie
  handling of, 47–48
  properties of, 48–49
Raschel knit, 248, 252
Rayon(s), 107, 383
  Bemberg, 92t, 93

Rayon(s) (*cont.*)
  characteristics of, 92–93t
  cold-stretched, 94, 96
  commercial, physical properties of, 101
  cross-linked
    manufacture of, 106
    properties of, 104–106
  defined, 91–92
  dimensional stabilization of, 292
  Fiber E, 179
  finishing of, 291–92
  Fortisan, 101, 103, 106
  high-tenacity, 106
  production of, 96
    cuprammonium process, 99–100
    viscose process, 98–99, 102–103
  properties of, 93–94
  quality of, standards for, 416
  use of, 95t, 402, 404
    in dish toweling, 384–85
  Viscose, 93, 384
  yarns, sizes of, 102
Rayon Rules, 90
Rayon standard, 420
Renovation methods, 364–68t
Repeat, in weaving, 235
Replacement cost, determining of, 370–71t
Research, 2. *See also* Market research
  consumer, into acceptance of new fiber, 185, 187
Research triangle, 348
Resilience, defined, 12
Resin(s)
  bonding method, 271
  finish, side effects of, 324–25
  use in durable-press process, 320–21
Rib knit
  circular, 250
  flat, 250
Rigmel finish, 301
Right face of fabric, identifying of, 234–35
Rippling, 43, 300
Roden, John J., 269
Roving, 44
  of cotton yarn, 194

Rug(s), 245, 404. *See also* Carpets
  backing of, 402
  characteristics of, 398
  construction of, 400–401
    nylon fibers in, 401
  worldwide production of, 405*t*
Rug method, of weaving, 240, 244

S

Saaba, 208
Sales-appeal, finishes for. *See* Esthetic
  finishes
Sales promotion, problems of, 190
Sanforizing process, methods of, 300
  for cotton, 300–301
Sanitizing, 313
Saponification, 106
Saran, 310
  characteristics of, 175–76
  fiber, properties of, 176
  manufacture of, 177
  trade names for, 176
  uses of, 176
    in tufted fabrics, 404
Satin weaves, characteristics of, 232
Schiffli design, 239
Scotchgard, Dual Action, 323
Scutching, 44
Seed hairs, 49
Selection, by consumer, 2
  influences on, 376–77
    psychological, 368–75
  technical aspects of, 361–63
  of textiles, aids to, 348–55
    skill development in, 407–409
Sericulture, 88
  description of, 77–79
Serviceability, 368. *See also* Performance
  criteria for, 5
  designations of, 364–68*t*
  rating of textiles, 409, 411–12*t*
  renovation methods, 364–68*t*
Shaft number, 231
Shape, 2U, 207

Shearing operation, 258, 294
  rough shearing, 258
  of worsteds, 294
Sheets. *See* Bed sheets
Shower curtains, fabrics for, 385
Shrinkage. *See also* Preshrinking
  problems of, 409*t*
  relaxation shrinkage, 300
  of wool, 65
Silk, 407
  characteristics of, 84–85*t*
  count of, 81–82
  finishing of, 292–93
  grading of, 82–83
  origin of, 76
  production of, 75–76
    sericulture, 77–79
  properties of, 79–80
  weighting of, 83, 86, 286, 293
  wild, 79
  yarn
    spun-silk, 83
    throwing of, 80–81
Silver, dyeing of, 333
Sizing, 239
  of cotton cloth, 288
Slipcover fabrics, 407
Slubber, 194
Snagging, problems of, 409*t*
Soil deposition, 325
  problems of, 409*t*
Soil-release agents, 296
Soil-resistant finishes, 322
  methods of, 323–24
  properties of, 322–23
Sonochemical process, 255
Source fibers, 179
Spandelle, 173
Spandex fibers, 172
  listing of, 174*t*
  properties of, 173–75
Specific gravity, of fiber, 11, 12
Specking, 293
Spinnability, 10
  physical properties for, 9
Spinning
  of acetate, 112
  of cotton yarn, 194

Spinning, of cotton yarn (*cont.*)
    American system, 196–97
  of fiber, 88–90
  of nylon filament, 131
  of yarn, 200
Spot-resistant finishes, 314
Spunize, 208
Stabilization, 300. *See also* Dimensional stabilization
Stain-resistant finishes, 314
Standards. *See also* L-22 standard
  commercial, 348
  performance. *See* Performance, standards
  for textile items
    organizations concerned with, 424
    setting of, 348–49
Staple fibers, 10
  defined, 9
  steel, 123
Static electricity, 177
  factors related to, 316–17
  finishes resistant to, 317
  problems of, 14
Steaming, 292
  of wool, 294
Stenciling, method of, 335
Stitch-thru constructions, 272, 278*t*, 279–80, 400
Stitching, methods of, 278–79
Stout, Evelyn, 33
Stretch yarns, 133, 205
  cotton, 213–14
Stretching
  of fibers, cold stretch, 94–96
  of silk, 293
Structural design. *See* Design, structural
Suint, 65
Sunn fiber, 48
Super-loft, 208
Sure Care, 360
  label, 355, 361
Swivel design, 239
Synthetic(s)
  fabrics, 15
  fibers, 68
    denier of, 198*t*

Synthetic(s), fibers (*cont.*)
  development of, 76
  staining sensitivity of, 314
  use in blankets, 394, 397
  woven, finishing process for, 295–96

T

Tabby, 224
Table linens, fabrics for, 385
Tachikawa, Schozo, 105
Taffeta, 224
Tapa fibers, 48
Taslan, 208, 211
Teflon fluorocarbon, 178
Tempresito, 314
Tenacity, 10
Tensile strength, defined, 10
Tentering, 292
  of cotton cloth, 290
  of linen, 291
  of silk, 293
Terry cloth, 383–84
Terry-weave method, 242–43
Test methods, requirements of, 419
Tetrafluoroethylene fibers
  nytril, 179
  source, 179
  teflon fluorocarbon, 178
Texstyle Creators of New York, 336
Textile(s)
  adaptation of, 430–31
  air pollution and, 422–23
  classification of, 9, 14–15
  fiber
    information on, availability of, 4–5, 432–37
    consumption of, future of, 429*t*
    future of, 425–26, 429–30
  nonwoven, 266
  products
    end-use volumes of, 427–28*t*
    evaluation of, 362
    grouping of, 419
  professional opportunities in, 8

Textile(s) (*cont.*)
  study of, conversion factors for, 439–40*t*
Textile Distributors Institute (TDI), 350
Textile Economics Bureau, 181
Textile Fiber Products Identification Act (TFPIA), 14, 15, 58, 75, 96, 106, 126*n*, 171, 178–79, 361, 393
  purpose of, 344–45
Textile finishing
  chemicals for, 296
  functional, 290
  growth of, 296, 298
  trade names for, 297–99*t*
Textralized, 208
  production of, 208
Textured printing, 338
Textured yarn(s)
  bulk, 205–206
    Helanca, 206–207
  cotton, stretchable, 213–14
  future trends in, 214–16
  production of, 208
  stretch, 205–206
    Agilon, 207
Thermal properties, 2
Thermoplastic fiber(s), 15, 106–107
  bonding, 271
  burn damage from, 312
  heat of combustion of, 311*t*
Thermoplasticity, in manufactured fibers, 125
Thornel, 123
Throwing of yarn, 200
Tigering, 258
Tie-dyeing, 335
Touch fiber, 212
Tow, 101
Towels, 383
  dish, 384–85
  terry cloth, 383–84
Transfer paper, textile printing from, 339
Trevira polyester, fiber, 163
Triacetate, 106
Tricot knit, 252

Tricot knit (*cont.*)
  structure of, 137
Trilok, 169–70
Trilon, 405
Tufted fabric(s), 398, 400
  fibers for, 402–404
  manufacture of, 245, 403
Twill weave
  characteristics of, 229–31
  fibers for, 230*t*
  herringbone, 231–32
  properties of, 232
  satin weave, 232–34
Twinned fibers, 211–13
Twinned yarns, 229
Tycora, 211
Tygan, 176

U

Unbalanced fabrics, 225–28
Underwear, knitting of, 254
Unions, 334
United States
  consumption of polypropylene fibers, 171*t*
  consumption of textile fibers, 180
  exports of man-made fibers, 188*t*, 190
  imports of man-made textiles, 186*t*
  legislation on flammability, 306–310, 312
    status of, 307*t*
  production in
    of cotton, 24–30
    of knitted fabrics, 263*t*
    of nylon, 130
    of silk, 76
U.S. Bureau of Standards, 300, 341
U.S. Congress
  FTC and, 342
  laws related to consumer consciousness, 361
U.S. Department of Agriculture, 213
  Market Research Division, 376
U.S. Department of Commerce, 245, 306, 347, 357, 402

U.S. Dept. of Commerce (*cont.*)
  flammability specifications by, 345–46
U.S. Department of Health, Education and Welfare, 304, 306, 347
U.S. Social Security Administration, 347
U.S. Weather Bureau, 381
Upholstery fabrics
  classification of, 406
  fibers for, 404–407

V

Value, defined, 377–80
Veblen, Thorstein, 373
Velon, 176
Verel modacrylic, 154
Vicŭna, 74
Vinal fibers, 178
Vinyl, expanded, 406
Vinylon, 178
Vinyon
  characteristics of, 177
  use of, 178
Viscose
  process, steps in, 98–99
  rayon, 384
Voltex, 123, 279
Vulcanized rubber, 11
Vycron polyester, 162
Vyrene, 173

W

Wales, 229, 241
Want(s), 377–78
  related to value, 379t
Ward, F. J., 305
Warmth retention, limitations of, 314
Warp
  knits, types of, 252
  knitting, 246

Warp (*cont.*)
  yarns, 217
Wash-and-wear finishes. *See also* Durable-press fabrics
  care of, 318
  characteristics of, 317
  limitations of, 318–20
  process of, 318
  trade names of, 319
Water
  action of, on wool, 63
  solution, resistance to, testing of, 313
Water-repellent finishes
  criteria for, 301–311
  factors in, 2
  materials for, 302–303
  penetration-resistance, 302
  permanent, 303–304
    trademark for, 303t, 304
Wear, factors in, 423
Weave(s). *See* Woven structures
Weaving
  defined, 217
  mechanism of, 217–18, 220
  of pile, 240, 243–44
  double-cloth, 241–42
  rug method, 244
  filling pile, 240–41
  terry weave, 242–43
  wire, 243–44
Weaving loom(s), 222, 233
  Jacquard, 235–37
  structure of, 217–18
Weft knit. *See* Filling knit
White light rays, 326
Wilkinson, G. B., 265n, 317
Wool, 11. *See also* Hair fibers ,
  behavior of, chemical, 62–64
  characteristics of, 84–85t, 294
    chemical, 59–60t
    performance, 68–70
    physical, 59t
  chlored, 63
  crimp in, 10
  effect of water on, 63
  fiber, history of, 52–53
  fineness of, 198t

Wool (*cont.*)
    finishing of, 293–94
    flammability of, 309
    garments, care of, 64
    grading of, 55–57
    growing of, 53–54
    hairs, minor, 74–75
    labeling of, for blankets, 392–93
    from llama family, 72, 74
    molecular structure of, 50–52
    mothproofing of, 315
    pashm, 72
    problems with, 409t
    processing of, 65–66
    products, classification of, Federal
        Wool Products Labeling Act
        and, 57–58
    properties of, 58
        capillarity and porosity, 62
        elasticity, 61–62
        fiber length, 60
        hydroscopic moisture, 62
    reprocessed, 343
    reused, 343
    use of, 402
        in carpets, 399
        in tufted fabrics, 403
    virgin, 343
    weighting of, 294
    worsteds. *See* Worsteds
    yarn
        manufacture of, 67–68
        numbering system of, 197, 199
Wool Products Labeling Act, 75, 361
    definition of wool fiber by, 343
    blankets and, 392–93
Wool Product Law, 393
Worsteds
    finishing of, 294
    processing of, 66–67
    system, 199

Woven apparel, versus knit, 262t
Woven structure(s), 222–23. *See also*
        Plain weave
    identification of, 234–35
    novelty weaves, 235–39
    synthetic, finishing process of, 295–
        96
    twill weave, 229–34
    USA standard of performance for,
        351–52t

Y

Yarn(s), 1
    anchorage, 300
    classification of, 201–202
    continuous filament, 200
    count system of, 438–39t
    defined, 191
    dyeing of, 333–34
    fiber joining in, 211–13
    forms of, 191
    numbering system of, 205, 438–39t
    properties of, 192
    simple, 204
    spinning of, 200
    tensile strength of, 392
    twist, 200–201
    uniformity in, 202, 204

Z

Zefran acrylic, 148
Zefrome, 148
Zelan, 304